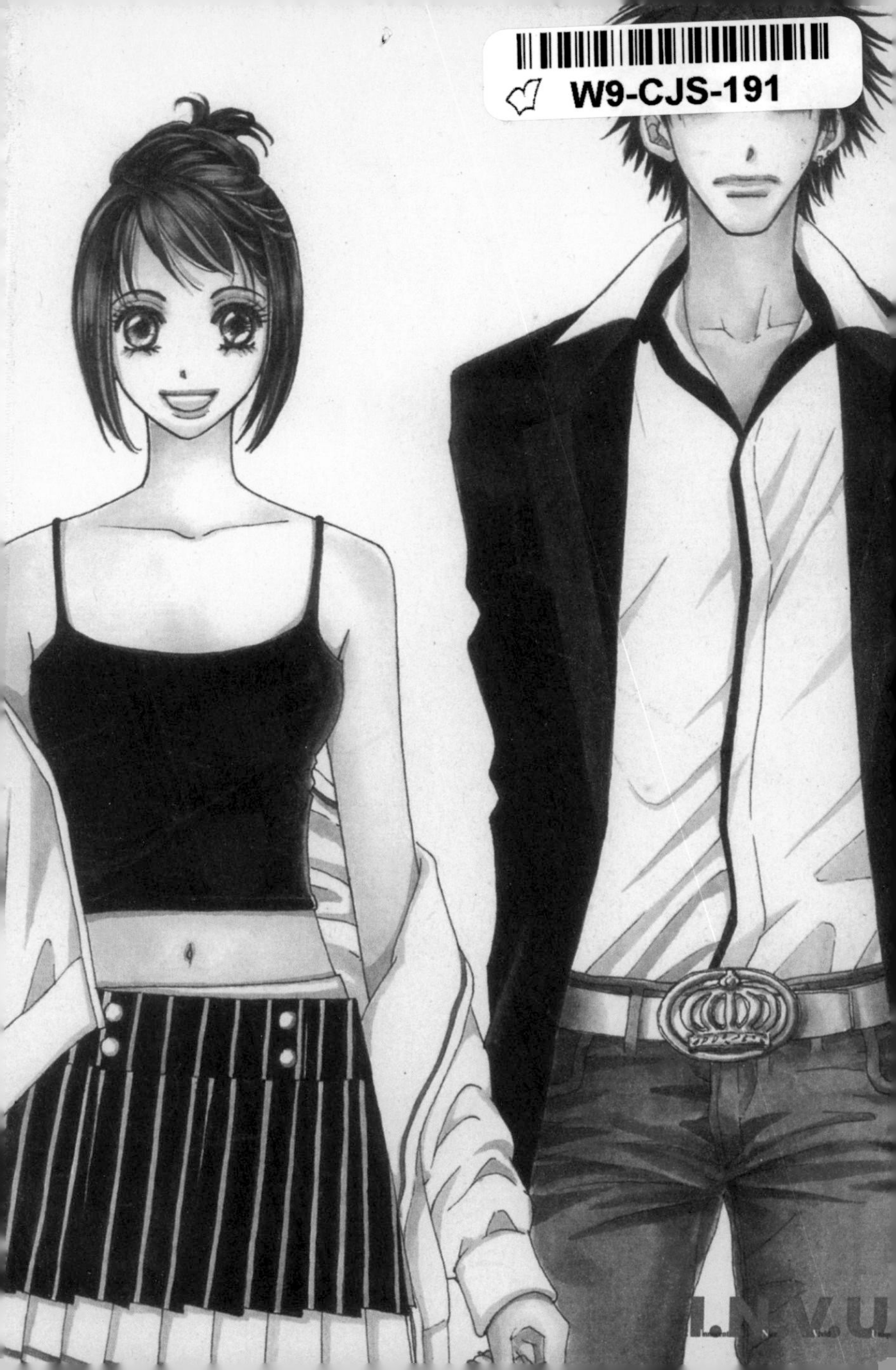
I.N.V.U

I ENVY YOU

I.N.V.U

Innocent · Nice · Vivid · Unique

I.N.V.U. Volume 4
Created by Kim Kang Won

Translation - Lauren Na
English Adaptation - Kristin Bailey Murphy
Copy Editor - Stephanie Duchin
Retouch and Lettering - Star Print Brokers
Production Artist - Gavin Hignight
Graphic Designer - Jennifer Carbajal

Editor - Lillian Diaz-Przybyl
Digital Imaging Manager - Chris Buford
Pre-Production Supervisor - Erika Terriquez
Art Director - Anne Marie Horne
Production Manager - Elisabeth Brizzi
Managing Editor - Vy Nguyen
VP of Production - Ron Klamert
Editor-in-Chief - Rob Tokar
Publisher - Mike Kiley
President and C.O.O. - John Parker
C.E.O. and Chief Creative Officer - Stuart Levy

A  Manga

TOKYOPOP and are trademarks or registered trademarks of TOKYOPOP Inc.

TOKYOPOP Inc.
5900 Wilshire Blvd. Suite 2000
Los Angeles, CA 90036

E-mail: info@TOKYOPOP.com
Come visit us online at www.TOKYOPOP.com

ISBN: 978-1-4278-0495-2

First TOKYOPOP printing: September 2007
10 9 8 7 6 5 4 3 2 1
Printed in the USA

I.N.V.U.

4

by
Kim Kang Won

HAMBURG // LONDON // LOS ANGELES // TOKYO

I ENVY YOU!

토요일
괜찮지?
뭐야?

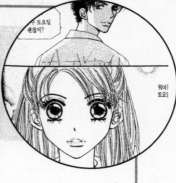

DUE TO HER MOTHER'S SUDDEN DECISION TO STUDY ABROAD, SEY IS FORCED TO LIVE WITH HALI'S FAMILY AND DECIDES TO LOOK FOR A JOB. HER FRIEND, REA, HELPS HER FIND PART-TIME WORK BY INTRODUCING HER TO SIHO, A BOY WHO GOES TO THEIR HIGH SCHOOL. BECAUSE OF SEY'S ERROR AT THE GAS STATION, THE OWNER (SIHO) INCURS A FINANCIAL LOSS. IN ORDER TO PAY HIM BACK, SEY OFFERS TO HELP HIM WITH HIS STUDIES AND PROMISES TO GO ON A DATE WITH HIM IF HE DOES WELL ON HIS UPCOMING SCIENCE EXAM. SIHO STEALS A KISS FROM SEY, AND SHE'S UNSURE OF HOW TO REACT TO HIS AGGRESSIVE "PLAYBOY" ATTITUDE. THE EXAM RESULTS ARE POSTED—SIHO'S PASSED, AND HE'S MAKING SEY LIVE UP TO HER PROMISE!

두근
선생님…?
두근
두근

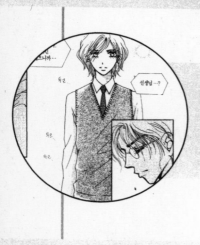

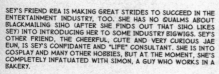

MEANWHILE, HALI HAS BEEN FORCED TO PLAY THE ROLE OF HER DEAD BROTHER, TERRY. SHE TRANSFERS TO THE SAME SCHOOL THAT HALI ATTENDS, AND THERE SHE MEETS HER JUNIOR-HIGH TUTOR, HAJUN. HALI HAS NO QUALMS ABOUT HONESTLY REVEALING HER LOVE FOR HAJUN, BUT HE IGNORES HIS FEELINGS FOR HER, TREATING HER JUST LIKE ANOTHER ONE OF HIS STUDENTS. WHEN HALI "COINCIDENTALLY" BEGINS A CAREER IN THE ENTERTAINMENT INDUSTRY, HAJUN'S RESOLVE NOT TO CARE FOR HER IS SHAKEN-ESPECIALLY SINCE HE KNOWS THAT HALI'S IN THE INDUSTRY TO ESCAPE FROM BEING "TERRY."

밀어붙여~~
엑!

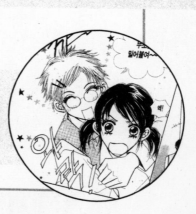

SEY'S FRIEND REA IS MAKING GREAT STRIDES TO SUCCEED IN THE ENTERTAINMENT INDUSTRY, TOO. SHE HAS NO QUALMS ABOUT BLACKMAILING SIHO (AFTER SHE FINDS OUT THAT SIHO LIKES SEY) INTO INTRODUCING HER TO SOME INDUSTRY BIGWIGS. SEY'S OTHER FRIEND, THE CHEERFUL, CUTE AND VERY CURIOUS JAE EUN, IS SEY'S CONFIDANTE AND "LIFE" CONSULTANT. SHE IS INTO COSPLAY AND MANY OTHER HOBBIES, BUT AT THE MOMENT, SHE'S COMPLETELY INFATUATED WITH SIMON, A GUY WHO WORKS IN A BAKERY.

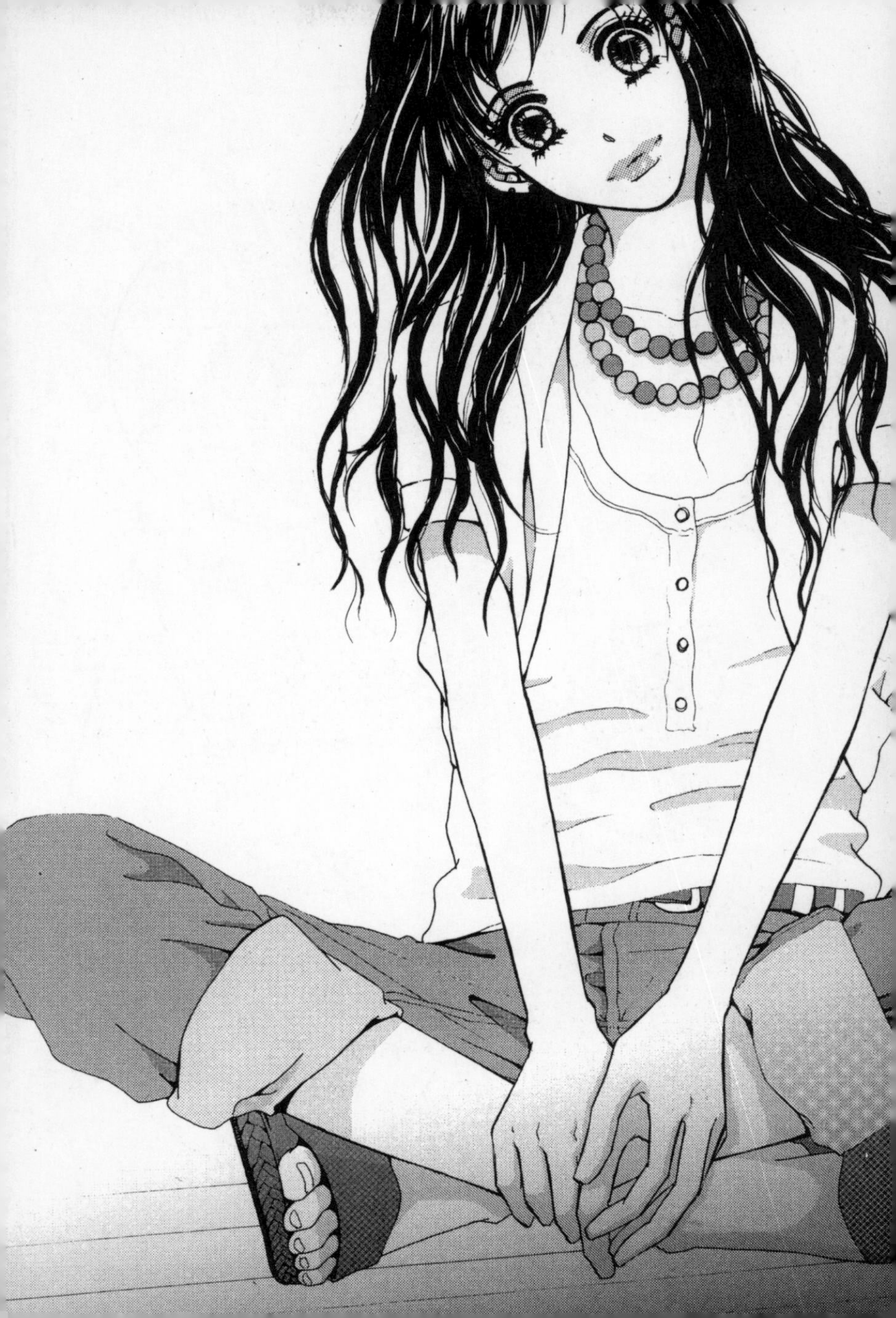

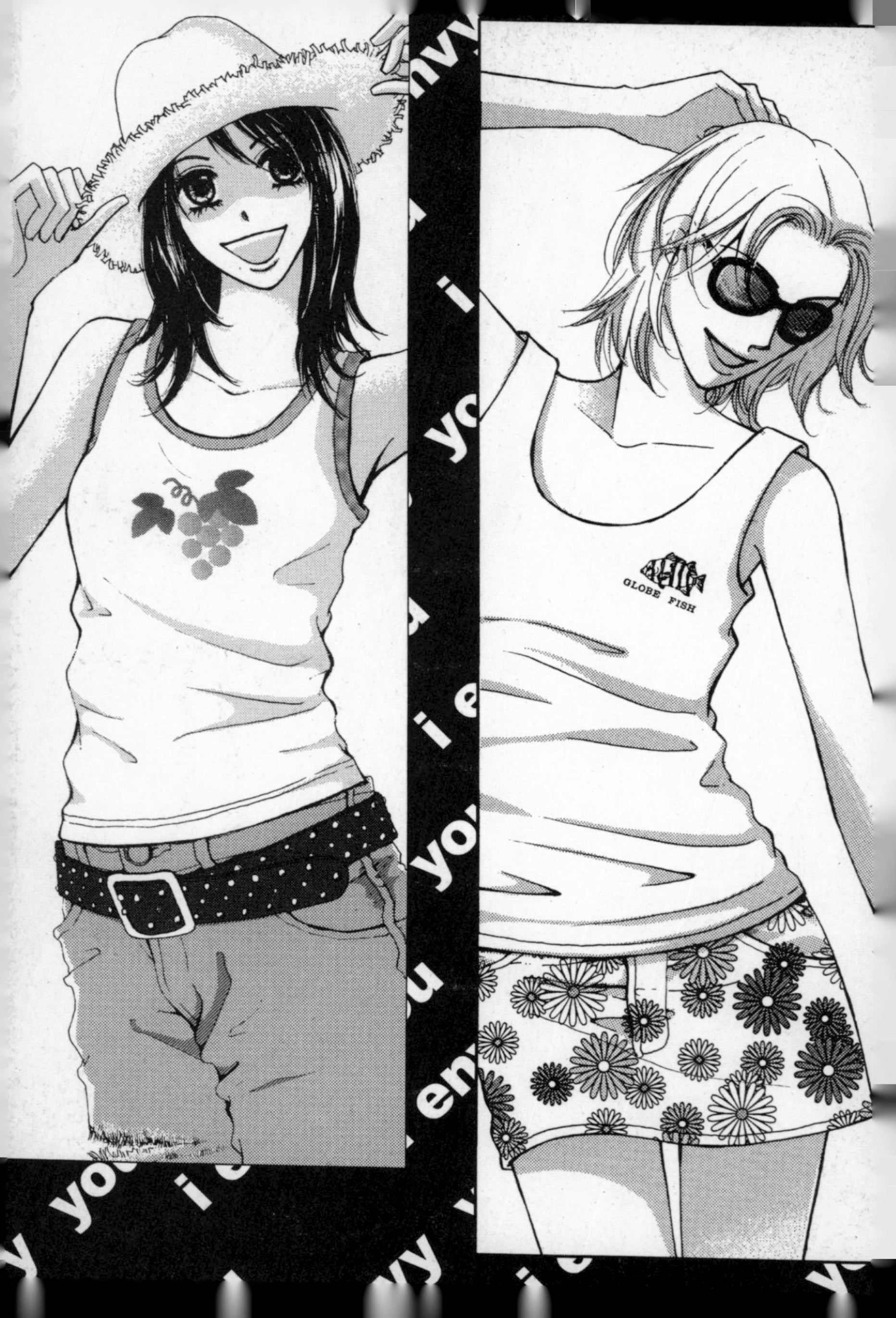
GLOBE FISH

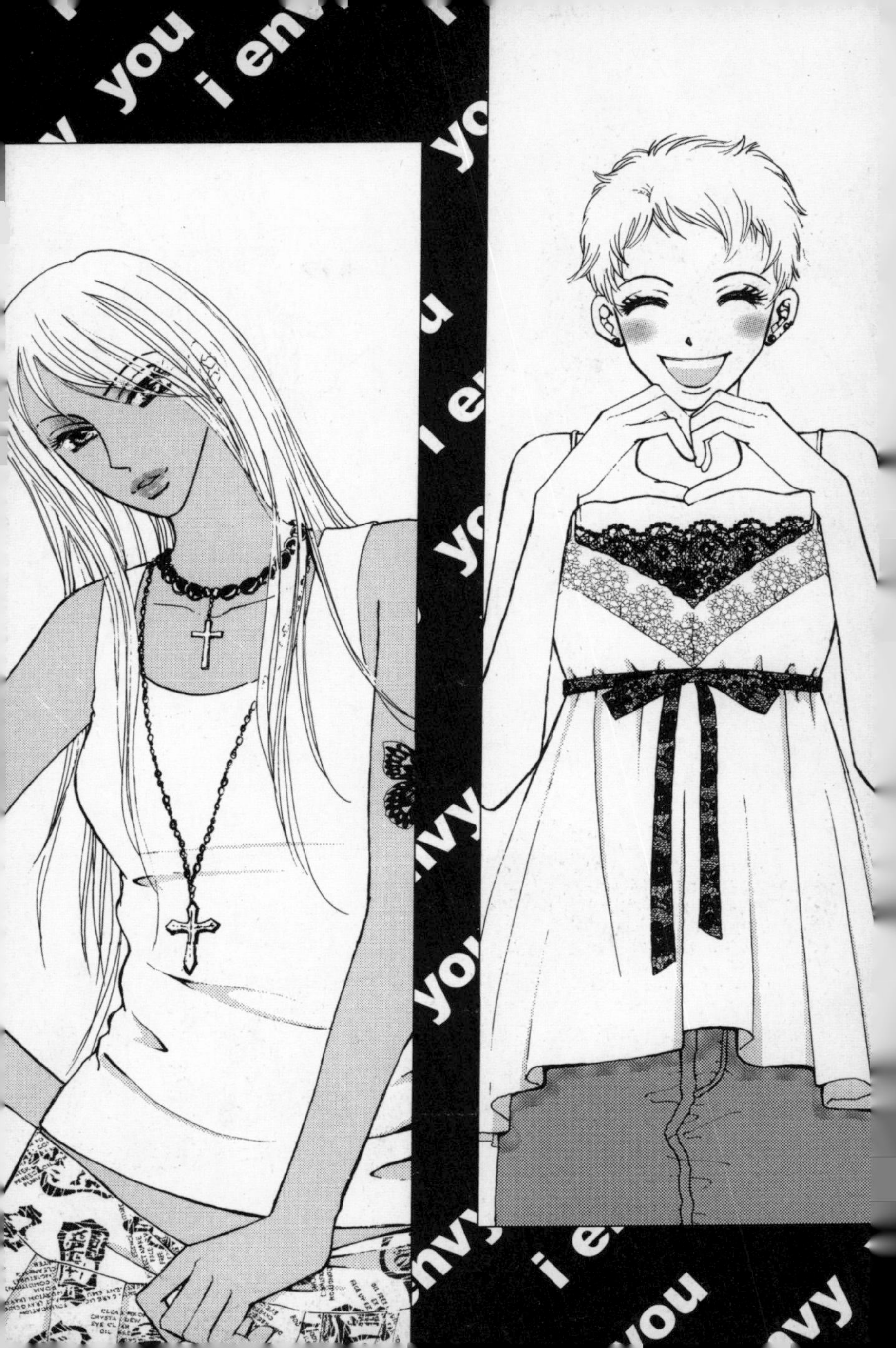

i envy you
i envy you
i envy you
i envy you

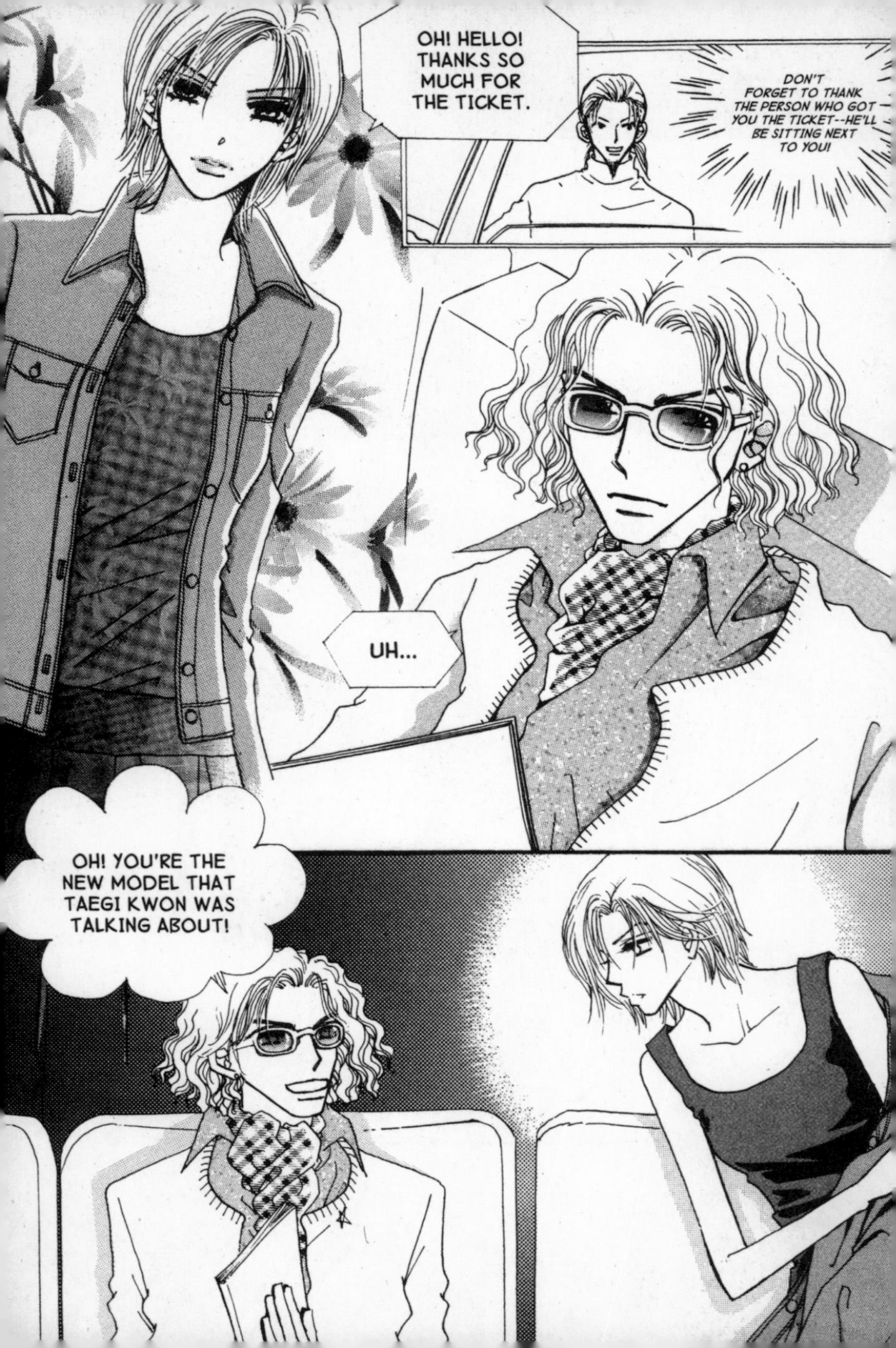
OH! HELLO! THANKS SO MUCH FOR THE TICKET.
DON'T FORGET TO THANK THE PERSON WHO GOT YOU THE TICKET--HE'LL BE SITTING NEXT TO YOU!
UH...
OH! YOU'RE THE NEW MODEL THAT TAEGI KWON WAS TALKING ABOUT!

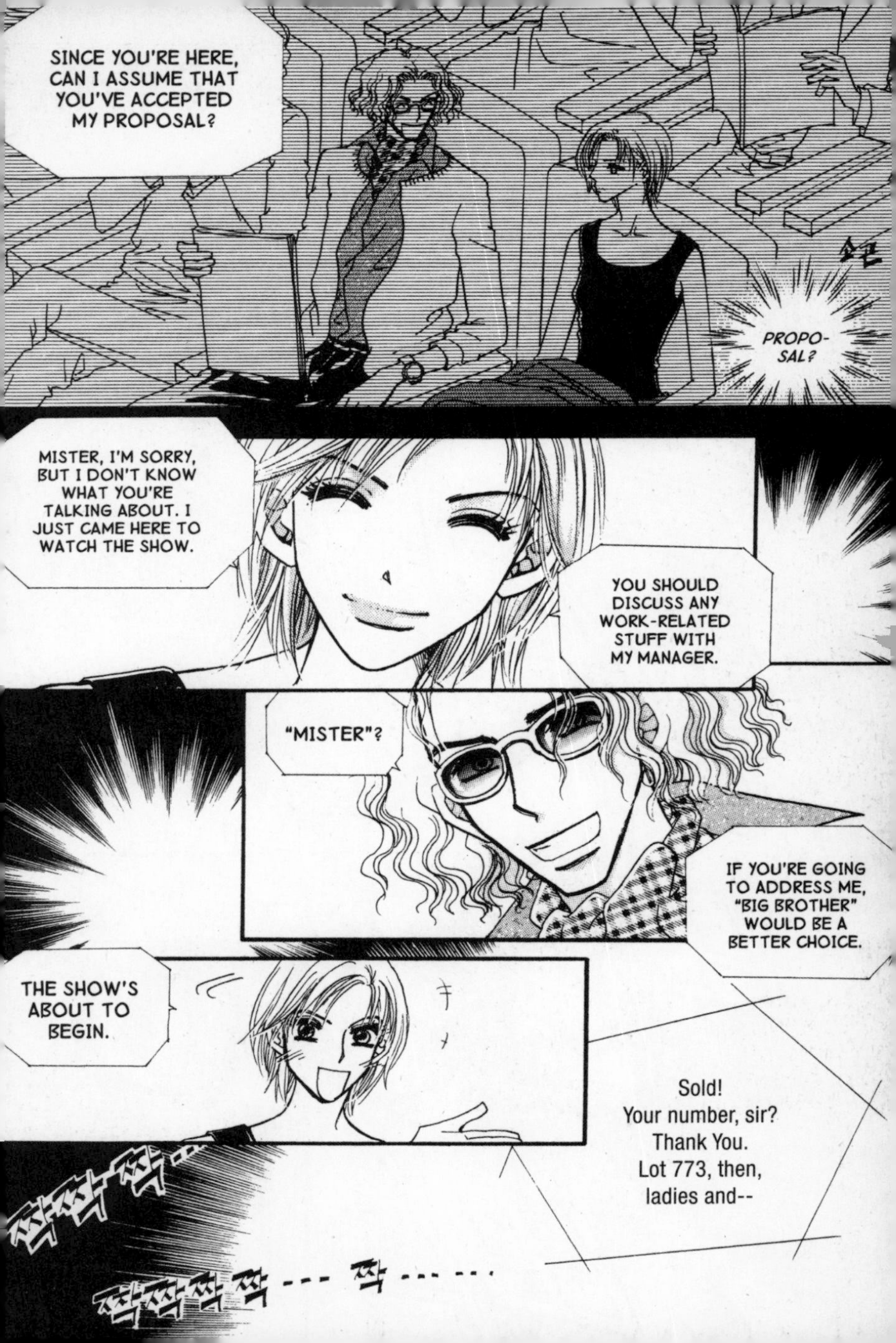
SINCE YOU'RE HERE, CAN I ASSUME THAT YOU'VE ACCEPTED MY PROPOSAL?
PROPO-SAL?
MISTER, I'M SORRY, BUT I DON'T KNOW WHAT YOU'RE TALKING ABOUT. I JUST CAME HERE TO WATCH THE SHOW.
YOU SHOULD DISCUSS ANY WORK-RELATED STUFF WITH MY MANAGER.
"MISTER"?
IF YOU'RE GOING TO ADDRESS ME, "BIG BROTHER" WOULD BE A BETTER CHOICE.
THE SHOW'S ABOUT TO BEGIN.
Sold!
Your number, sir?
Thank You.
Lot 773, then,
ladies and--

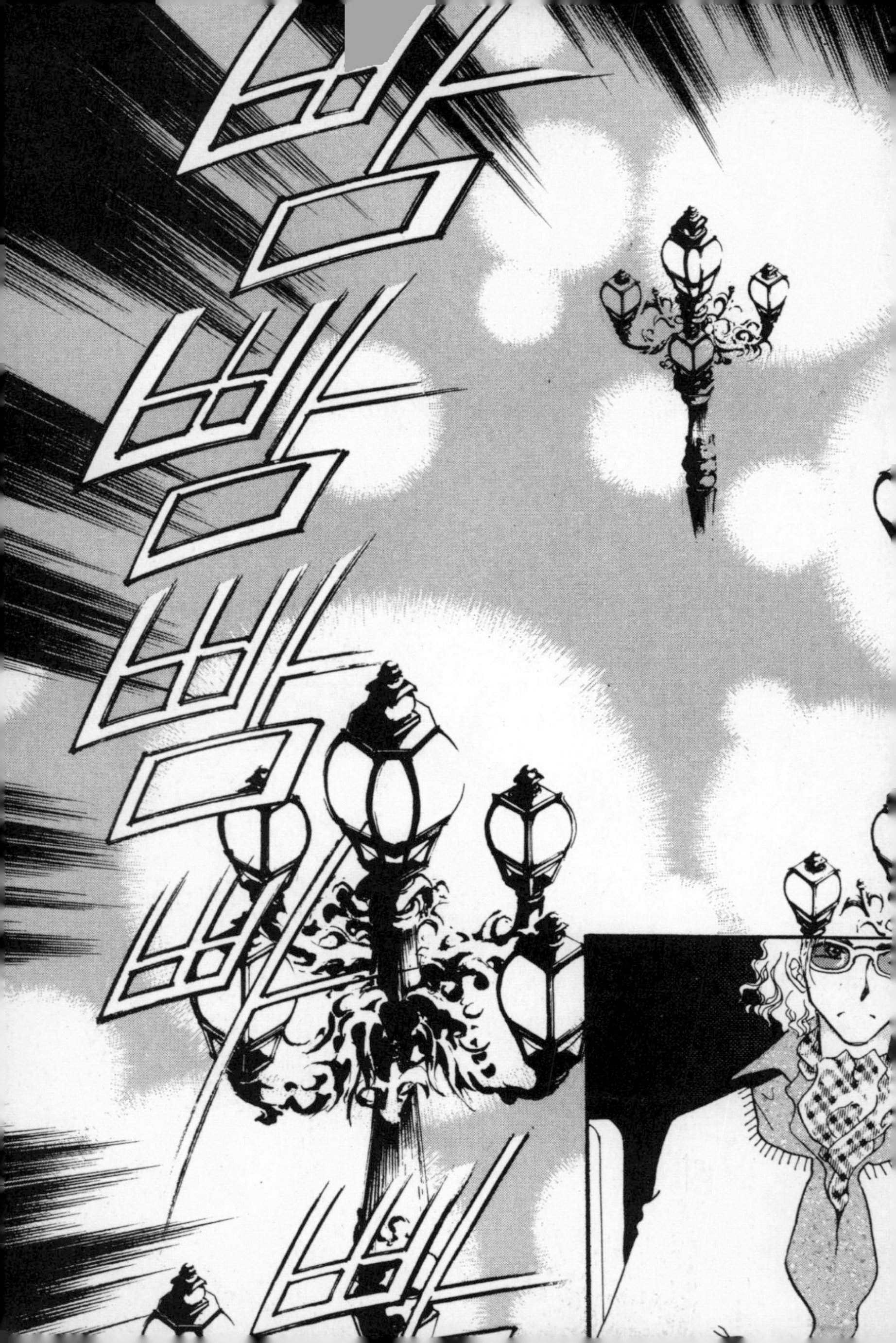

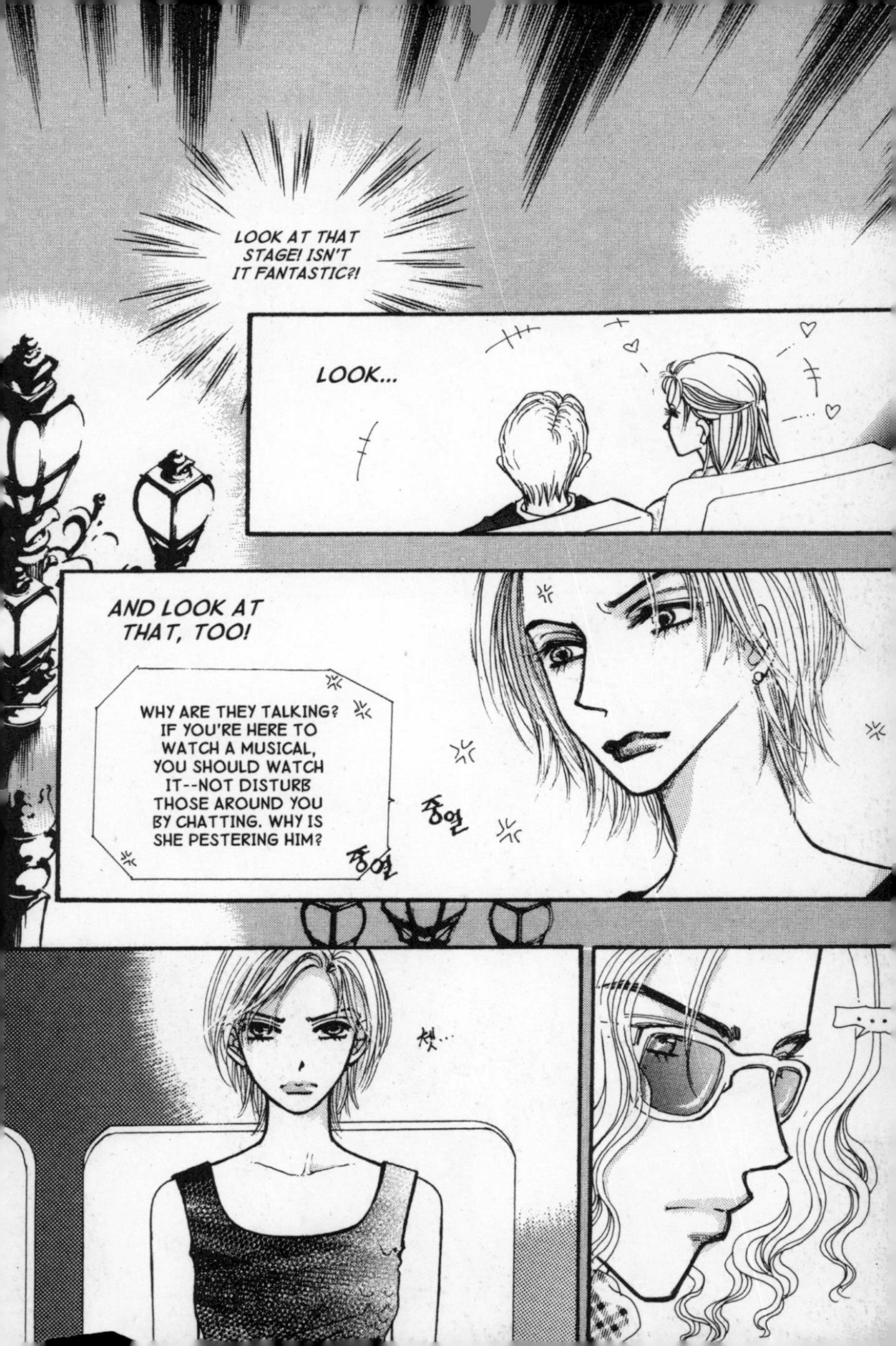
LOOK AT THAT STAGE! ISN'T IT FANTASTIC?!
LOOK...
AND LOOK AT THAT, TOO!
WHY ARE THEY TALKING? IF YOU'RE HERE TO WATCH A MUSICAL, YOU SHOULD WATCH IT--NOT DISTURB THOSE AROUND YOU BY CHATTING. WHY IS SHE PESTERING HIM?
중얼
중얼
쳇...
...

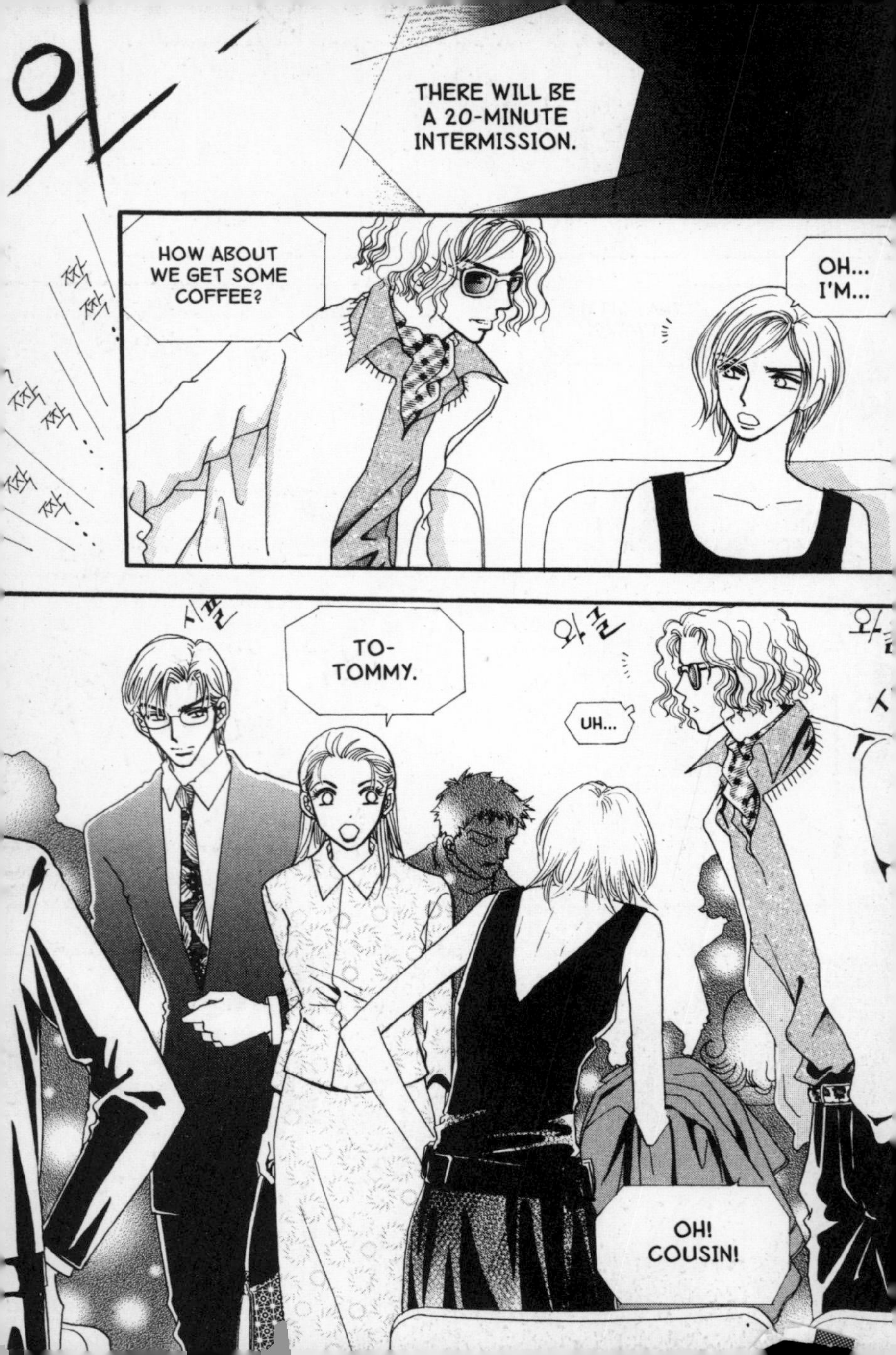

와
THERE WILL BE A 20-MINUTE INTERMISSION.
짝 짝...
HOW ABOUT WE GET SOME COFFEE?
OH... I'M...
시끌
TO-TOMMY.
와글
UH...
OH! COUSIN!

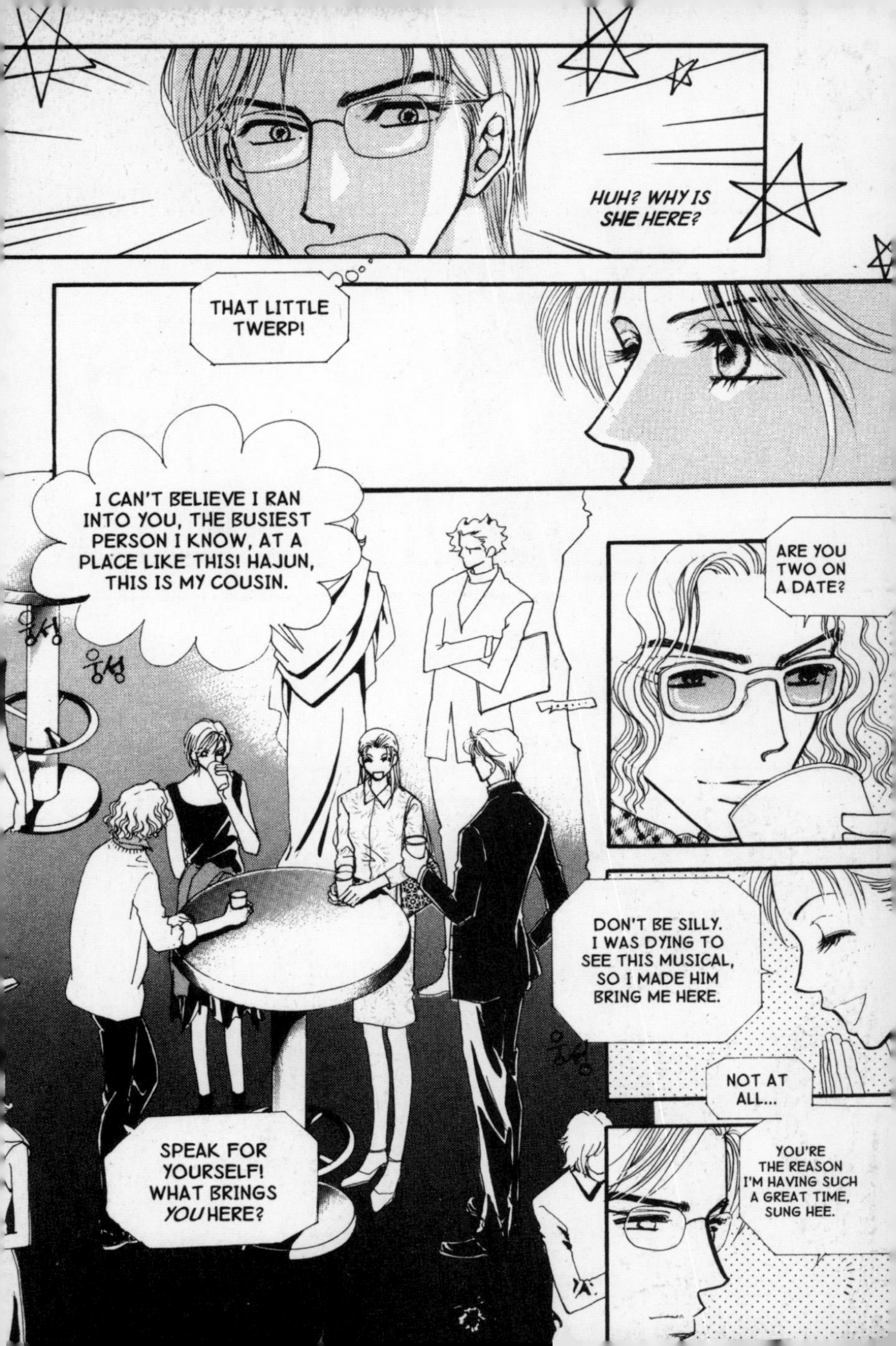
HUH? WHY IS SHE HERE?
THAT LITTLE TWERP!
I CAN'T BELIEVE I RAN INTO YOU, THE BUSIEST PERSON I KNOW, AT A PLACE LIKE THIS! HAJUN, THIS IS MY COUSIN.
웅성
웅성
SPEAK FOR YOURSELF! WHAT BRINGS *YOU* HERE?
웅성
ARE YOU TWO ON A DATE?
DON'T BE SILLY. I WAS DYING TO SEE THIS MUSICAL, SO I MADE HIM BRING ME HERE.
NOT AT ALL...
YOU'RE THE REASON I'M HAVING SUCH A GREAT TIME, SUNG HEE.

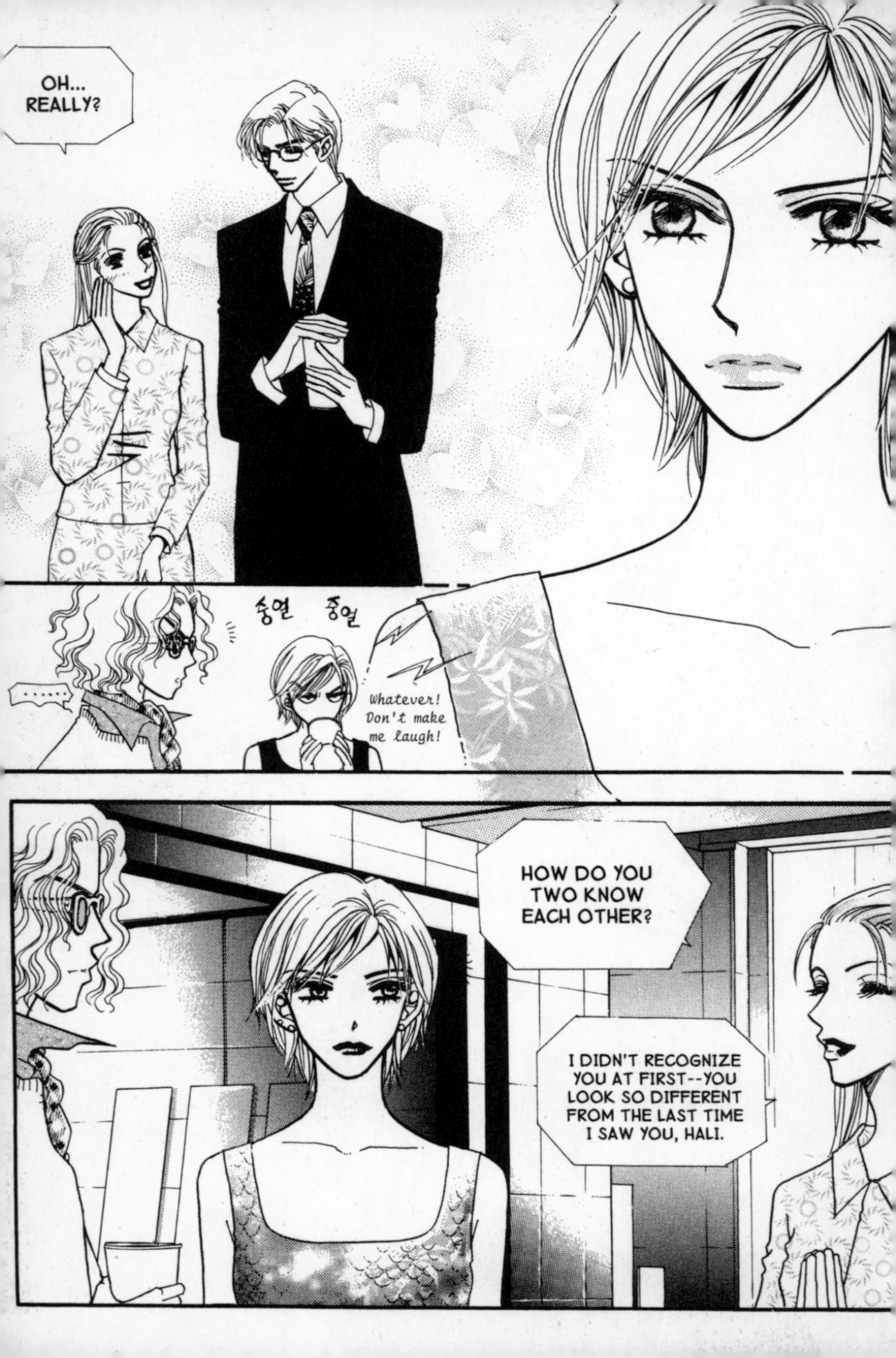
OH... REALLY?
......
중얼 중얼
Whatever! Don't make me laugh!
HOW DO YOU TWO KNOW EACH OTHER?
I DIDN'T RECOGNIZE YOU AT FIRST--YOU LOOK SO DIFFERENT FROM THE LAST TIME I SAW YOU, HALI.

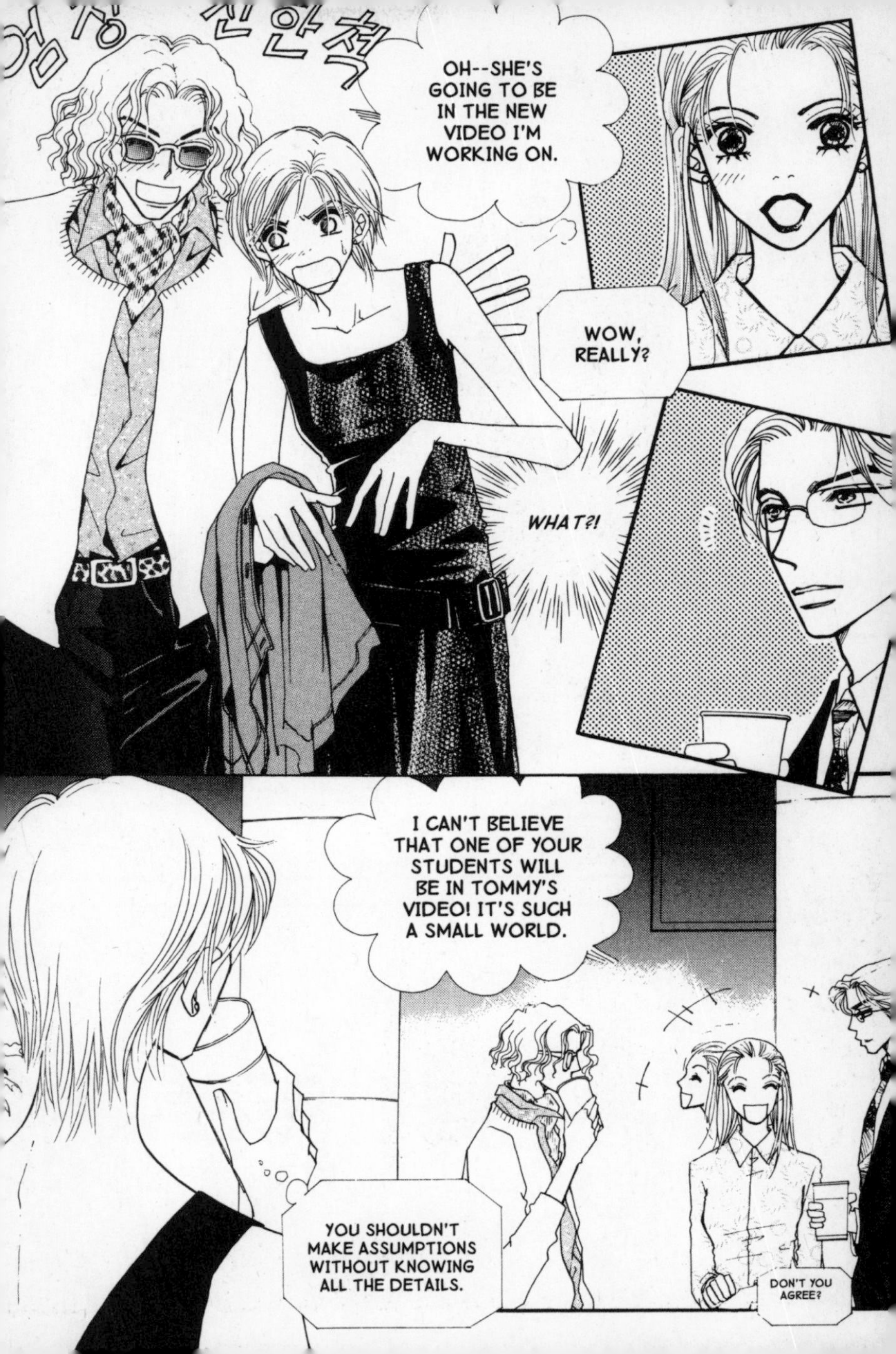
OH--SHE'S GOING TO BE IN THE NEW VIDEO I'M WORKING ON.
WOW, REALLY?
WHAT?!
I CAN'T BELIEVE THAT ONE OF YOUR STUDENTS WILL BE IN TOMMY'S VIDEO! IT'S SUCH A SMALL WORLD.
YOU SHOULDN'T MAKE ASSUMPTIONS WITHOUT KNOWING ALL THE DETAILS.
DON'T YOU AGREE?

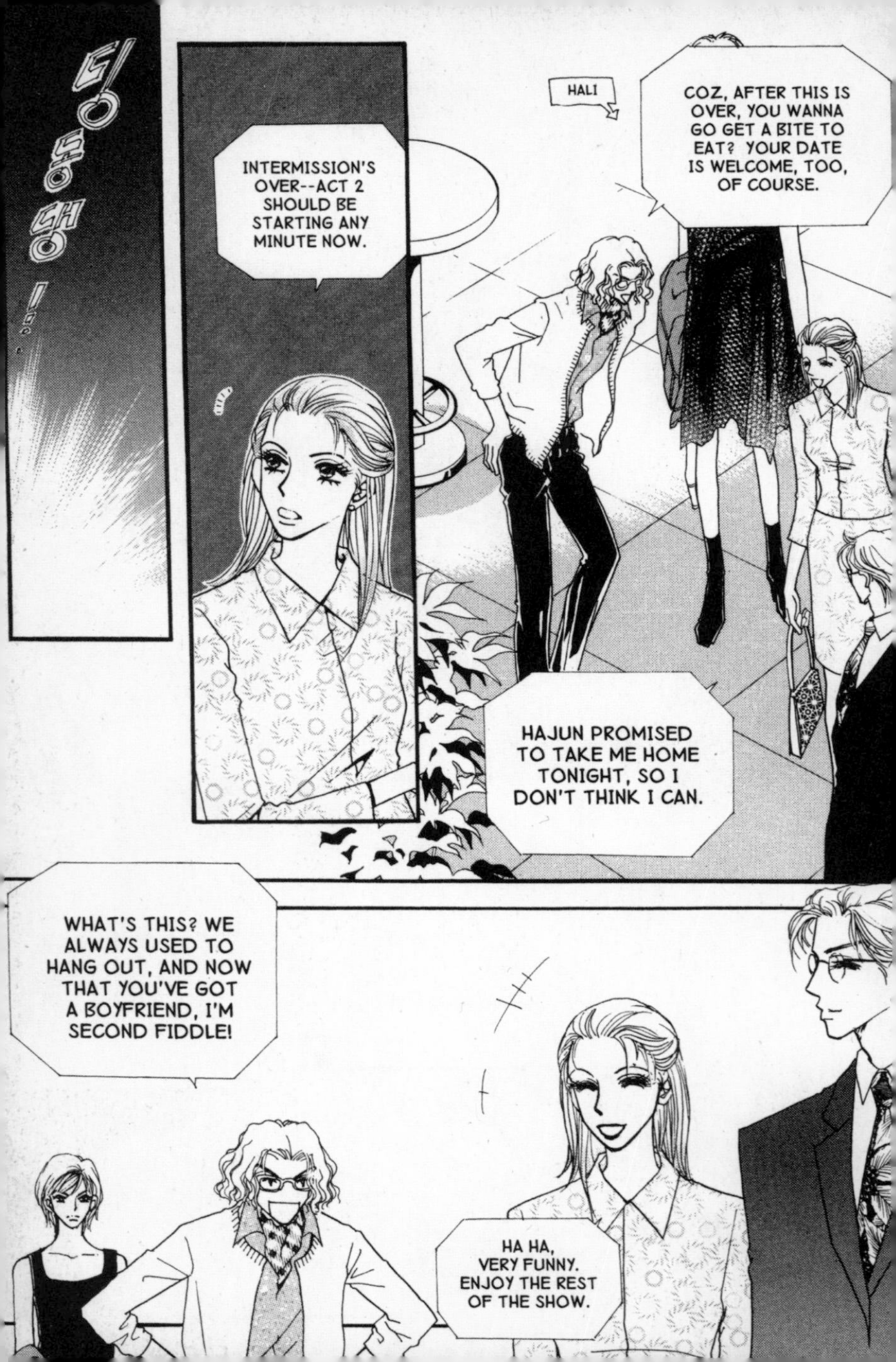
INTERMISSION'S OVER--ACT 2 SHOULD BE STARTING ANY MINUTE NOW.
HALI
COZ, AFTER THIS IS OVER, YOU WANNA GO GET A BITE TO EAT? YOUR DATE IS WELCOME, TOO, OF COURSE.
HAJUN PROMISED TO TAKE ME HOME TONIGHT, SO I DON'T THINK I CAN.
WHAT'S THIS? WE ALWAYS USED TO HANG OUT, AND NOW THAT YOU'VE GOT A BOYFRIEND, I'M SECOND FIDDLE!
HA HA, VERY FUNNY. ENJOY THE REST OF THE SHOW.

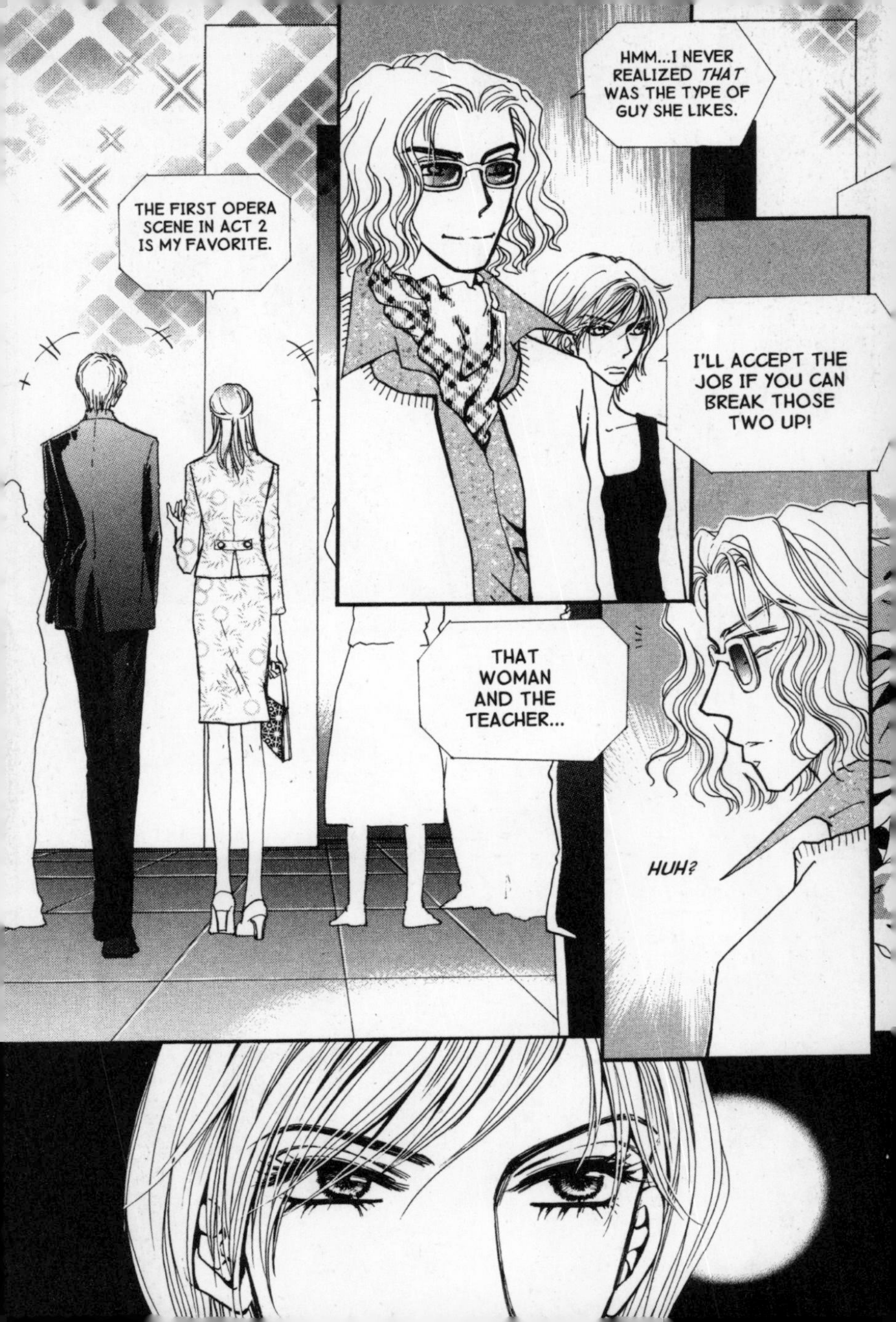
THE FIRST OPERA SCENE IN ACT 2 IS MY FAVORITE.
HMM...I NEVER REALIZED *THAT* WAS THE TYPE OF GUY SHE LIKES.
I'LL ACCEPT THE JOB IF YOU CAN BREAK THOSE TWO UP!
HUH?
THAT WOMAN AND THE TEACHER...

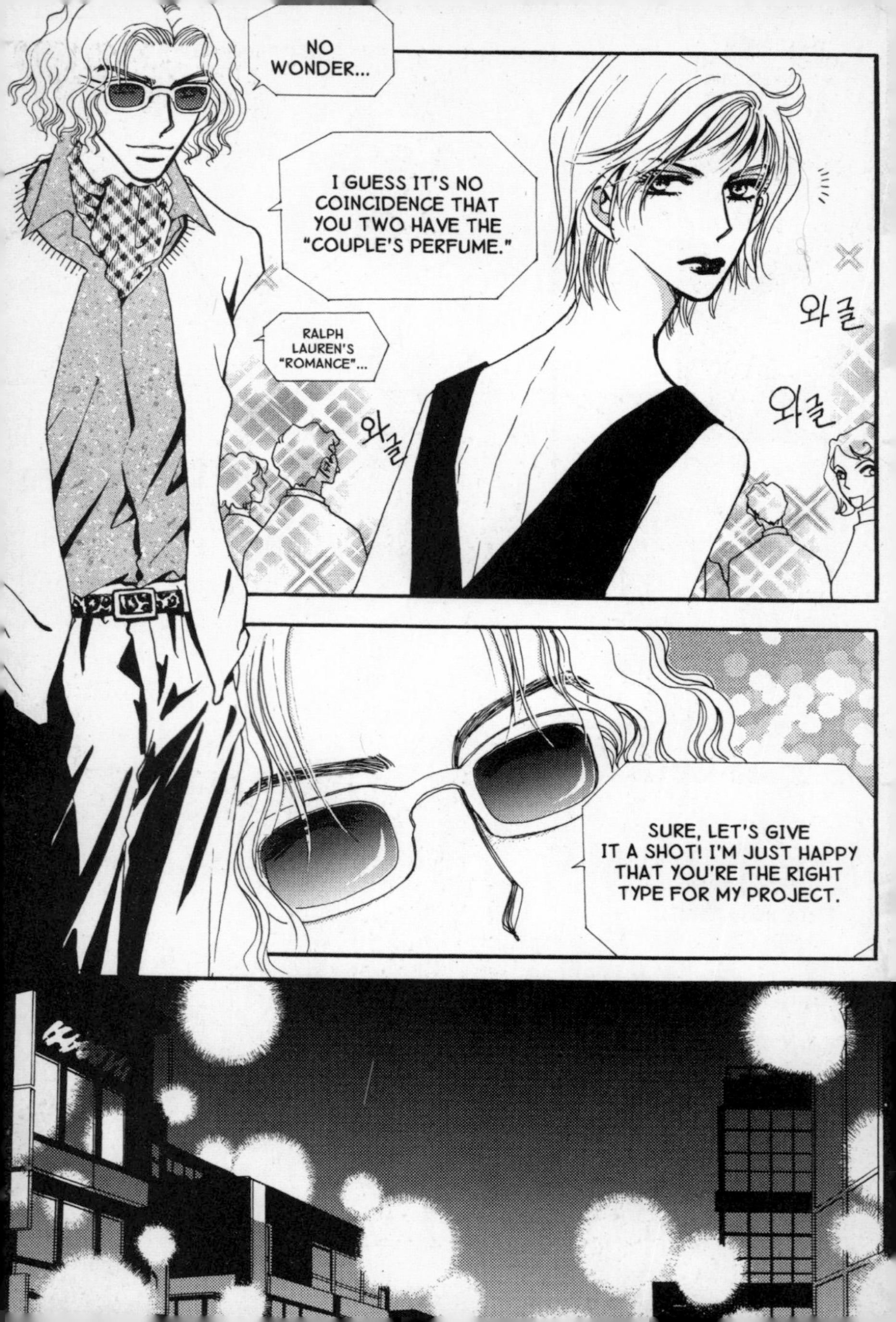
NO WONDER...
I GUESS IT'S NO COINCIDENCE THAT YOU TWO HAVE THE "COUPLE'S PERFUME."
RALPH LAUREN'S "ROMANCE"...
와글
와글
와글
SURE, LET'S GIVE IT A SHOT! I'M JUST HAPPY THAT YOU'RE THE RIGHT TYPE FOR MY PROJECT.

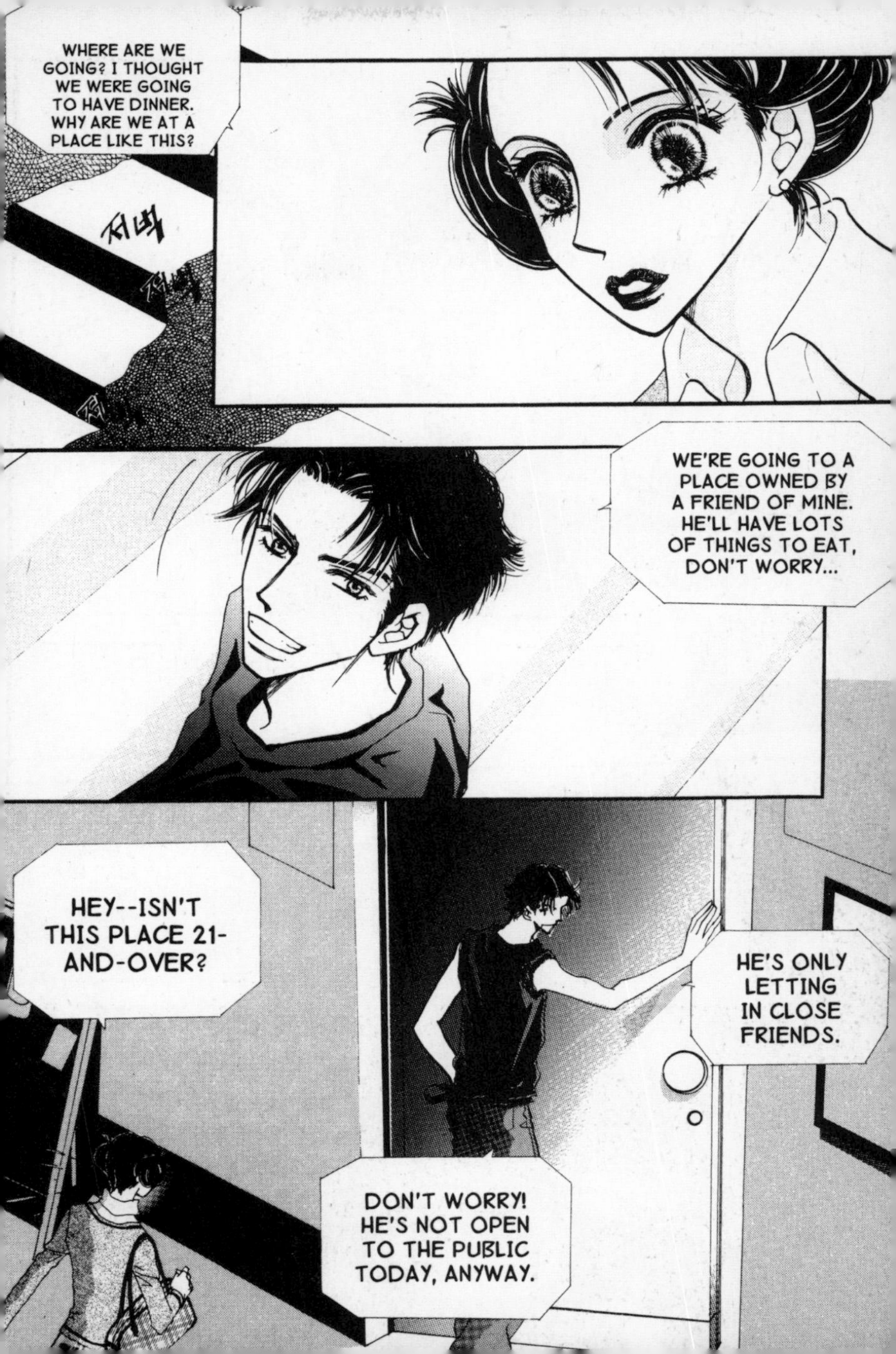
WHERE ARE WE GOING? I THOUGHT WE WERE GOING TO HAVE DINNER. WHY ARE WE AT A PLACE LIKE THIS?
저벅
저벅
WE'RE GOING TO A PLACE OWNED BY A FRIEND OF MINE. HE'LL HAVE LOTS OF THINGS TO EAT, DON'T WORRY...
HEY--ISN'T THIS PLACE 21-AND-OVER?
HE'S ONLY LETTING IN CLOSE FRIENDS.
DON'T WORRY! HE'S NOT OPEN TO THE PUBLIC TODAY, ANYWAY.

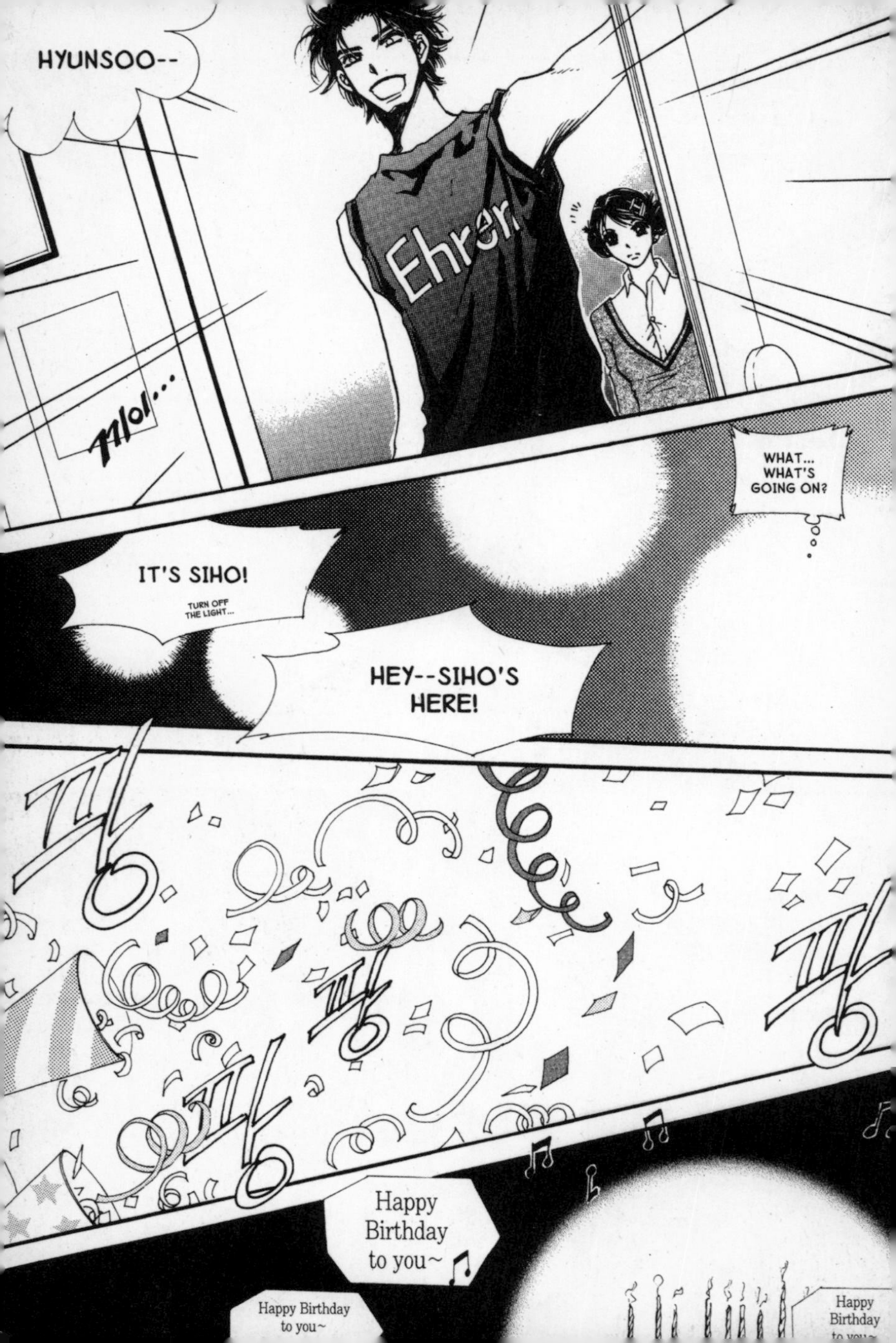
HYUNSOO--
WHAT... WHAT'S GOING ON?
IT'S SIHO!
TURN OFF THE LIGHT...
HEY--SIHO'S HERE!
Happy Birthday to you~
Happy Birthday to you~
Happy Birthday

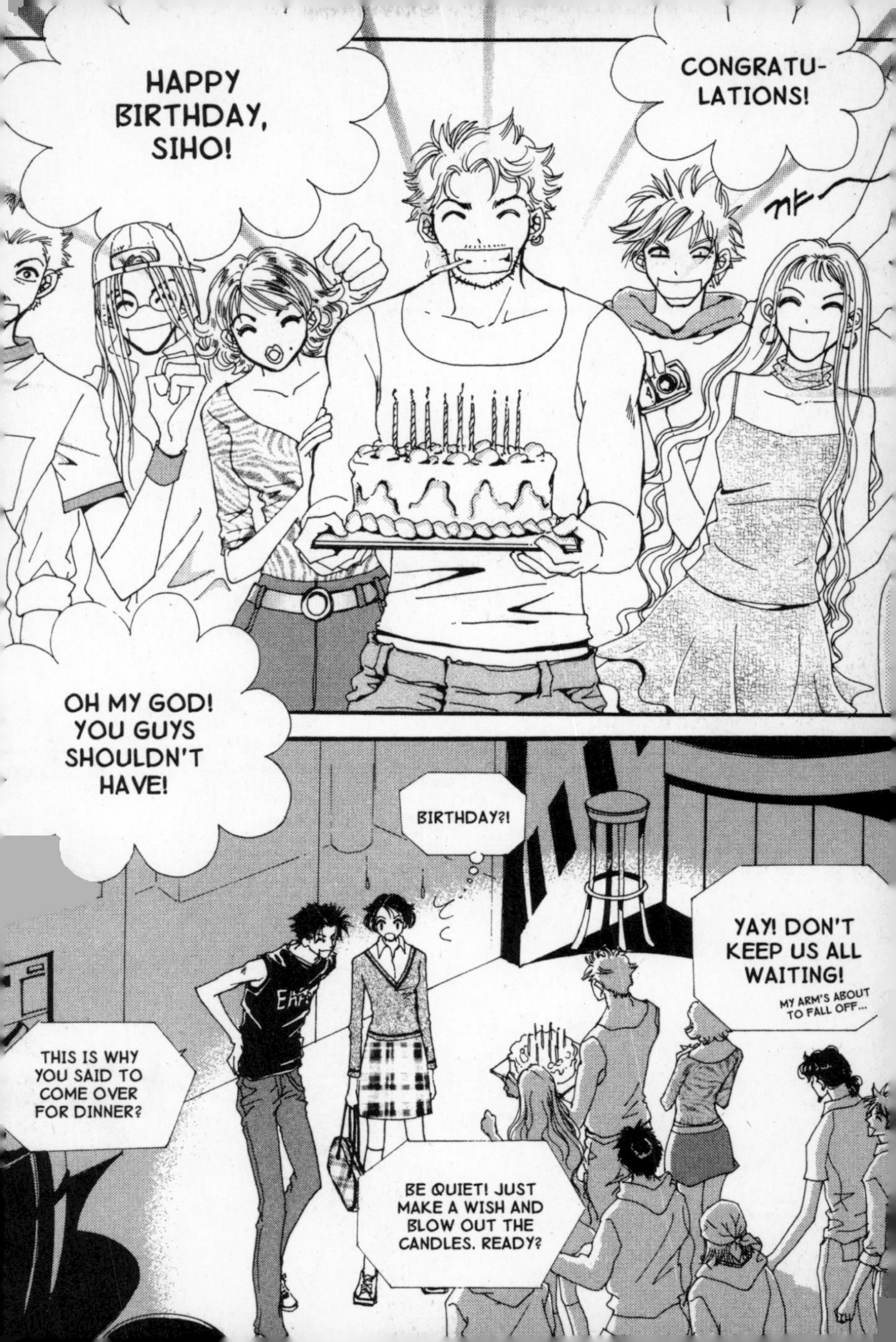
CONGRATU-
LATIONS!
HAPPY BIRTHDAY, SIHO!
OH MY GOD! YOU GUYS SHOULDN'T HAVE!
YAY! DON'T KEEP US ALL WAITING!
MY ARM'S ABOUT TO FALL OFF...
BIRTHDAY?!
THIS IS WHY YOU SAID TO COME OVER FOR DINNER?
BE QUIET! JUST MAKE A WISH AND BLOW OUT THE CANDLES. READY?

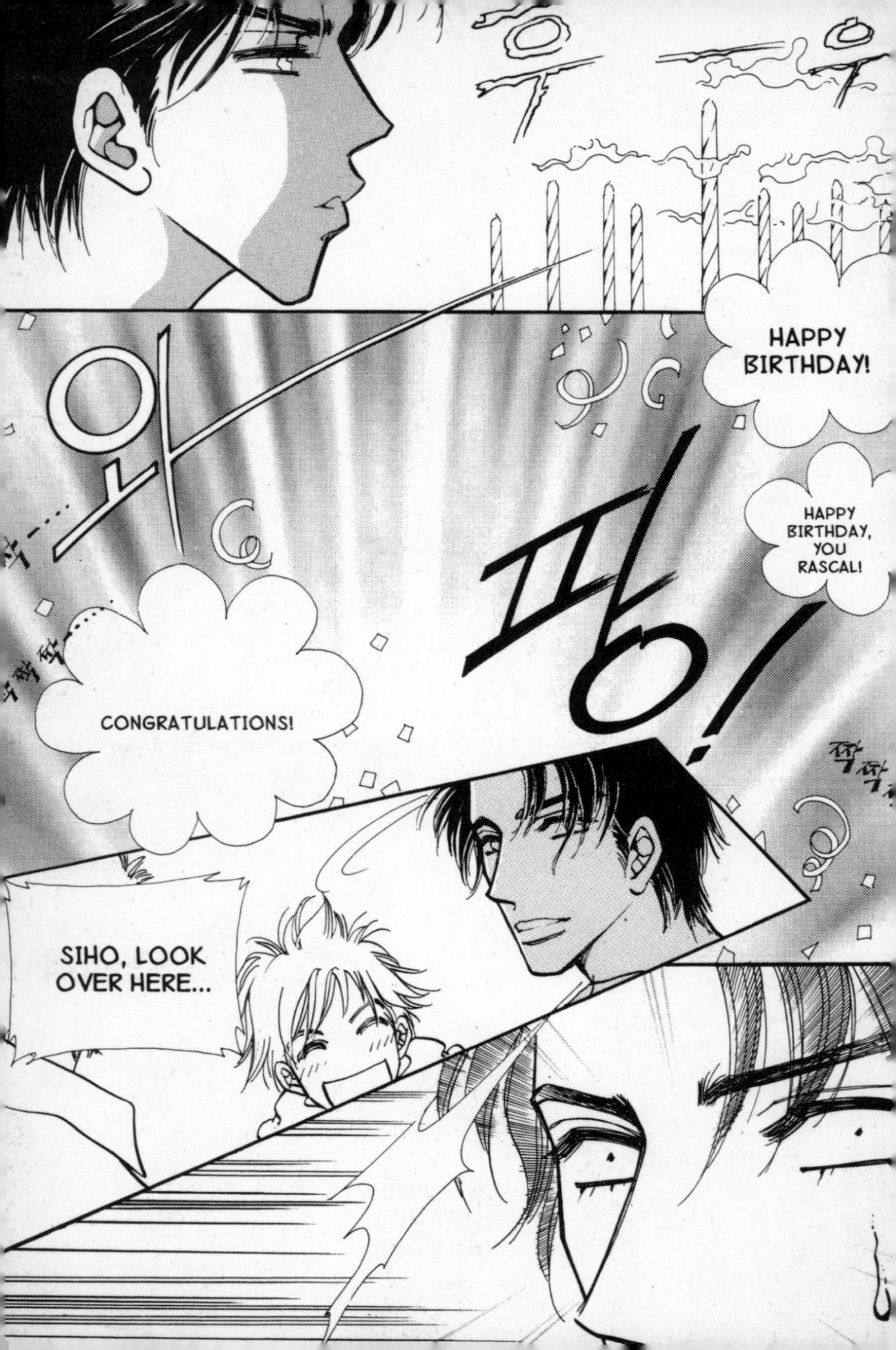
와
팡!
HAPPY BIRTHDAY!
HAPPY BIRTHDAY, YOU RASCAL!
CONGRATULATIONS!
SIHO, LOOK OVER HERE...

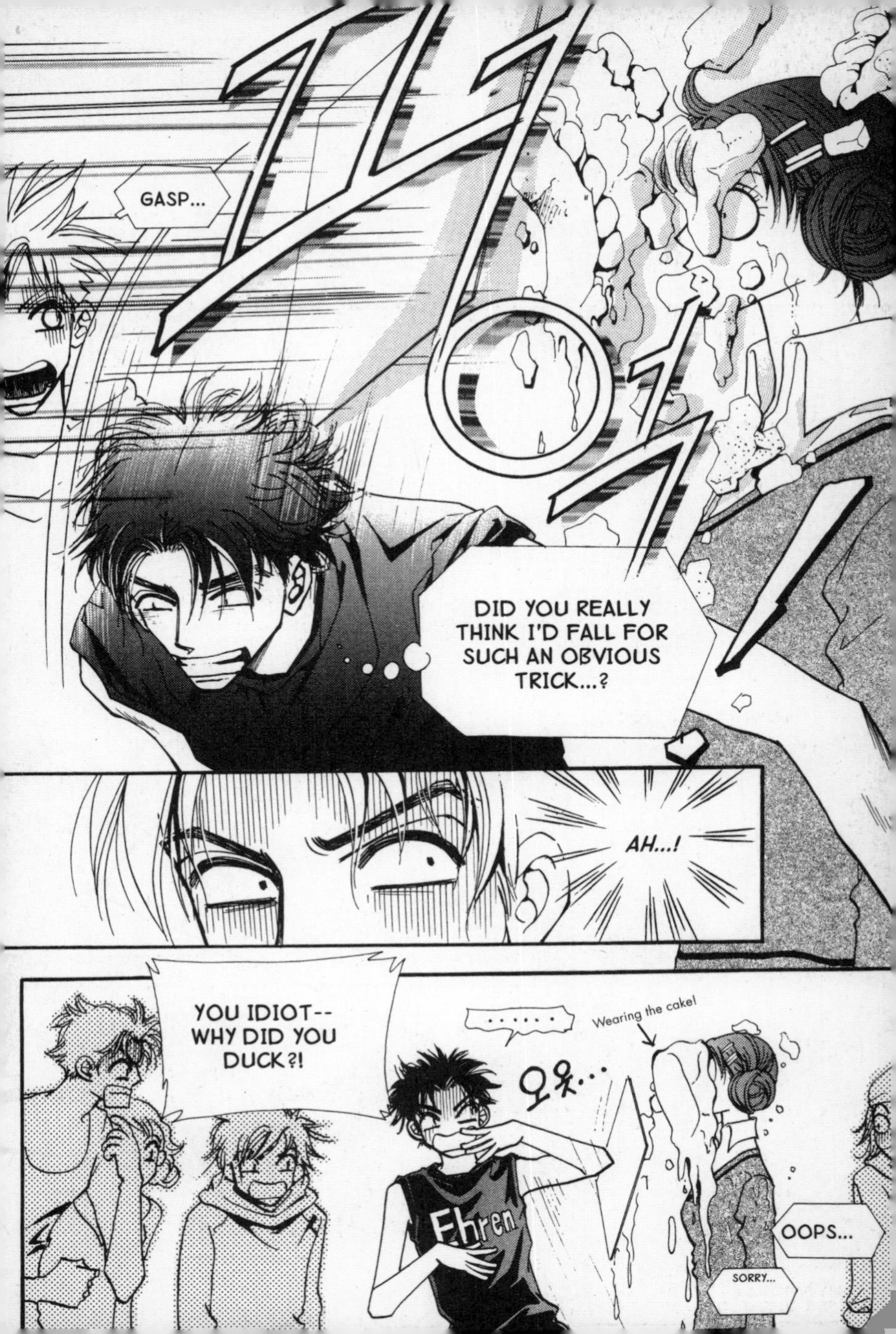
GASP...
DID YOU REALLY THINK I'D FALL FOR SUCH AN OBVIOUS TRICK...?
AH...!
OOPS...
SORRY...
Wearing the cake!
オ옷...
......
YOU IDIOT-- WHY DID YOU DUCK?!

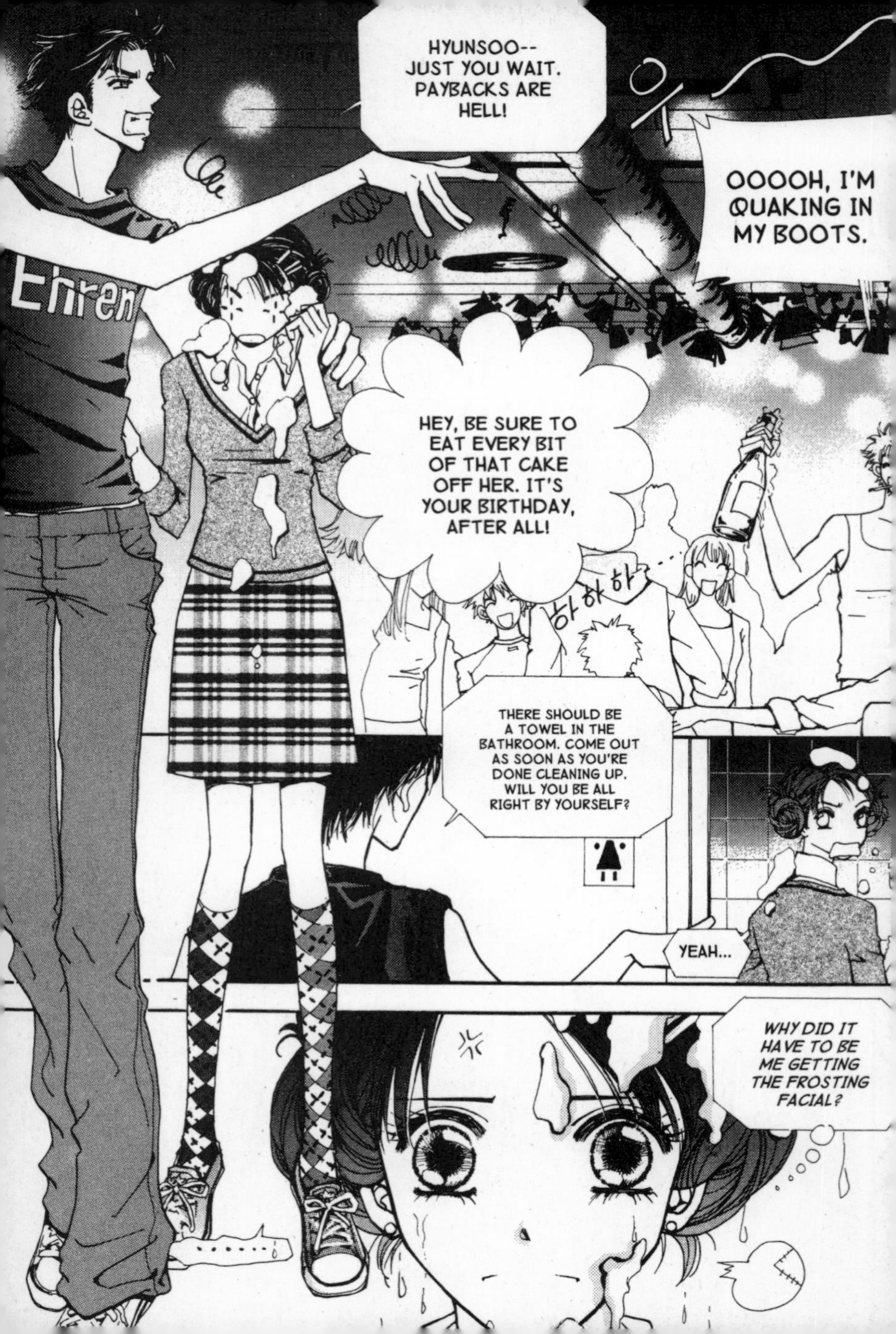
HYUNSOO-- JUST YOU WAIT. PAYBACKS ARE HELL!
OOOOH, I'M QUAKING IN MY BOOTS.
HEY, BE SURE TO EAT EVERY BIT OF THAT CAKE OFF HER. IT'S YOUR BIRTHDAY, AFTER ALL!
하하하
THERE SHOULD BE A TOWEL IN THE BATHROOM. COME OUT AS SOON AS YOU'RE DONE CLEANING UP. WILL YOU BE ALL RIGHT BY YOURSELF?
YEAH...
WHY DID IT HAVE TO BE ME GETTING THE FROSTING FACIAL?

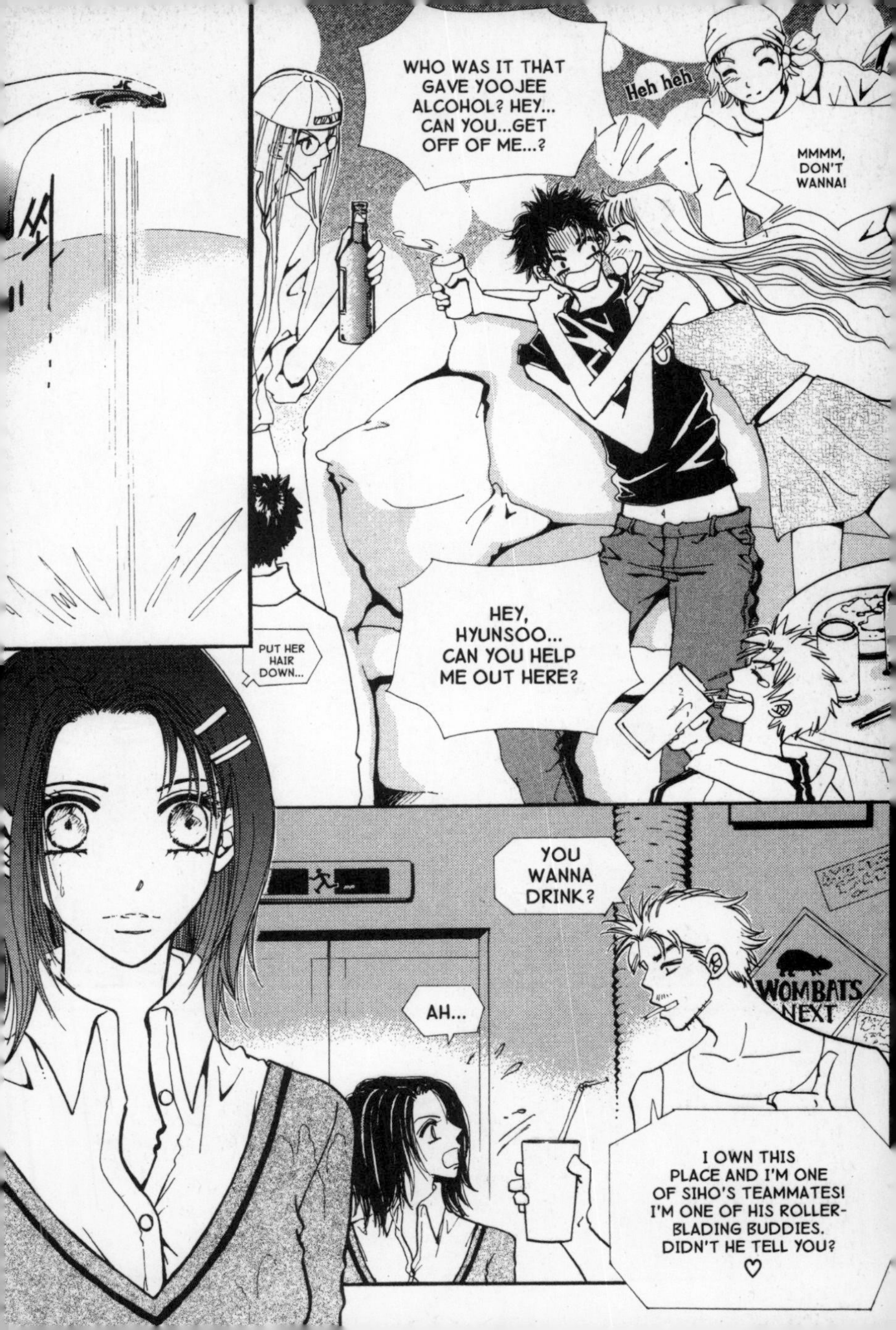
쏴
WHO WAS IT THAT GAVE YOOJEE ALCOHOL? HEY... CAN YOU...GET OFF OF ME...?
Heh heh
MMMM, DON'T WANNA!
PUT HER HAIR DOWN...
HEY, HYUNSOO... CAN YOU HELP ME OUT HERE?
YOU WANNA DRINK?
AH...
WOMBATS NEXT
I OWN THIS PLACE AND I'M ONE OF SIHO'S TEAMMATES! I'M ONE OF HIS ROLLER-BLADING BUDDIES. DIDN'T HE TELL YOU? ♡

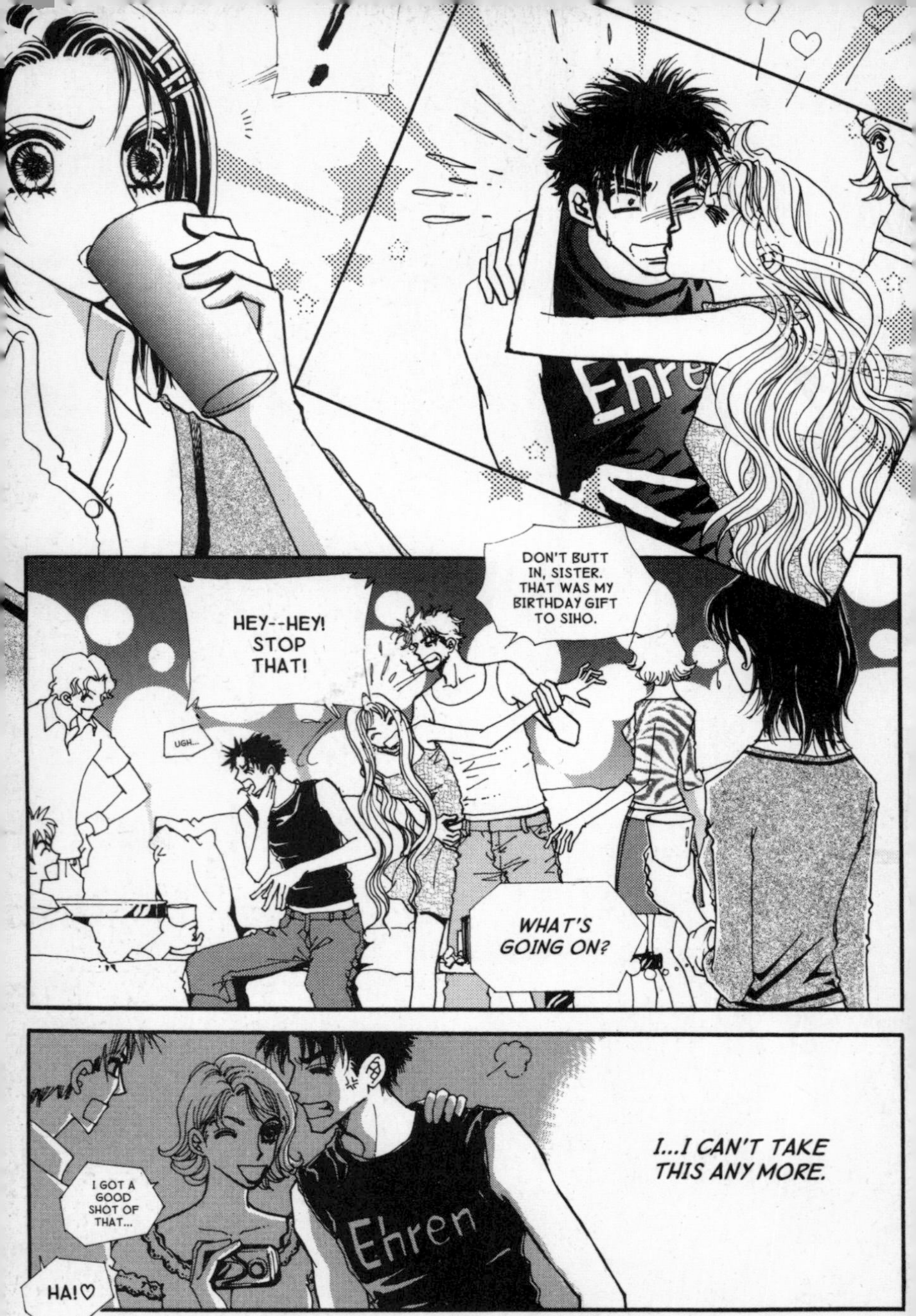
HEY--HEY! STOP THAT!
UGH...
DON'T BUTT IN, SISTER. THAT WAS MY BIRTHDAY GIFT TO SIHO.
WHAT'S GOING ON?
I GOT A GOOD SHOT OF THAT...
HA!♡
I...I CAN'T TAKE THIS ANY MORE.

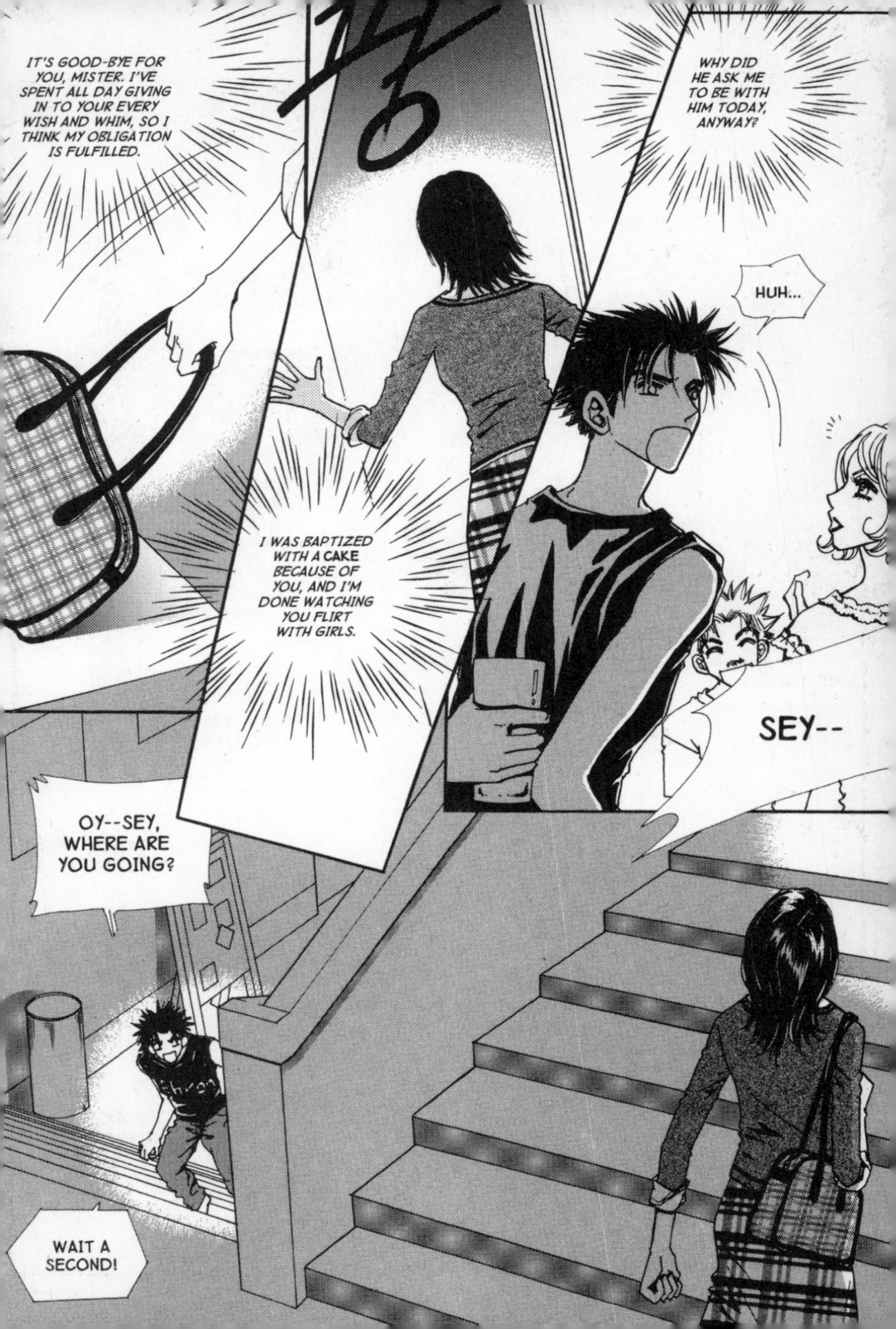
WHY DID HE ASK ME TO BE WITH HIM TODAY, ANYWAY?
HUH...
SEY--
I WAS BAPTIZED WITH A CAKE BECAUSE OF YOU, AND I'M DONE WATCHING YOU FLIRT WITH GIRLS.
IT'S GOOD-BYE FOR YOU, MISTER. I'VE SPENT ALL DAY GIVING IN TO YOUR EVERY WISH AND WHIM, SO I THINK MY OBLIGATION IS FULFILLED.
OY--SEY, WHERE ARE YOU GOING?
WAIT A SECOND!

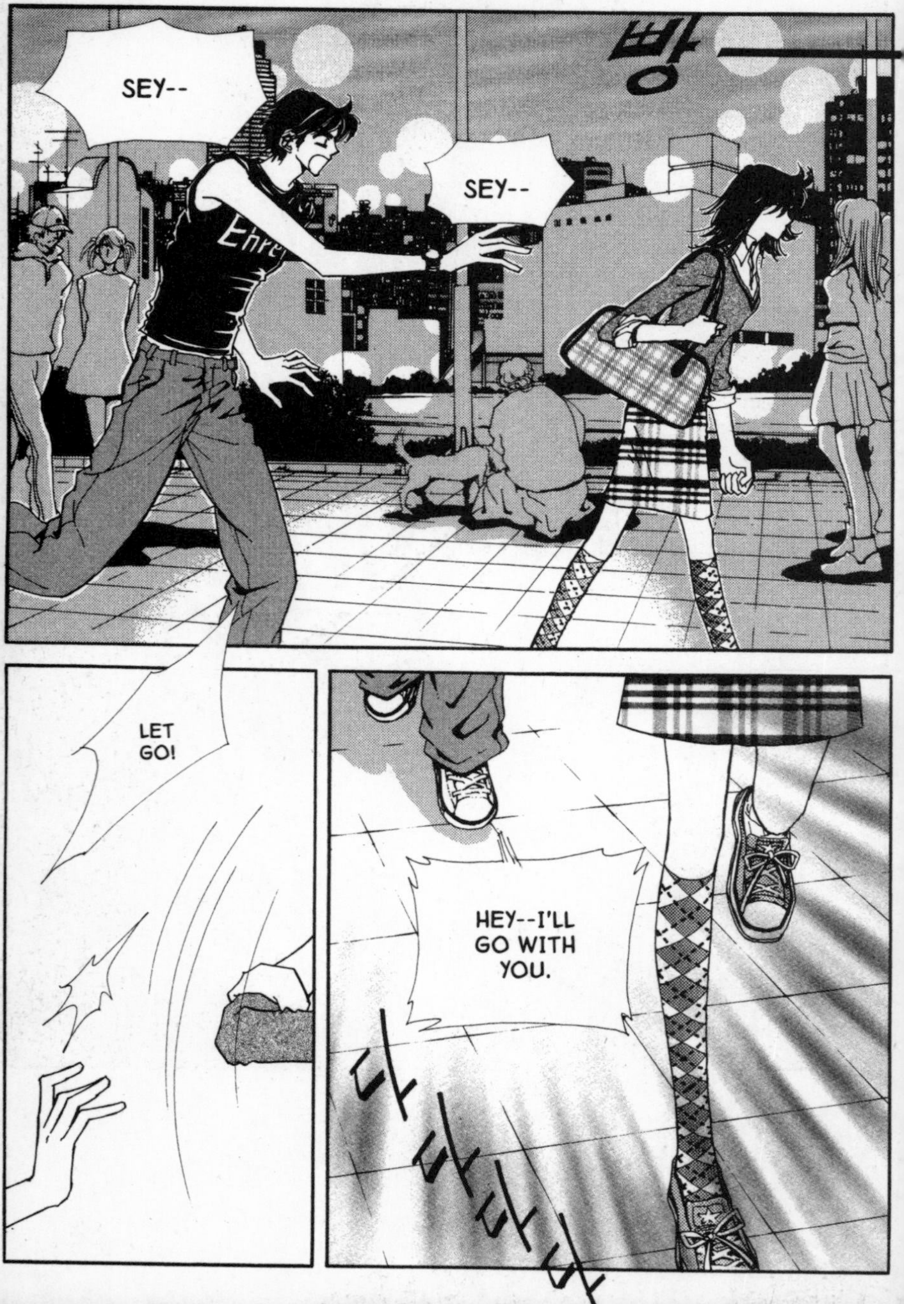
SEY--
SEY--
빵—
LET GO!
HEY--I'LL GO WITH YOU.
다다다다다

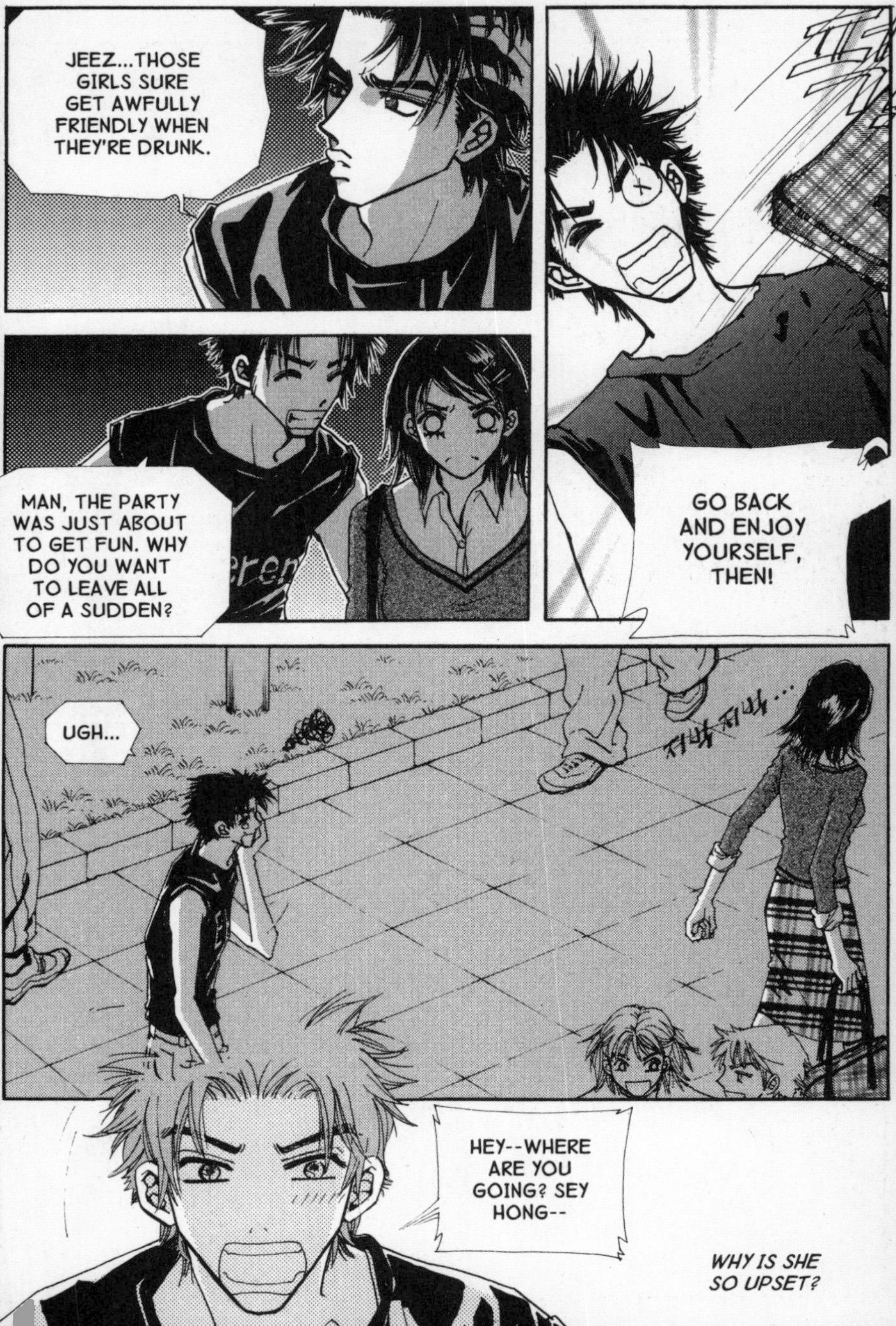
JEEZ...THOSE GIRLS SURE GET AWFULLY FRIENDLY WHEN THEY'RE DRUNK.
MAN, THE PARTY WAS JUST ABOUT TO GET FUN. WHY DO YOU WANT TO LEAVE ALL OF A SUDDEN?
GO BACK AND ENJOY YOURSELF, THEN!
UGH...
HEY--WHERE ARE YOU GOING? SEY HONG--
WHY IS SHE SO UPSET?

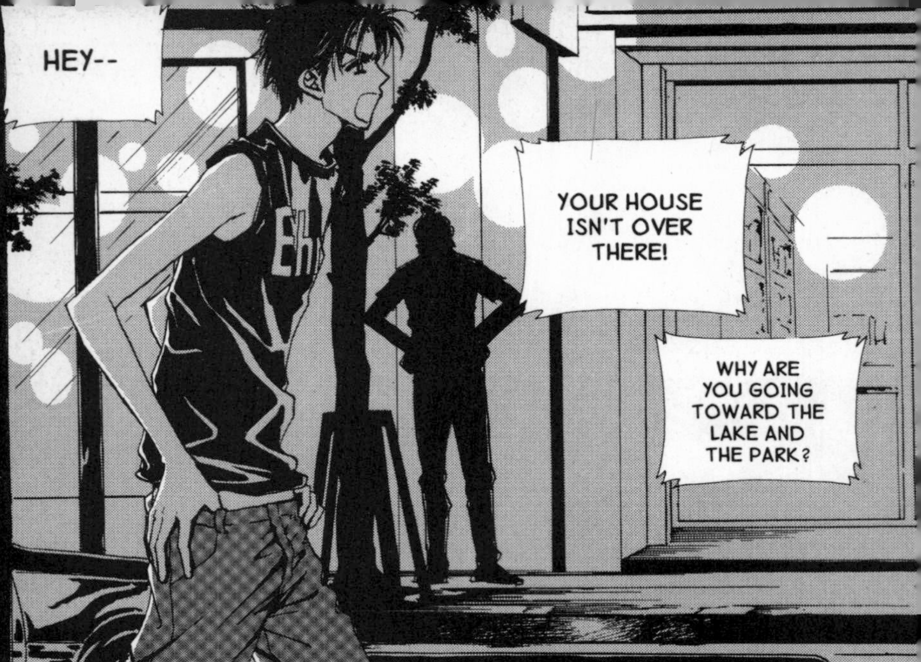
HEY--
YOUR HOUSE ISN'T OVER THERE!
WHY ARE YOU GOING TOWARD THE LAKE AND THE PARK?

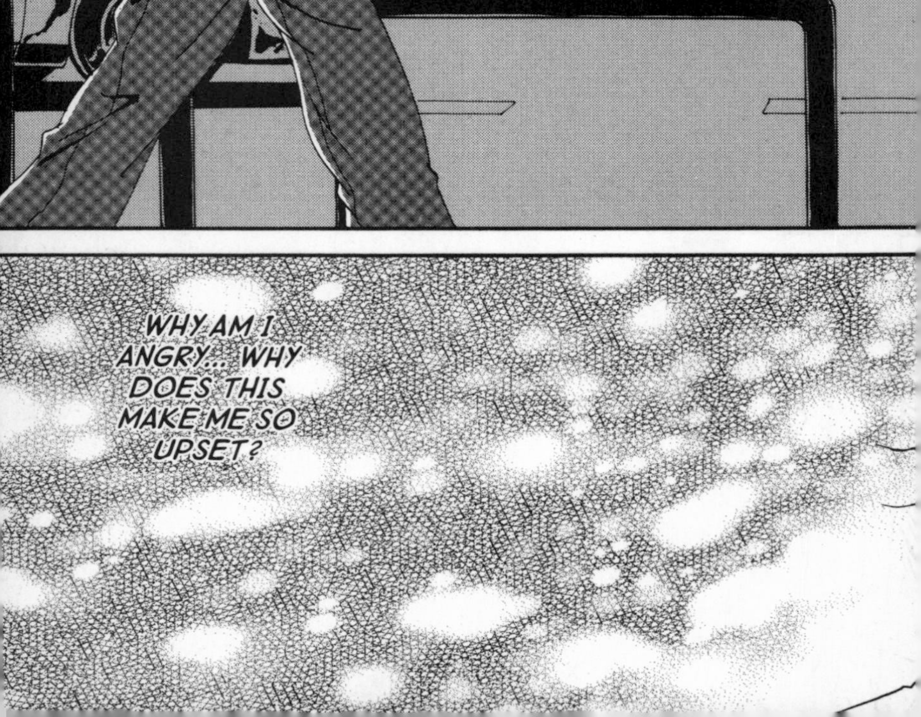
WHY AM I ANGRY... WHY DOES THIS MAKE ME SO UPSET?

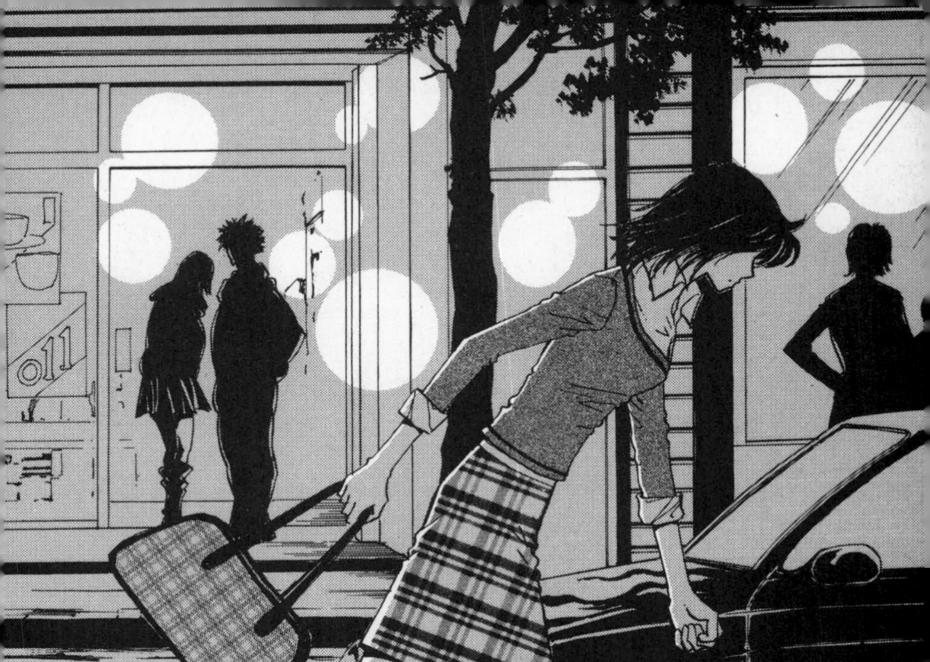
011

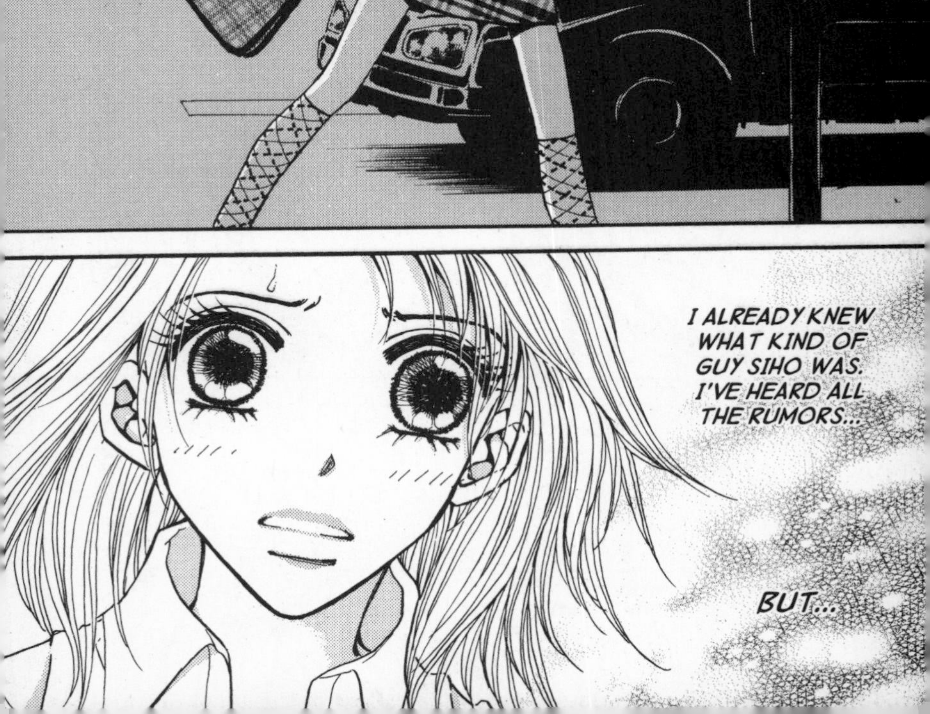
I ALREADY KNEW WHAT KIND OF GUY SIHO WAS. I'VE HEARD ALL THE RUMORS...
BUT...

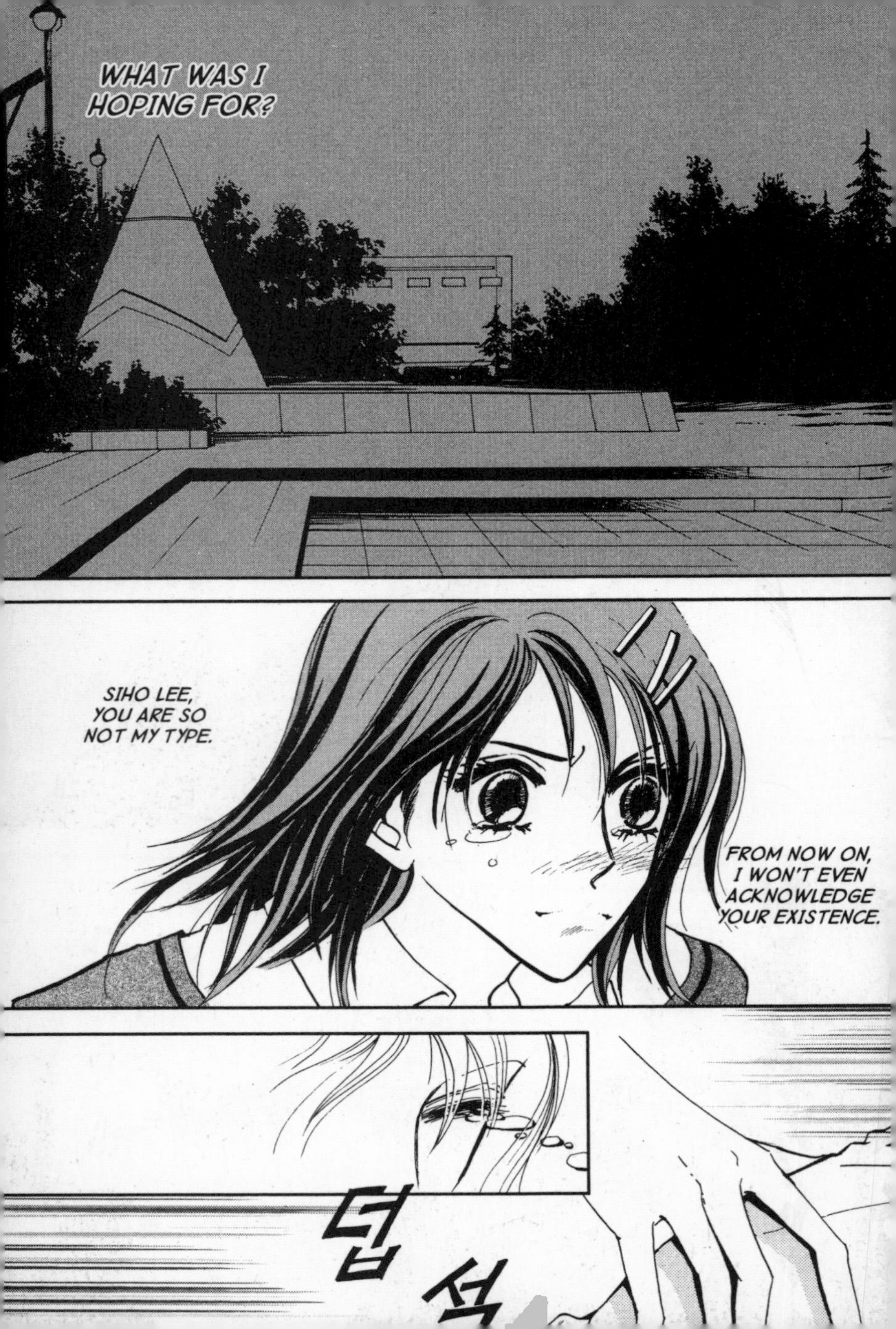
WHAT WAS I HOPING FOR?
SIHO LEE, YOU ARE SO NOT MY TYPE.
FROM NOW ON, I WON'T EVEN ACKNOWLEDGE YOUR EXISTENCE.
덥석

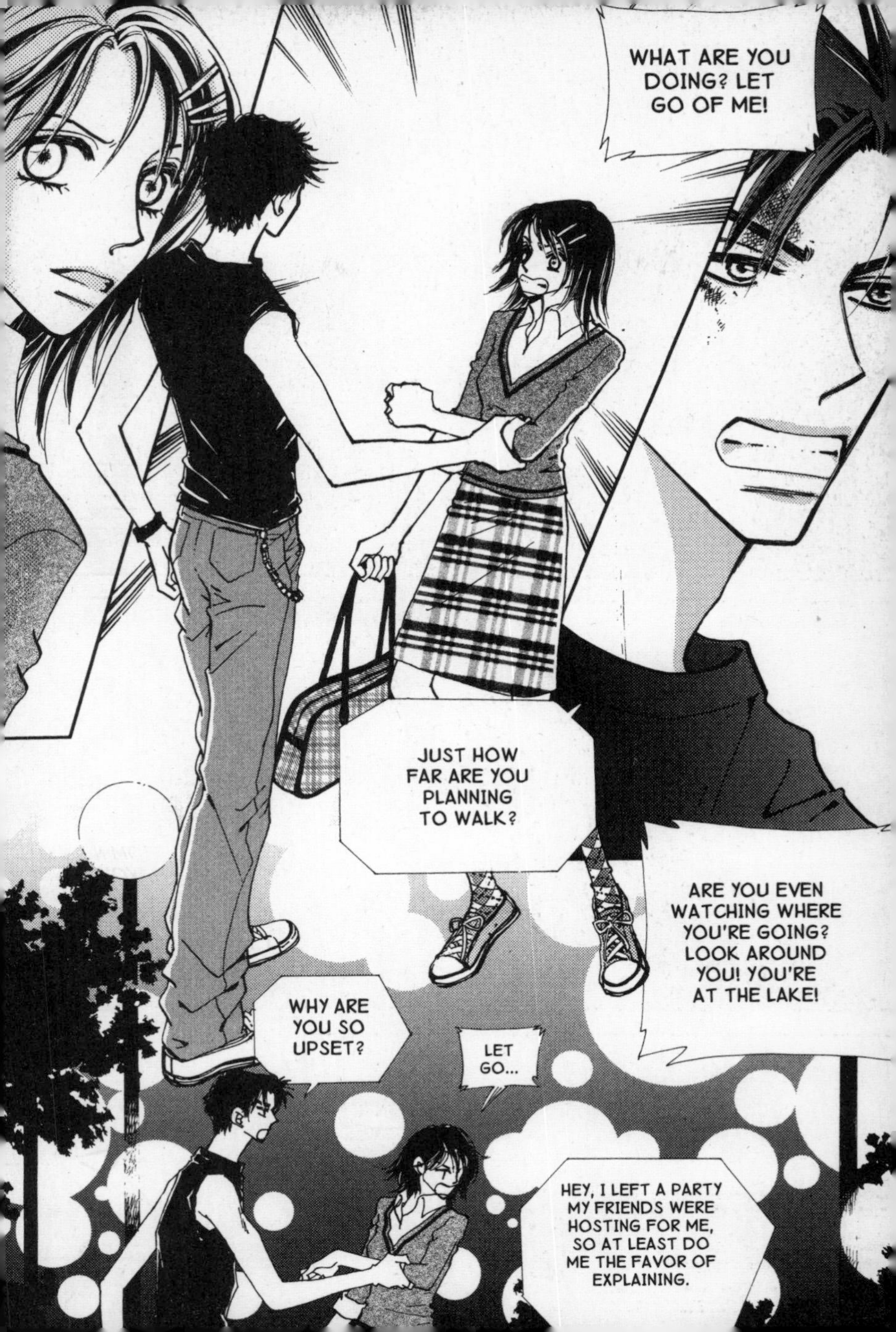
WHAT ARE YOU DOING? LET GO OF ME!
JUST HOW FAR ARE YOU PLANNING TO WALK?
ARE YOU EVEN WATCHING WHERE YOU'RE GOING? LOOK AROUND YOU! YOU'RE AT THE LAKE!
LET GO...
WHY ARE YOU SO UPSET?
HEY, I LEFT A PARTY MY FRIENDS WERE HOSTING FOR ME, SO AT LEAST DO ME THE FAVOR OF EXPLAINING.

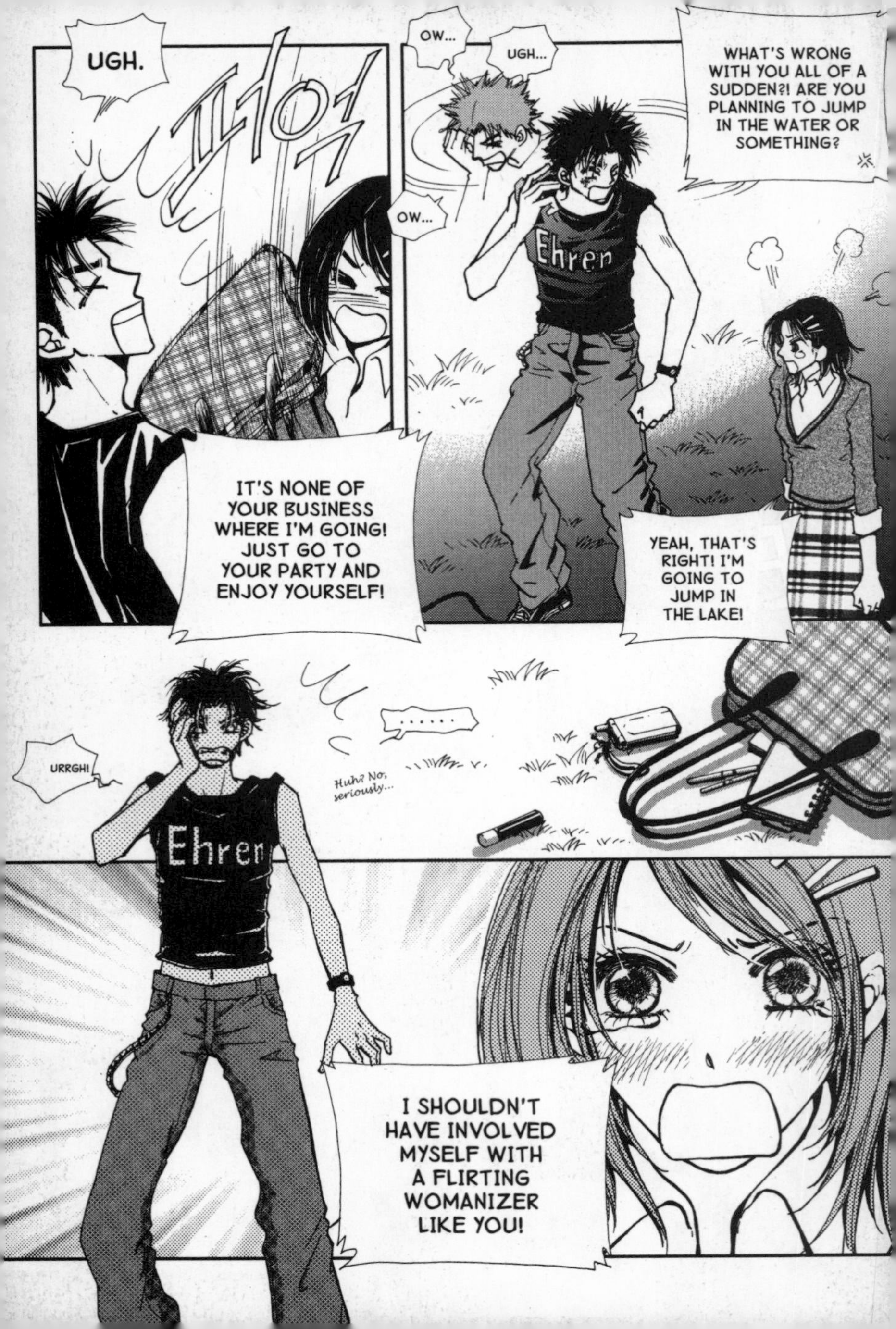
UGH.
OW...
UGH...
OW...
WHAT'S WRONG WITH YOU ALL OF A SUDDEN?! ARE YOU PLANNING TO JUMP IN THE WATER OR SOMETHING?
IT'S NONE OF YOUR BUSINESS WHERE I'M GOING! JUST GO TO YOUR PARTY AND ENJOY YOURSELF!
YEAH, THAT'S RIGHT! I'M GOING TO JUMP IN THE LAKE!
Ehren
URRGH!
......
Huh? No, seriously...
Ehren
I SHOULDN'T HAVE INVOLVED MYSELF WITH A FLIRTING WOMANIZER LIKE YOU!

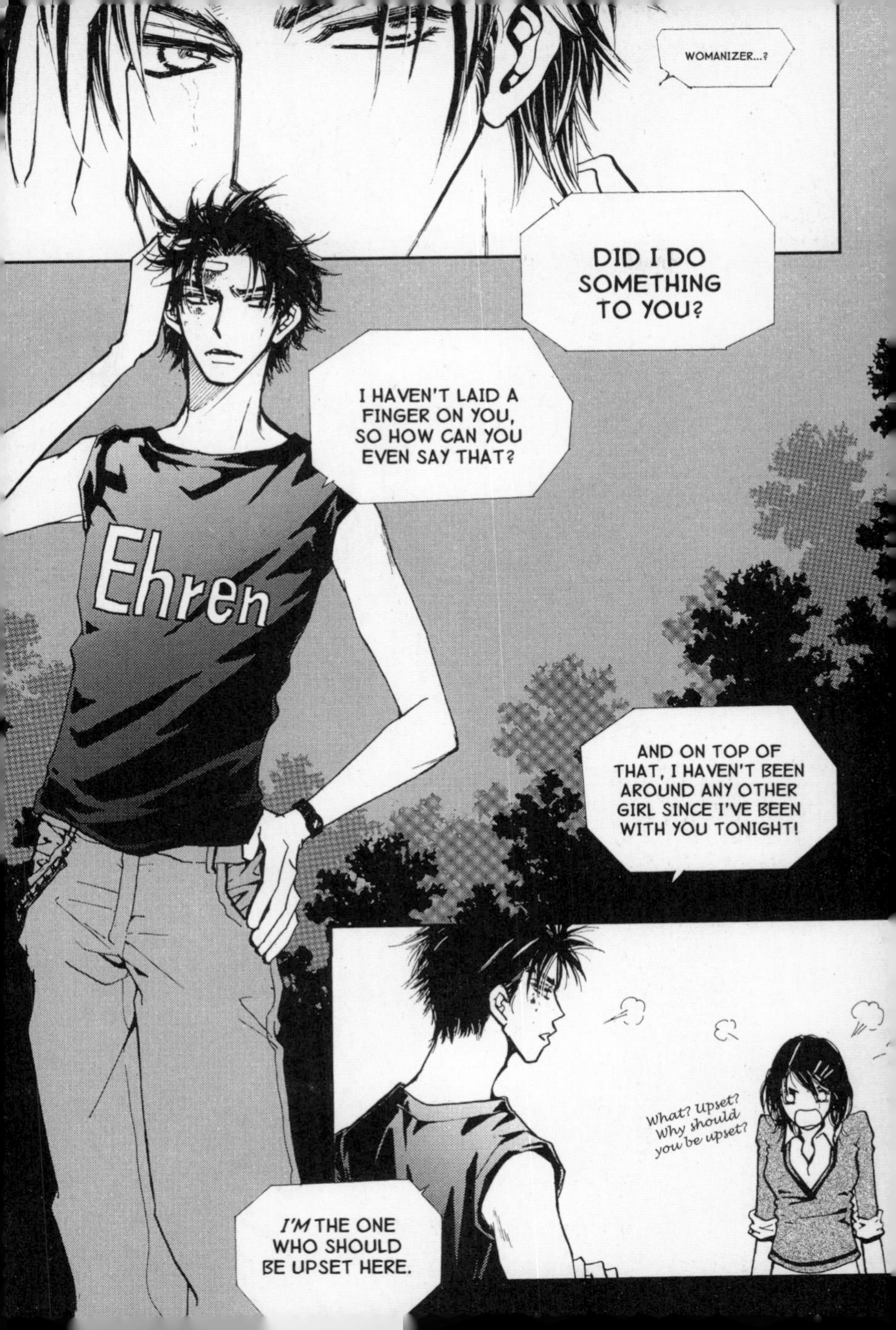
WOMANIZER...?
DID I DO SOMETHING TO YOU?
I HAVEN'T LAID A FINGER ON YOU, SO HOW CAN YOU EVEN SAY THAT?
Ehren
AND ON TOP OF THAT, I HAVEN'T BEEN AROUND ANY OTHER GIRL SINCE I'VE BEEN WITH YOU TONIGHT!
What? Upset? Why should you be upset?
I'M THE ONE WHO SHOULD BE UPSET HERE.

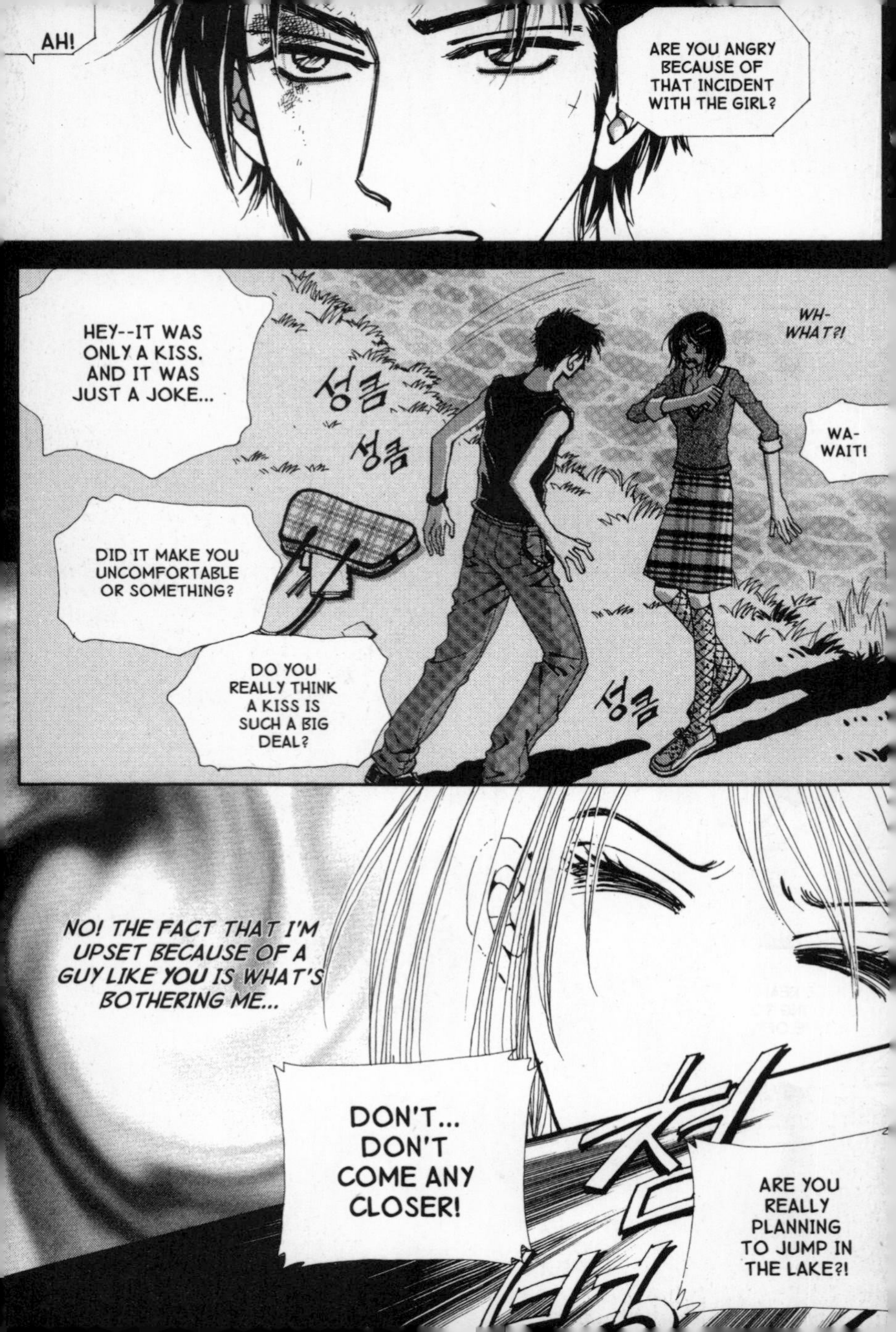
AH!
ARE YOU ANGRY BECAUSE OF THAT INCIDENT WITH THE GIRL?
HEY--IT WAS ONLY A KISS. AND IT WAS JUST A JOKE...
성큼
성큼
DID IT MAKE YOU UNCOMFORTABLE OR SOMETHING?
DO YOU REALLY THINK A KISS IS SUCH A BIG DEAL?
성큼
WH- WHAT?!
WA- WAIT!
NO! THE FACT THAT I'M UPSET BECAUSE OF A GUY LIKE YOU IS WHAT'S BOTHERING ME...
DON'T... DON'T COME ANY CLOSER!
ARE YOU REALLY PLANNING TO JUMP IN THE LAKE?!

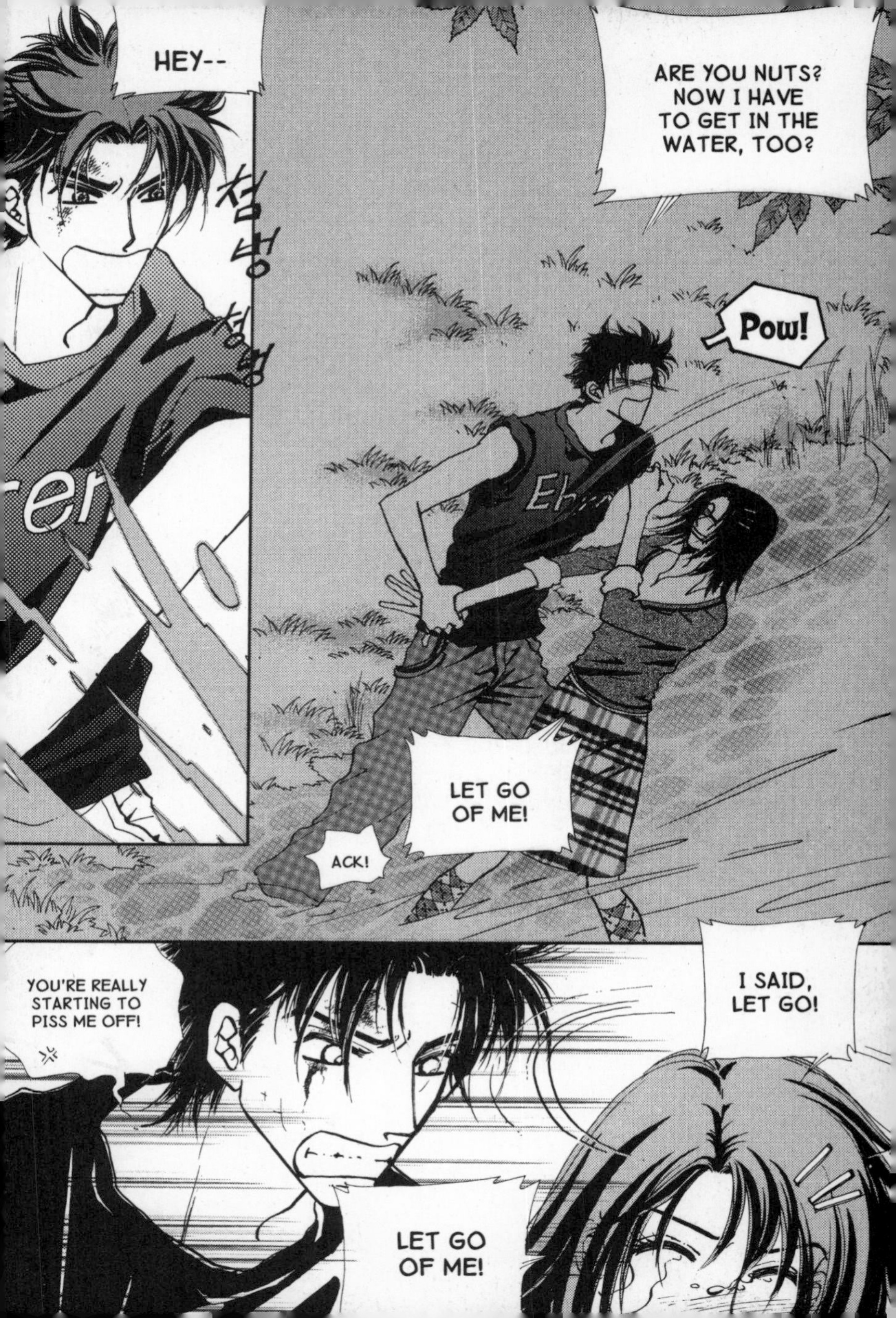
HEY--
첨벙 첨벙
ARE YOU NUTS? NOW I HAVE TO GET IN THE WATER, TOO?
Pow!
LET GO OF ME!
ACK!
YOU'RE REALLY STARTING TO PISS ME OFF!
I SAID, LET GO!
LET GO OF ME!

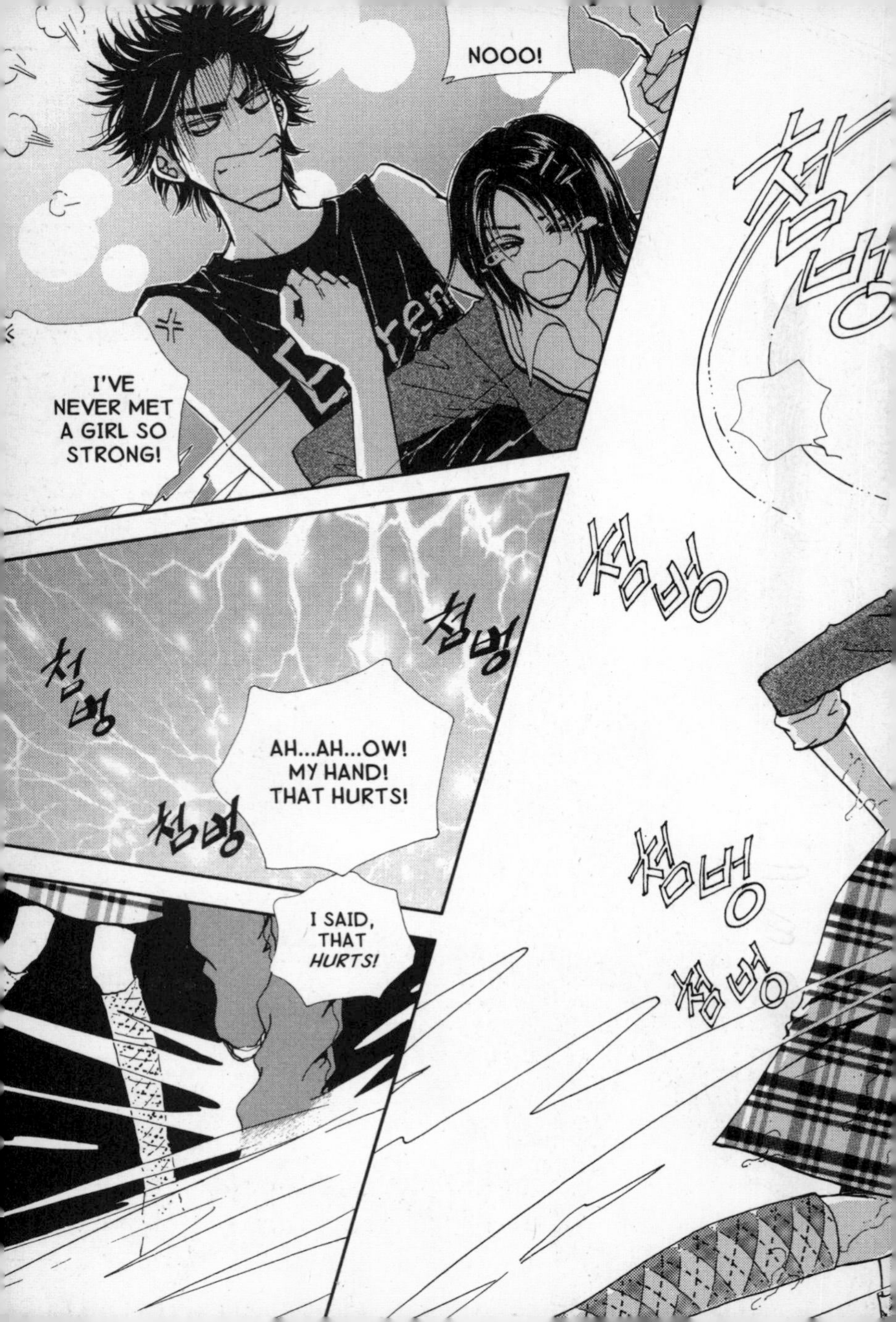
NOOO!
I'VE NEVER MET A GIRL SO STRONG!
첨벙
첨벙
첨벙
첨벙
첨벙
AH...AH...OW! MY HAND! THAT HURTS!
첨벙
첨벙
I SAID, THAT *HURTS!*

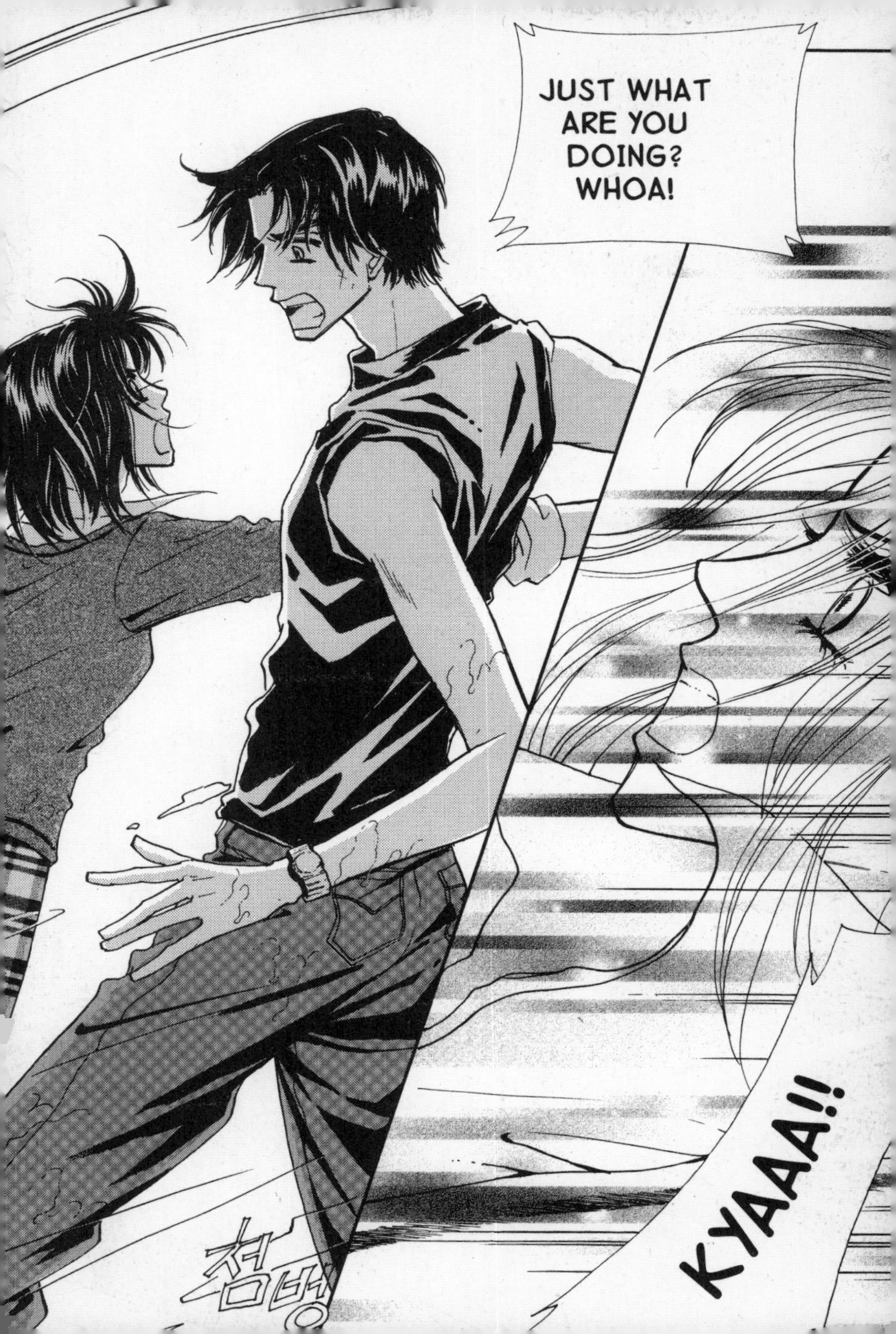
JUST WHAT ARE YOU DOING? WHOA!
KYAAA!!
첨벙

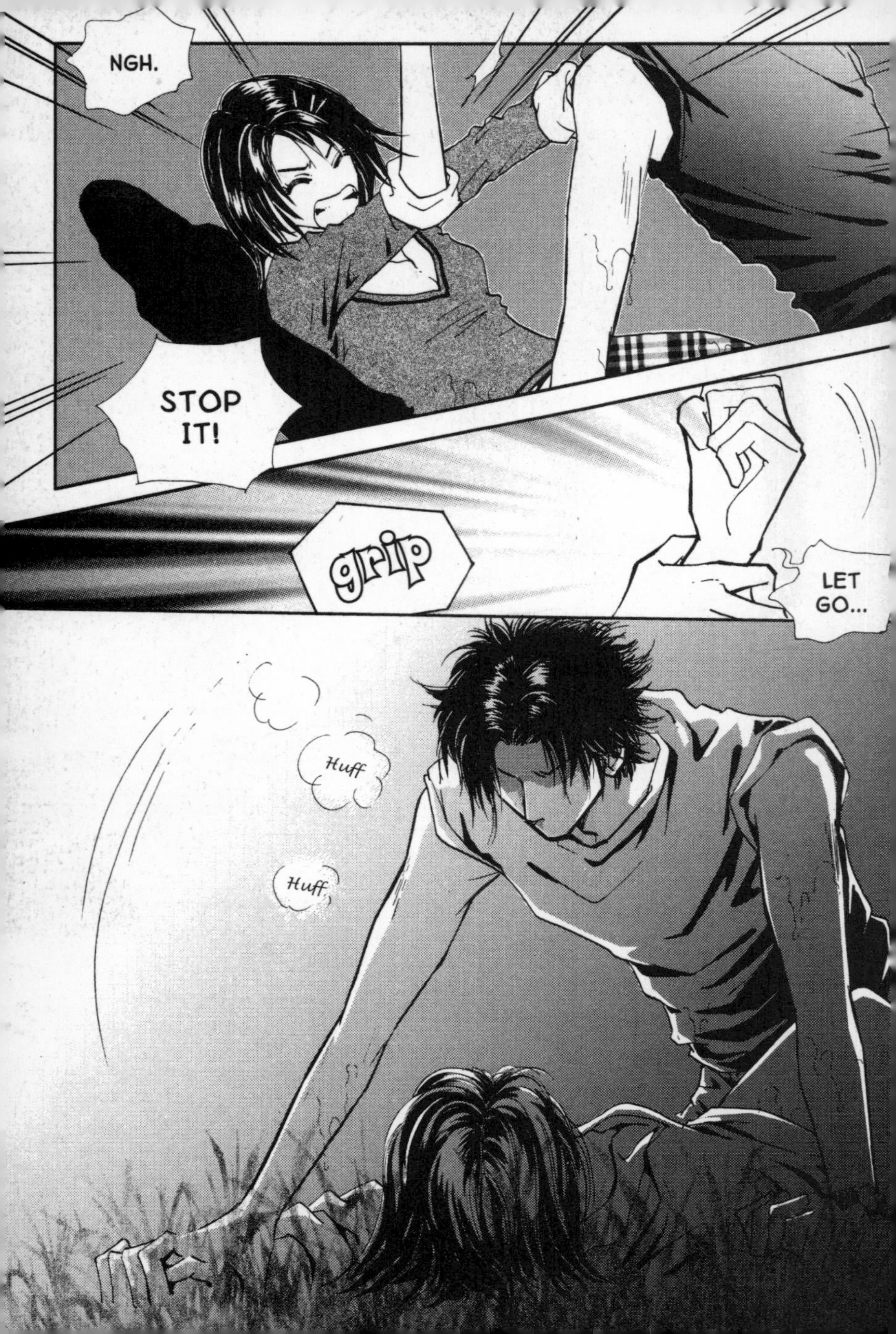
NGH.
STOP IT!
grip
LET GO...
Huff
Huff

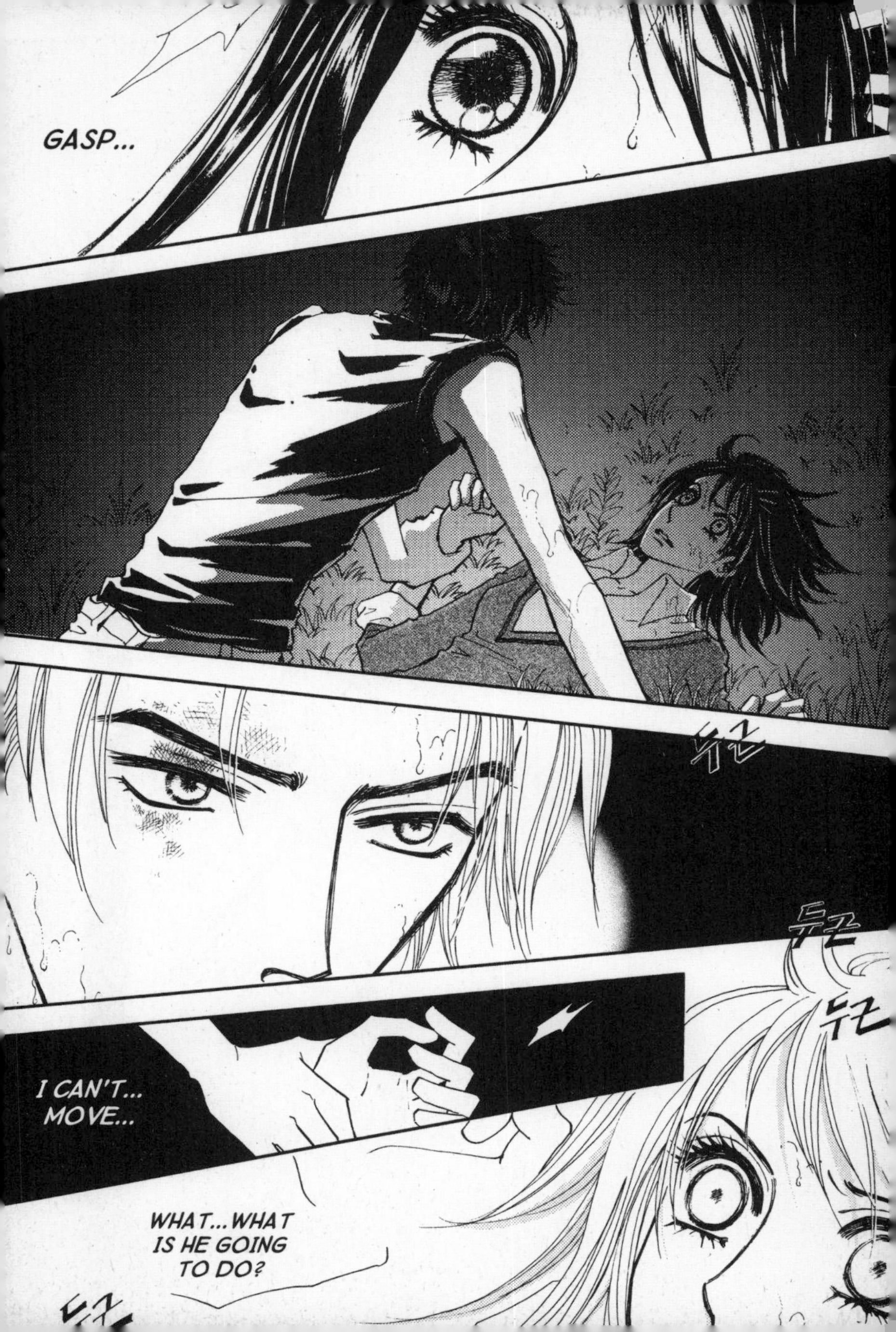
GASP...
I CAN'T... MOVE...
WHAT...WHAT IS HE GOING TO DO?

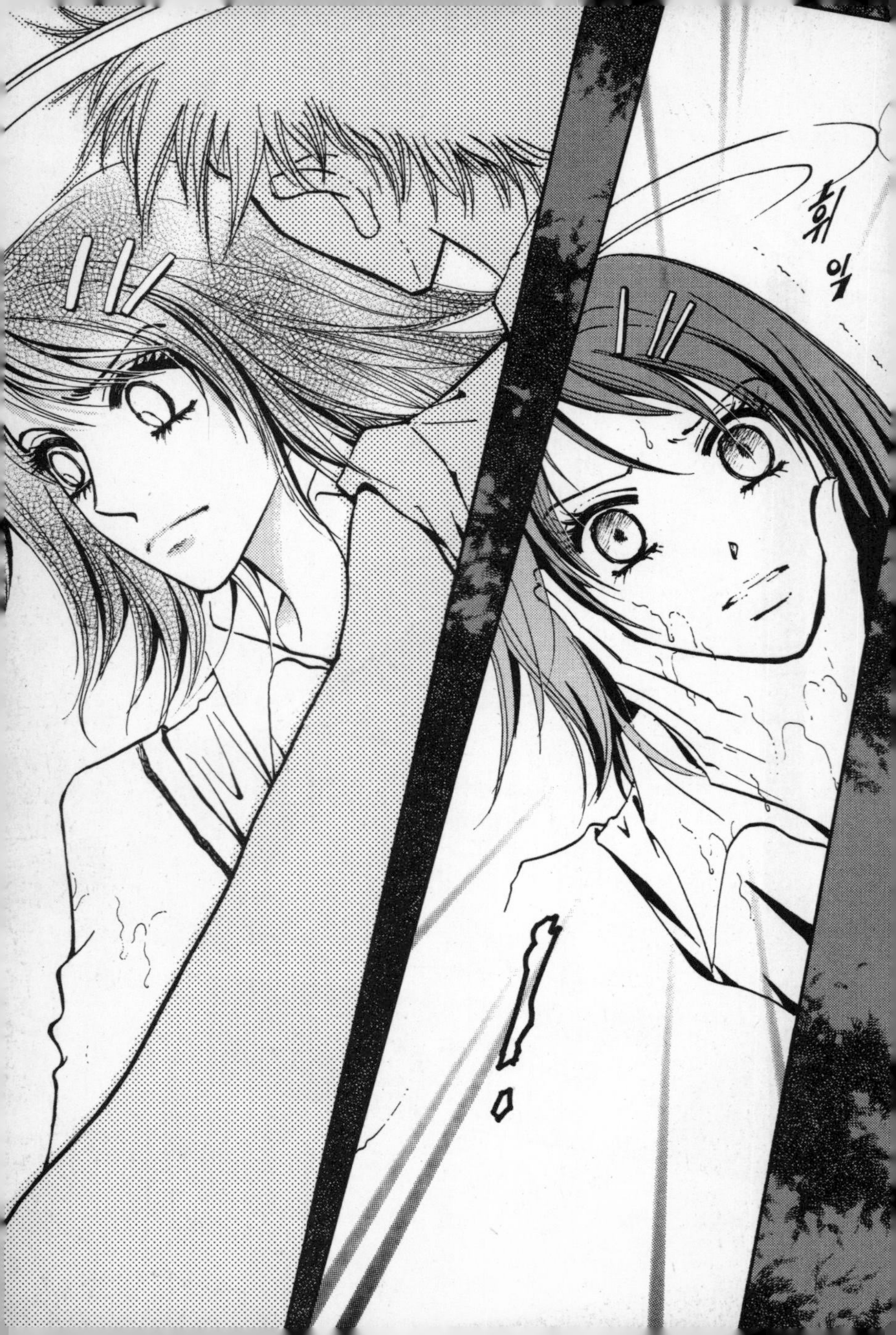
휘익

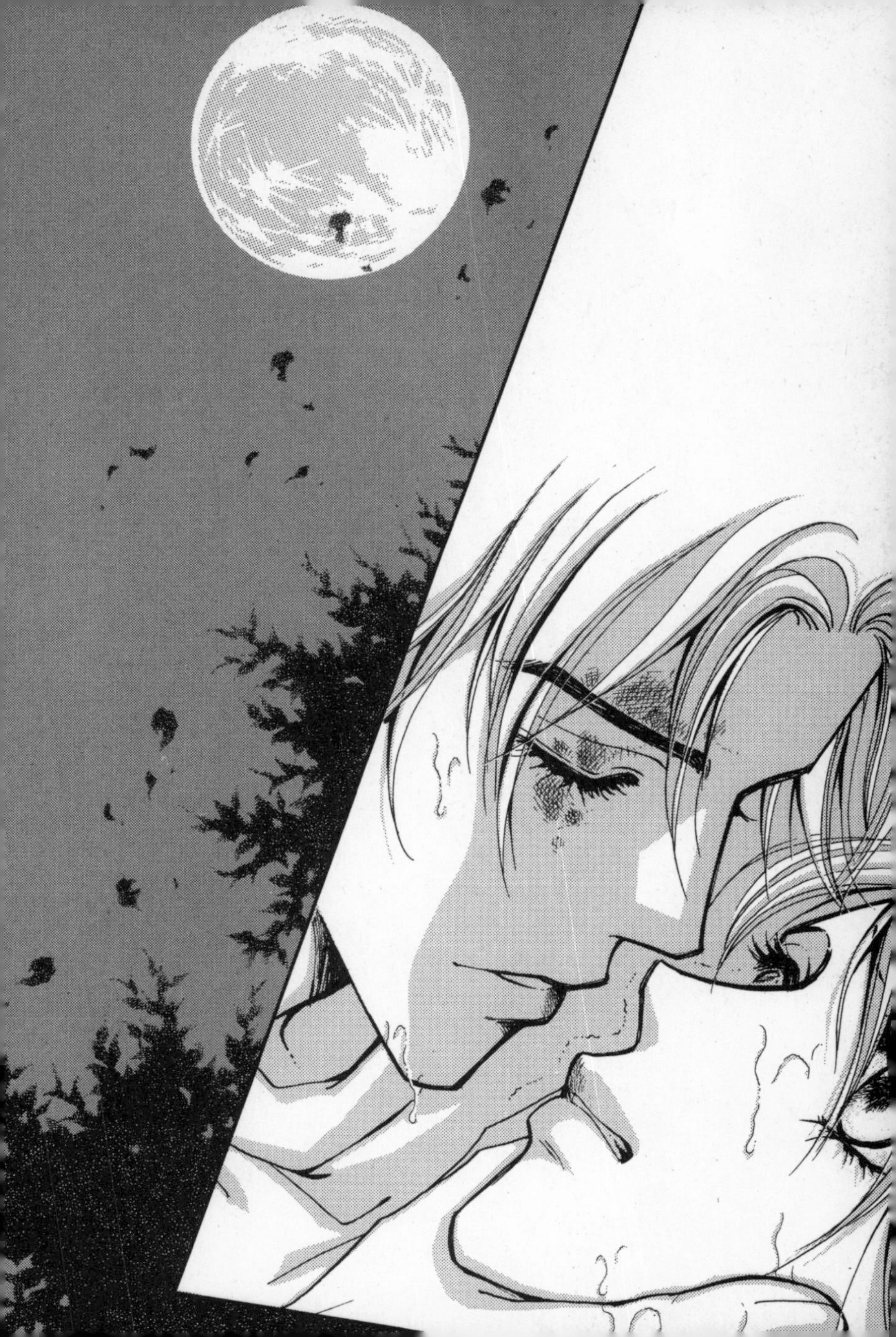

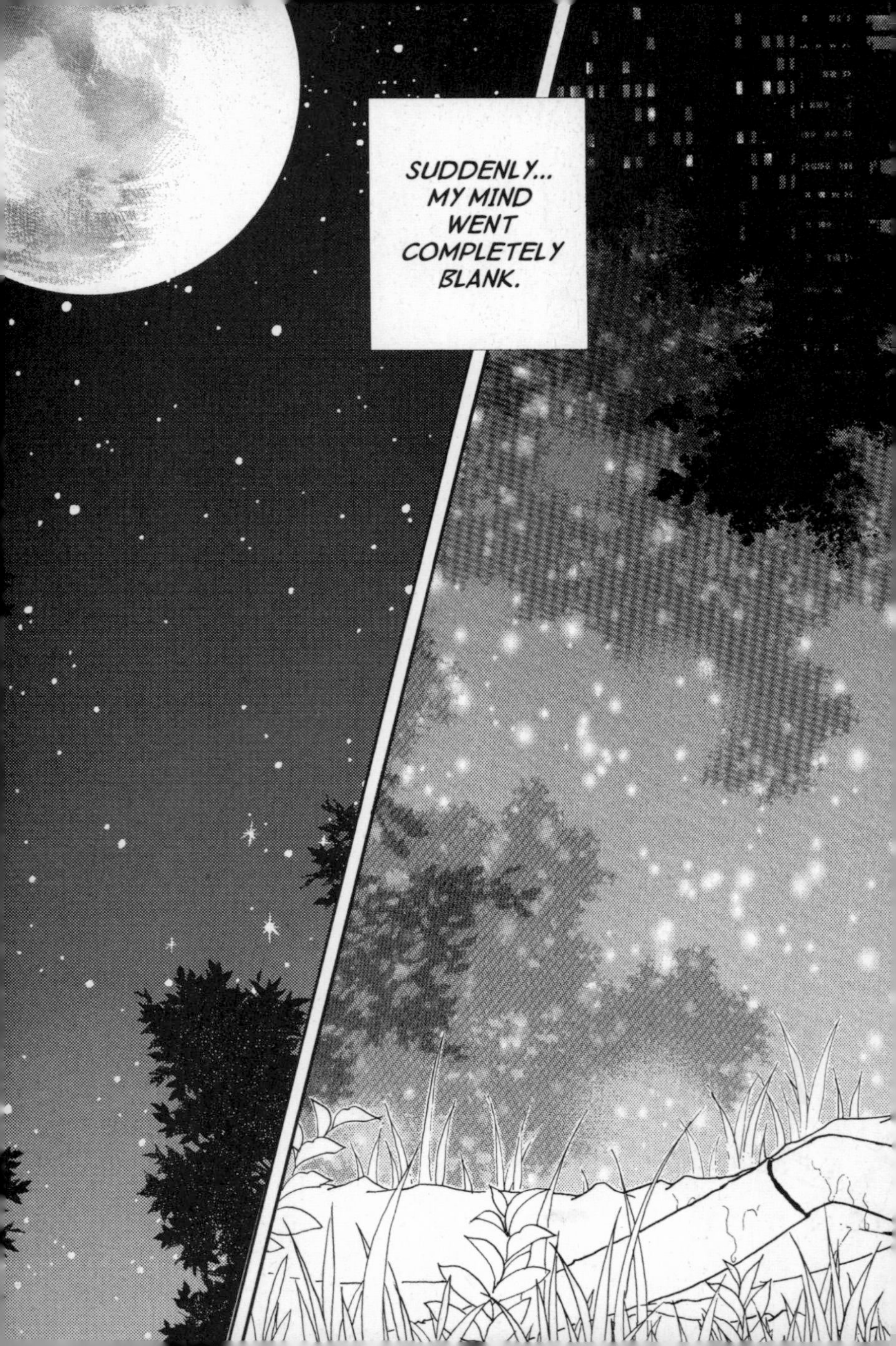
SUDDENLY... MY MIND WENT COMPLETELY BLANK.

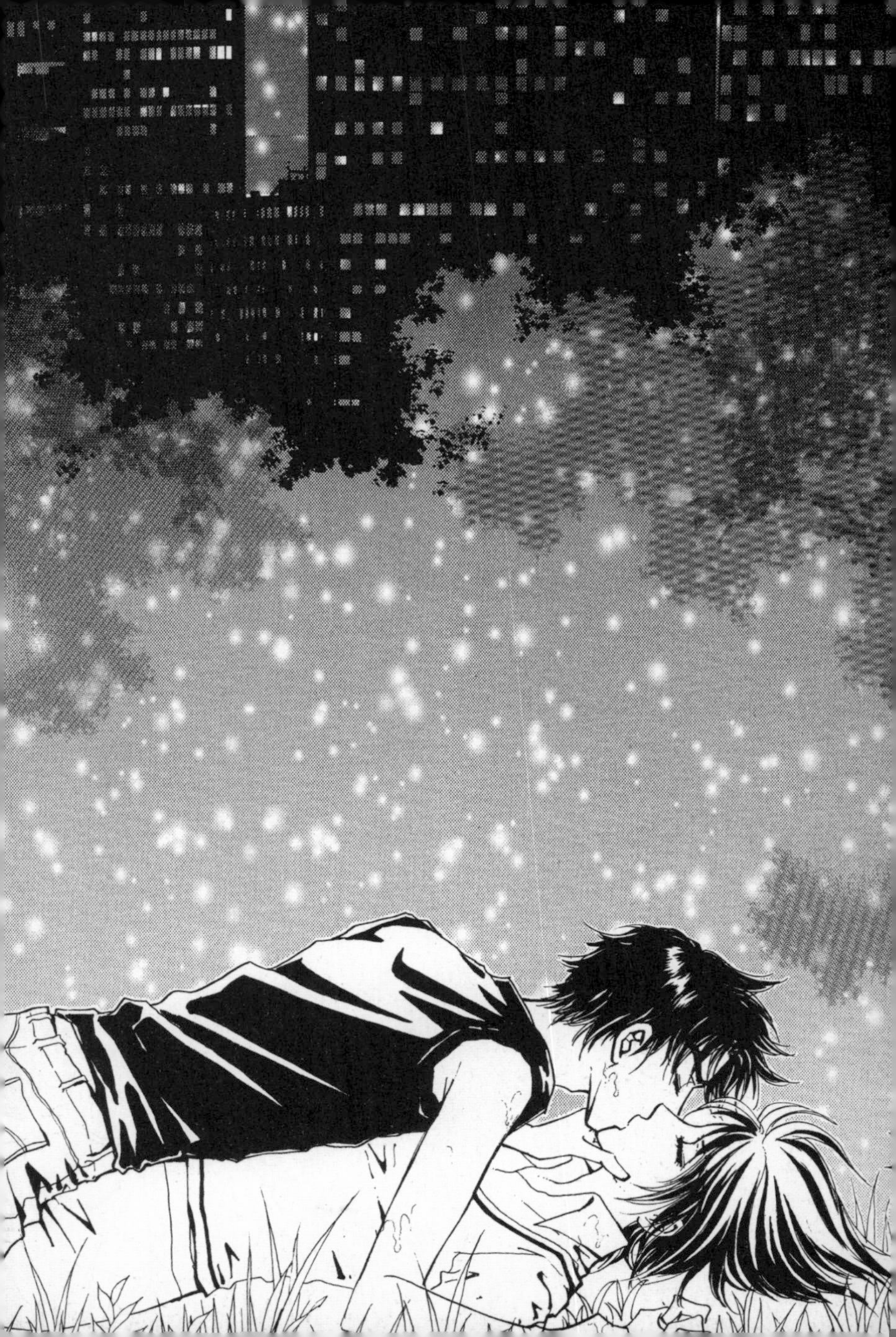

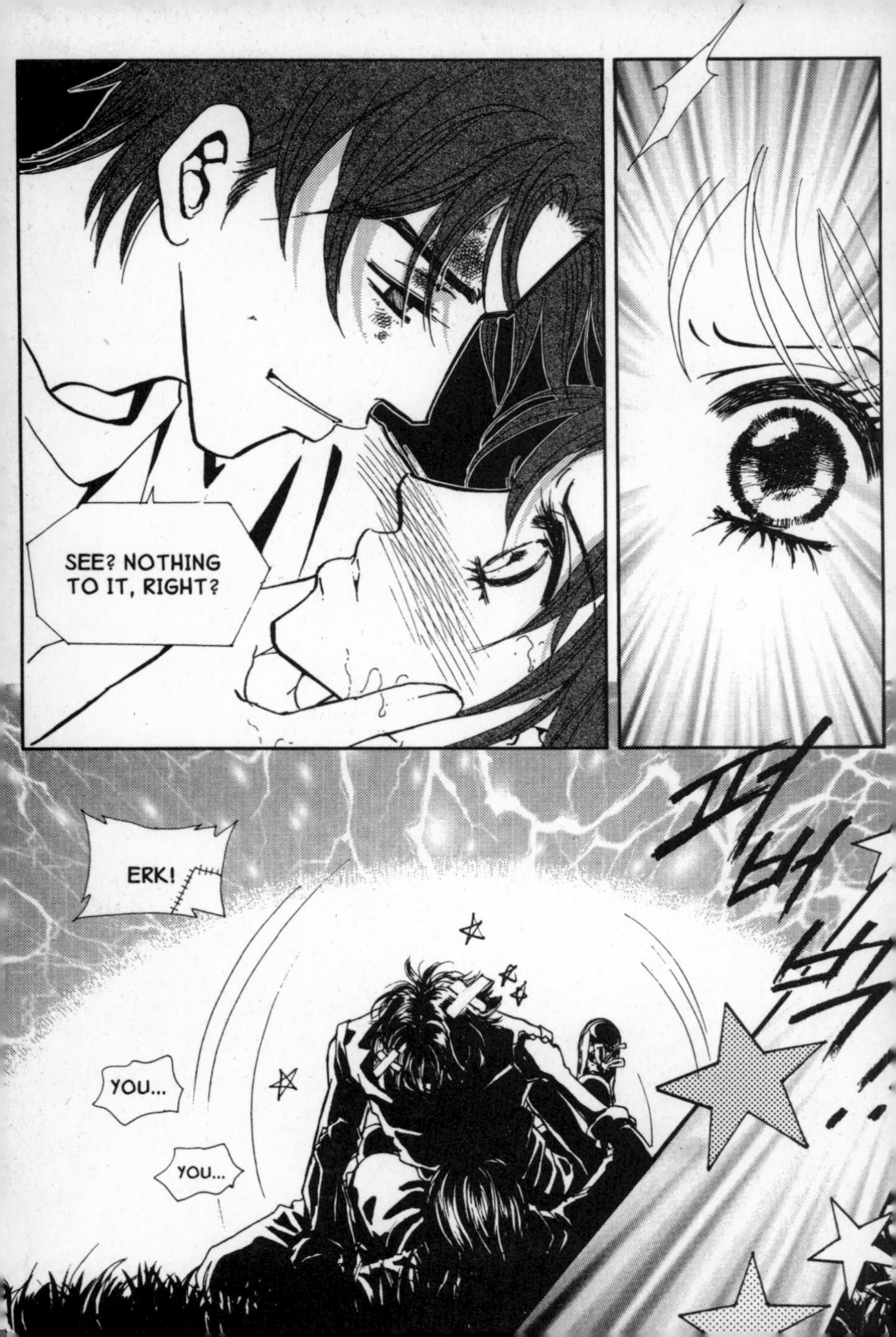
SEE? NOTHING TO IT, RIGHT?
ERK!
퍼버벅
YOU...
YOU...

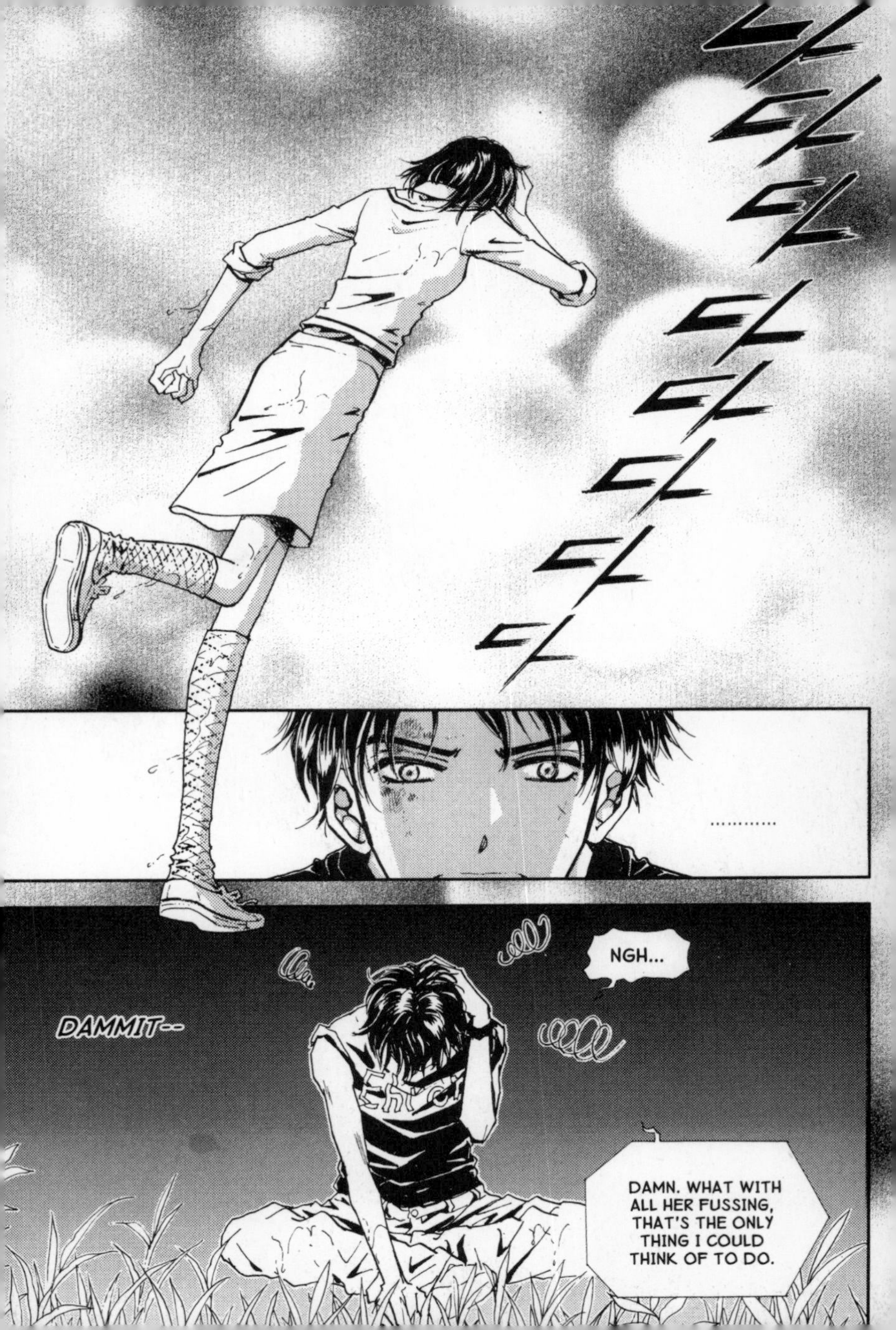
…………
DAMMIT--
NGH...
DAMN. WHAT WITH ALL HER FUSSING, THAT'S THE ONLY THING I COULD THINK OF TO DO.

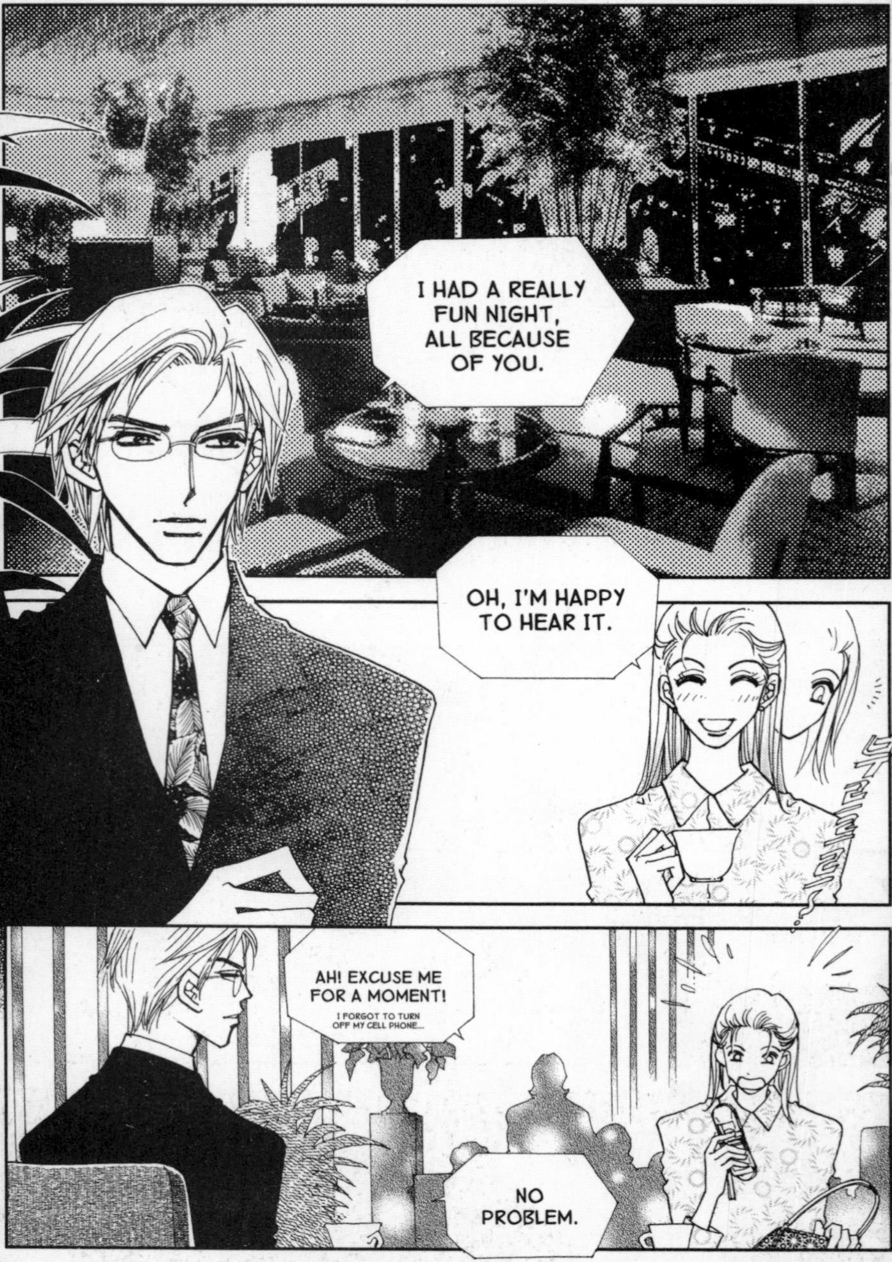
I HAD A REALLY FUN NIGHT, ALL BECAUSE OF YOU.
OH, I'M HAPPY TO HEAR IT.
AH! EXCUSE ME FOR A MOMENT!
I FORGOT TO TURN OFF MY CELL PHONE...
NO PROBLEM.

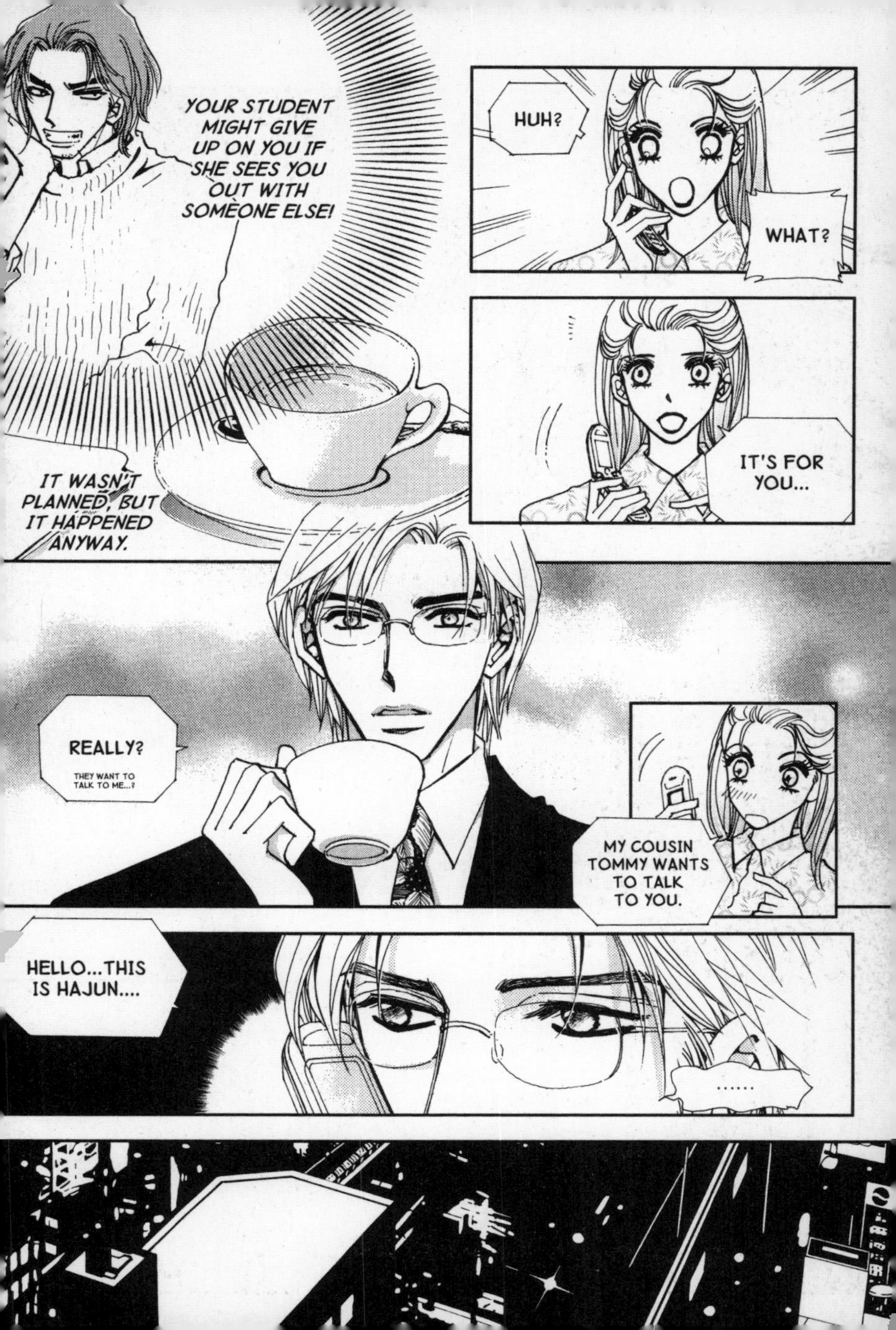
YOUR STUDENT MIGHT GIVE UP ON YOU IF SHE SEES YOU OUT WITH SOMEONE ELSE!
IT WASN'T PLANNED, BUT IT HAPPENED ANYWAY.
HUH?
WHAT?
IT'S FOR YOU...
REALLY?
THEY WANT TO TALK TO ME...?
MY COUSIN TOMMY WANTS TO TALK TO YOU.
HELLO...THIS IS HAJUN....
......

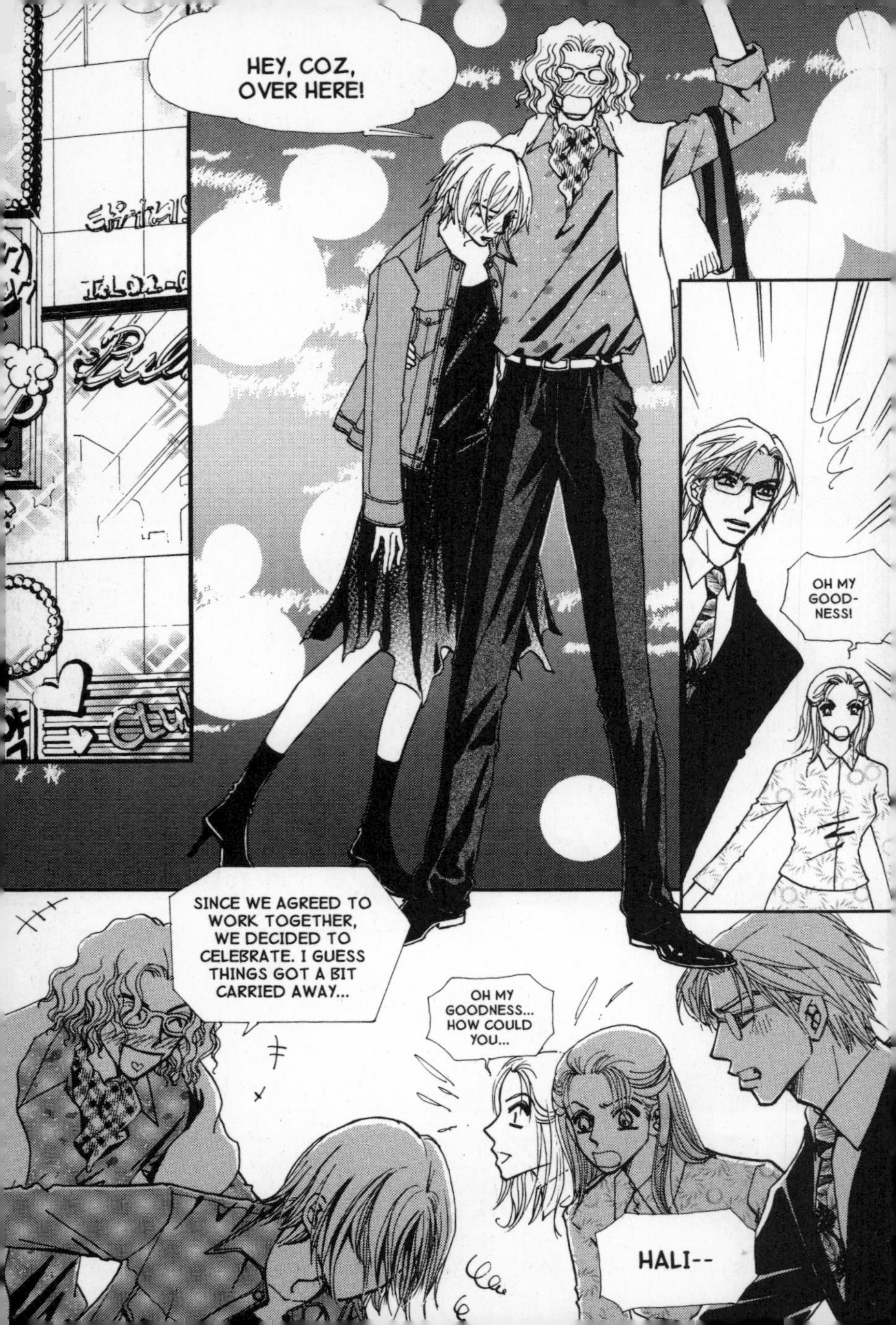
HEY, COZ, OVER HERE!
OH MY GOOD-NESS!
OH MY GOODNESS... HOW COULD YOU...
SINCE WE AGREED TO WORK TOGETHER, WE DECIDED TO CELEBRATE. I GUESS THINGS GOT A BIT CARRIED AWAY...
HALI--

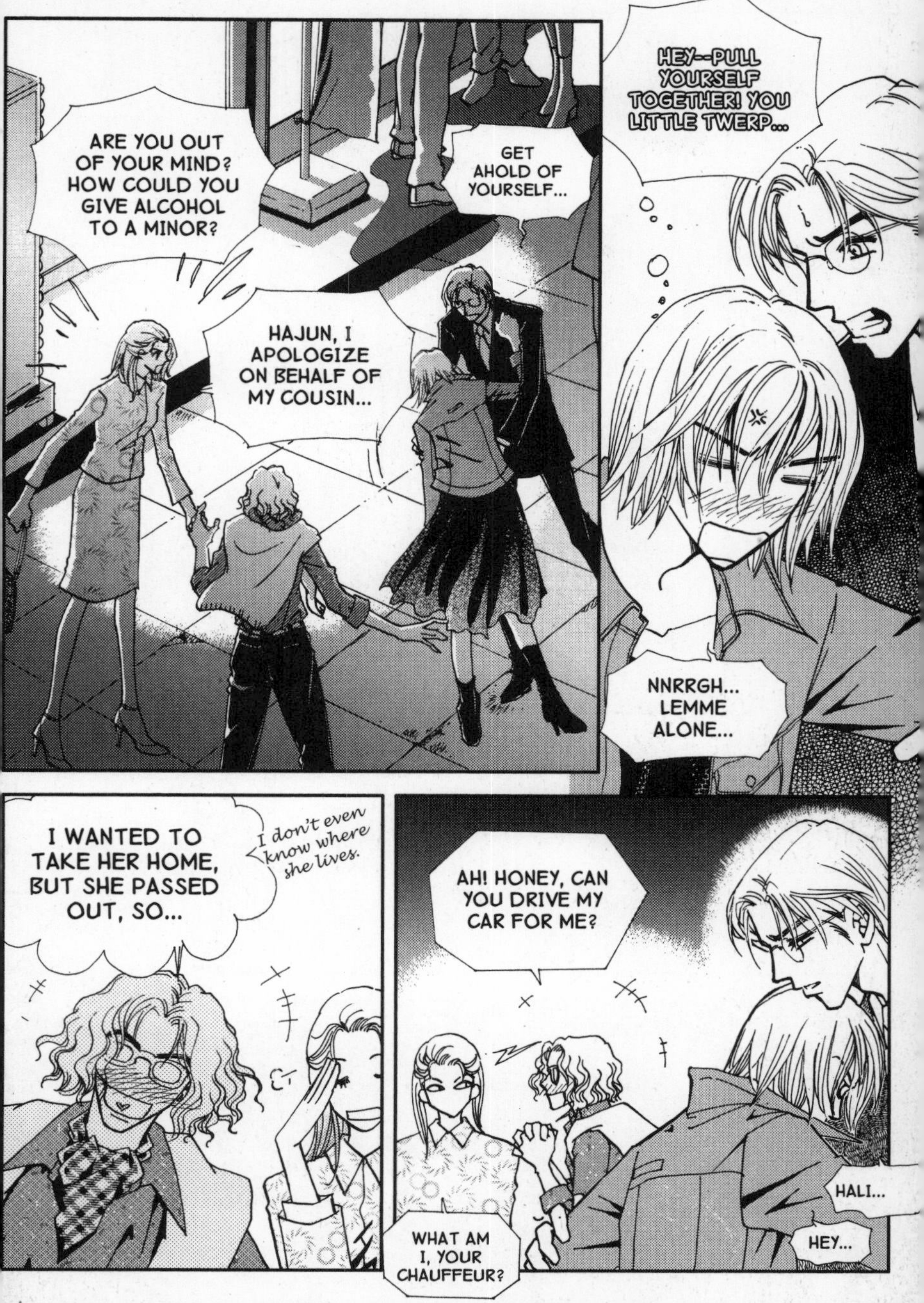
ARE YOU OUT OF YOUR MIND? HOW COULD YOU GIVE ALCOHOL TO A MINOR?
GET AHOLD OF YOURSELF...
HAJUN, I APOLOGIZE ON BEHALF OF MY COUSIN...
HEY--PULL YOURSELF TOGETHER! YOU LITTLE TWERP...
NNRRGH... LEMME ALONE...
I WANTED TO TAKE HER HOME, BUT SHE PASSED OUT, SO...
I don't even know where she lives.
AH! HONEY, CAN YOU DRIVE MY CAR FOR ME?
WHAT AM I, YOUR CHAUFFEUR?
HALI...
HEY...

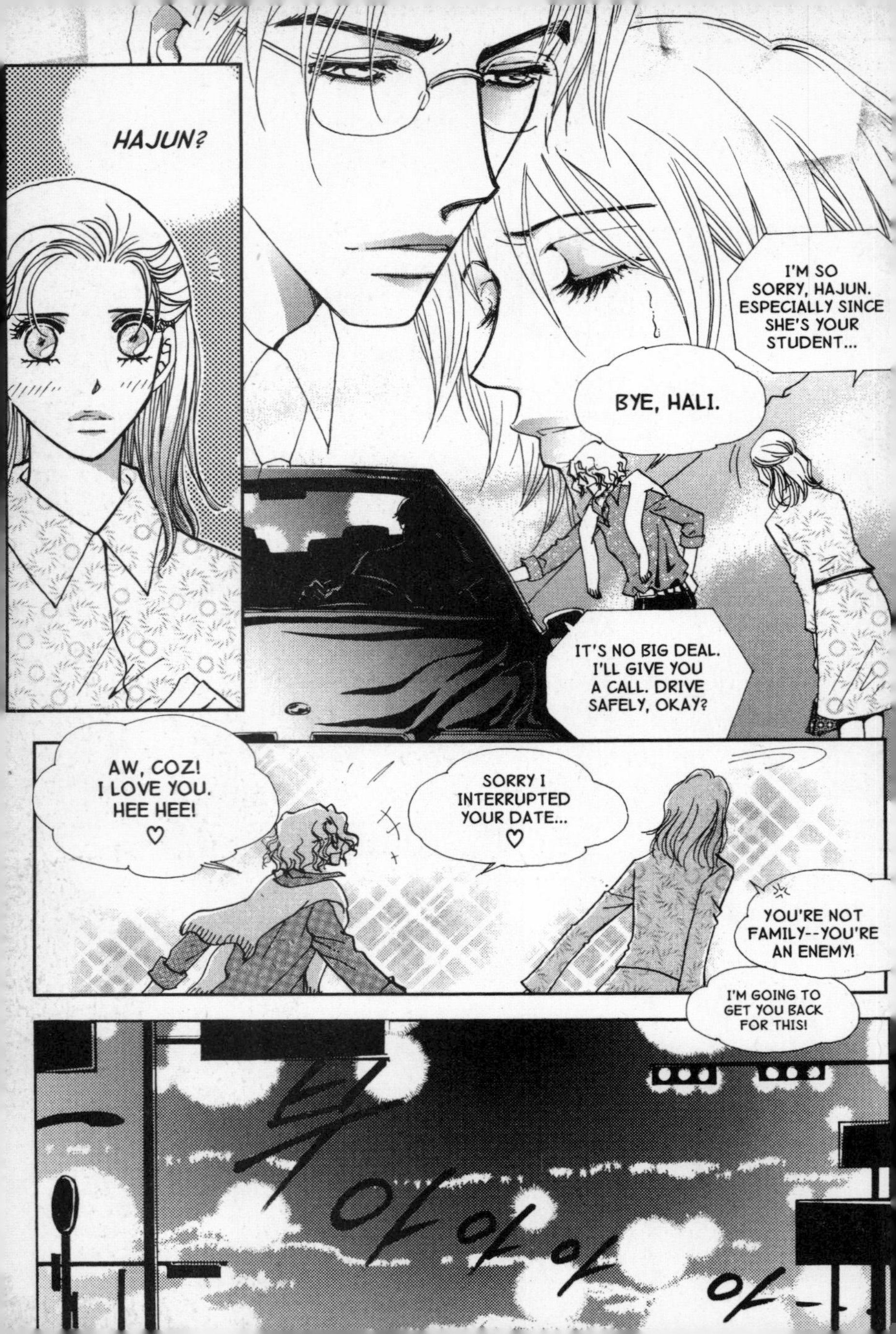
HAJUN?
I'M SO SORRY, HAJUN. ESPECIALLY SINCE SHE'S YOUR STUDENT...
BYE, HALI.
IT'S NO BIG DEAL. I'LL GIVE YOU A CALL. DRIVE SAFELY, OKAY?
AW, COZ! I LOVE YOU. HEE HEE! ♡
SORRY I INTERRUPTED YOUR DATE... ♡
YOU'RE NOT FAMILY--YOU'RE AN ENEMY!
I'M GOING TO GET YOU BACK FOR THIS!

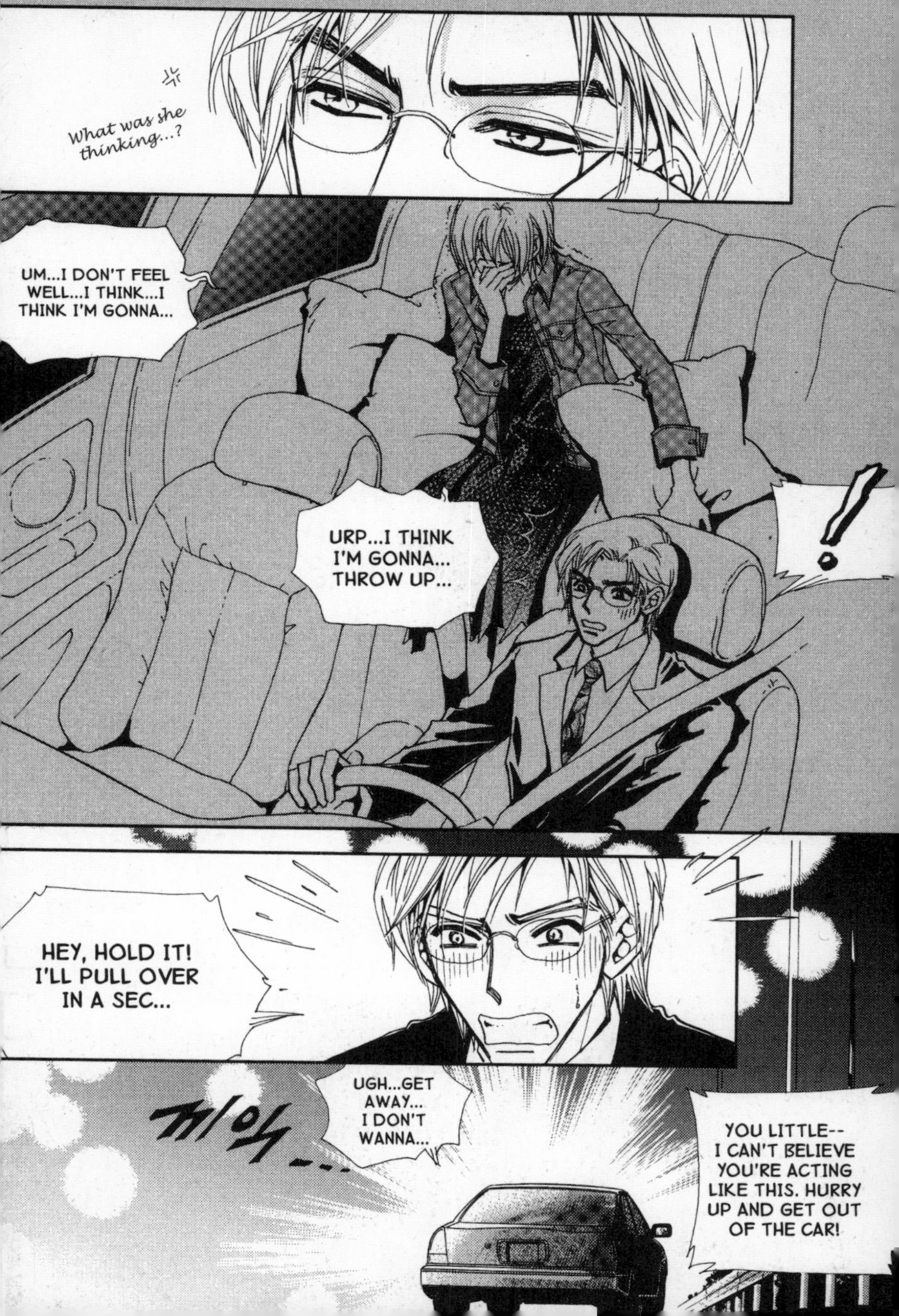
What was she thinking...?
UM...I DON'T FEEL WELL...I THINK...I THINK I'M GONNA...
URP...I THINK I'M GONNA... THROW UP...
!
HEY, HOLD IT! I'LL PULL OVER IN A SEC...
끼이익...
UGH...GET AWAY... I DON'T WANNA...
YOU LITTLE-- I CAN'T BELIEVE YOU'RE ACTING LIKE THIS. HURRY UP AND GET OUT OF THE CAR!

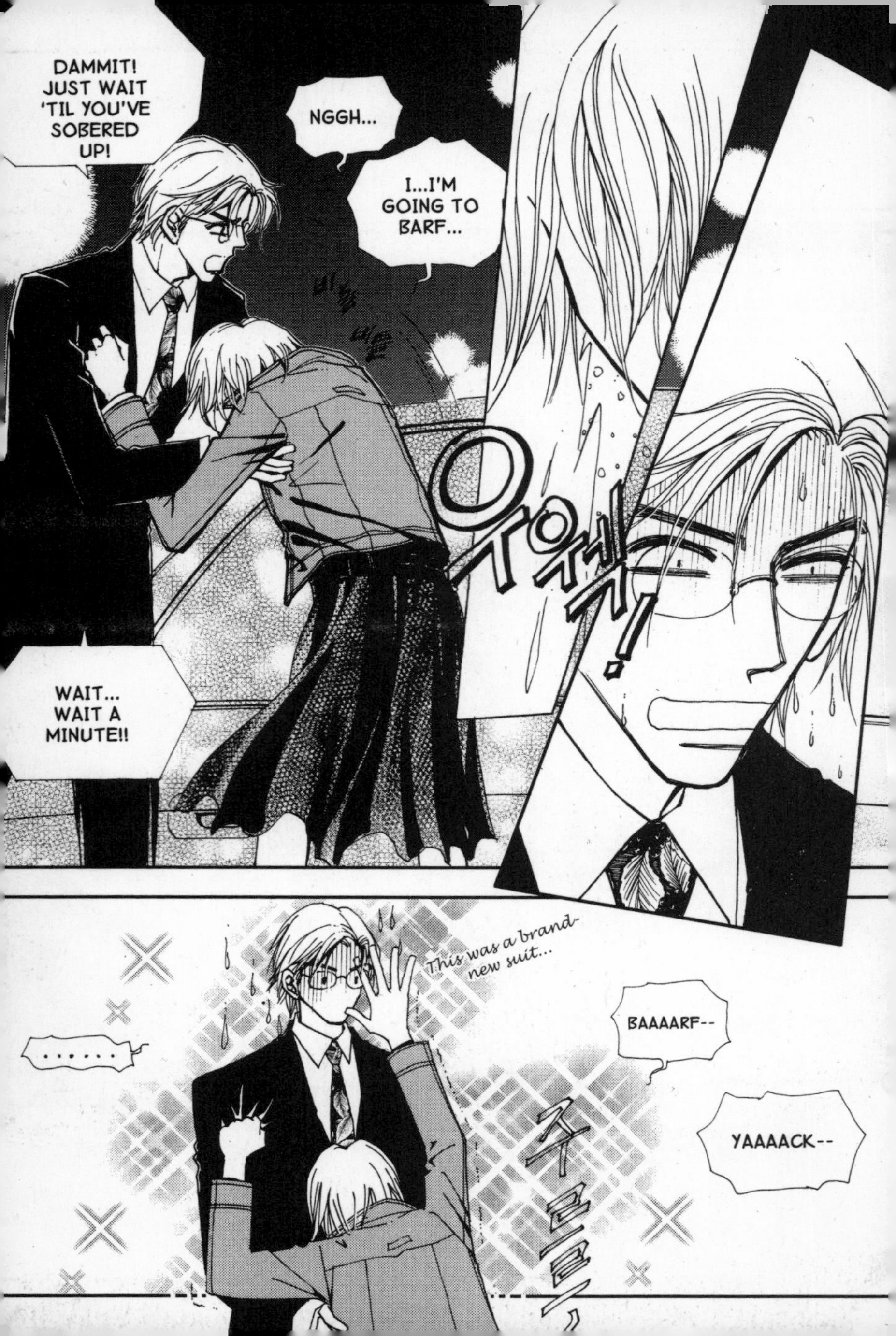
DAMMIT! JUST WAIT 'TIL YOU'VE SOBERED UP!
NGGH...
I...I'M GOING TO BARF...
WAIT... WAIT A MINUTE!!
This was a brand-new suit...
......
BAAAARF--
YAAAACK--

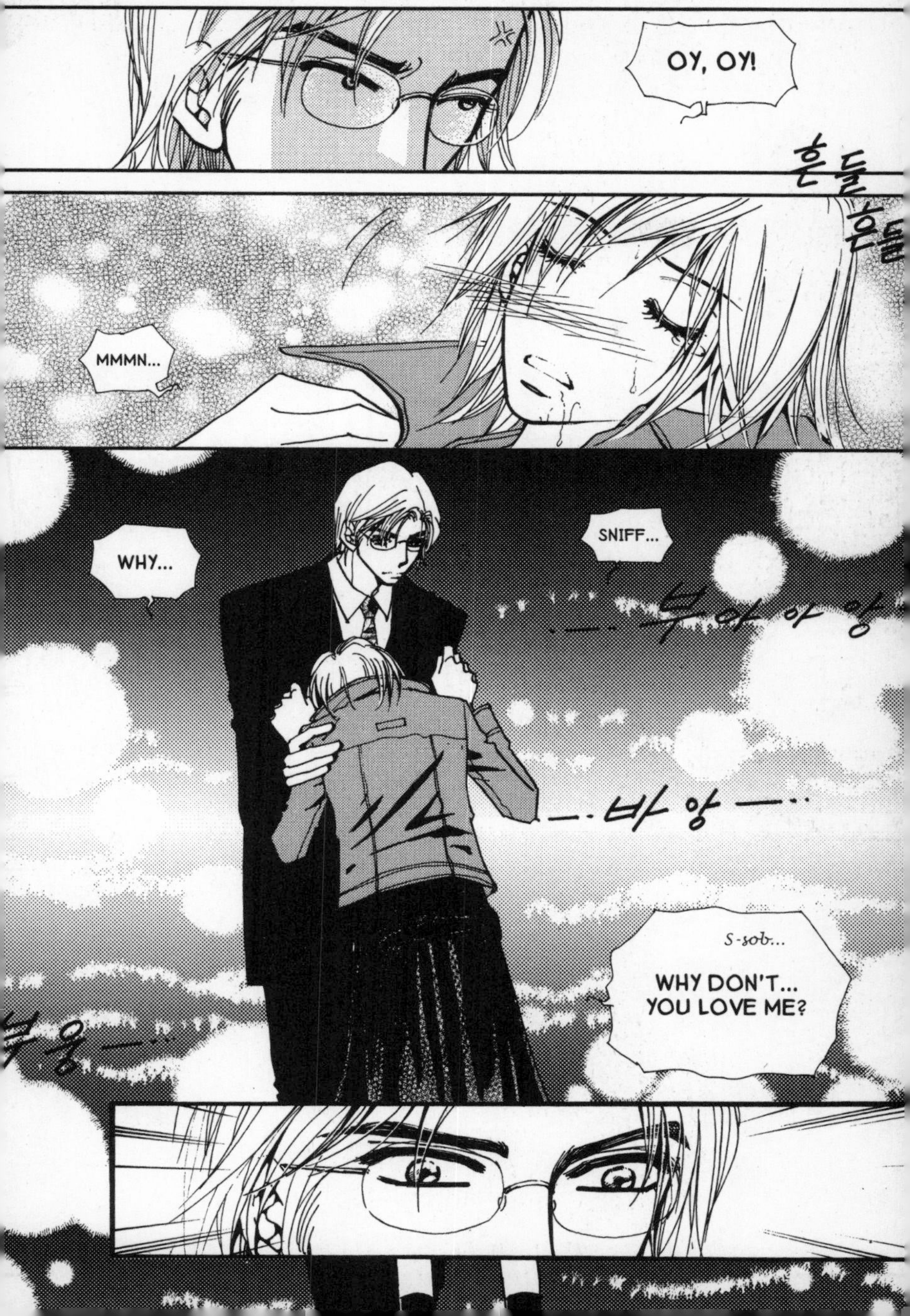
OY, OY!
흔들흔들
MMMN...
WHY...
SNIFF...
부아아앙
바앙
S-sob...
WHY DON'T... YOU LOVE ME?
부웅

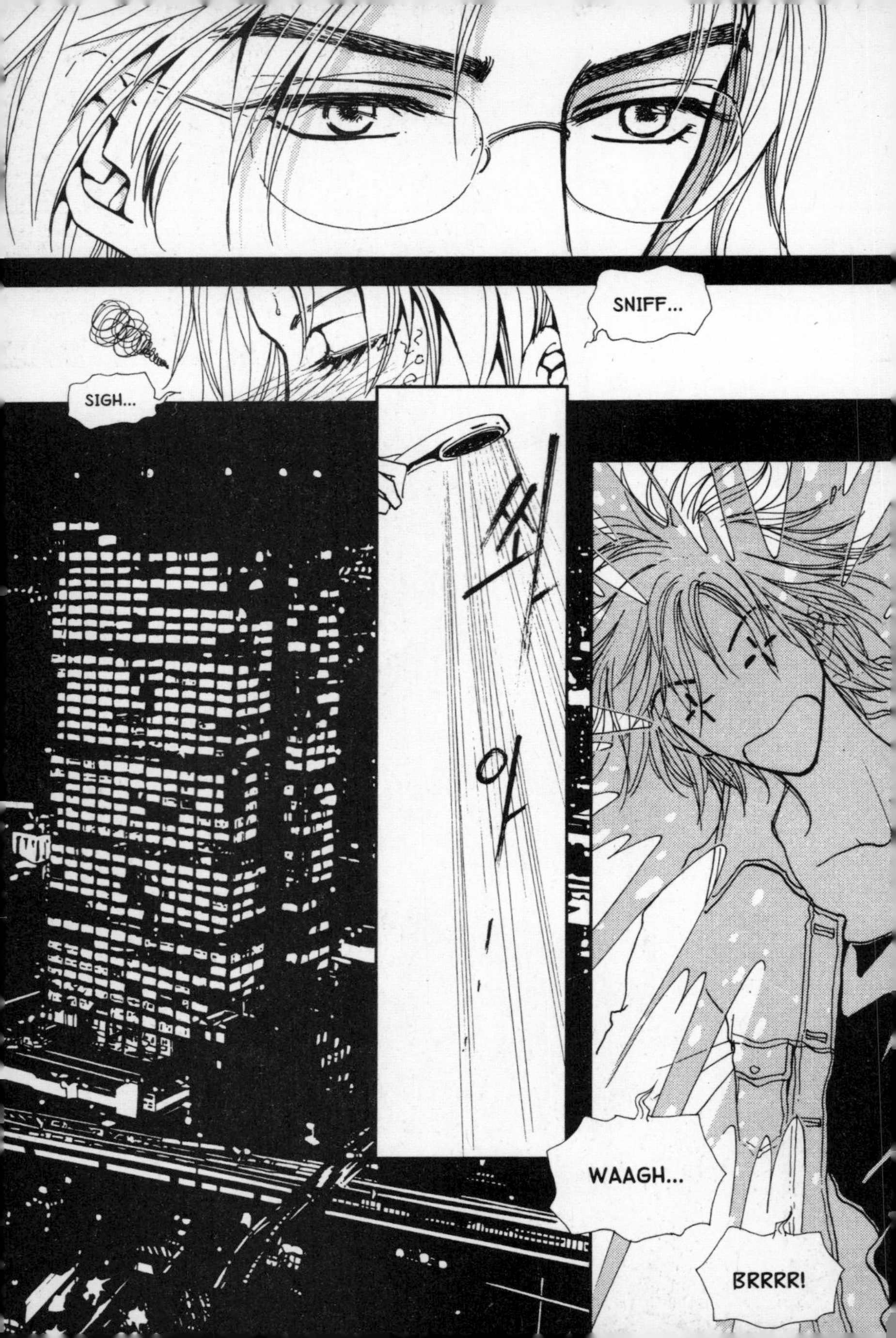
SNIFF...
SIGH...
WAAGH...
BRRRR!

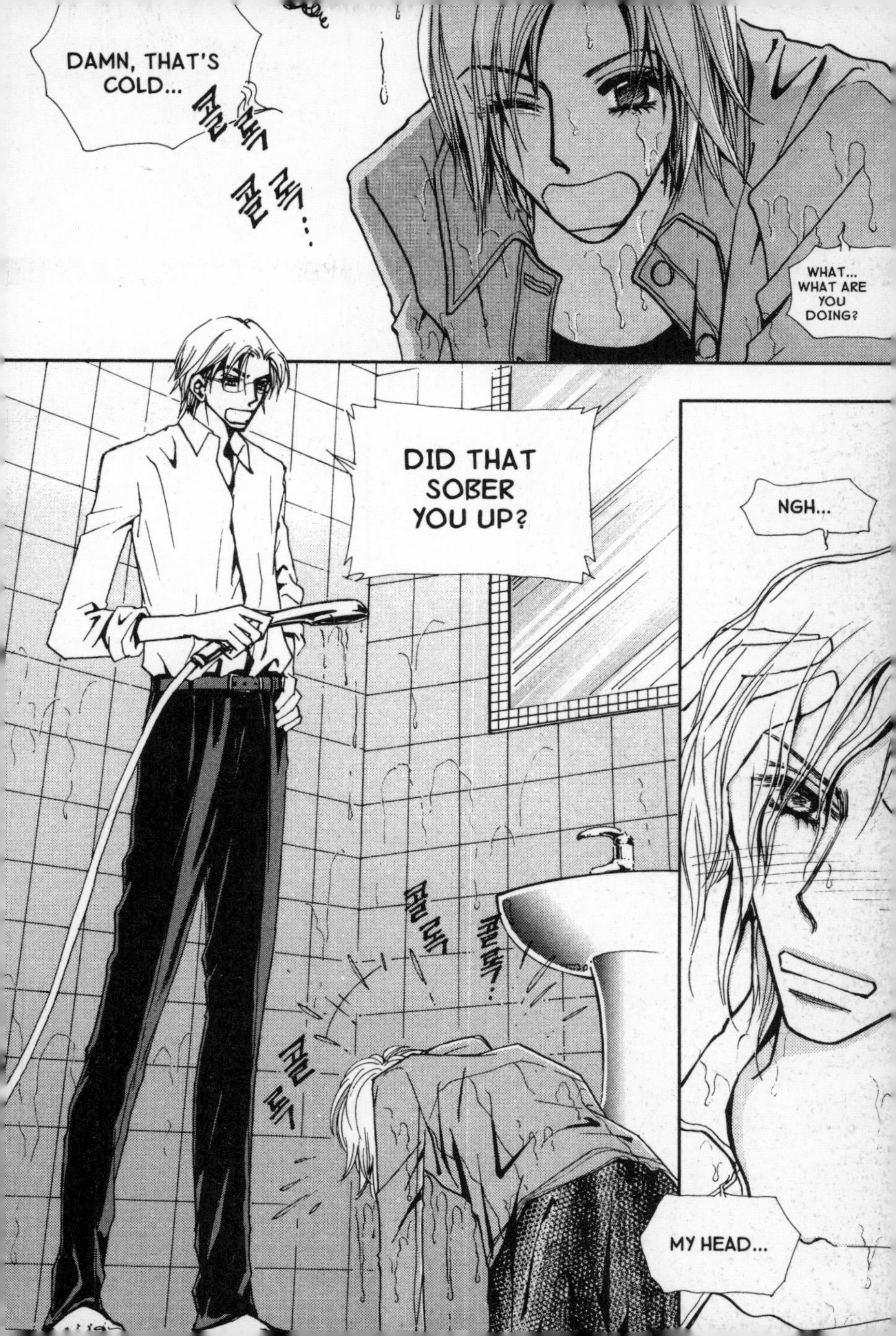
DAMN, THAT'S COLD...
콜록 콜록...
WHAT... WHAT ARE YOU DOING?
DID THAT SOBER YOU UP?
콜록 콜록...
콜록
NGH...
MY HEAD...

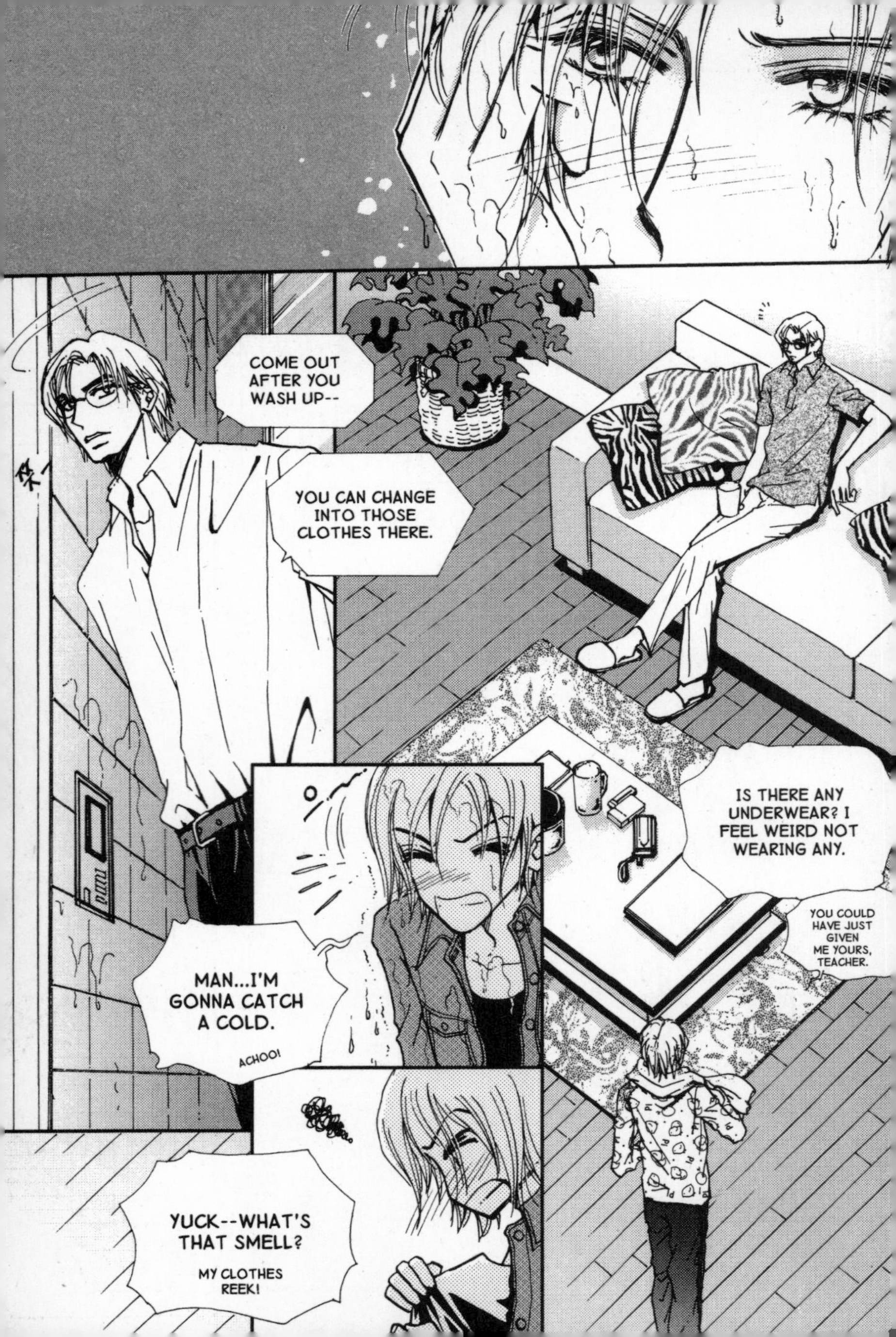
COME OUT AFTER YOU WASH UP--
YOU CAN CHANGE INTO THOSE CLOTHES THERE.
MAN...I'M GONNA CATCH A COLD.
ACHOO!
YUCK--WHAT'S THAT SMELL?
MY CLOTHES REEK!
IS THERE ANY UNDERWEAR? I FEEL WEIRD NOT WEARING ANY.
YOU COULD HAVE JUST GIVEN ME YOURS, TEACHER.

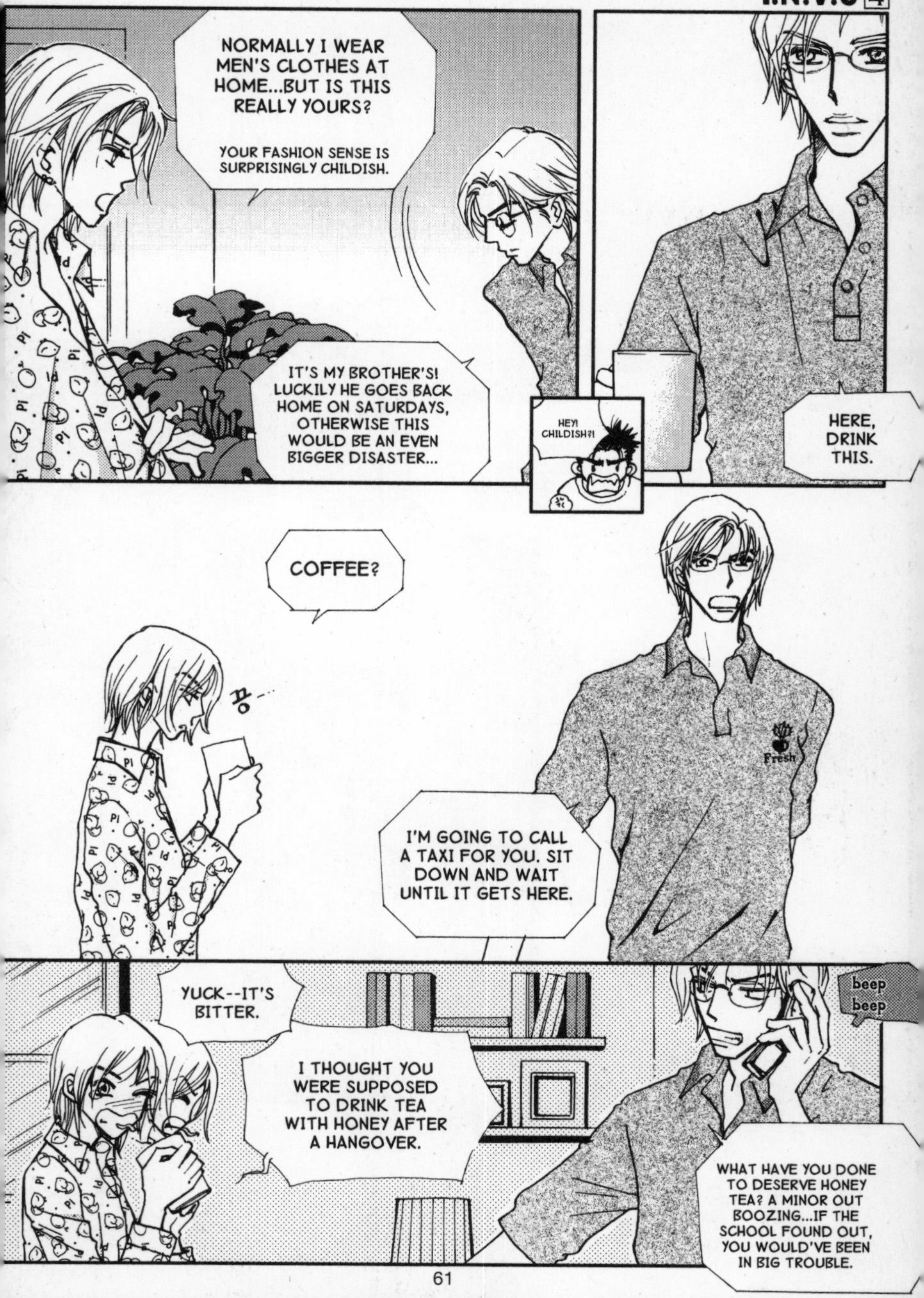
NORMALLY I WEAR MEN'S CLOTHES AT HOME...BUT IS THIS REALLY YOURS?
YOUR FASHION SENSE IS SURPRISINGLY CHILDISH.
IT'S MY BROTHER'S! LUCKILY HE GOES BACK HOME ON SATURDAYS, OTHERWISE THIS WOULD BE AN EVEN BIGGER DISASTER...
HEY! CHILDISH?!
HERE, DRINK THIS.
COFFEE?
I'M GOING TO CALL A TAXI FOR YOU. SIT DOWN AND WAIT UNTIL IT GETS HERE.
YUCK--IT'S BITTER.
I THOUGHT YOU WERE SUPPOSED TO DRINK TEA WITH HONEY AFTER A HANGOVER.
beep beep
WHAT HAVE YOU DONE TO DESERVE HONEY TEA? A MINOR OUT BOOZING...IF THE SCHOOL FOUND OUT, YOU WOULD'VE BEEN IN BIG TROUBLE.

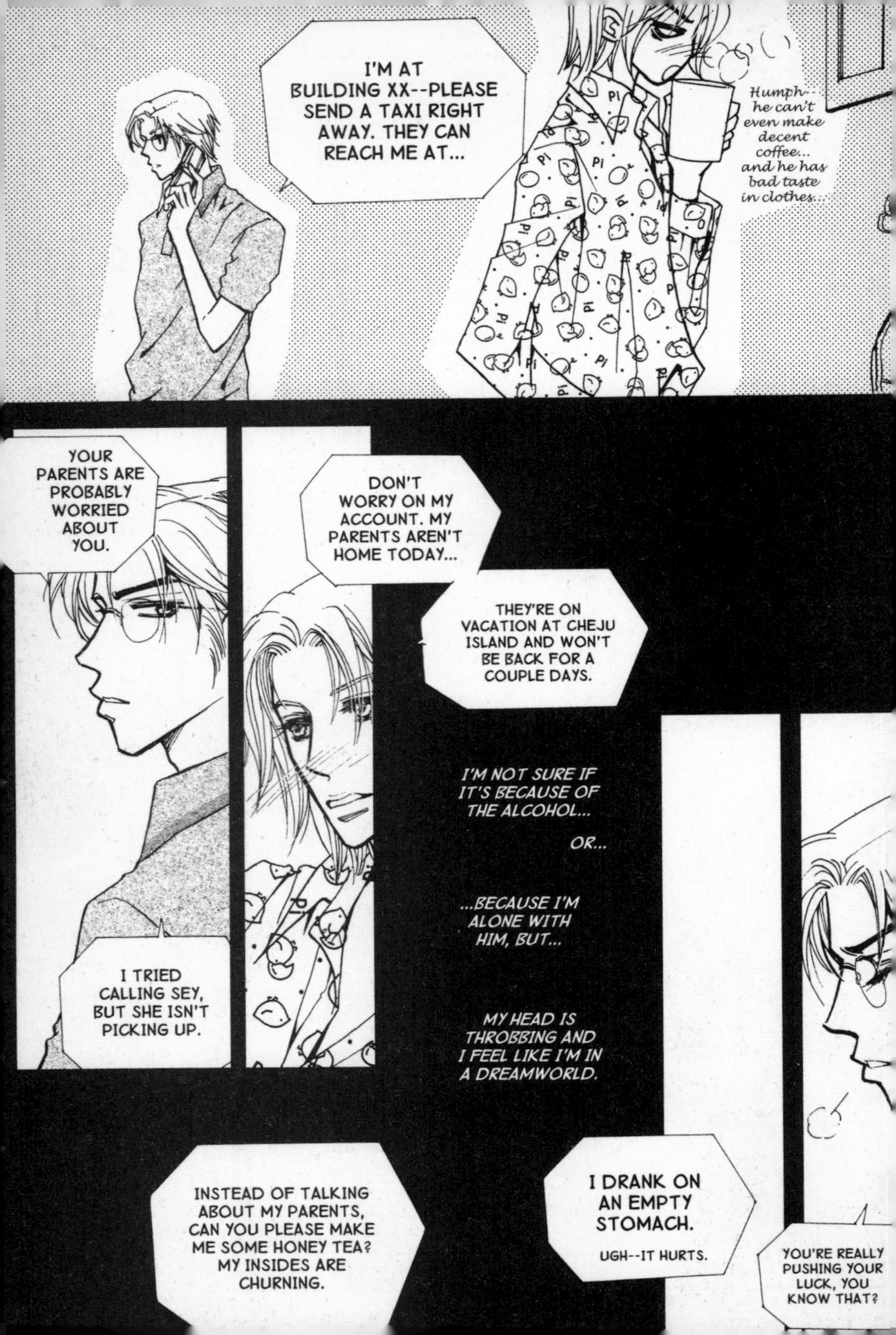
I'M AT BUILDING XX--PLEASE SEND A TAXI RIGHT AWAY. THEY CAN REACH ME AT...
Humph-- he can't even make decent coffee... and he has bad taste in clothes...
YOUR PARENTS ARE PROBABLY WORRIED ABOUT YOU.
I TRIED CALLING SEY, BUT SHE ISN'T PICKING UP.
DON'T WORRY ON MY ACCOUNT. MY PARENTS AREN'T HOME TODAY...
THEY'RE ON VACATION AT CHEJU ISLAND AND WON'T BE BACK FOR A COUPLE DAYS.
I'M NOT SURE IF IT'S BECAUSE OF THE ALCOHOL...
OR...
...BECAUSE I'M ALONE WITH HIM, BUT...
MY HEAD IS THROBBING AND I FEEL LIKE I'M IN A DREAMWORLD.
INSTEAD OF TALKING ABOUT MY PARENTS, CAN YOU PLEASE MAKE ME SOME HONEY TEA? MY INSIDES ARE CHURNING.
I DRANK ON AN EMPTY STOMACH.
UGH--IT HURTS.
YOU'RE REALLY PUSHING YOUR LUCK, YOU KNOW THAT?

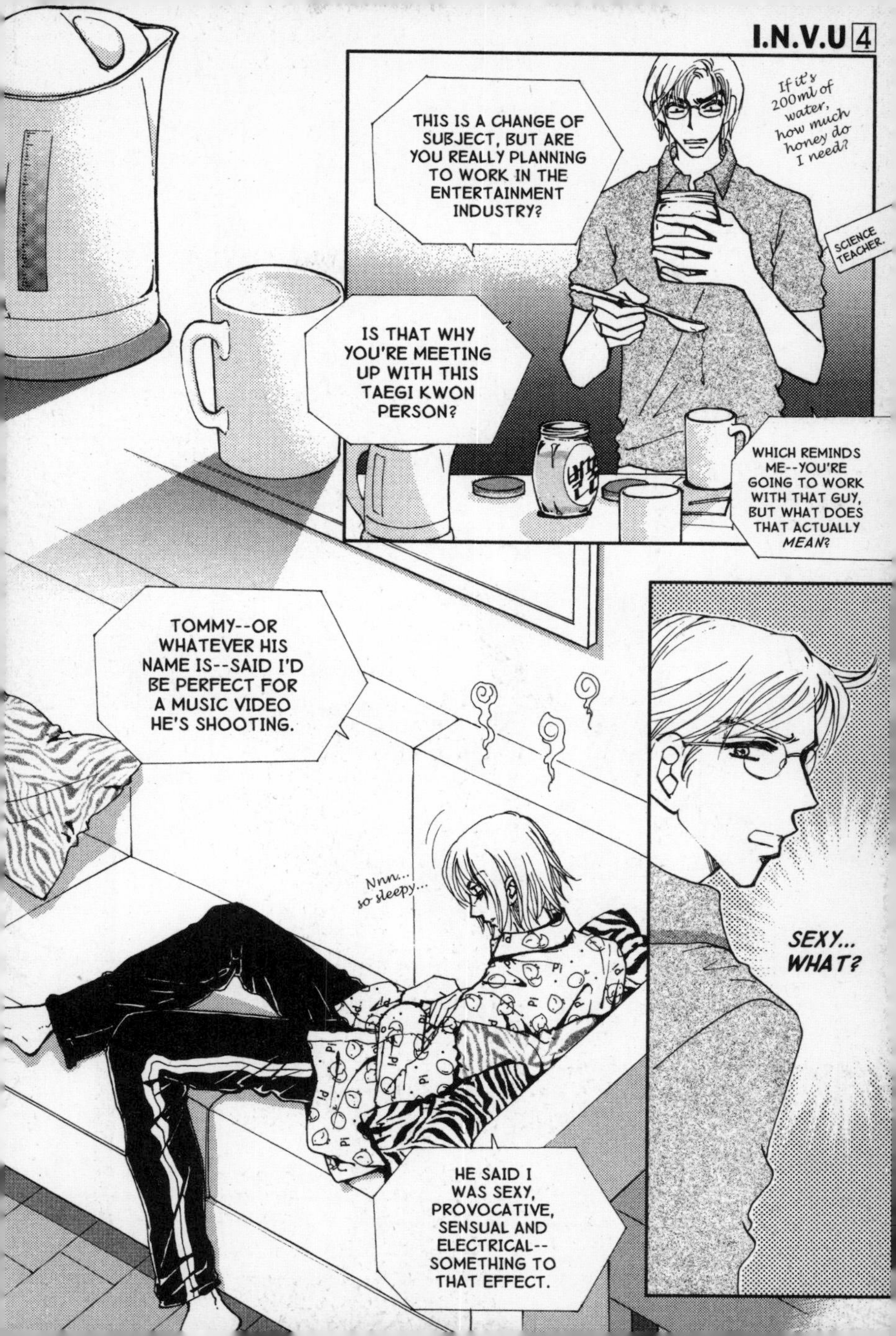
THIS IS A CHANGE OF SUBJECT, BUT ARE YOU REALLY PLANNING TO WORK IN THE ENTERTAINMENT INDUSTRY?
If it's 200ml of water, how much honey do I need?
SCIENCE TEACHER.
IS THAT WHY YOU'RE MEETING UP WITH THIS TAEGI KWON PERSON?
WHICH REMINDS ME--YOU'RE GOING TO WORK WITH THAT GUY, BUT WHAT DOES THAT ACTUALLY *MEAN*?
TOMMY--OR WHATEVER HIS NAME IS--SAID I'D BE PERFECT FOR A MUSIC VIDEO HE'S SHOOTING.
Nnn... so sleepy...
HE SAID I WAS SEXY, PROVOCATIVE, SENSUAL AND ELECTRICAL--SOMETHING TO THAT EFFECT.
SEXY... WHAT?

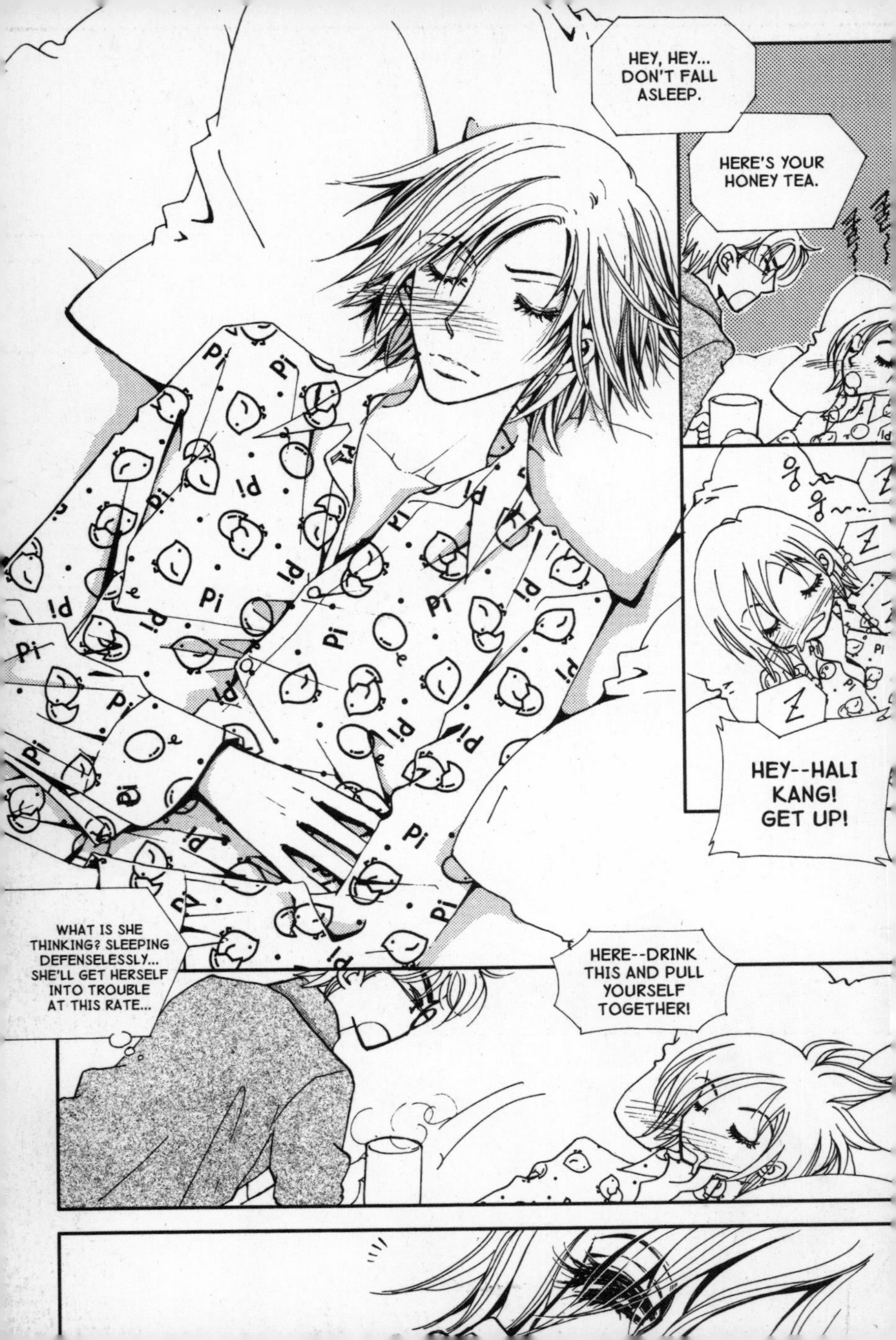
HEY, HEY... DON'T FALL ASLEEP.
HERE'S YOUR HONEY TEA.
HEY--HALI KANG! GET UP!
HERE--DRINK THIS AND PULL YOURSELF TOGETHER!
WHAT IS SHE THINKING? SLEEPING DEFENSELESSLY... SHE'LL GET HERSELF INTO TROUBLE AT THIS RATE...

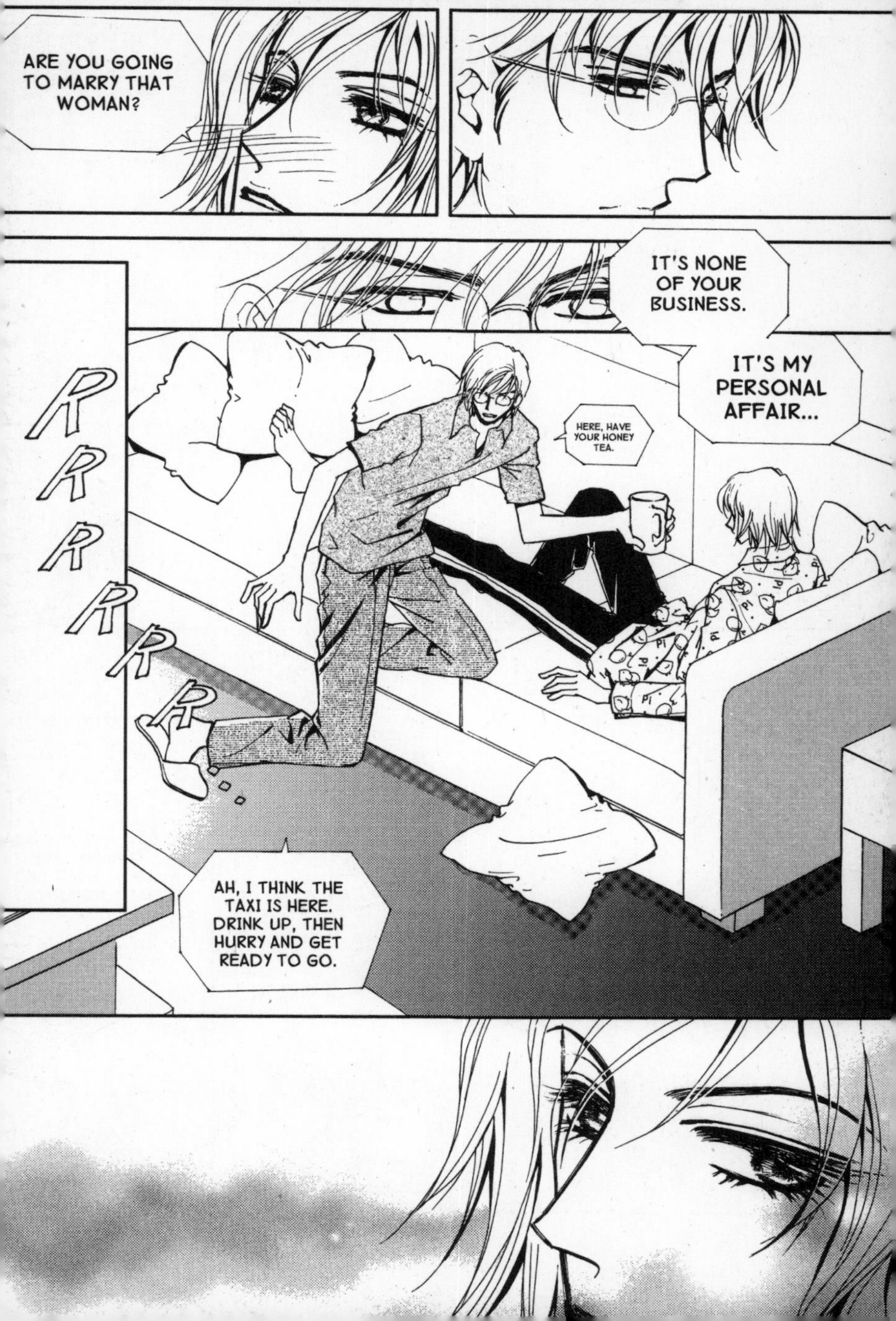
ARE YOU GOING TO MARRY THAT WOMAN?
IT'S NONE OF YOUR BUSINESS.
IT'S MY PERSONAL AFFAIR...
HERE, HAVE YOUR HONEY TEA.
RRRRRR
AH, I THINK THE TAXI IS HERE. DRINK UP, THEN HURRY AND GET READY TO GO.

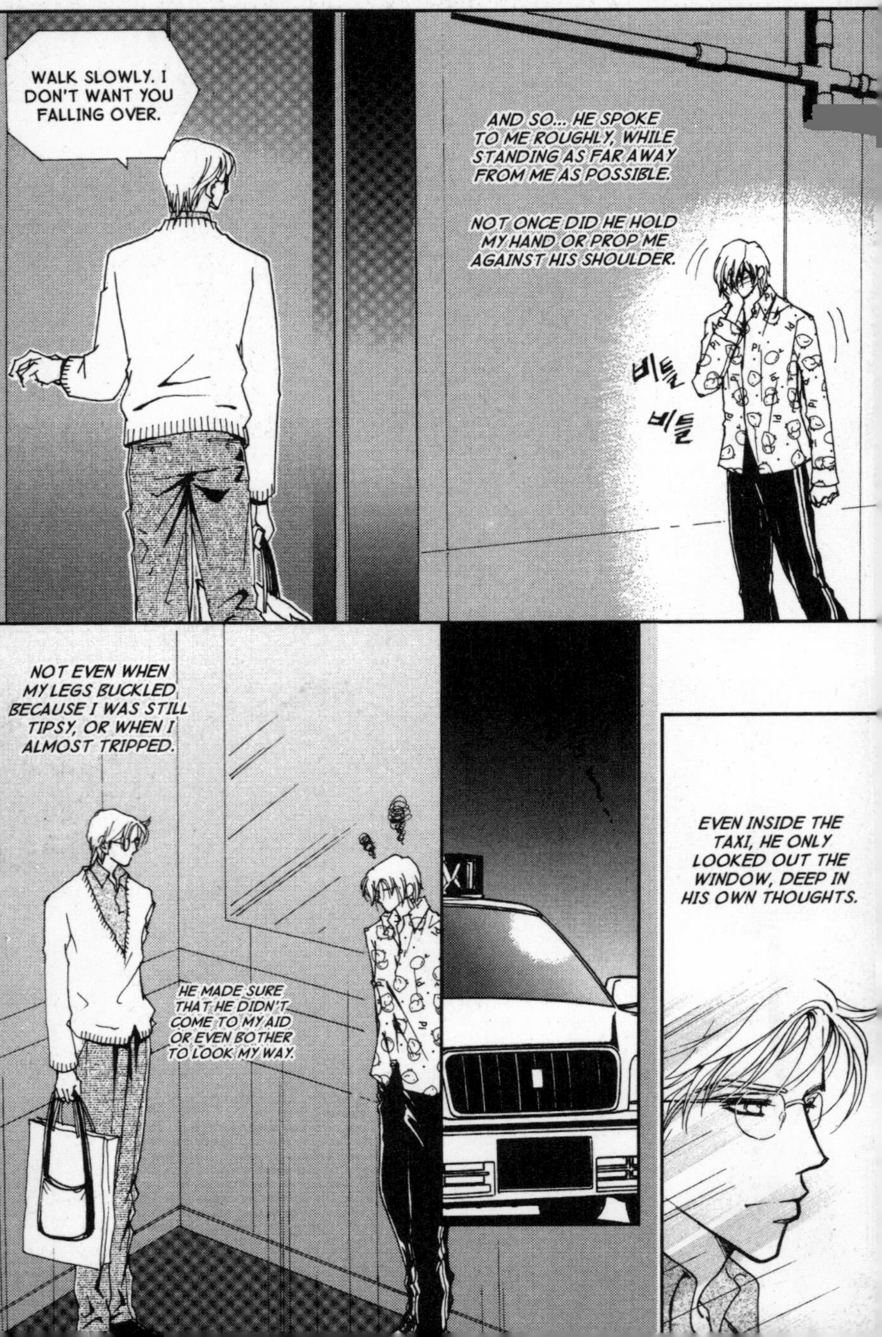
WALK SLOWLY. I DON'T WANT YOU FALLING OVER.
AND SO... HE SPOKE TO ME ROUGHLY, WHILE STANDING AS FAR AWAY FROM ME AS POSSIBLE.
NOT ONCE DID HE HOLD MY HAND OR PROP ME AGAINST HIS SHOULDER.
비틀
비틀
NOT EVEN WHEN MY LEGS BUCKLED BECAUSE I WAS STILL TIPSY, OR WHEN I ALMOST TRIPPED.
HE MADE SURE THAT HE DIDN'T COME TO MY AID OR EVEN BOTHER TO LOOK MY WAY.
EVEN INSIDE THE TAXI, HE ONLY LOOKED OUT THE WINDOW, DEEP IN HIS OWN THOUGHTS.

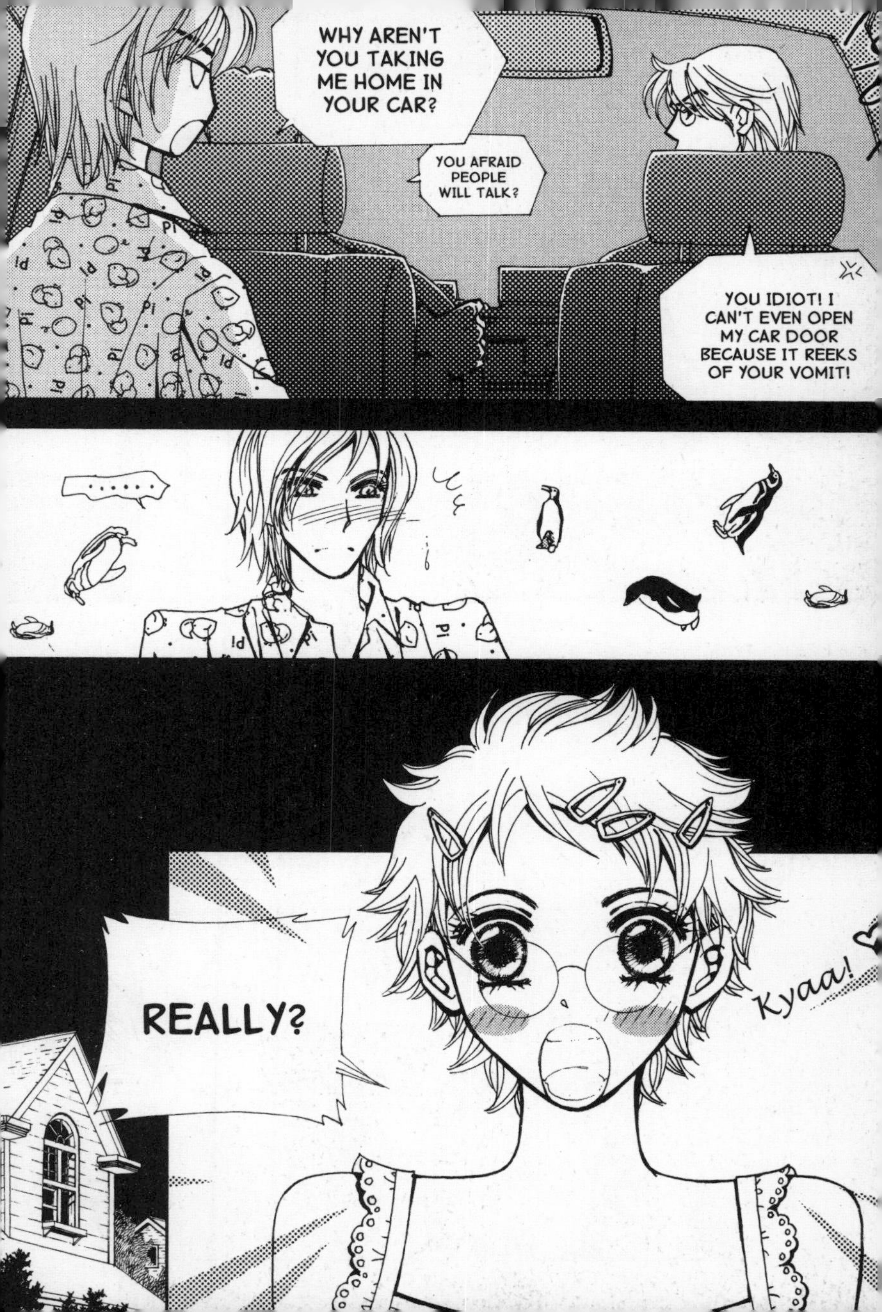
WHY AREN'T YOU TAKING ME HOME IN YOUR CAR?
YOU AFRAID PEOPLE WILL TALK?
YOU IDIOT! I CAN'T EVEN OPEN MY CAR DOOR BECAUSE IT REEKS OF YOUR VOMIT!
......
Kyaa!
REALLY?

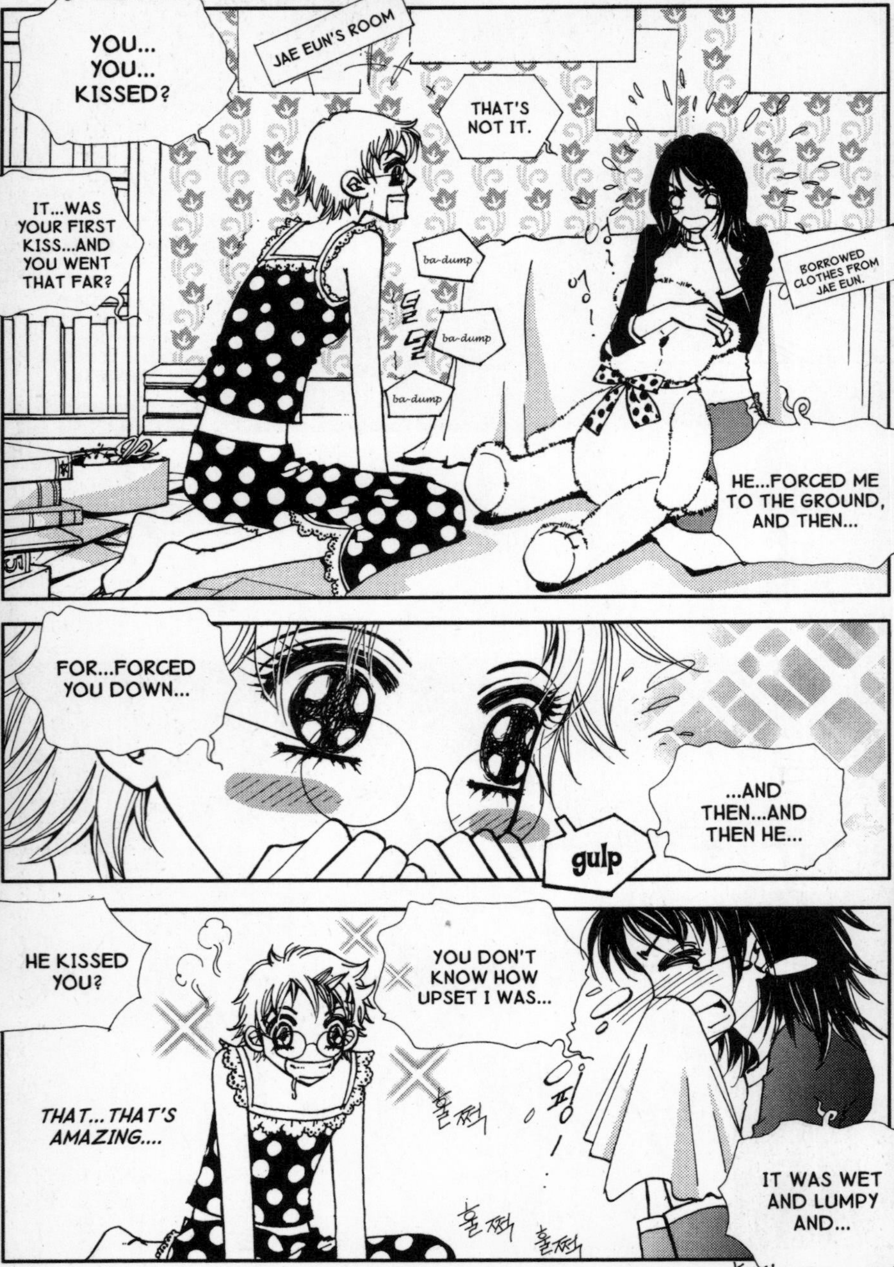
YOU... YOU... KISSED?
JAE EUN'S ROOM
THAT'S NOT IT.
IT...WAS YOUR FIRST KISS...AND YOU WENT THAT FAR?
ba-dump
ba-dump
ba-dump
BORROWED CLOTHES FROM JAE EUN.
HE...FORCED ME TO THE GROUND, AND THEN...
FOR...FORCED YOU DOWN...
...AND THEN...AND THEN HE...
gulp
HE KISSED YOU?
YOU DON'T KNOW HOW UPSET I WAS...
THAT...THAT'S AMAZING....
훌쩍
IT WAS WET AND LUMPY AND...
훌쩍
훌쩍
훌쩍

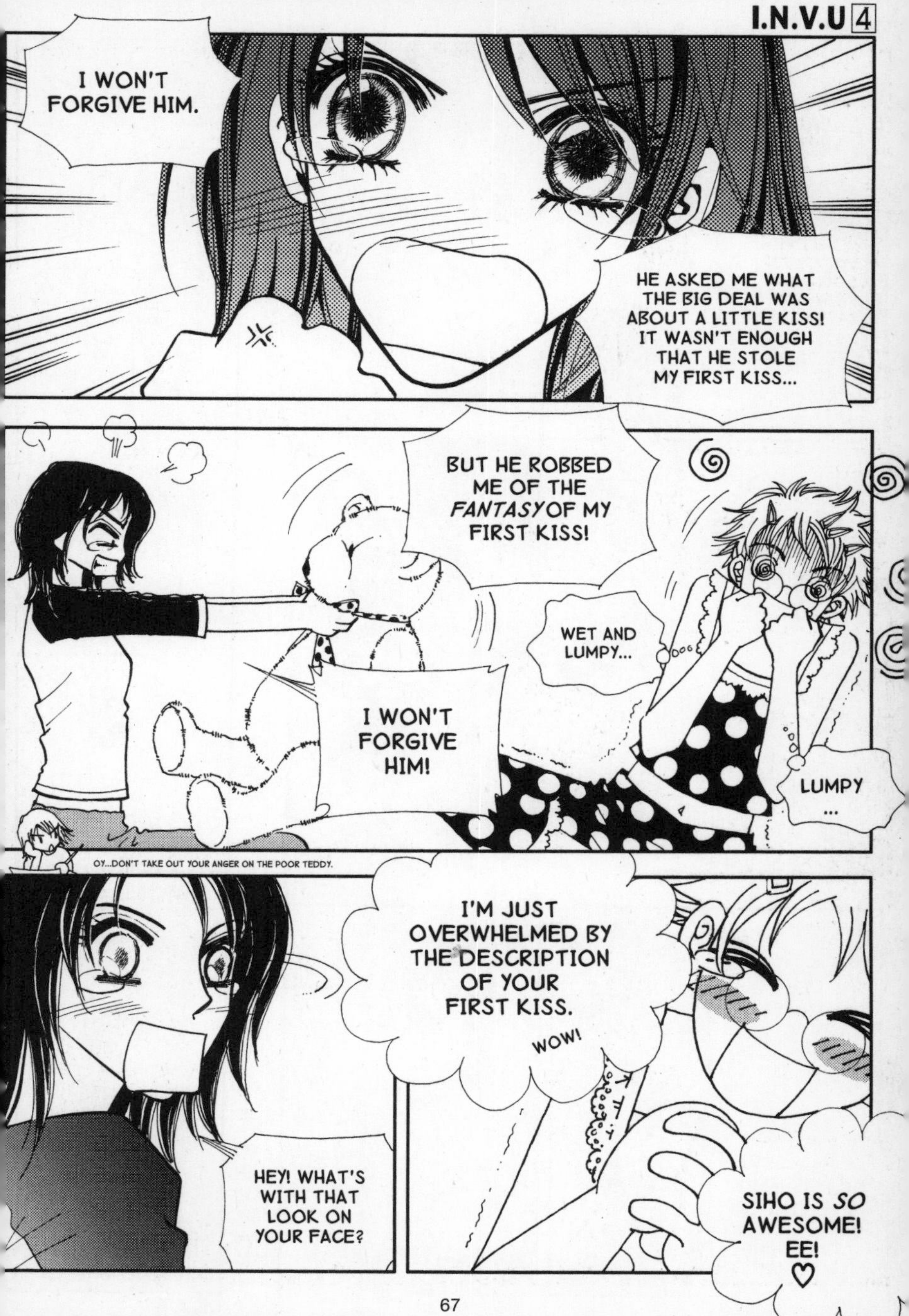
I WON'T FORGIVE HIM.
HE ASKED ME WHAT THE BIG DEAL WAS ABOUT A LITTLE KISS! IT WASN'T ENOUGH THAT HE STOLE MY FIRST KISS...
BUT HE ROBBED ME OF THE *FANTASY* OF MY FIRST KISS!
I WON'T FORGIVE HIM!
WET AND LUMPY...
LUMPY ...
OY...DON'T TAKE OUT YOUR ANGER ON THE POOR TEDDY.
HEY! WHAT'S WITH THAT LOOK ON YOUR FACE?
I'M JUST OVERWHELMED BY THE DESCRIPTION OF YOUR FIRST KISS.
WOW!
SIHO IS *SO* AWESOME! EE! ♡

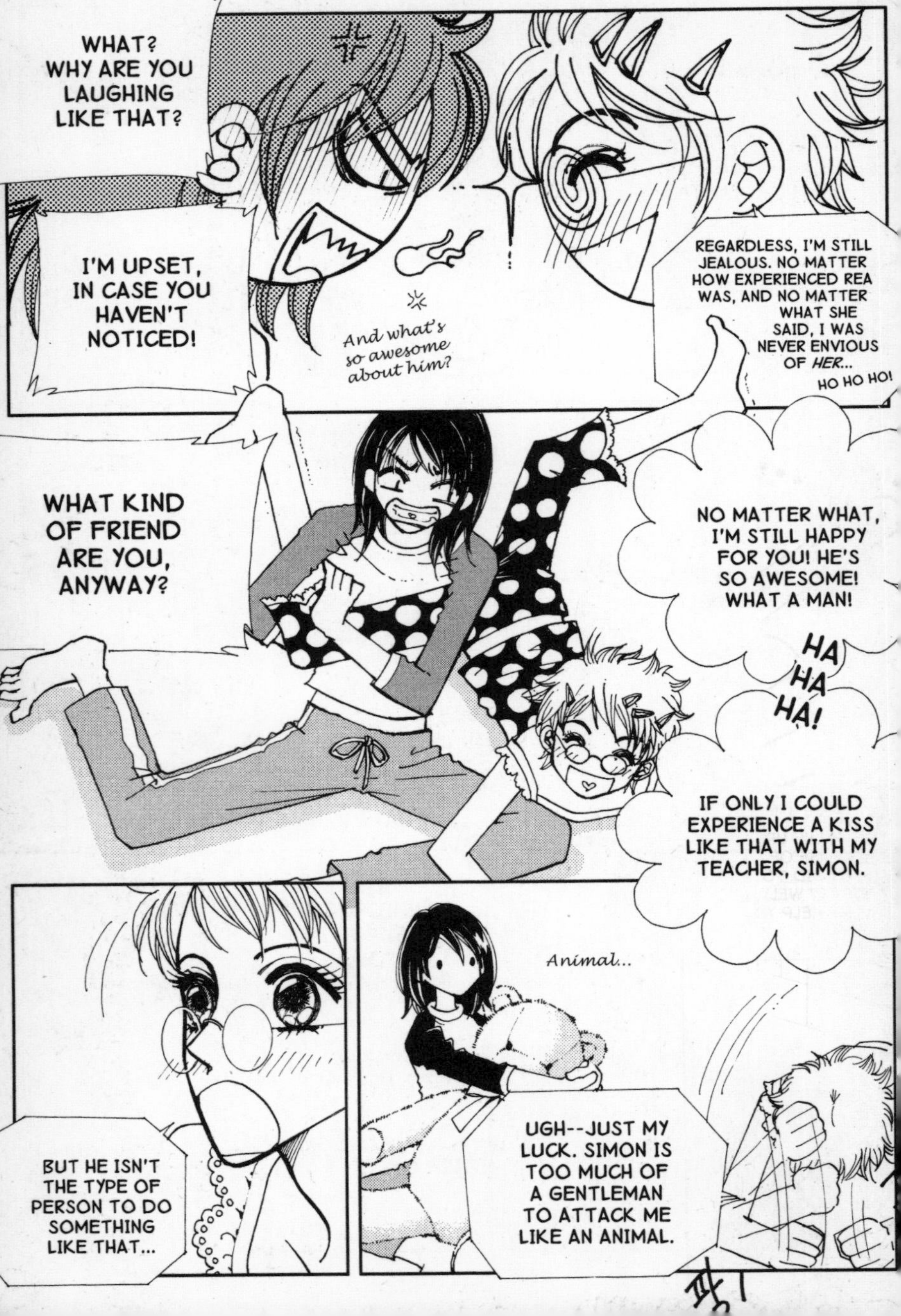
REGARDLESS, I'M STILL JEALOUS. NO MATTER HOW EXPERIENCED REA WAS, AND NO MATTER WHAT SHE SAID, I WAS NEVER ENVIOUS OF *HER*...
HO HO HO!
WHAT? WHY ARE YOU LAUGHING LIKE THAT?
I'M UPSET, IN CASE YOU HAVEN'T NOTICED!
And what's so awesome about him?
NO MATTER WHAT, I'M STILL HAPPY FOR YOU! HE'S SO AWESOME! WHAT A MAN!
HA HA HA!
WHAT KIND OF FRIEND ARE YOU, ANYWAY?
IF ONLY I COULD EXPERIENCE A KISS LIKE THAT WITH MY TEACHER, SIMON.
UGH--JUST MY LUCK. SIMON IS TOO MUCH OF A GENTLEMAN TO ATTACK ME LIKE AN ANIMAL.
Animal...
BUT HE ISN'T THE TYPE OF PERSON TO DO SOMETHING LIKE THAT...

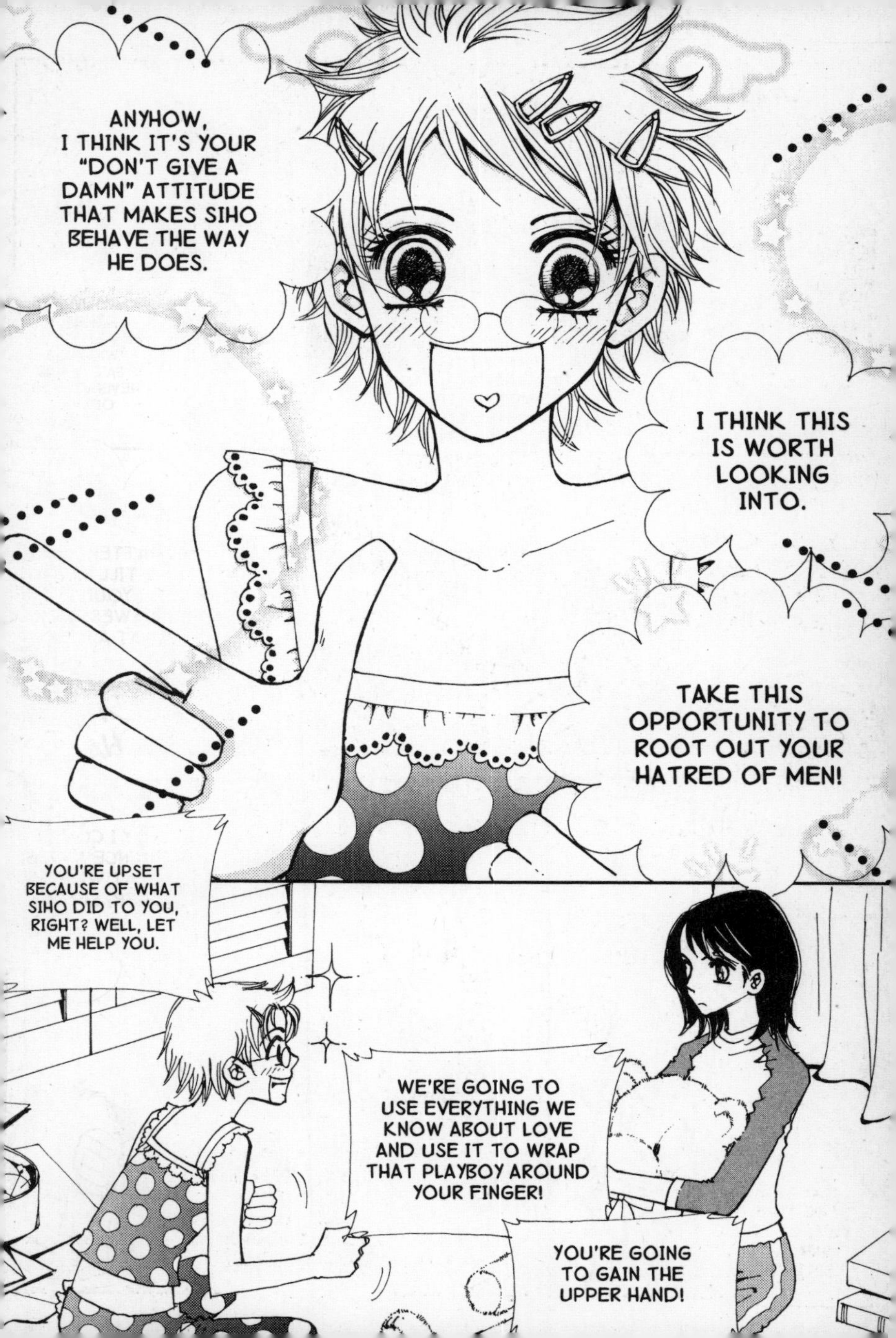
ANYHOW, I THINK IT'S YOUR "DON'T GIVE A DAMN" ATTITUDE THAT MAKES SIHO BEHAVE THE WAY HE DOES.
I THINK THIS IS WORTH LOOKING INTO.
TAKE THIS OPPORTUNITY TO ROOT OUT YOUR HATRED OF MEN!
YOU'RE UPSET BECAUSE OF WHAT SIHO DID TO YOU, RIGHT? WELL, LET ME HELP YOU.
WE'RE GOING TO USE EVERYTHING WE KNOW ABOUT LOVE AND USE IT TO WRAP THAT PLAYBOY AROUND YOUR FINGER!
YOU'RE GOING TO GAIN THE UPPER HAND!

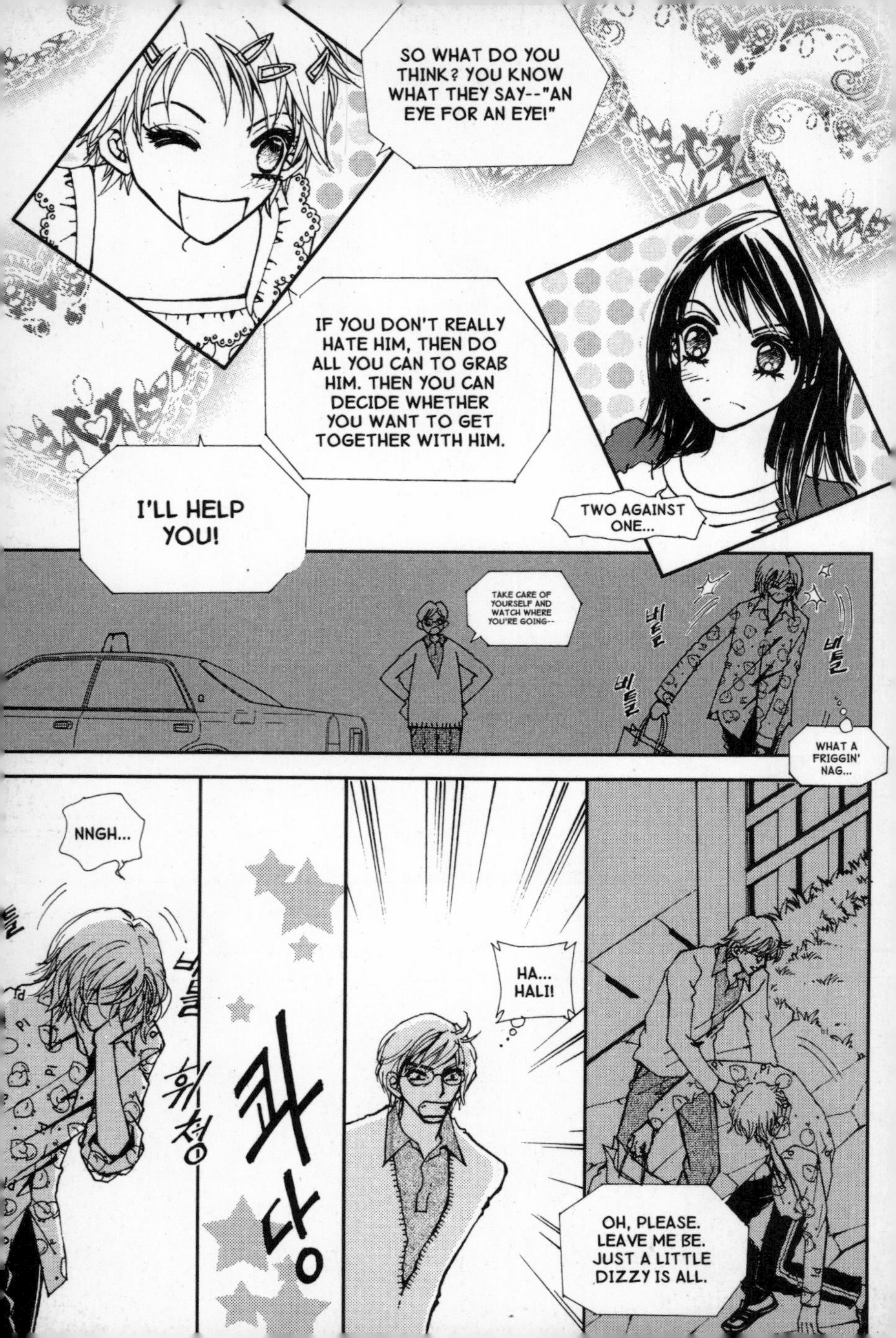
SO WHAT DO YOU THINK? YOU KNOW WHAT THEY SAY--"AN EYE FOR AN EYE!"
IF YOU DON'T REALLY HATE HIM, THEN DO ALL YOU CAN TO GRAB HIM. THEN YOU CAN DECIDE WHETHER YOU WANT TO GET TOGETHER WITH HIM.
I'LL HELP YOU!
TWO AGAINST ONE...
TAKE CARE OF YOURSELF AND WATCH WHERE YOU'RE GOING--
비틀
비틀
비틀
WHAT A FRIGGIN' NAG...
NNGH...
비틀
휘청
콰당
HA... HALI!
OH, PLEASE. LEAVE ME BE. JUST A LITTLE DIZZY IS ALL.

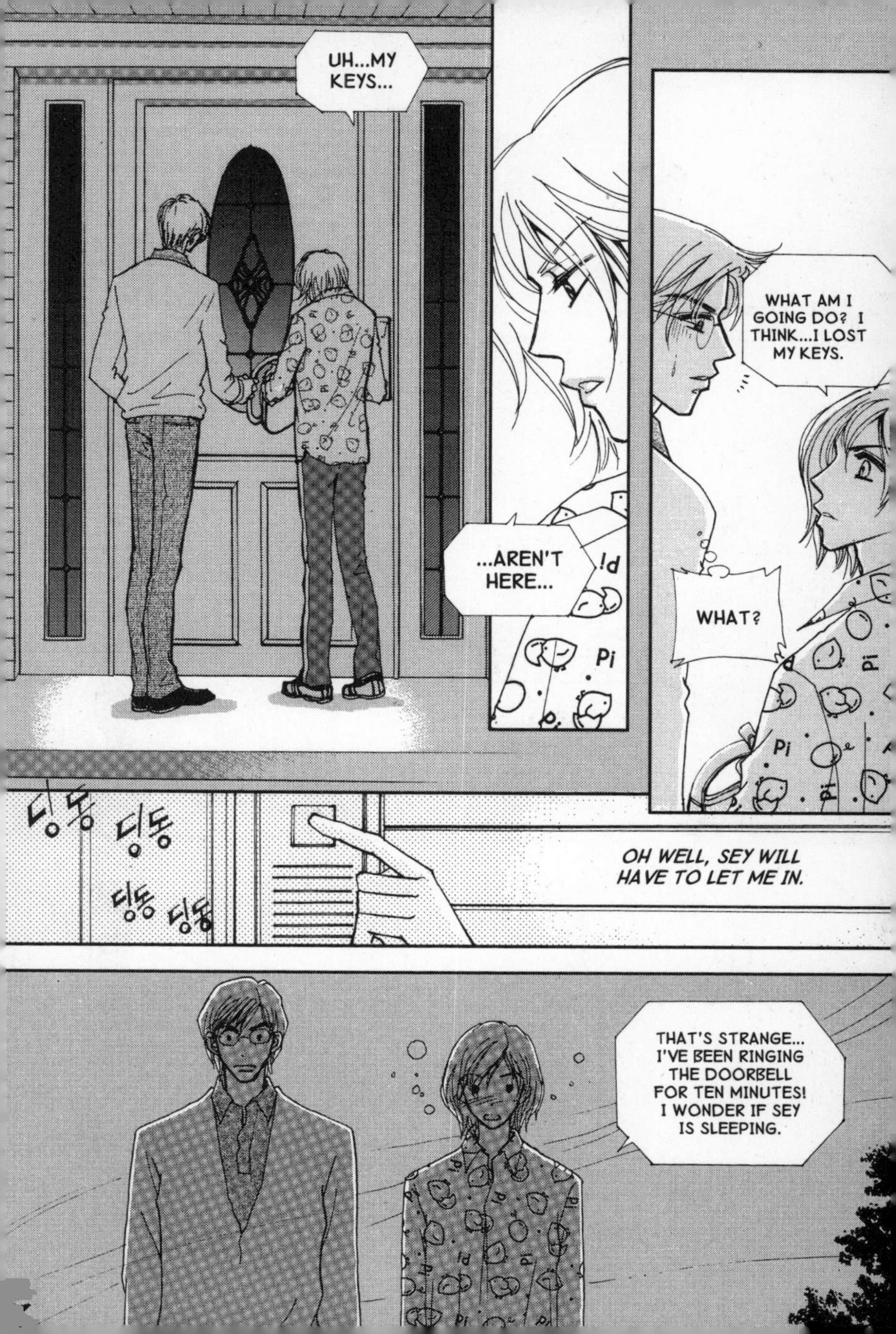
UH...MY KEYS...
...AREN'T HERE...
WHAT AM I GOING DO? I THINK...I LOST MY KEYS.
WHAT?
딩동 딩동
딩동 딩동
OH WELL, SEY WILL HAVE TO LET ME IN.
THAT'S STRANGE... I'VE BEEN RINGING THE DOORBELL FOR TEN MINUTES! I WONDER IF SEY IS SLEEPING.

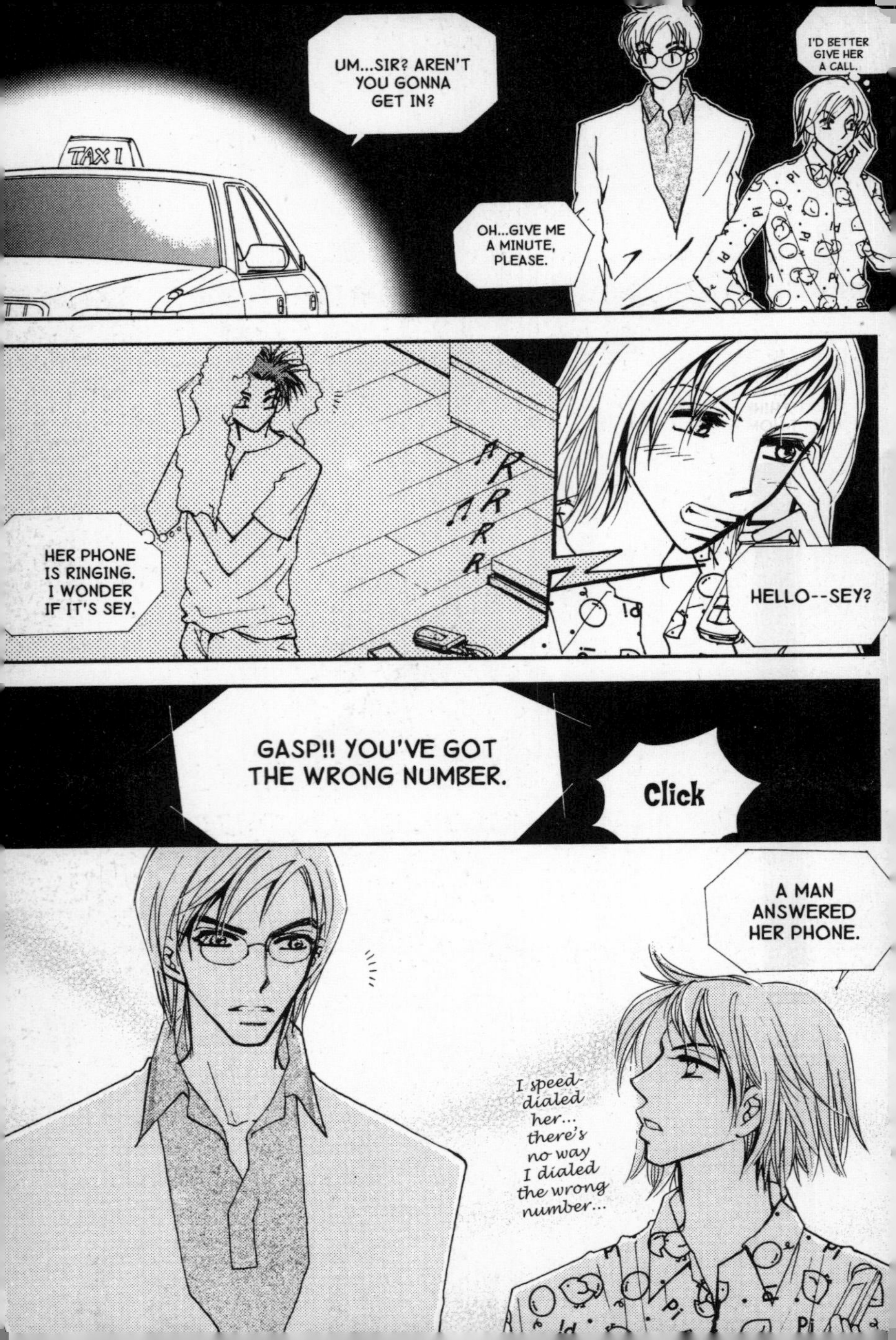
UM...SIR? AREN'T YOU GONNA GET IN?
OH...GIVE ME A MINUTE, PLEASE.
I'D BETTER GIVE HER A CALL.
HELLO--SEY?
RRRR
HER PHONE IS RINGING. I WONDER IF IT'S SEY.
Click
GASP!! YOU'VE GOT THE WRONG NUMBER.
A MAN ANSWERED HER PHONE.
I speed-dialed her... there's no way I dialed the wrong number...

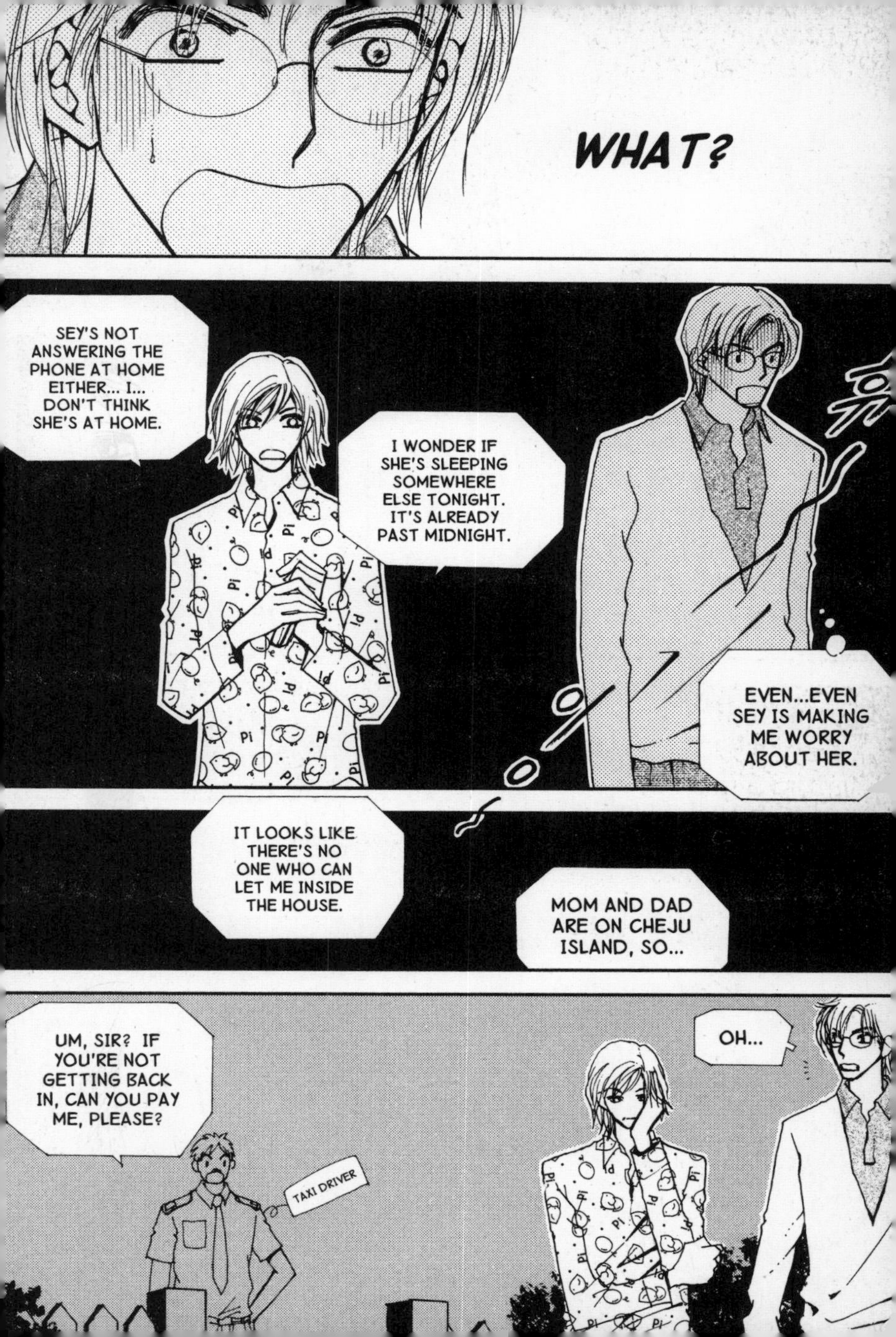
WHAT?
SEY'S NOT ANSWERING THE PHONE AT HOME EITHER... I... DON'T THINK SHE'S AT HOME.
I WONDER IF SHE'S SLEEPING SOMEWHERE ELSE TONIGHT. IT'S ALREADY PAST MIDNIGHT.
EVEN...EVEN SEY IS MAKING ME WORRY ABOUT HER.
IT LOOKS LIKE THERE'S NO ONE WHO CAN LET ME INSIDE THE HOUSE.
MOM AND DAD ARE ON CHEJU ISLAND, SO...
UM, SIR? IF YOU'RE NOT GETTING BACK IN, CAN YOU PAY ME, PLEASE?
TAXI DRIVER
OH...

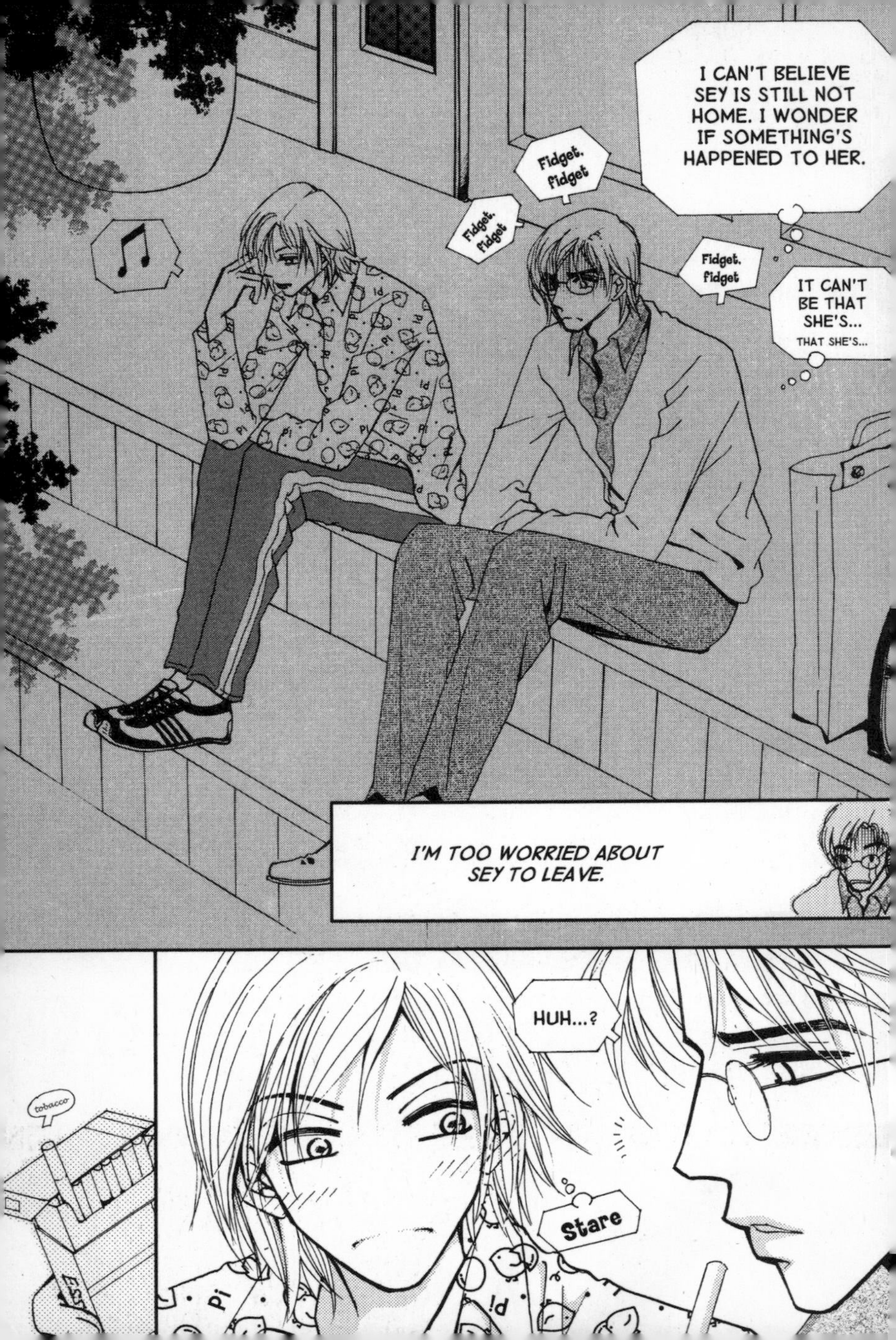

I CAN'T BELIEVE SEY IS STILL NOT HOME. I WONDER IF SOMETHING'S HAPPENED TO HER.
Fidget, fidget
Fidget, fidget
IT CAN'T BE THAT SHE'S... THAT SHE'S...
Fidget, fidget
Fidget, fidget
I'M TOO WORRIED ABOUT SEY TO LEAVE.
HUH...?
Stare
tobacco

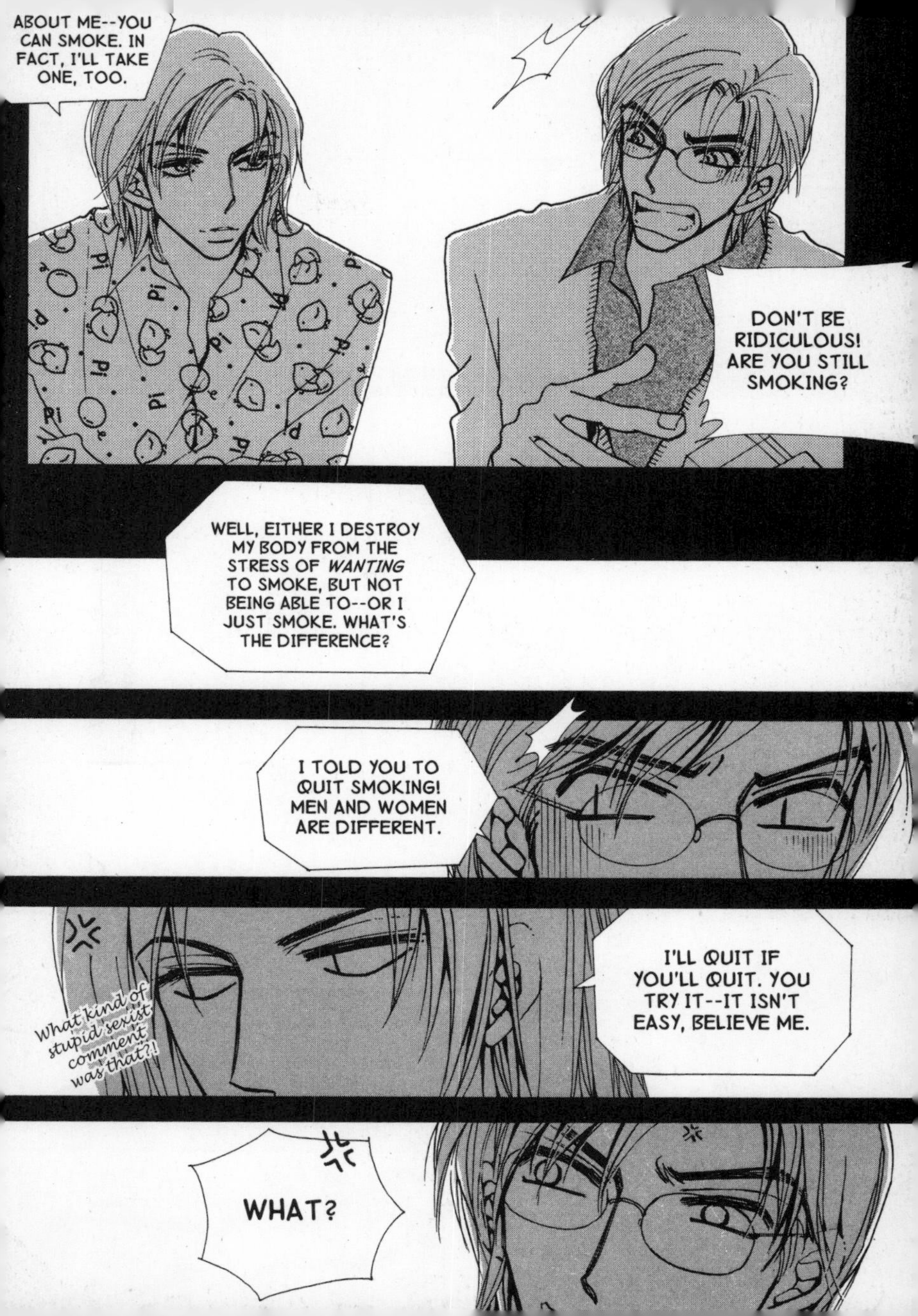
ABOUT ME--YOU CAN SMOKE. IN FACT, I'LL TAKE ONE, TOO.
DON'T BE RIDICULOUS! ARE YOU STILL SMOKING?
WELL, EITHER I DESTROY MY BODY FROM THE STRESS OF *WANTING* TO SMOKE, BUT NOT BEING ABLE TO--OR I JUST SMOKE. WHAT'S THE DIFFERENCE?
I TOLD YOU TO QUIT SMOKING! MEN AND WOMEN ARE DIFFERENT.
What kind of stupid sexist comment was that?!
I'LL QUIT IF YOU'LL QUIT. YOU TRY IT--IT ISN'T EASY, BELIEVE ME.
WHAT?

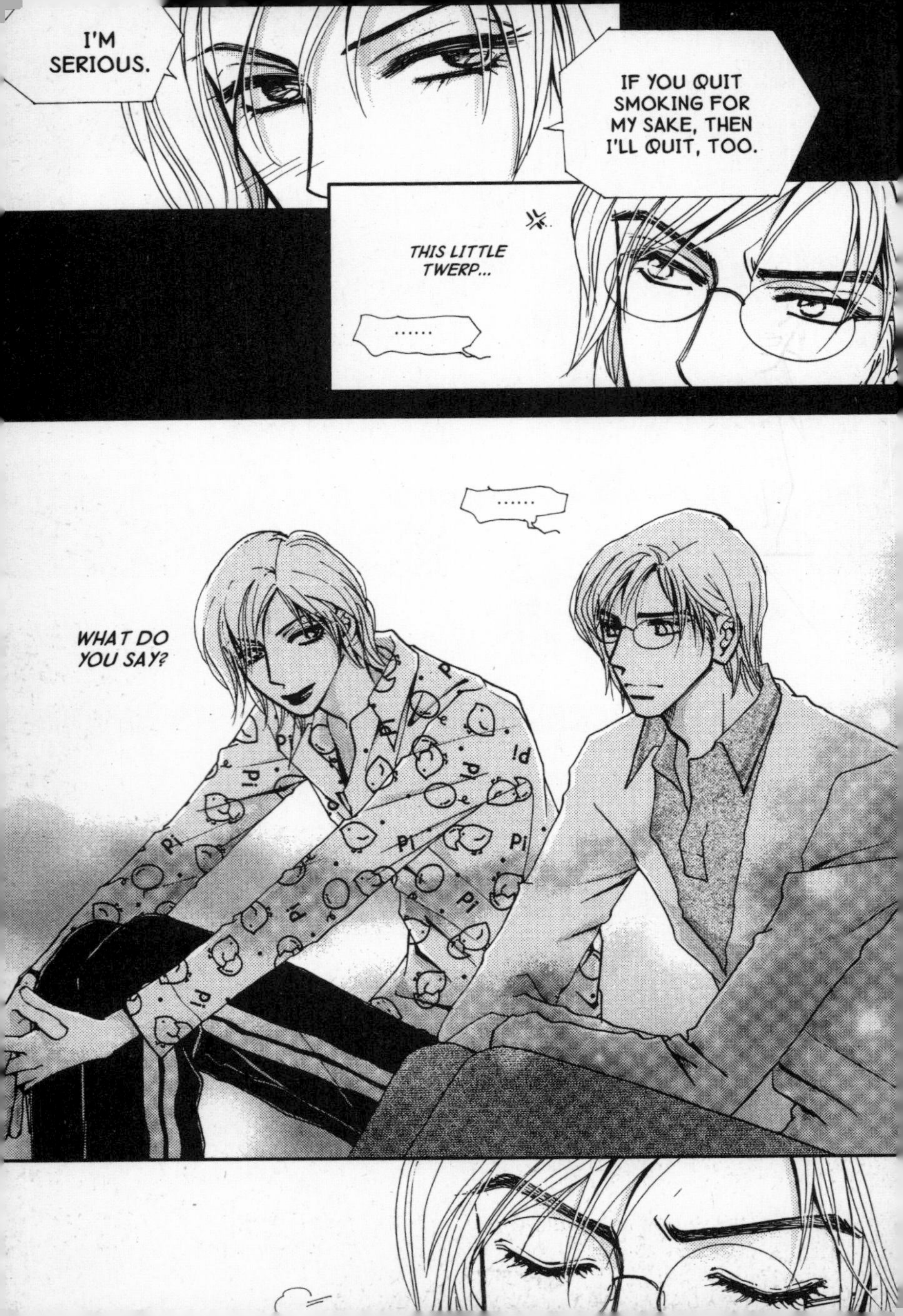
I'M SERIOUS.
IF YOU QUIT SMOKING FOR MY SAKE, THEN I'LL QUIT, TOO.
THIS LITTLE TWERP...
......
......
WHAT DO YOU SAY?

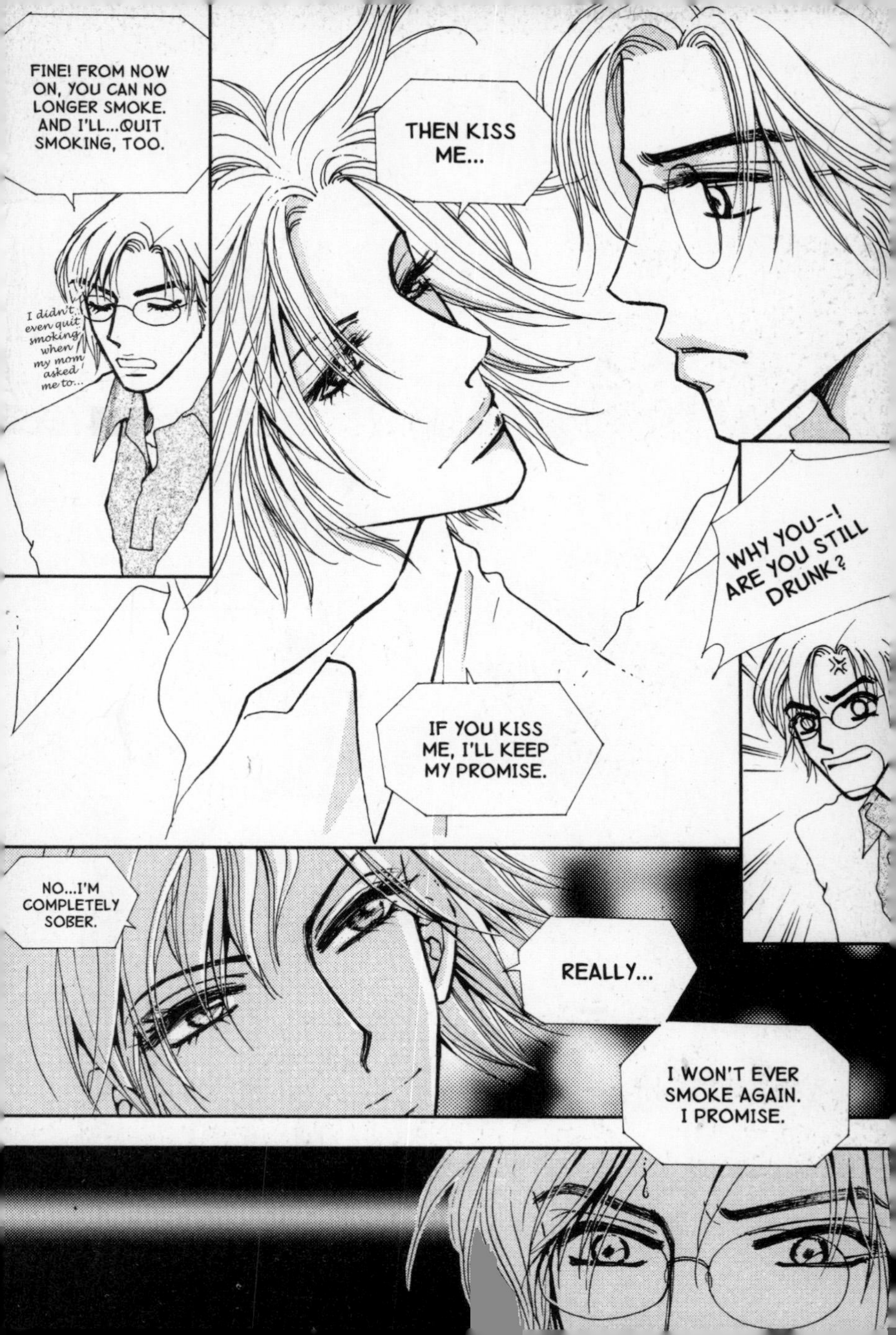
FINE! FROM NOW ON, YOU CAN NO LONGER SMOKE. AND I'LL...QUIT SMOKING, TOO.
I didn't even quit smoking when my mom asked me to...
THEN KISS ME...
IF YOU KISS ME, I'LL KEEP MY PROMISE.
WHY YOU--! ARE YOU STILL DRUNK?
NO...I'M COMPLETELY SOBER.
REALLY...
I WON'T EVER SMOKE AGAIN. I PROMISE.

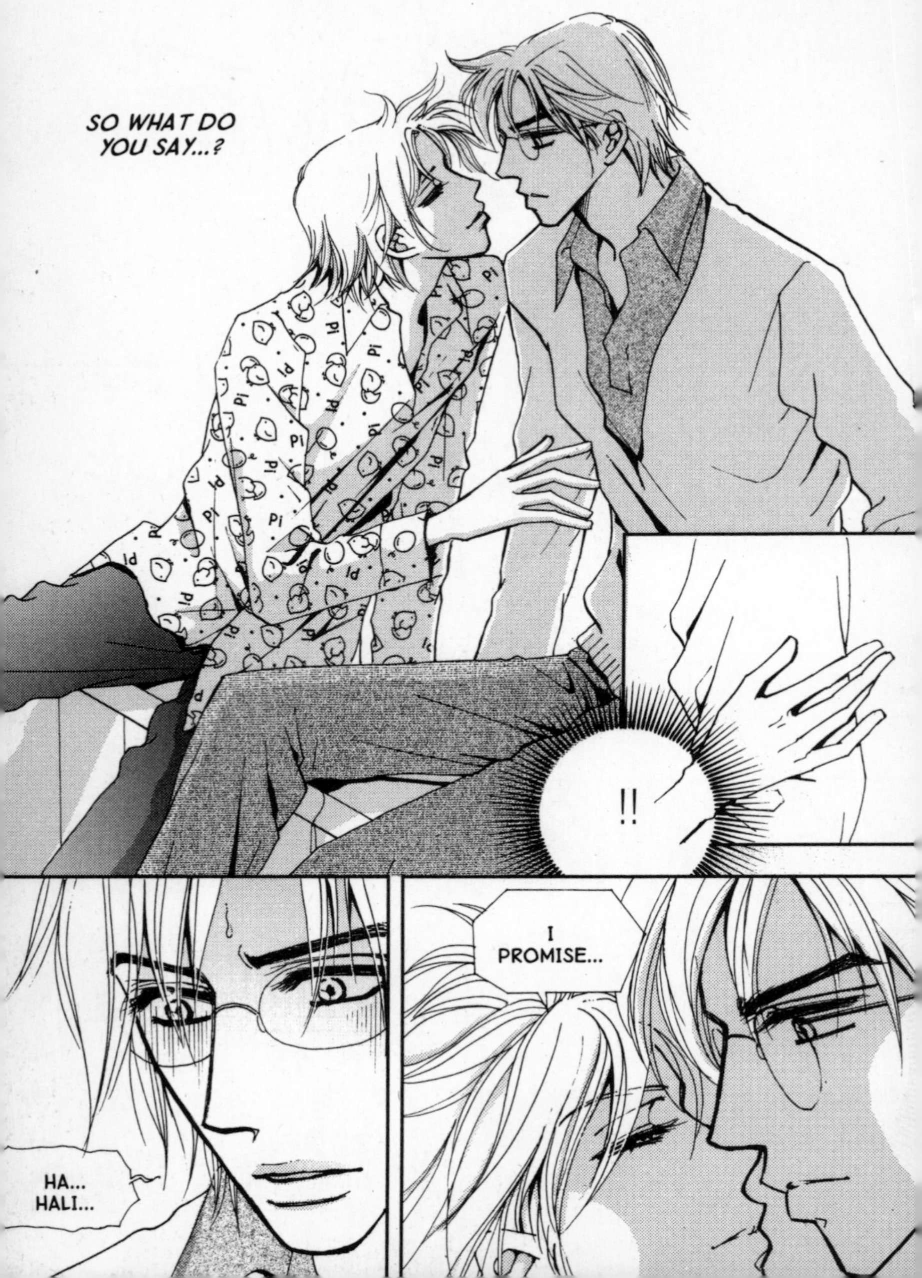
SO WHAT DO YOU SAY...?
!!
I PROMISE...
HA... HALI...

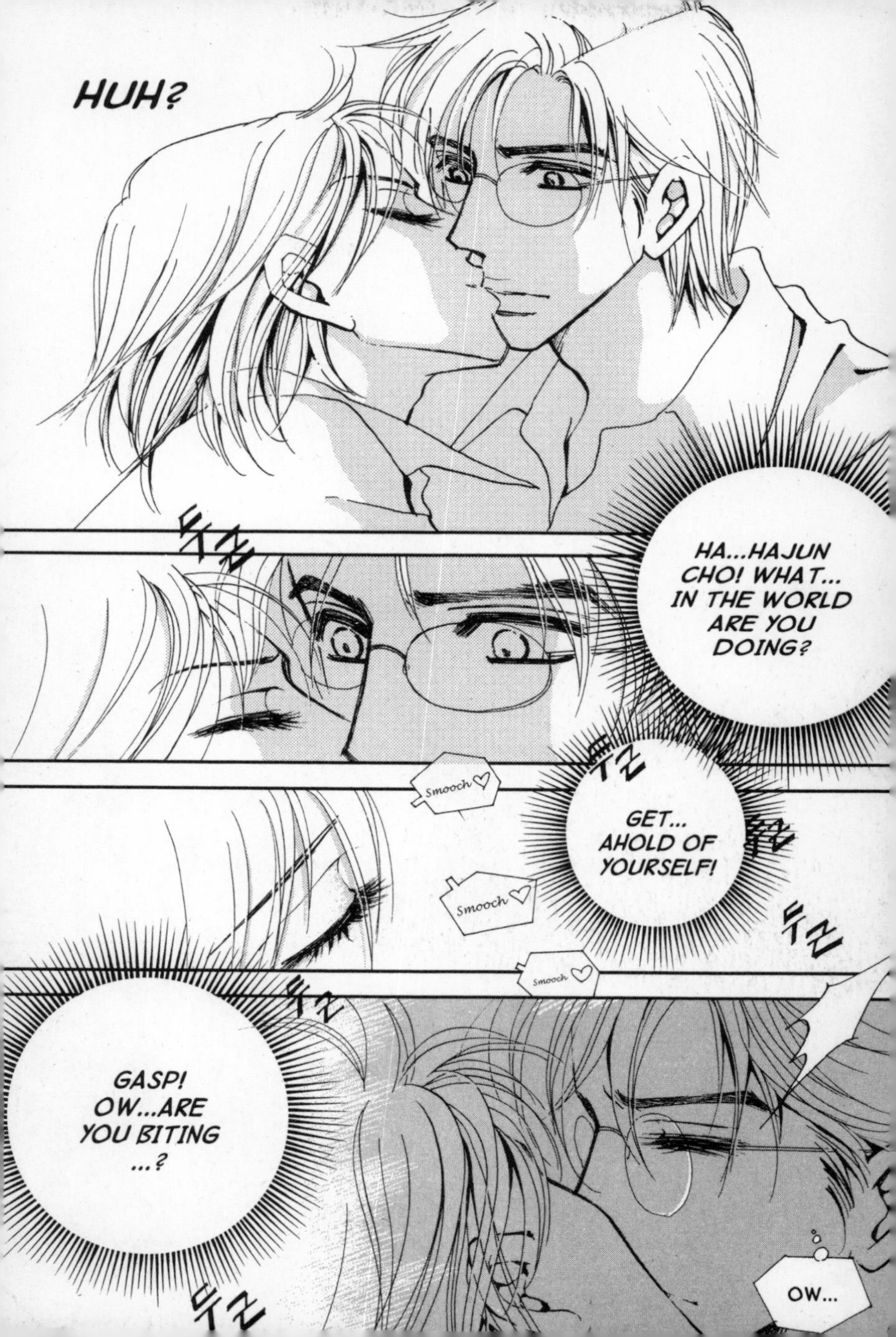
HUH?
HA...HAJUN CHO! WHAT... IN THE WORLD ARE YOU DOING?
Smooch♡
GET... AHOLD OF YOURSELF!
Smooch♡
Smooch♡
GASP! OW...ARE YOU BITING ...?
OW...

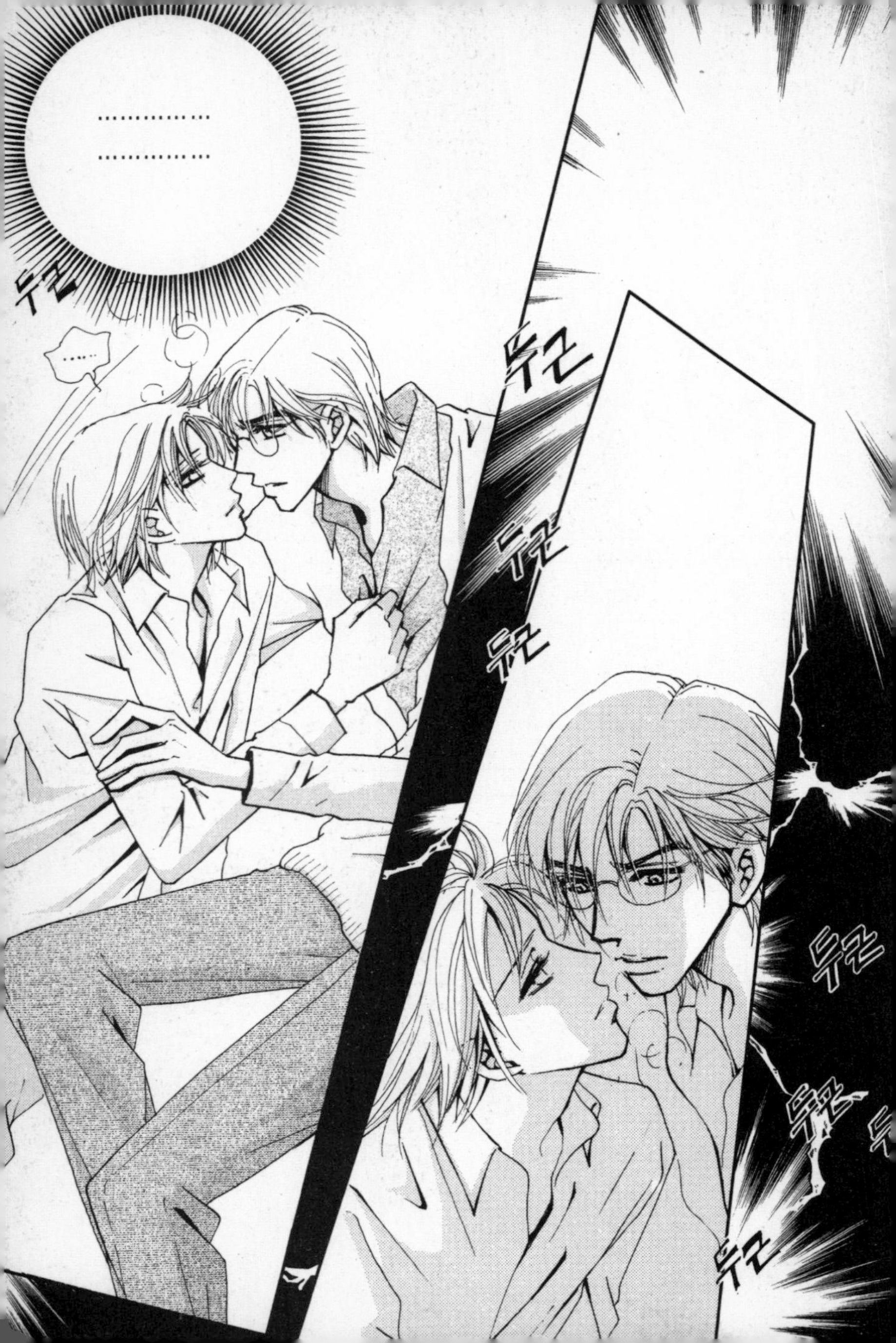

두근
두근
두근
두근
두근
두근
……
……
두근
……

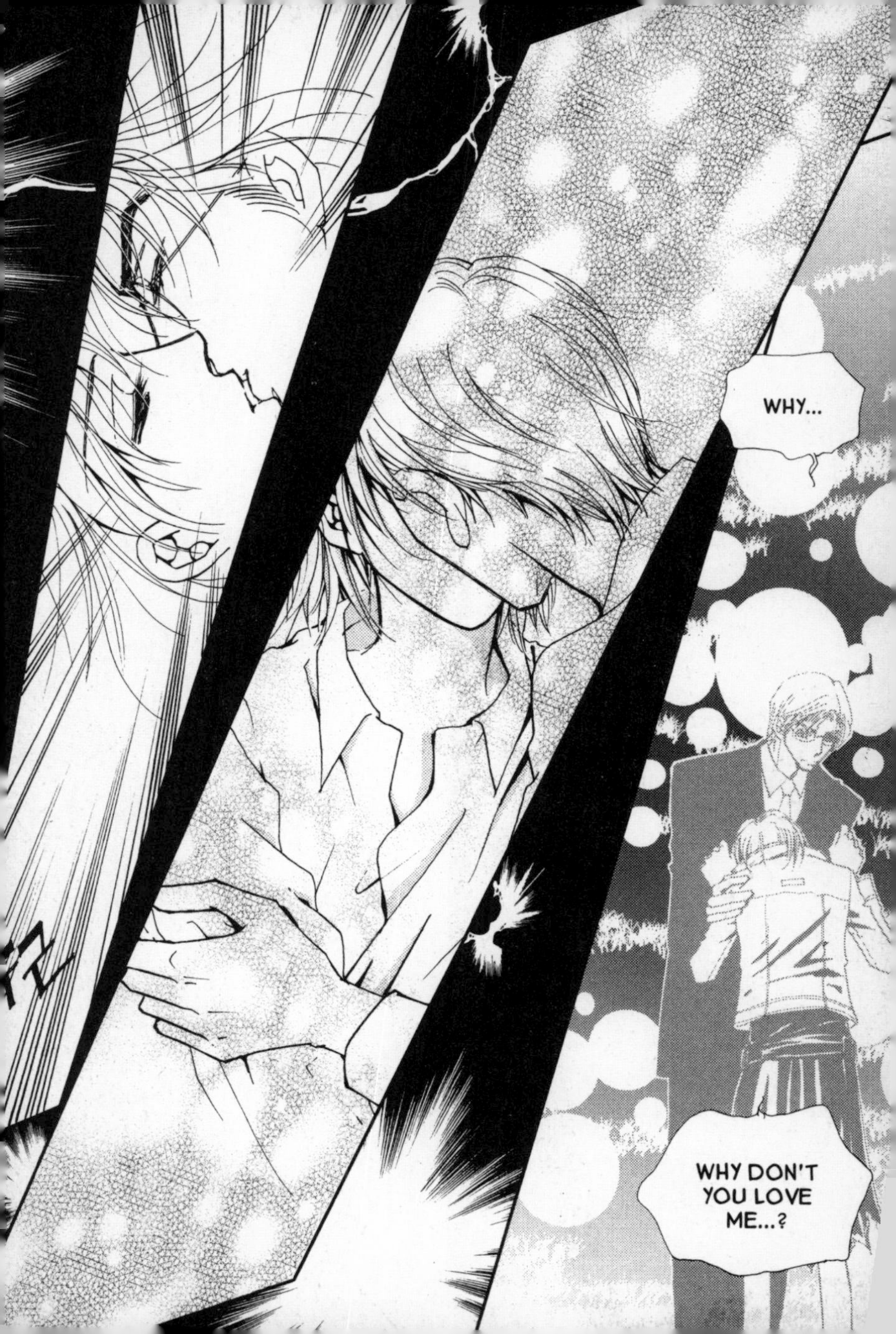
WHY...
WHY DON'T YOU LOVE ME...?

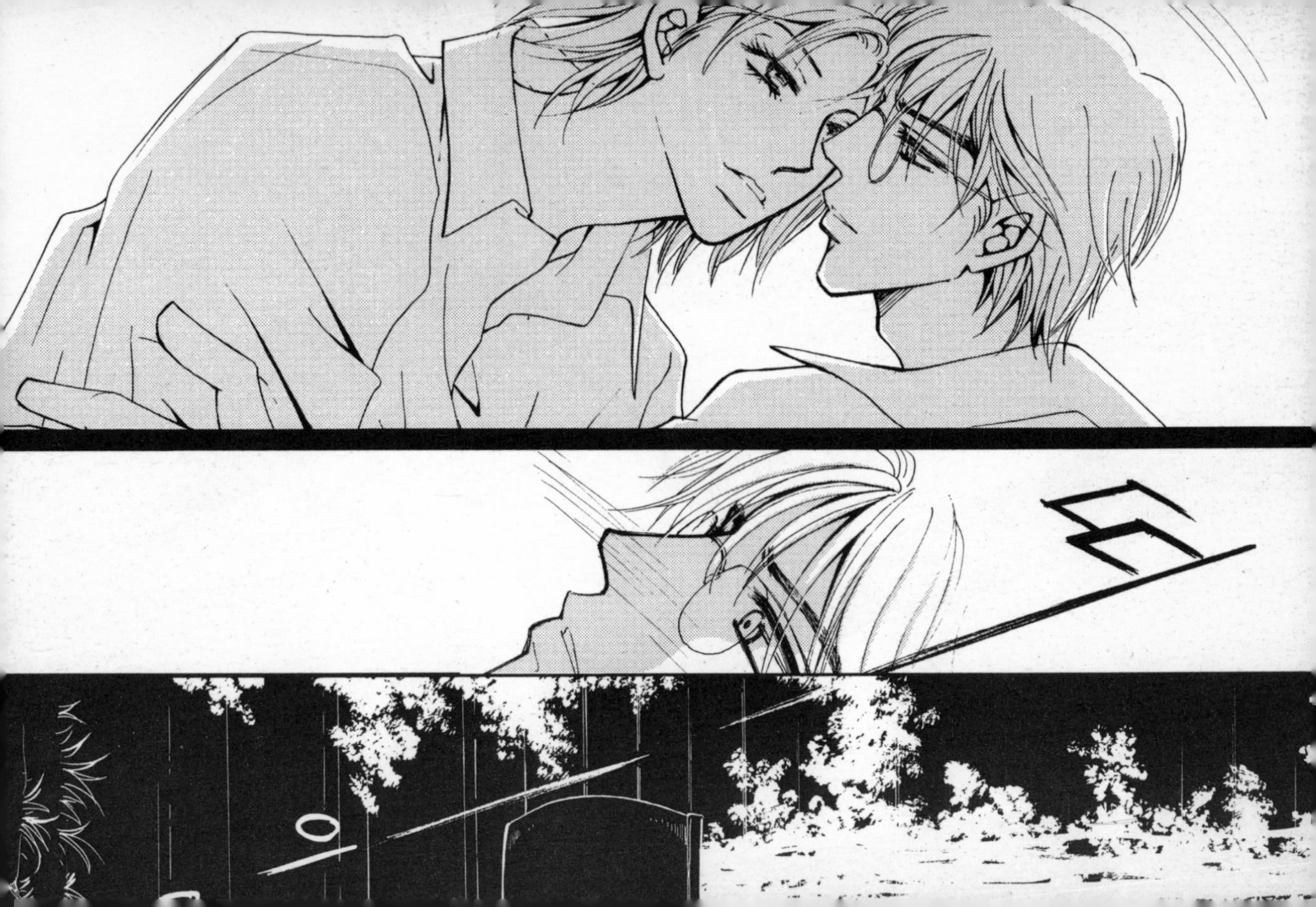

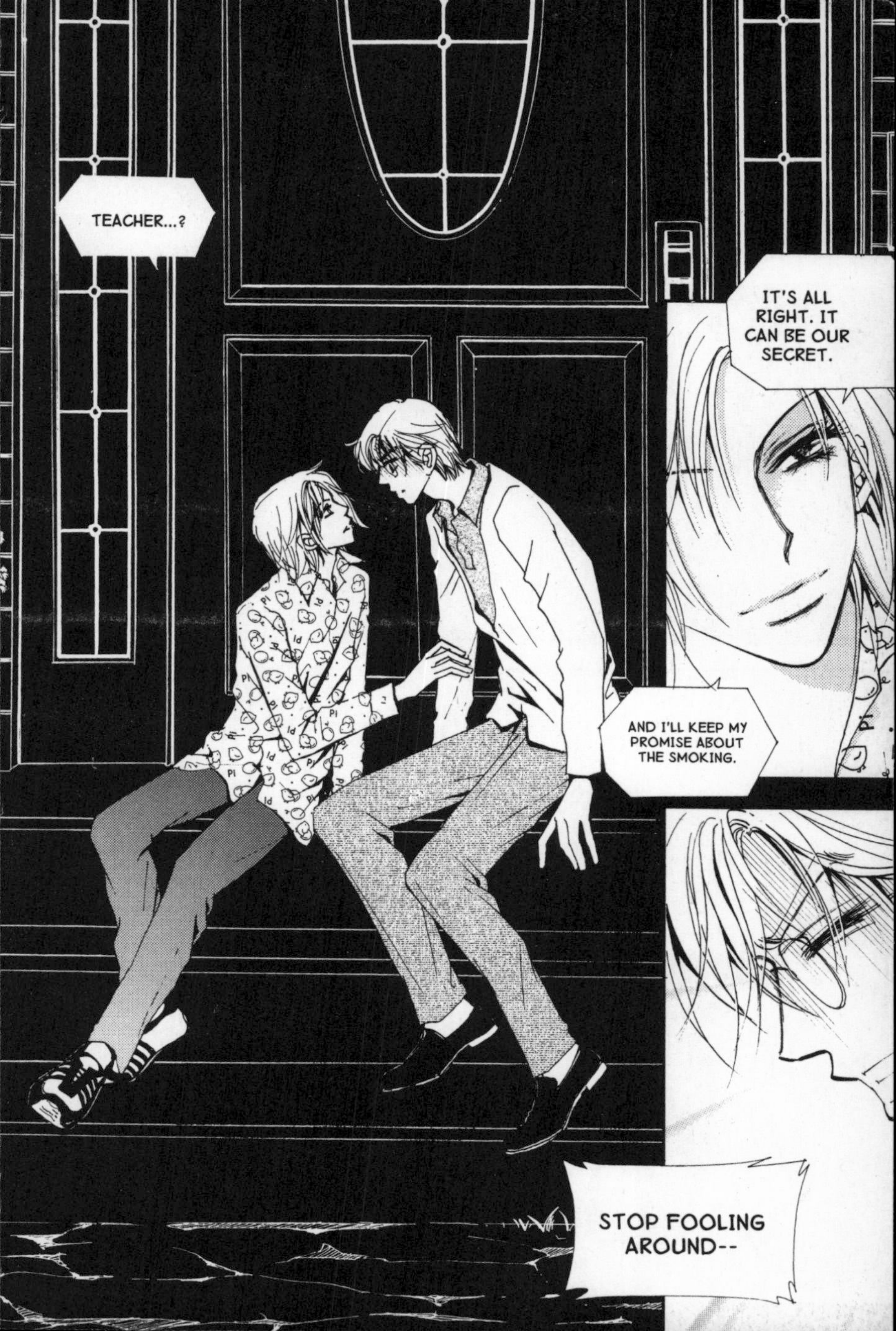
TEACHER...?
IT'S ALL RIGHT. IT CAN BE OUR SECRET.
AND I'LL KEEP MY PROMISE ABOUT THE SMOKING.
STOP FOOLING AROUND--

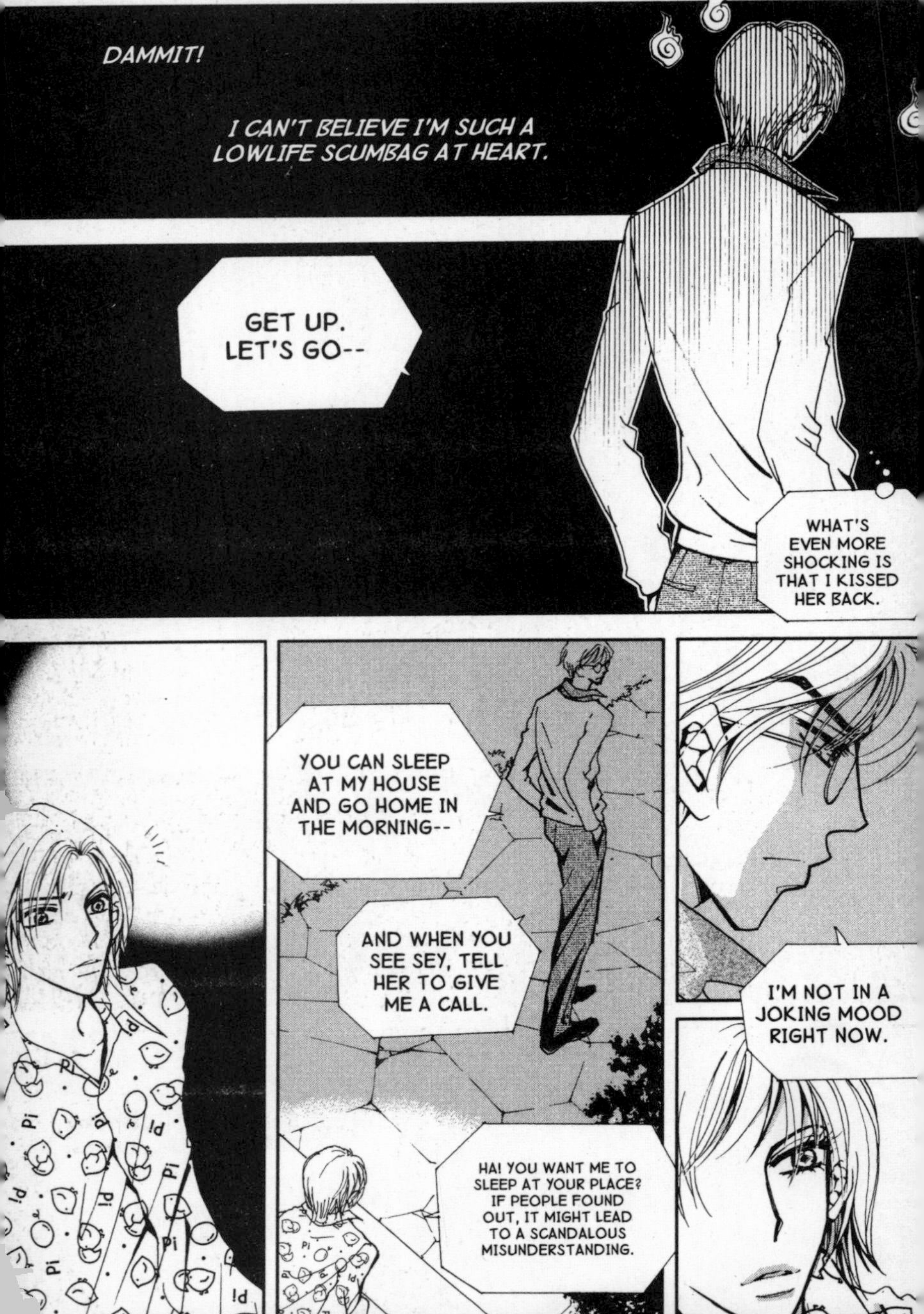
DAMMIT!
I CAN'T BELIEVE I'M SUCH A LOWLIFE SCUMBAG AT HEART.
WHAT'S EVEN MORE SHOCKING IS THAT I KISSED HER BACK.
GET UP. LET'S GO--
YOU CAN SLEEP AT MY HOUSE AND GO HOME IN THE MORNING--
AND WHEN YOU SEE SEY, TELL HER TO GIVE ME A CALL.
HA! YOU WANT ME TO SLEEP AT YOUR PLACE? IF PEOPLE FOUND OUT, IT MIGHT LEAD TO A SCANDALOUS MISUNDERSTANDING.
I'M NOT IN A JOKING MOOD RIGHT NOW.

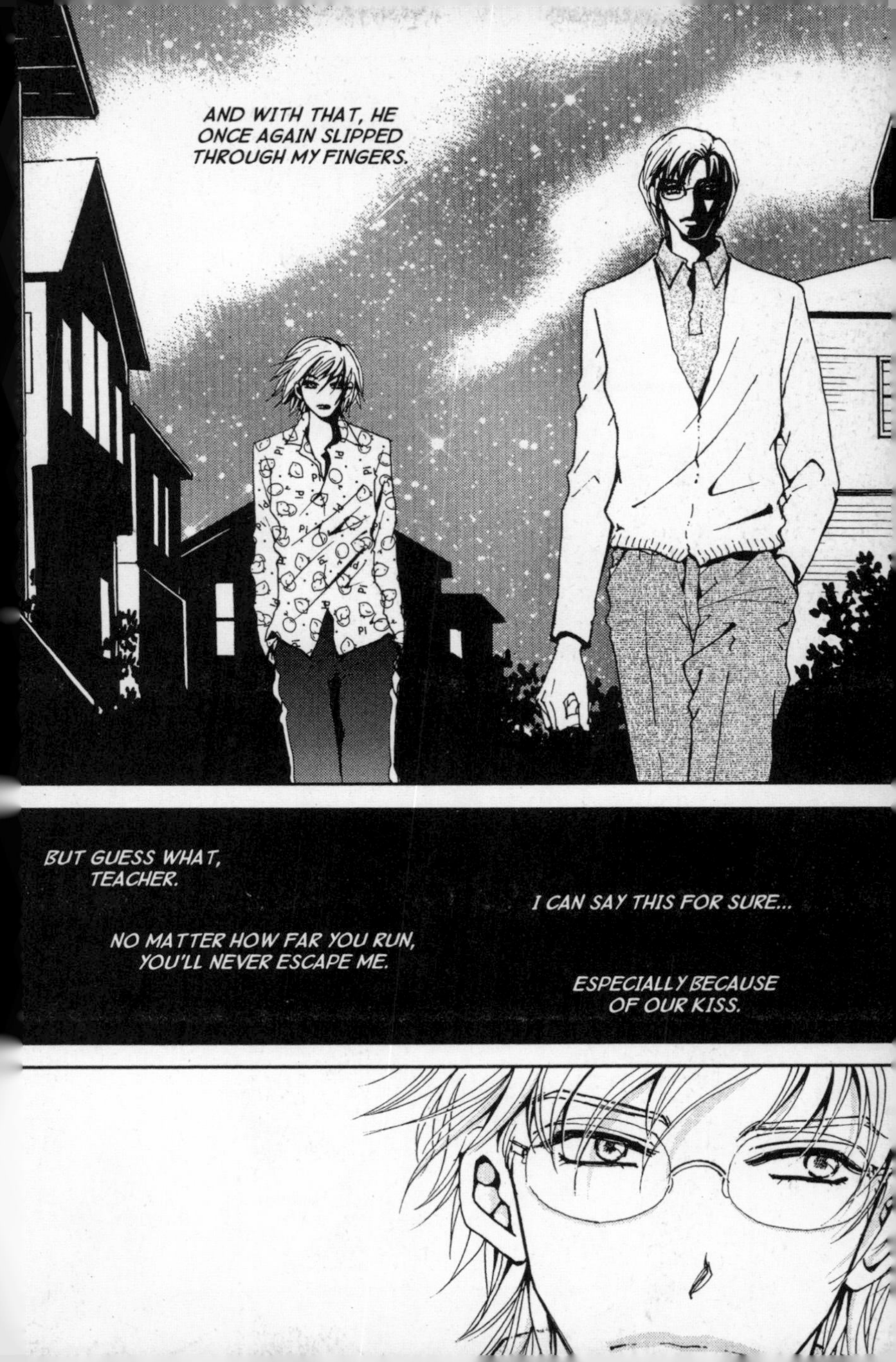
AND WITH THAT, HE ONCE AGAIN SLIPPED THROUGH MY FINGERS.
BUT GUESS WHAT, TEACHER.
NO MATTER HOW FAR YOU RUN, YOU'LL NEVER ESCAPE ME.
I CAN SAY THIS FOR SURE...
ESPECIALLY BECAUSE OF OUR KISS.

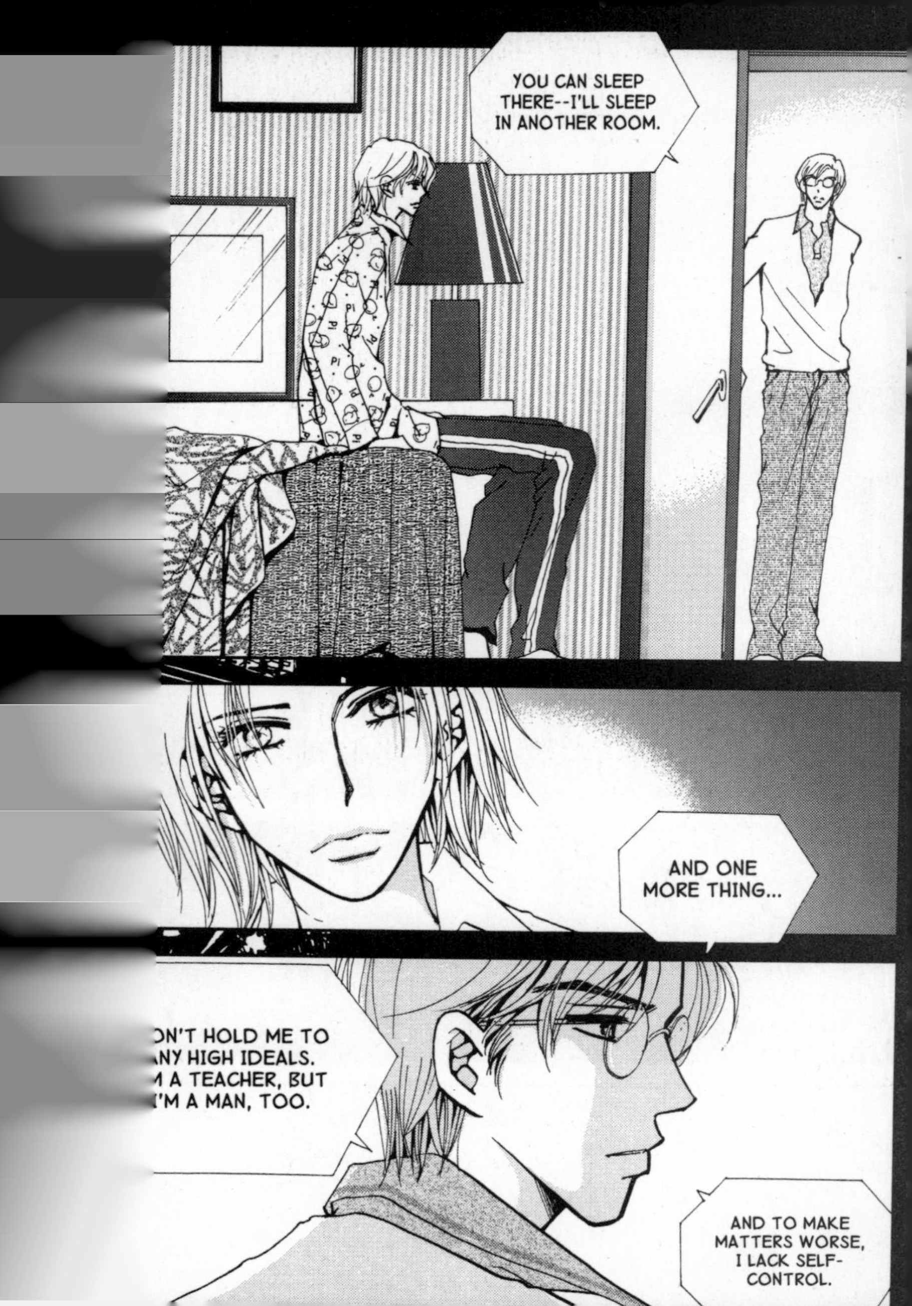
YOU CAN SLEEP THERE--I'LL SLEEP IN ANOTHER ROOM.
AND ONE MORE THING...
AND TO MAKE MATTERS WORSE, I LACK SELF-CONTROL.
ON'T HOLD ME TO ANY HIGH IDEALS. M A TEACHER, BUT 'M A MAN, TOO.

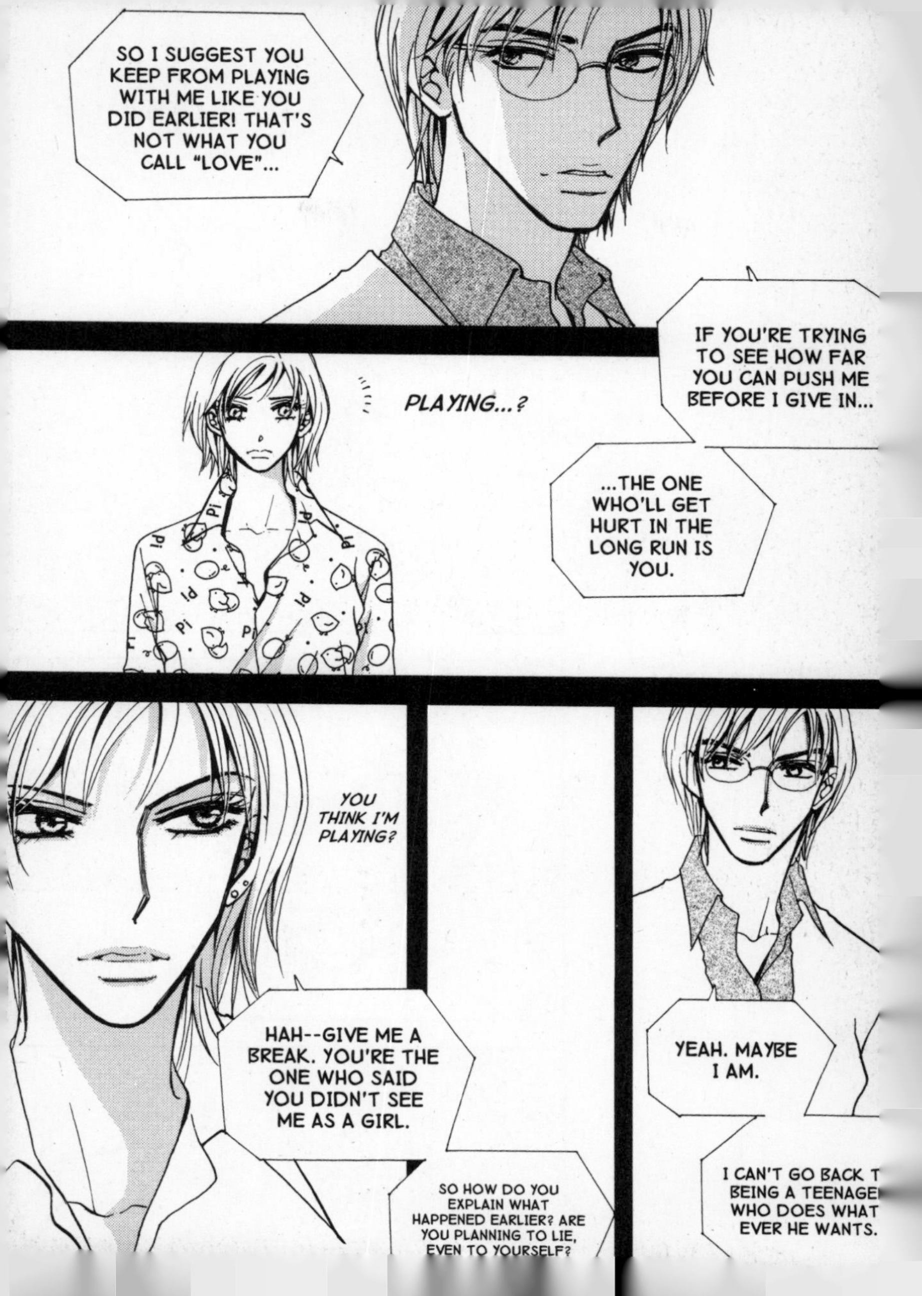
SO I SUGGEST YOU KEEP FROM PLAYING WITH ME LIKE YOU DID EARLIER! THAT'S NOT WHAT YOU CALL "LOVE"...
PLAYING...?
IF YOU'RE TRYING TO SEE HOW FAR YOU CAN PUSH ME BEFORE I GIVE IN...
...THE ONE WHO'LL GET HURT IN THE LONG RUN IS YOU.
YOU THINK I'M PLAYING?
HAH--GIVE ME A BREAK. YOU'RE THE ONE WHO SAID YOU DIDN'T SEE ME AS A GIRL.
SO HOW DO YOU EXPLAIN WHAT HAPPENED EARLIER? ARE YOU PLANNING TO LIE, EVEN TO YOURSELF?
YEAH. MAYBE I AM.
I CAN'T GO BACK T BEING A TEENAGE WHO DOES WHAT EVER HE WANTS.

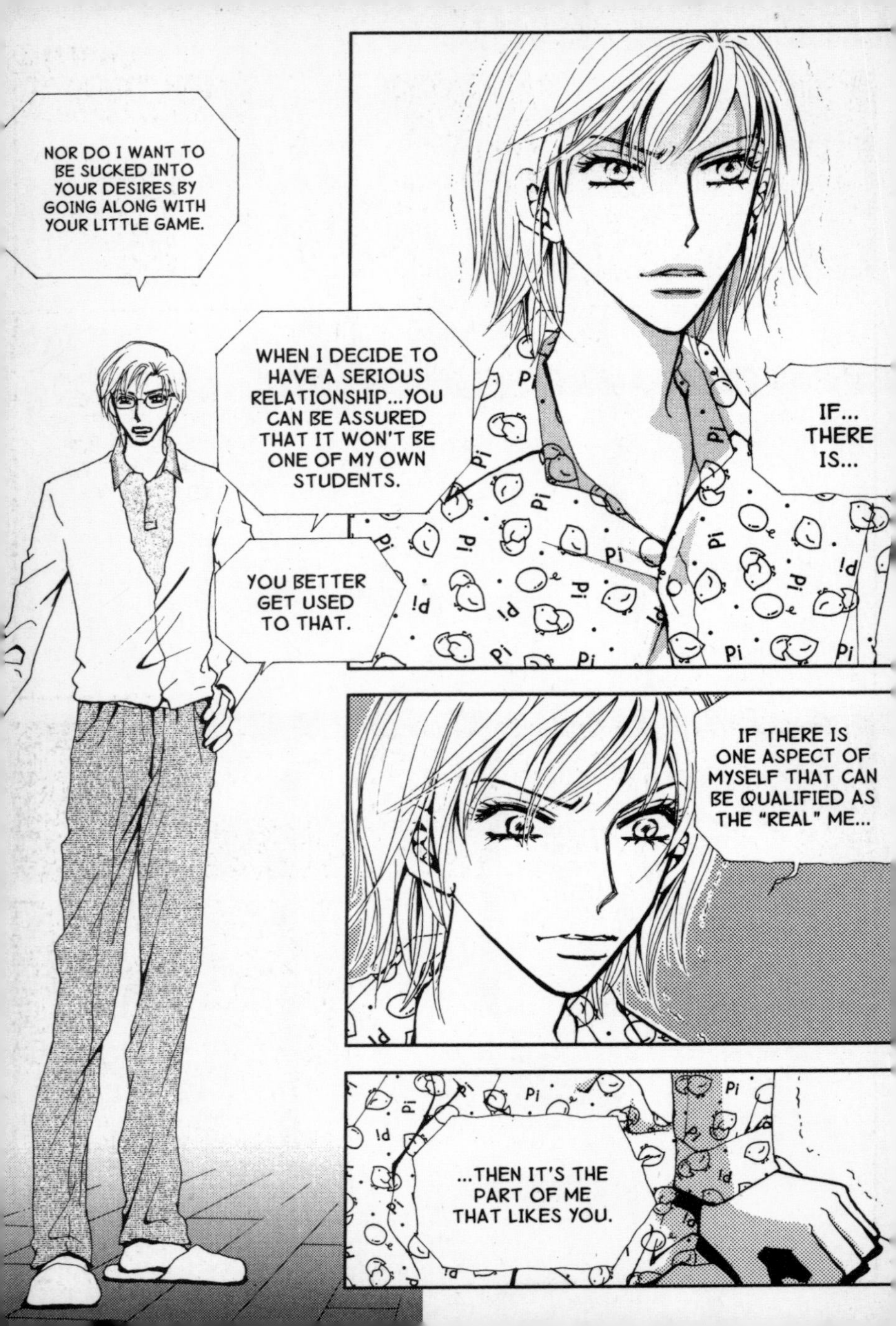
NOR DO I WANT TO BE SUCKED INTO YOUR DESIRES BY GOING ALONG WITH YOUR LITTLE GAME.
WHEN I DECIDE TO HAVE A SERIOUS RELATIONSHIP...YOU CAN BE ASSURED THAT IT WON'T BE ONE OF MY OWN STUDENTS.
YOU BETTER GET USED TO THAT.
IF... THERE IS...
IF THERE IS ONE ASPECT OF MYSELF THAT CAN BE QUALIFIED AS THE "REAL" ME...
...THEN IT'S THE PART OF ME THAT LIKES YOU.

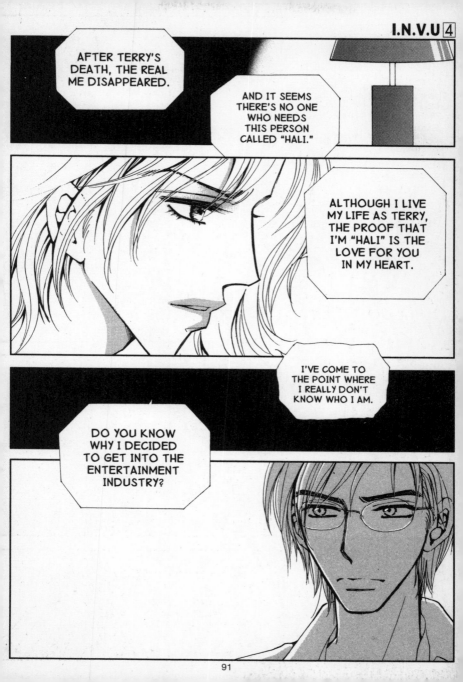

AFTER TERRY'S DEATH, THE REAL ME DISAPPEARED.

AND IT SEEMS THERE'S NO ONE WHO NEEDS THIS PERSON CALLED "HALI."

ALTHOUGH I LIVE MY LIFE AS TERRY, THE PROOF THAT I'M "HALI" IS THE LOVE FOR YOU IN MY HEART.

I'VE COME TO THE POINT WHERE I REALLY DON'T KNOW WHO I AM.

DO YOU KNOW WHY I DECIDED TO GET INTO THE ENTERTAINMENT INDUSTRY?

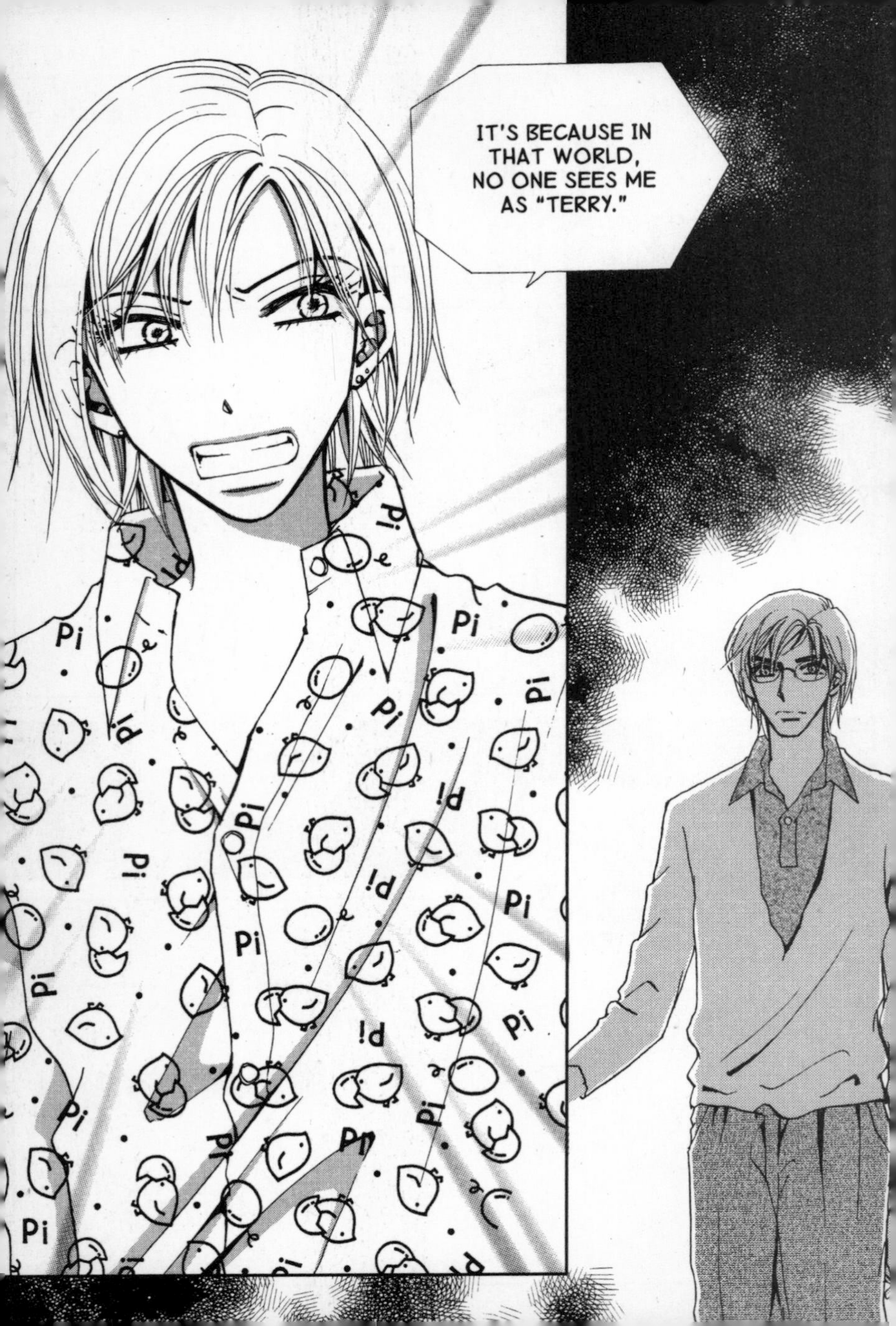
IT'S BECAUSE IN THAT WORLD, NO ONE SEES ME AS "TERRY."

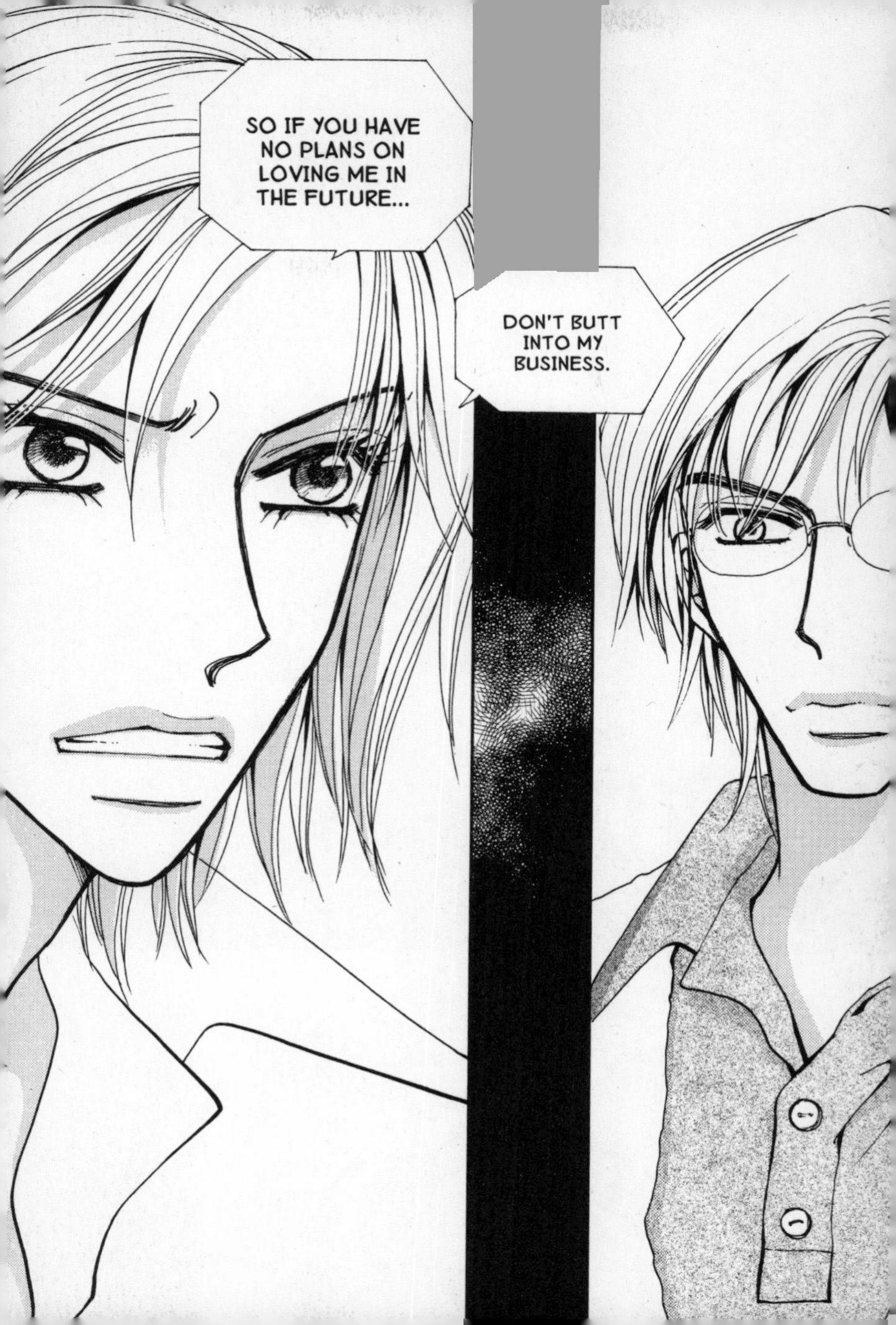
SO IF YOU HAVE NO PLANS ON LOVING ME IN THE FUTURE...
DON'T BUTT INTO MY BUSINESS.

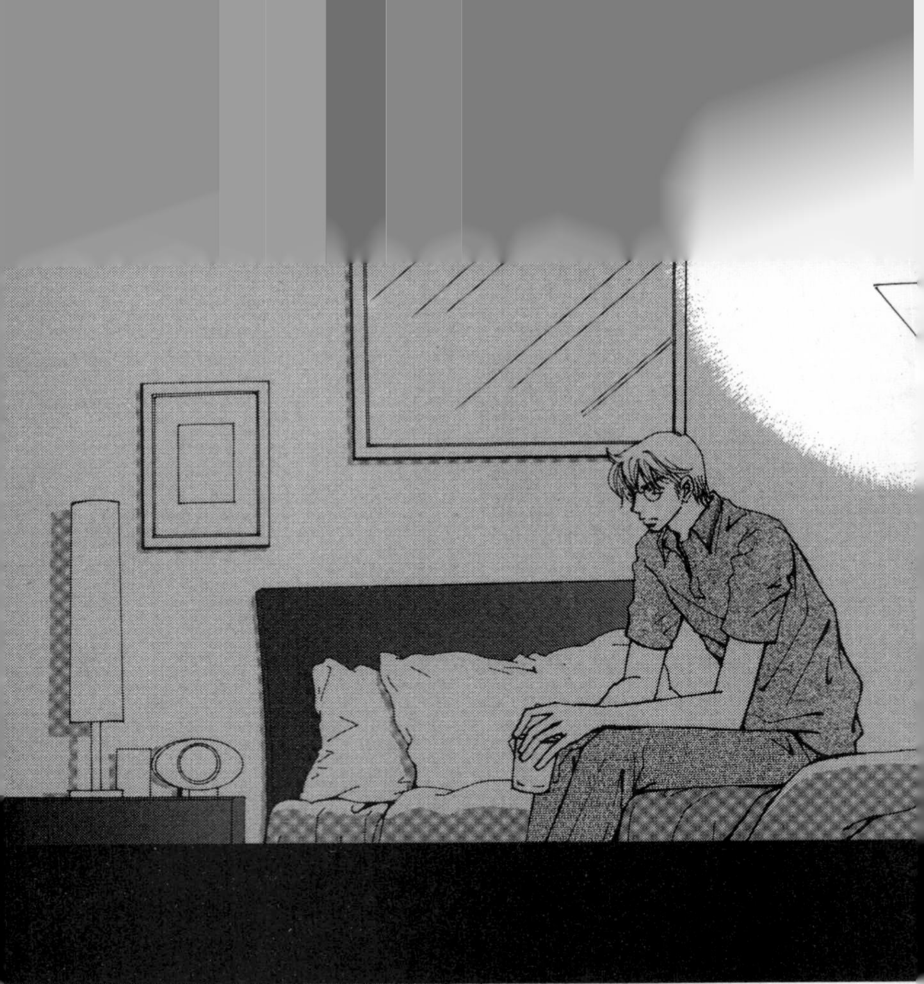
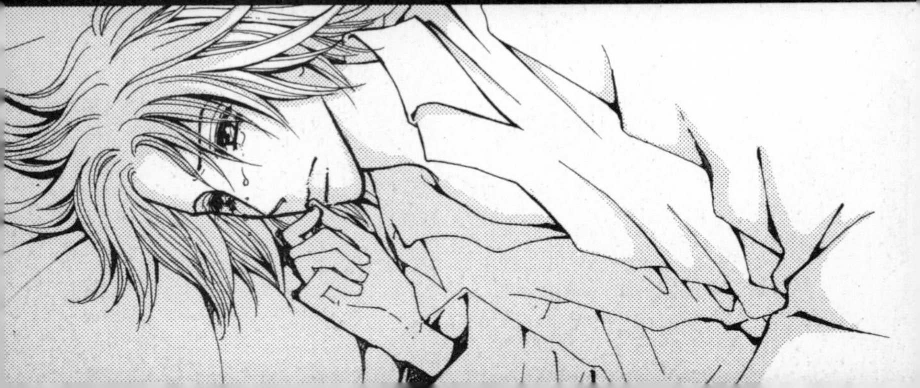

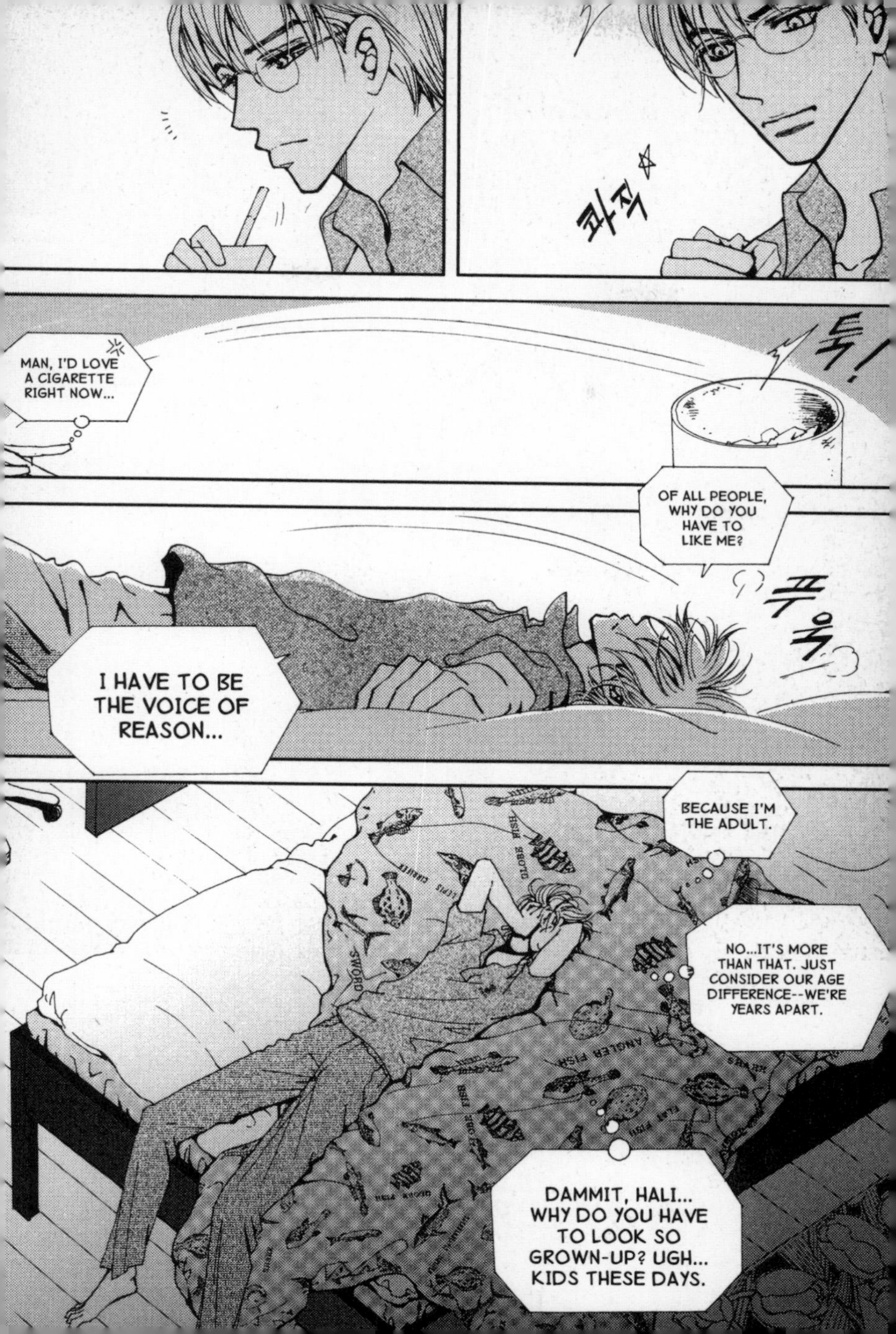
파직
MAN, I'D LOVE A CIGARETTE RIGHT NOW...
뚝!
OF ALL PEOPLE, WHY DO YOU HAVE TO LIKE ME?
푸욱
I HAVE TO BE THE VOICE OF REASON...
BECAUSE I'M THE ADULT.
NO...IT'S MORE THAN THAT. JUST CONSIDER OUR AGE DIFFERENCE--WE'RE YEARS APART.
DAMMIT, HALI... WHY DO YOU HAVE TO LOOK SO GROWN-UP? UGH... KIDS THESE DAYS.
ANGLER FISH
SWORD

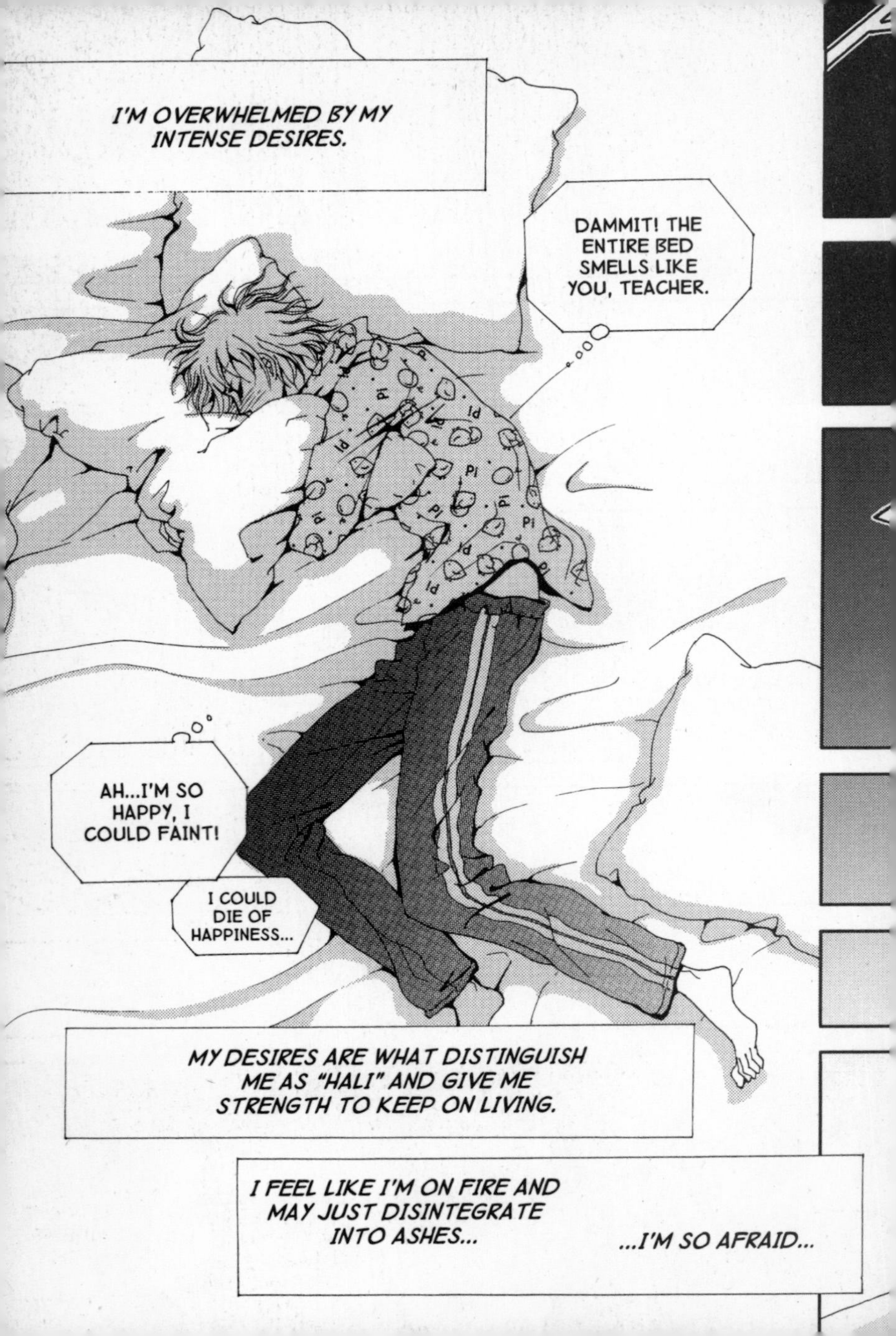
I'M OVERWHELMED BY MY INTENSE DESIRES.
DAMMIT! THE ENTIRE BED SMELLS LIKE YOU, TEACHER.
AH...I'M SO HAPPY, I COULD FAINT!
I COULD DIE OF HAPPINESS...
MY DESIRES ARE WHAT DISTINGUISH ME AS "HALI" AND GIVE ME STRENGTH TO KEEP ON LIVING.
I FEEL LIKE I'M ON FIRE AND MAY JUST DISINTEGRATE INTO ASHES...
...I'M SO AFRAID...

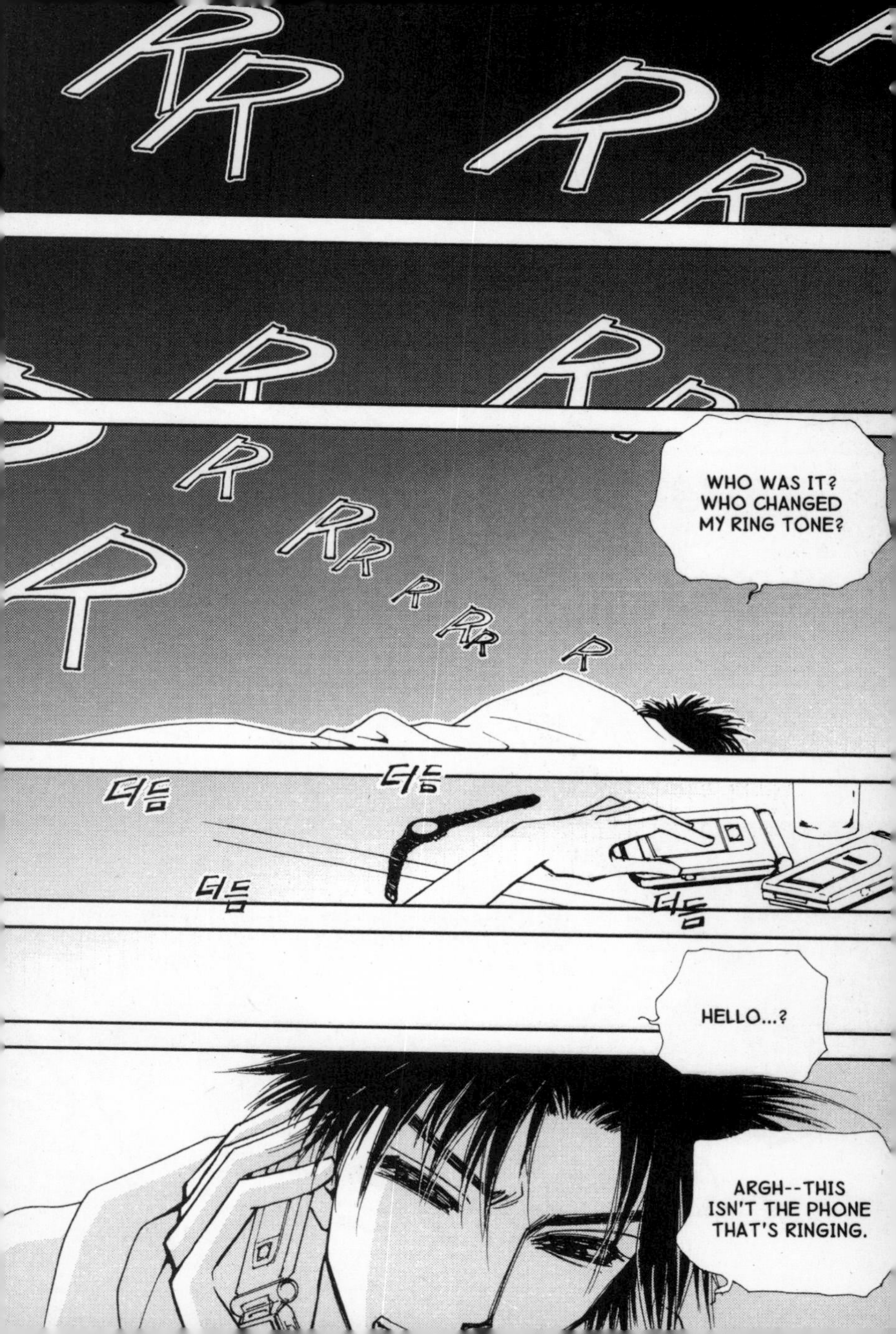
WHO WAS IT? WHO CHANGED MY RING TONE?
더듬
더듬
더듬
더듬
HELLO...?
ARGH--THIS ISN'T THE PHONE THAT'S RINGING.

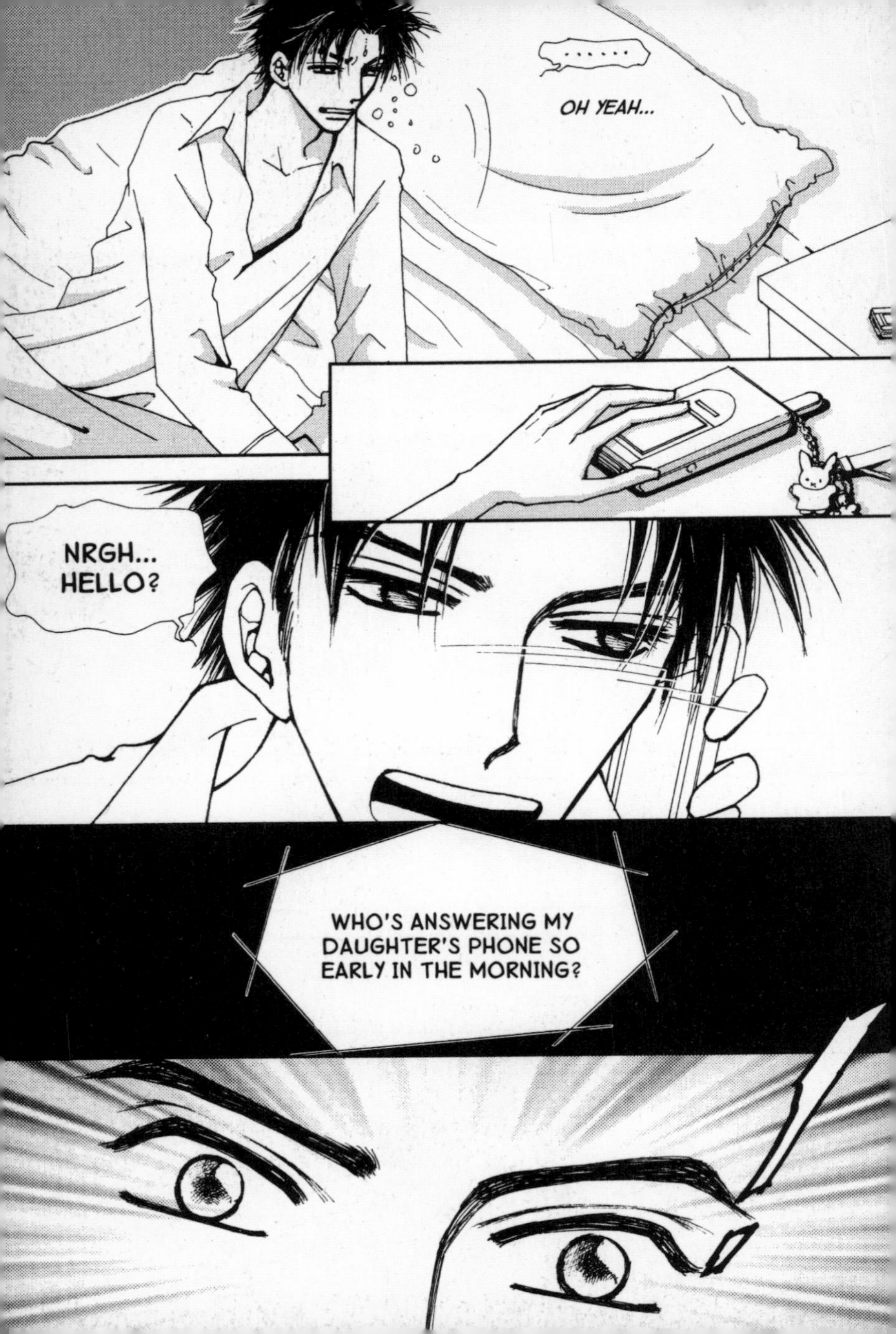
......
OH YEAH...
NRGH... HELLO?
WHO'S ANSWERING MY DAUGHTER'S PHONE SO EARLY IN THE MORNING?

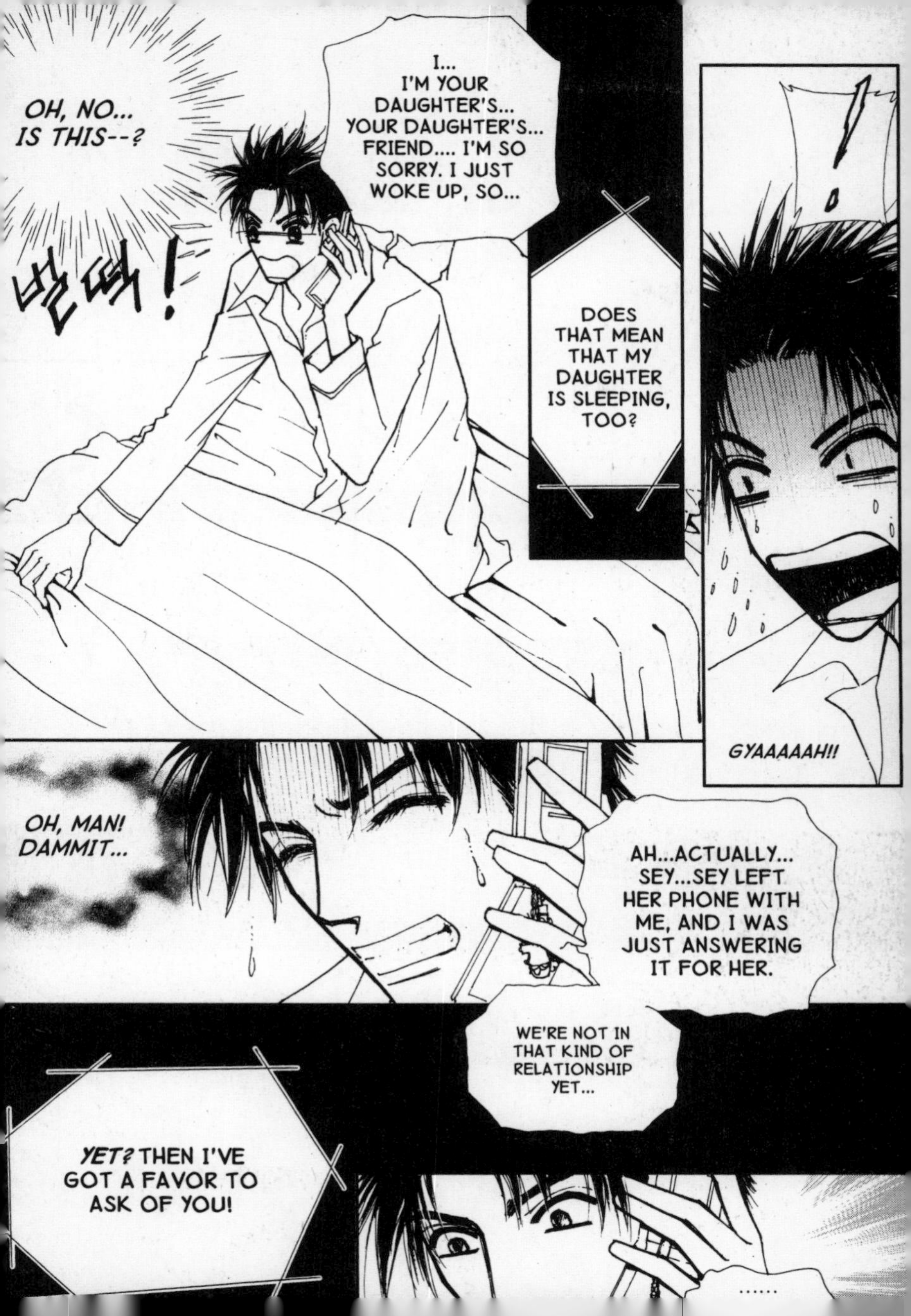
OH, NO... IS THIS--?
벌떡!
I... I'M YOUR DAUGHTER'S... YOUR DAUGHTER'S... FRIEND.... I'M SO SORRY. I JUST WOKE UP, SO...
DOES THAT MEAN THAT MY DAUGHTER IS SLEEPING, TOO?
!
GYAAAAAH!!
OH, MAN! DAMMIT...
AH...ACTUALLY... SEY...SEY LEFT HER PHONE WITH ME, AND I WAS JUST ANSWERING IT FOR HER.
WE'RE NOT IN THAT KIND OF RELATIONSHIP YET...
YET? THEN I'VE GOT A FAVOR TO ASK OF YOU!
......

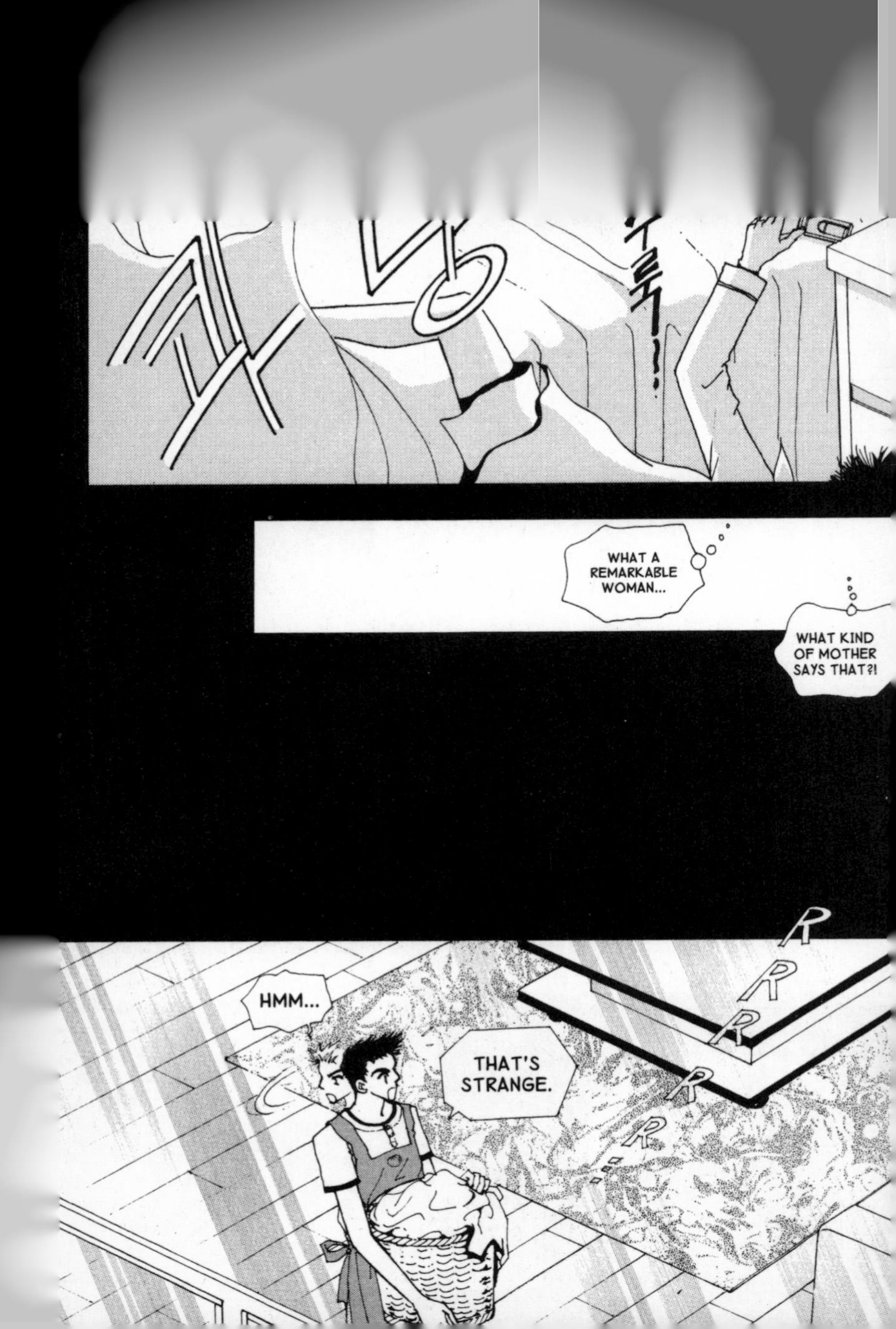
WHAT A REMARKABLE WOMAN...
WHAT KIND OF MOTHER SAYS THAT?!
RRRRR
HMM...
THAT'S STRANGE.

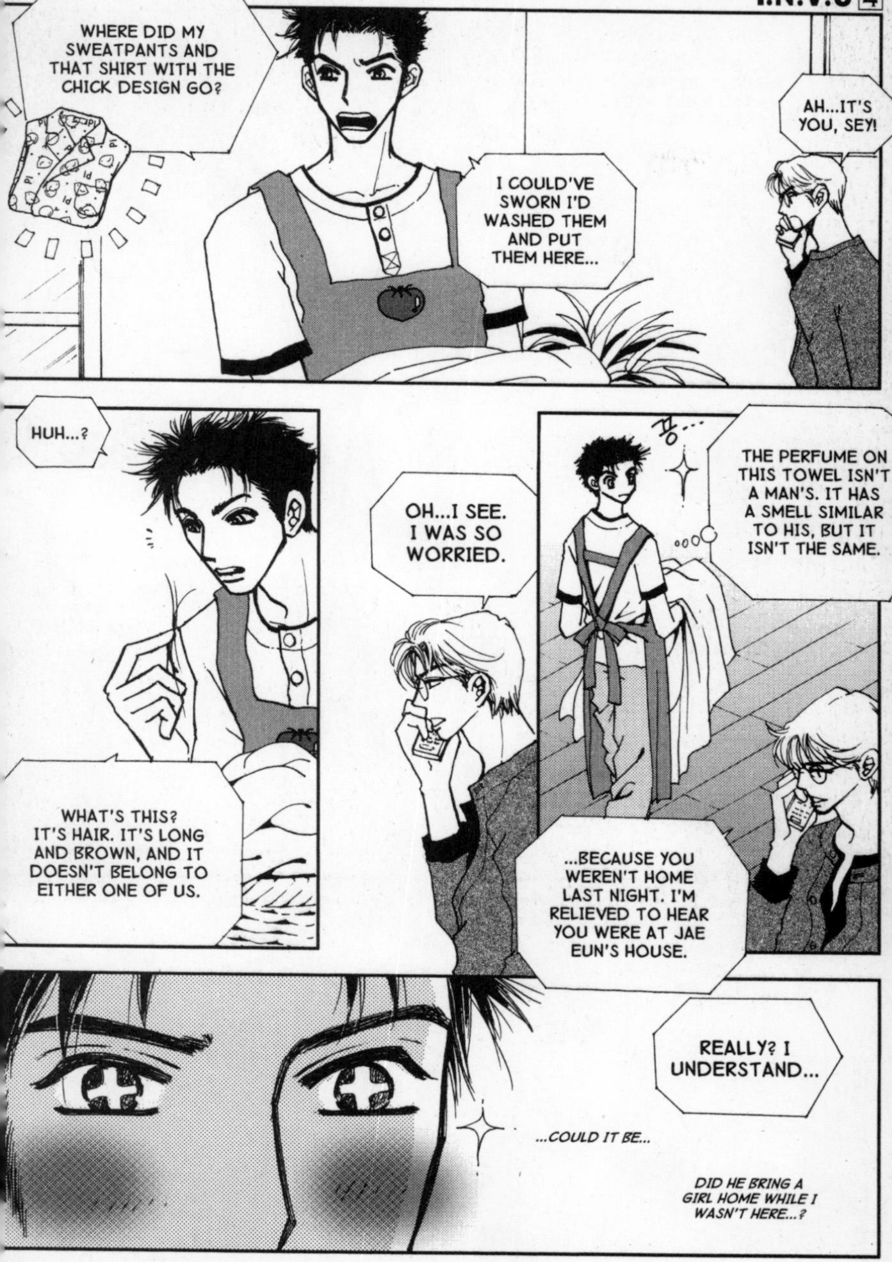
WHERE DID MY SWEATPANTS AND THAT SHIRT WITH THE CHICK DESIGN GO?
I COULD'VE SWORN I'D WASHED THEM AND PUT THEM HERE...
AH...IT'S YOU, SEY!
HUH...?
WHAT'S THIS? IT'S HAIR. IT'S LONG AND BROWN, AND IT DOESN'T BELONG TO EITHER ONE OF US.
OH...I SEE. I WAS SO WORRIED.
...BECAUSE YOU WEREN'T HOME LAST NIGHT. I'M RELIEVED TO HEAR YOU WERE AT JAE EUN'S HOUSE.
THE PERFUME ON THIS TOWEL ISN'T A MAN'S. IT HAS A SMELL SIMILAR TO HIS, BUT IT ISN'T THE SAME.
REALLY? I UNDERSTAND...
...COULD IT BE...
DID HE BRING A GIRL HOME WHILE I WASN'T HERE...?

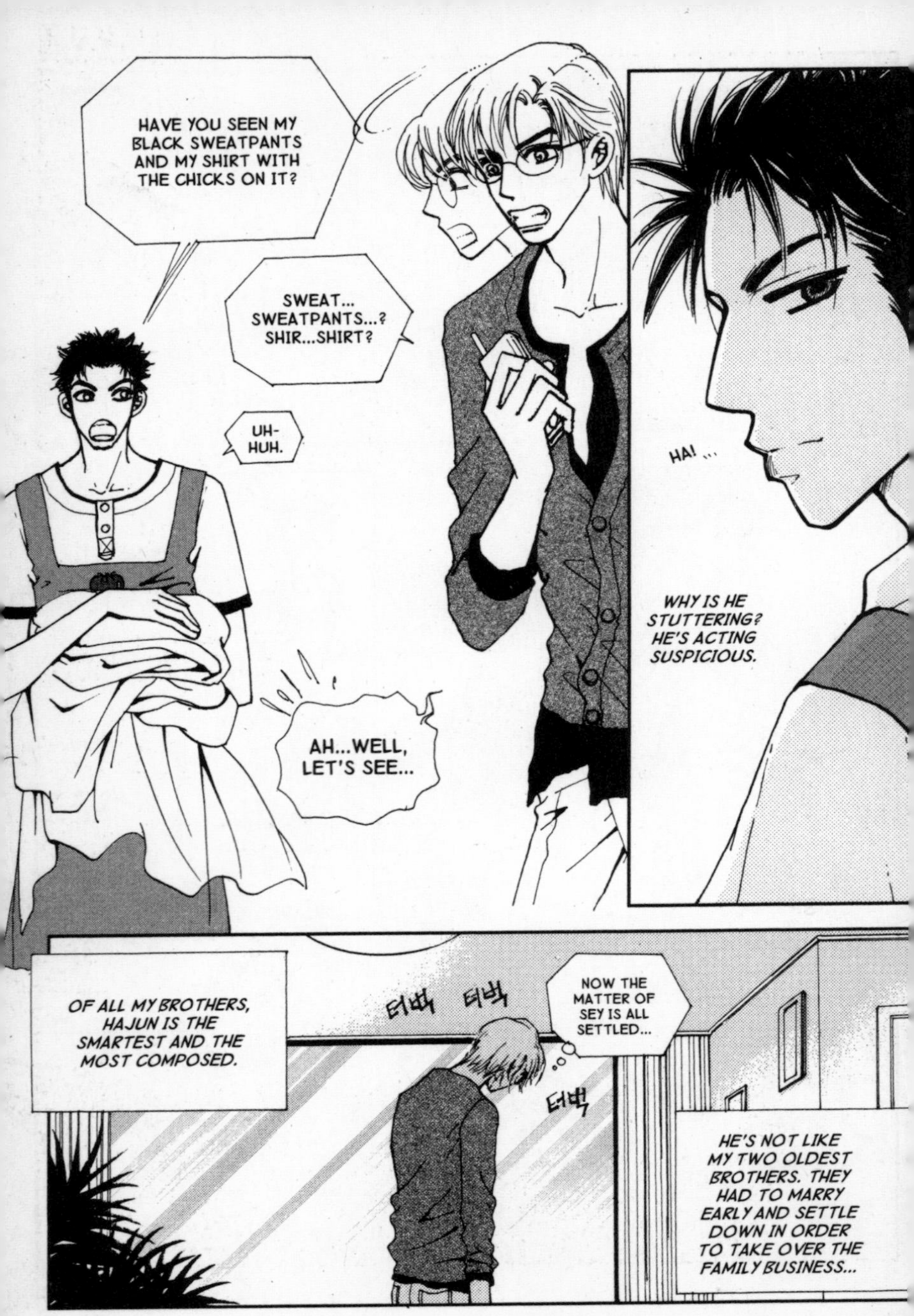
HAVE YOU SEEN MY BLACK SWEATPANTS AND MY SHIRT WITH THE CHICKS ON IT?
SWEAT... SWEATPANTS...? SHIR...SHIRT?
UH-HUH.
AH...WELL, LET'S SEE...
HA! ...
WHY IS HE STUTTERING? HE'S ACTING SUSPICIOUS.
OF ALL MY BROTHERS, HAJUN IS THE SMARTEST AND THE MOST COMPOSED.
터벅 터벅
NOW THE MATTER OF SEY IS ALL SETTLED...
터벅
HE'S NOT LIKE MY TWO OLDEST BROTHERS. THEY HAD TO MARRY EARLY AND SETTLE DOWN IN ORDER TO TAKE OVER THE FAMILY BUSINESS...

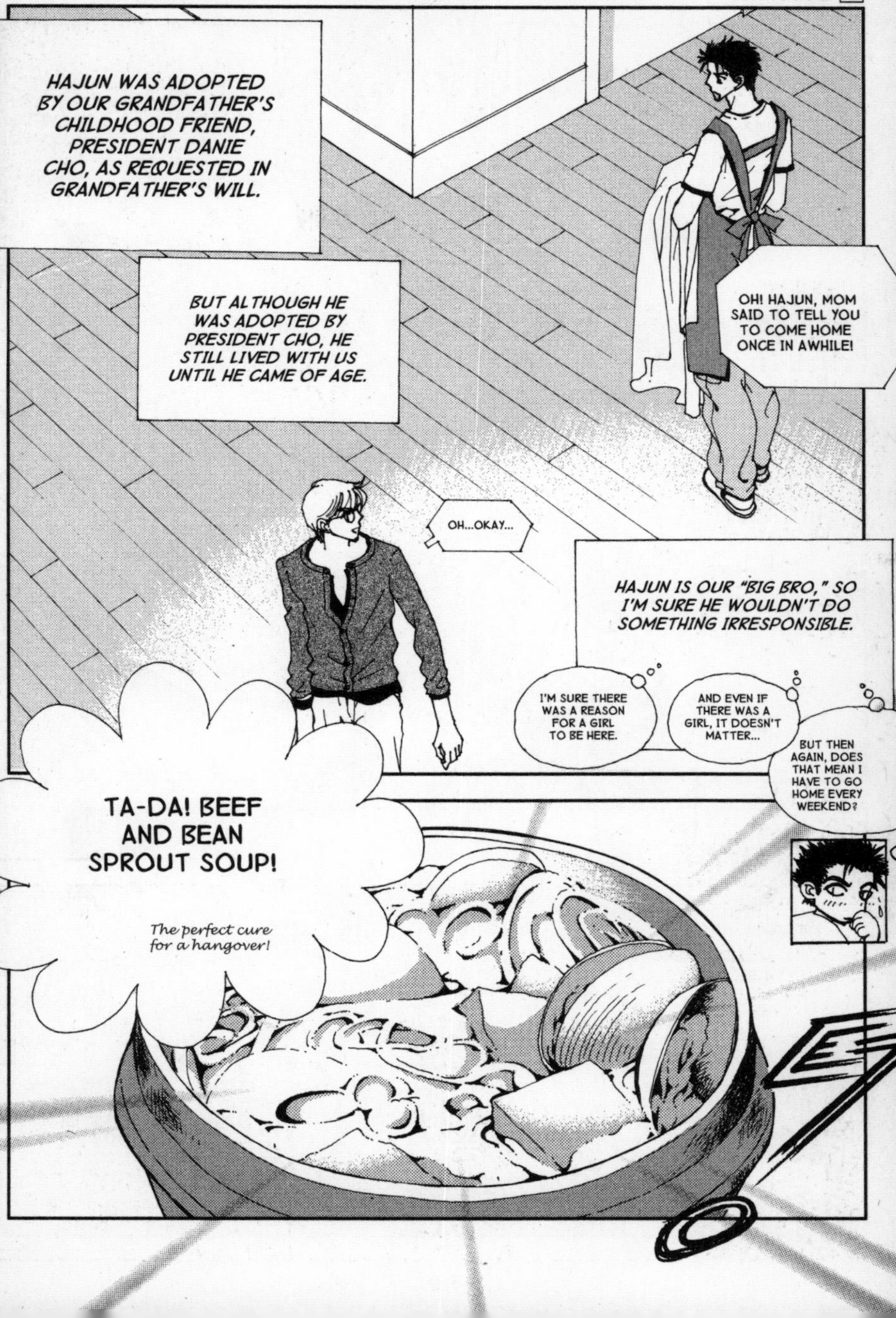
HAJUN WAS ADOPTED BY OUR GRANDFATHER'S CHILDHOOD FRIEND, PRESIDENT DANIE CHO, AS REQUESTED IN GRANDFATHER'S WILL.
BUT ALTHOUGH HE WAS ADOPTED BY PRESIDENT CHO, HE STILL LIVED WITH US UNTIL HE CAME OF AGE.
OH! HAJUN, MOM SAID TO TELL YOU TO COME HOME ONCE IN AWHILE!
OH...OKAY...
HAJUN IS OUR "BIG BRO," SO I'M SURE HE WOULDN'T DO SOMETHING IRRESPONSIBLE.
I'M SURE THERE WAS A REASON FOR A GIRL TO BE HERE.
AND EVEN IF THERE WAS A GIRL, IT DOESN'T MATTER...
BUT THEN AGAIN, DOES THAT MEAN I HAVE TO GO HOME EVERY WEEKEND?
TA-DA! BEEF AND BEAN SPROUT SOUP!
The perfect cure for a hangover!

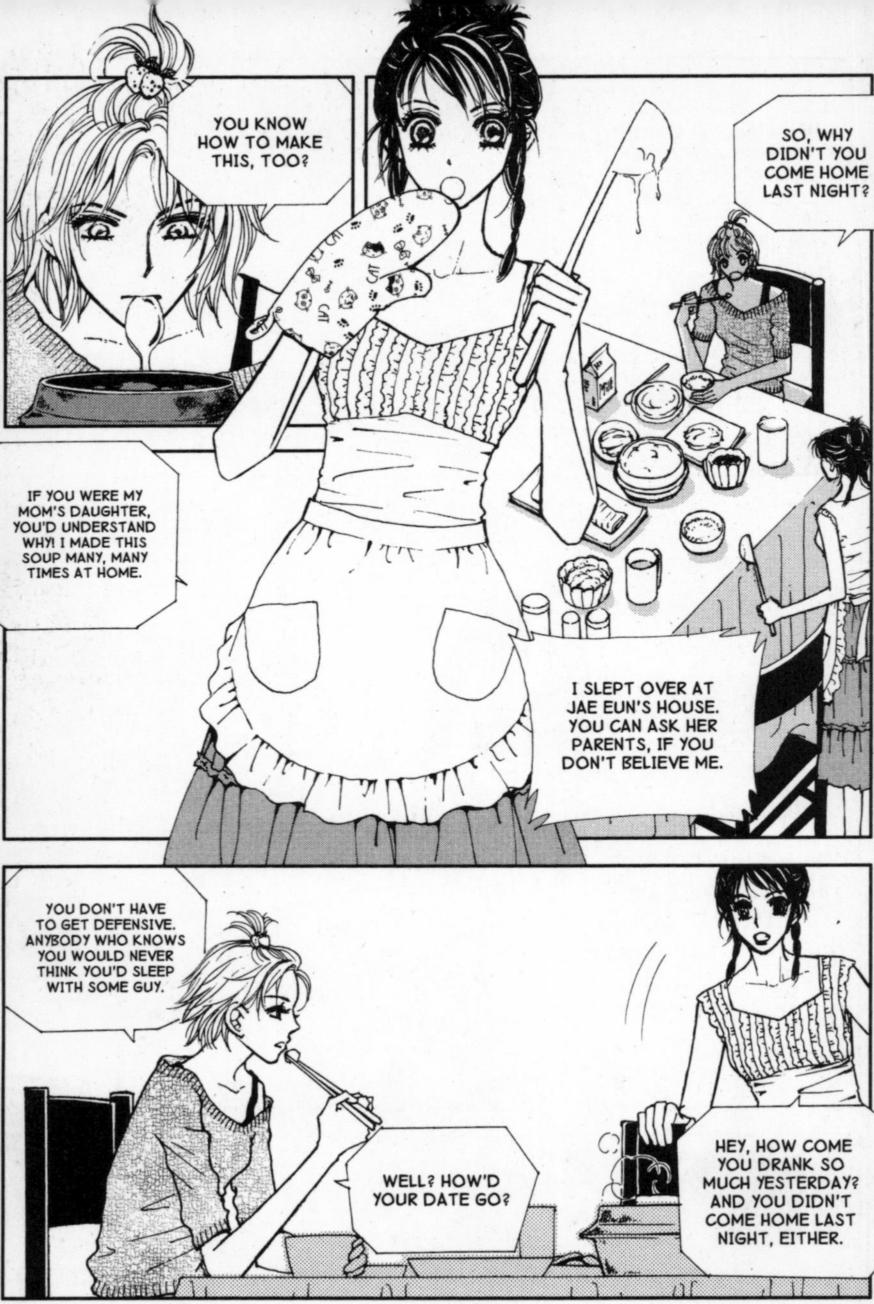
YOU KNOW HOW TO MAKE THIS, TOO?
IF YOU WERE MY MOM'S DAUGHTER, YOU'D UNDERSTAND WHY! I MADE THIS SOUP MANY, MANY TIMES AT HOME.
SO, WHY DIDN'T YOU COME HOME LAST NIGHT?
I SLEPT OVER AT JAE EUN'S HOUSE. YOU CAN ASK HER PARENTS, IF YOU DON'T BELIEVE ME.
YOU DON'T HAVE TO GET DEFENSIVE. ANYBODY WHO KNOWS YOU WOULD NEVER THINK YOU'D SLEEP WITH SOME GUY.
WELL? HOW'D YOUR DATE GO?
HEY, HOW COME YOU DRANK SO MUCH YESTERDAY? AND YOU DIDN'T COME HOME LAST NIGHT, EITHER.

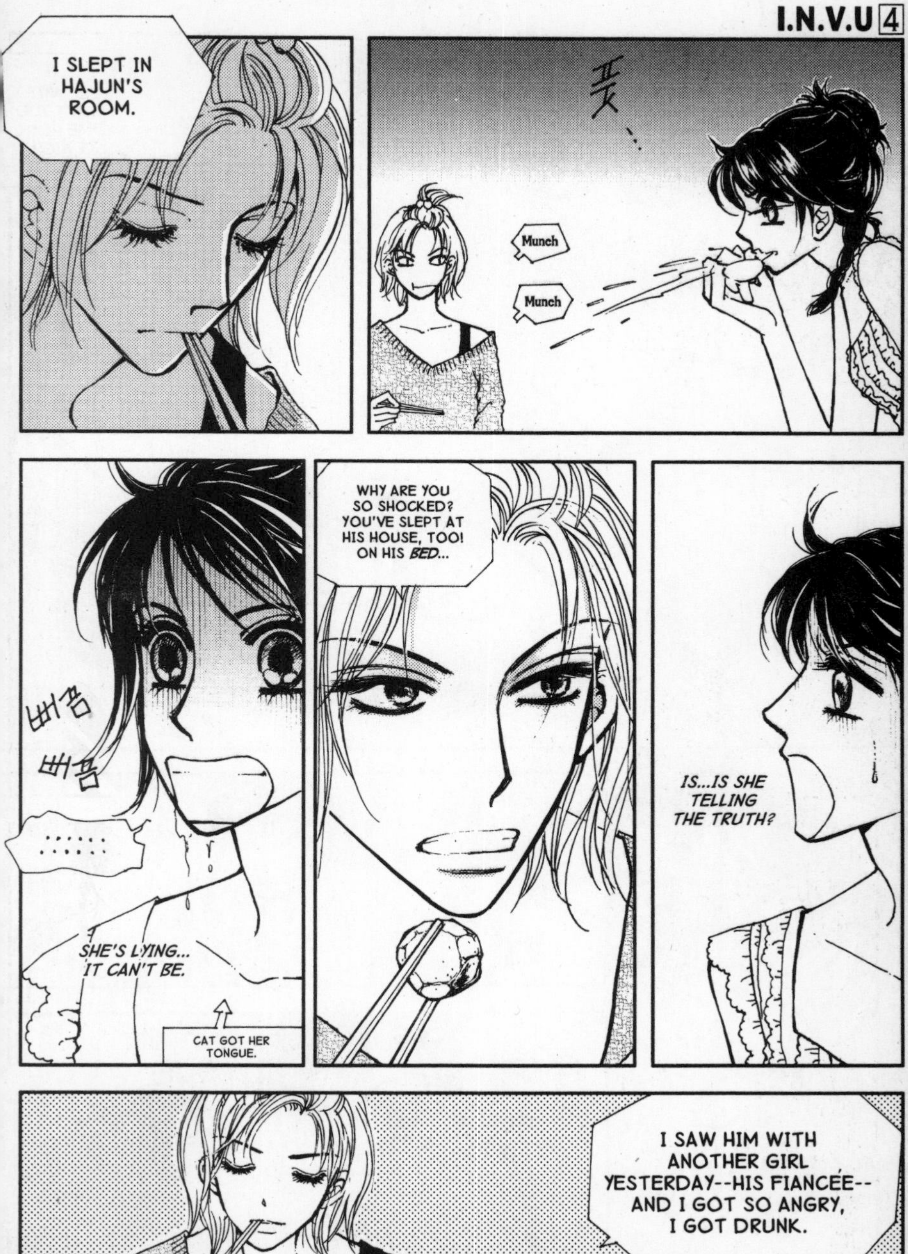
I SLEPT IN HAJUN'S ROOM.
Munch
Munch
WHY ARE YOU SO SHOCKED? YOU'VE SLEPT AT HIS HOUSE, TOO! ON HIS *BED*...
......
SHE'S LYING... IT CAN'T BE.
CAT GOT HER TONGUE.
IS...IS SHE TELLING THE TRUTH?
I SAW HIM WITH ANOTHER GIRL YESTERDAY--HIS FIANCÉE--AND I GOT SO ANGRY, I GOT DRUNK.

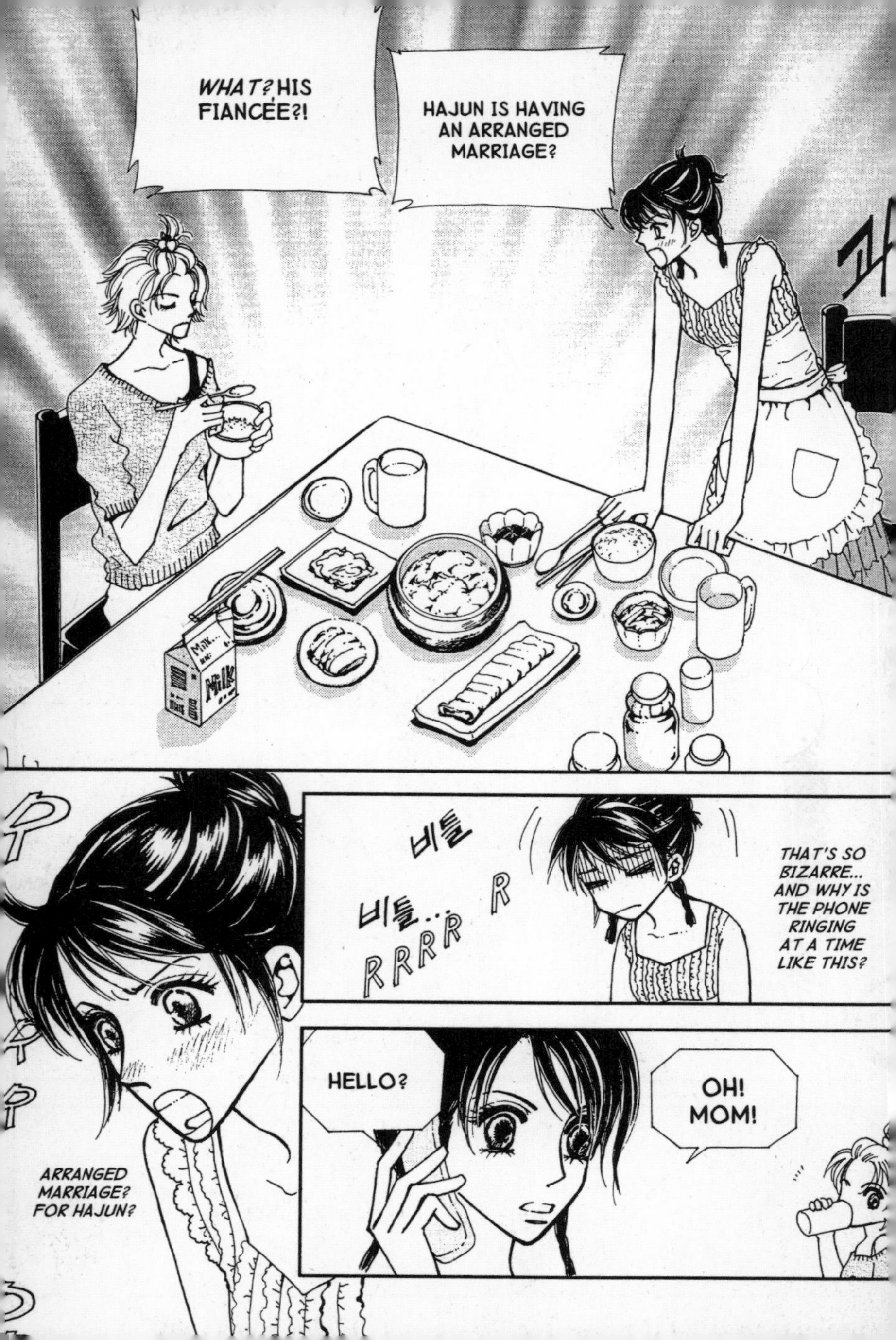
WHAT? HIS FIANCÉE?!
HAJUN IS HAVING AN ARRANGED MARRIAGE?
ARRANGED MARRIAGE? FOR HAJUN?
비틀
비틀...
RRRRR
THAT'S SO BIZARRE... AND WHY IS THE PHONE RINGING AT A TIME LIKE THIS?
HELLO?
OH! MOM!

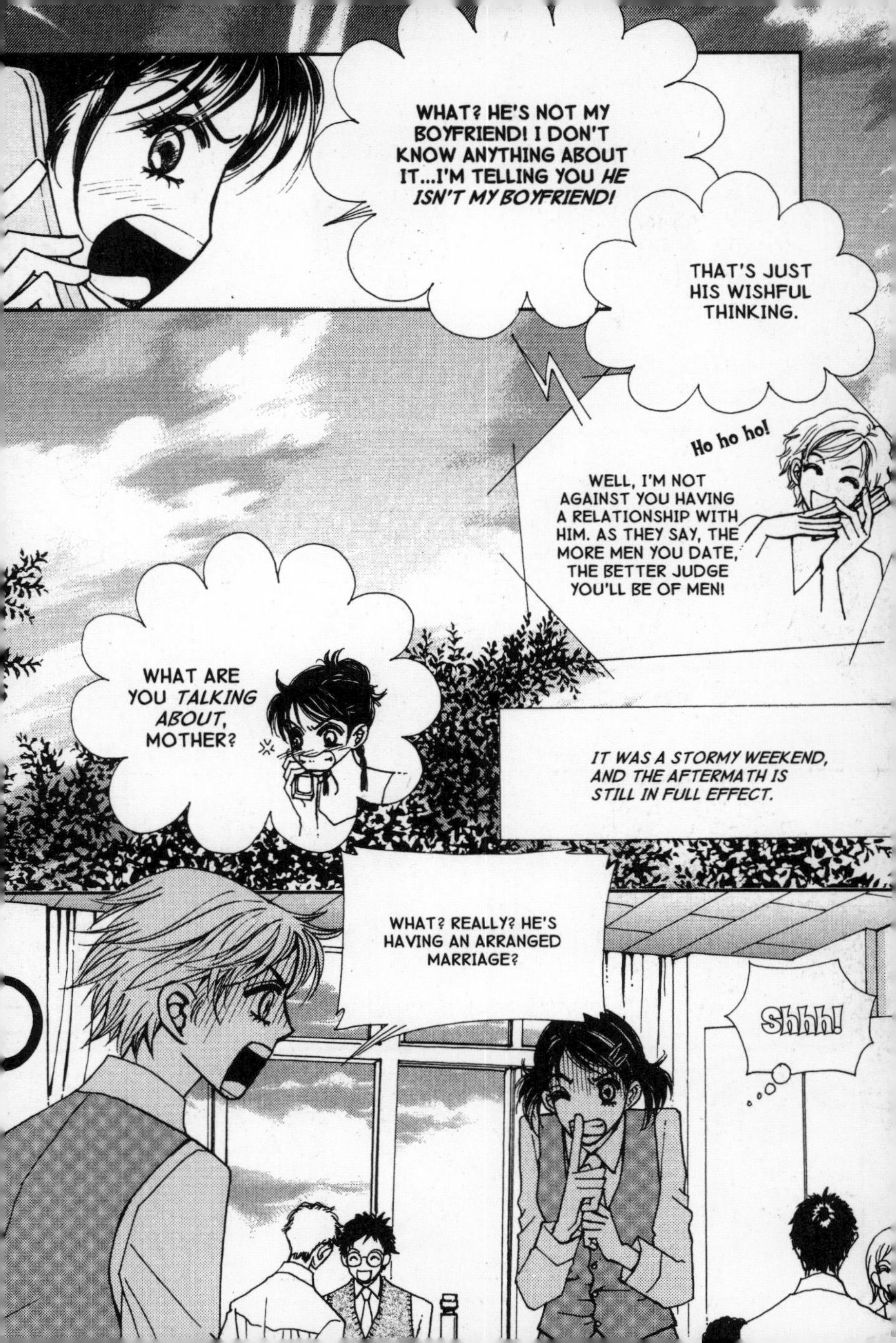
WHAT? HE'S NOT MY BOYFRIEND! I DON'T KNOW ANYTHING ABOUT IT...I'M TELLING YOU *HE ISN'T MY BOYFRIEND!*
THAT'S JUST HIS WISHFUL THINKING.
Ho ho ho!
WELL, I'M NOT AGAINST YOU HAVING A RELATIONSHIP WITH HIM. AS THEY SAY, THE MORE MEN YOU DATE, THE BETTER JUDGE YOU'LL BE OF MEN!
WHAT ARE YOU *TALKING ABOUT*, MOTHER?
IT WAS A STORMY WEEKEND, AND THE AFTERMATH IS STILL IN FULL EFFECT.
WHAT? REALLY? HE'S HAVING AN ARRANGED MARRIAGE?
Shhh!

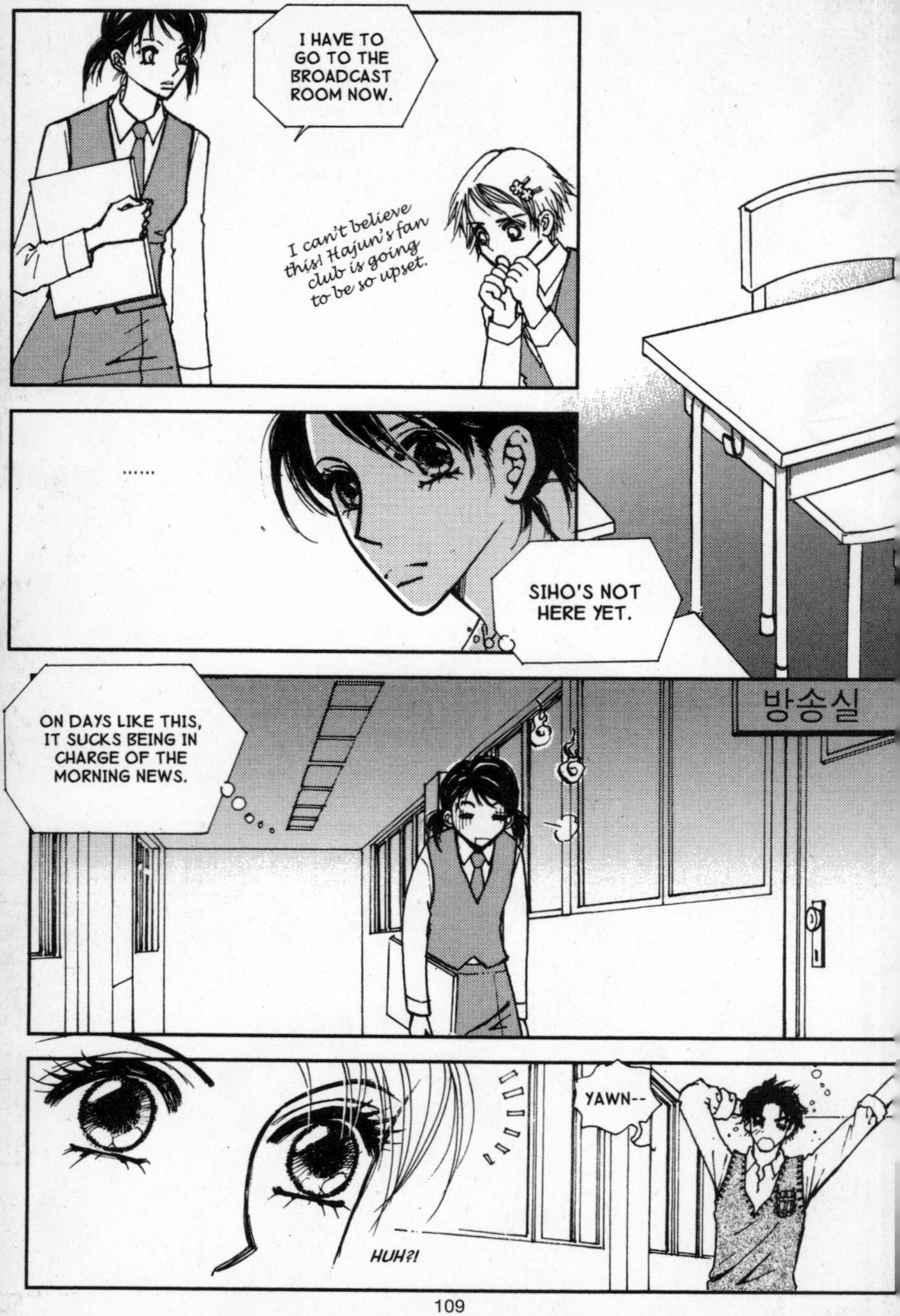
I HAVE TO GO TO THE BROADCAST ROOM NOW.
I can't believe this! Hajun's fan club is going to be so upset.
......
SIHO'S NOT HERE YET.
ON DAYS LIKE THIS, IT SUCKS BEING IN CHARGE OF THE MORNING NEWS.
방송실
YAWN--
HUH?!

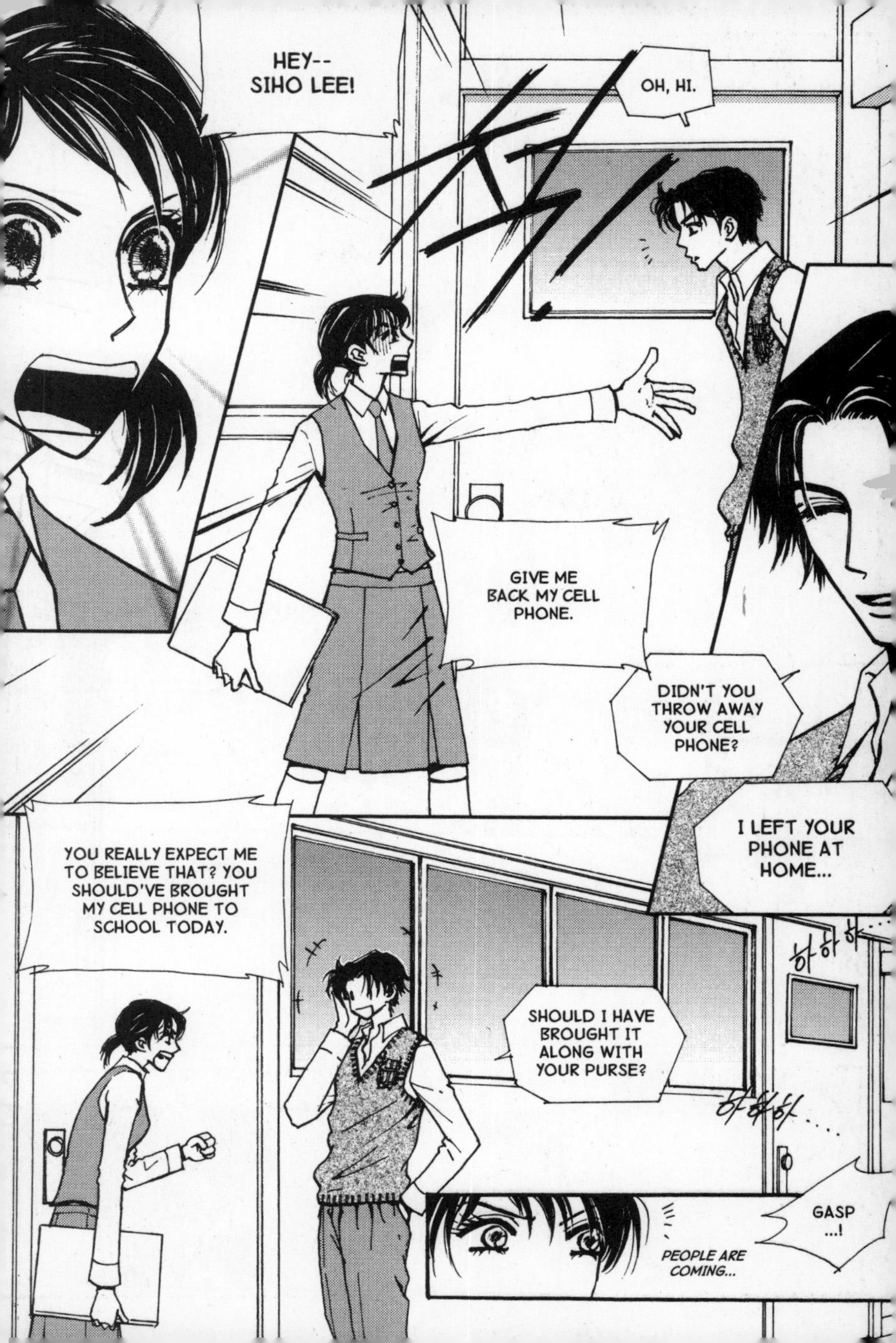
HEY--
SIHO LEE!
OH, HI.
GIVE ME BACK MY CELL PHONE.
DIDN'T YOU THROW AWAY YOUR CELL PHONE?
I LEFT YOUR PHONE AT HOME...
YOU REALLY EXPECT ME TO BELIEVE THAT? YOU SHOULD'VE BROUGHT MY CELL PHONE TO SCHOOL TODAY.
하하하...
SHOULD I HAVE BROUGHT IT ALONG WITH YOUR PURSE?
하하하...
GASP ...!
PEOPLE ARE COMING...

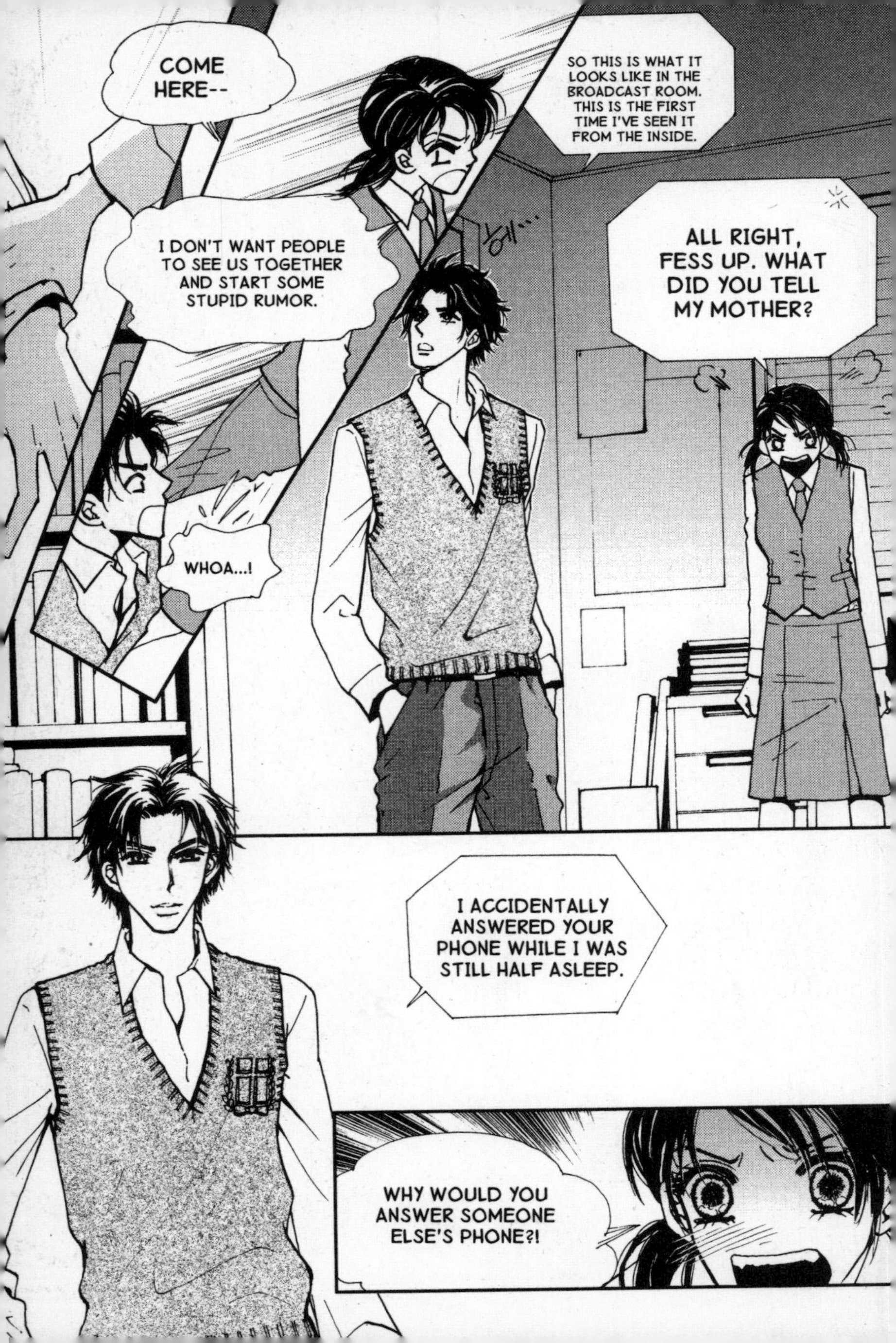
COME HERE--
I DON'T WANT PEOPLE TO SEE US TOGETHER AND START SOME STUPID RUMOR.
WHOA...!
SO THIS IS WHAT IT LOOKS LIKE IN THE BROADCAST ROOM. THIS IS THE FIRST TIME I'VE SEEN IT FROM THE INSIDE.
ALL RIGHT, FESS UP. WHAT DID YOU TELL MY MOTHER?
I ACCIDENTALLY ANSWERED YOUR PHONE WHILE I WAS STILL HALF ASLEEP.
WHY WOULD YOU ANSWER SOMEONE ELSE'S PHONE?!

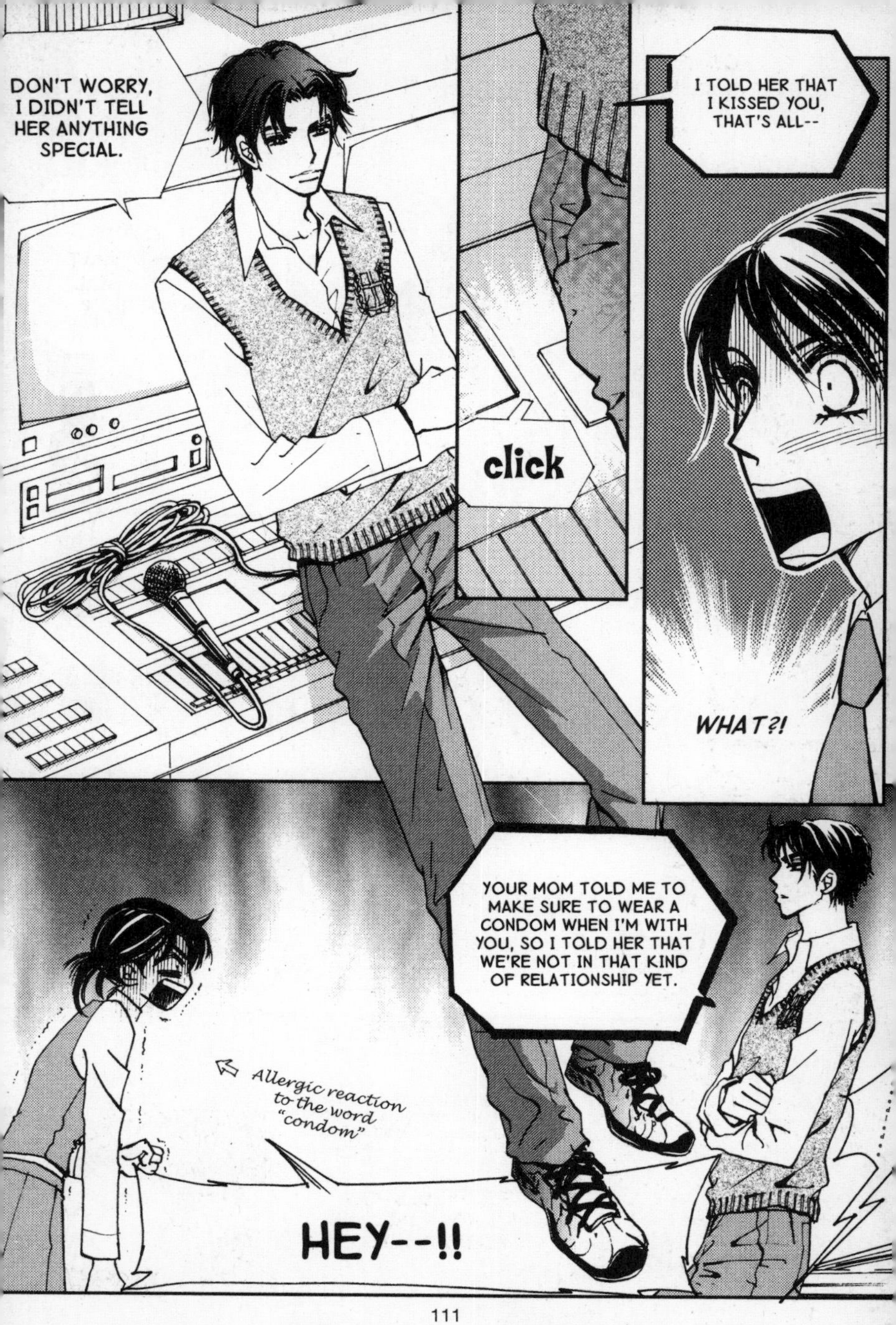
DON'T WORRY, I DIDN'T TELL HER ANYTHING SPECIAL.
click
I TOLD HER THAT I KISSED YOU, THAT'S ALL--
WHAT?!
YOUR MOM TOLD ME TO MAKE SURE TO WEAR A CONDOM WHEN I'M WITH YOU, SO I TOLD HER THAT WE'RE NOT IN THAT KIND OF RELATIONSHIP YET.
Allergic reaction to the word "condom"
HEY--!!

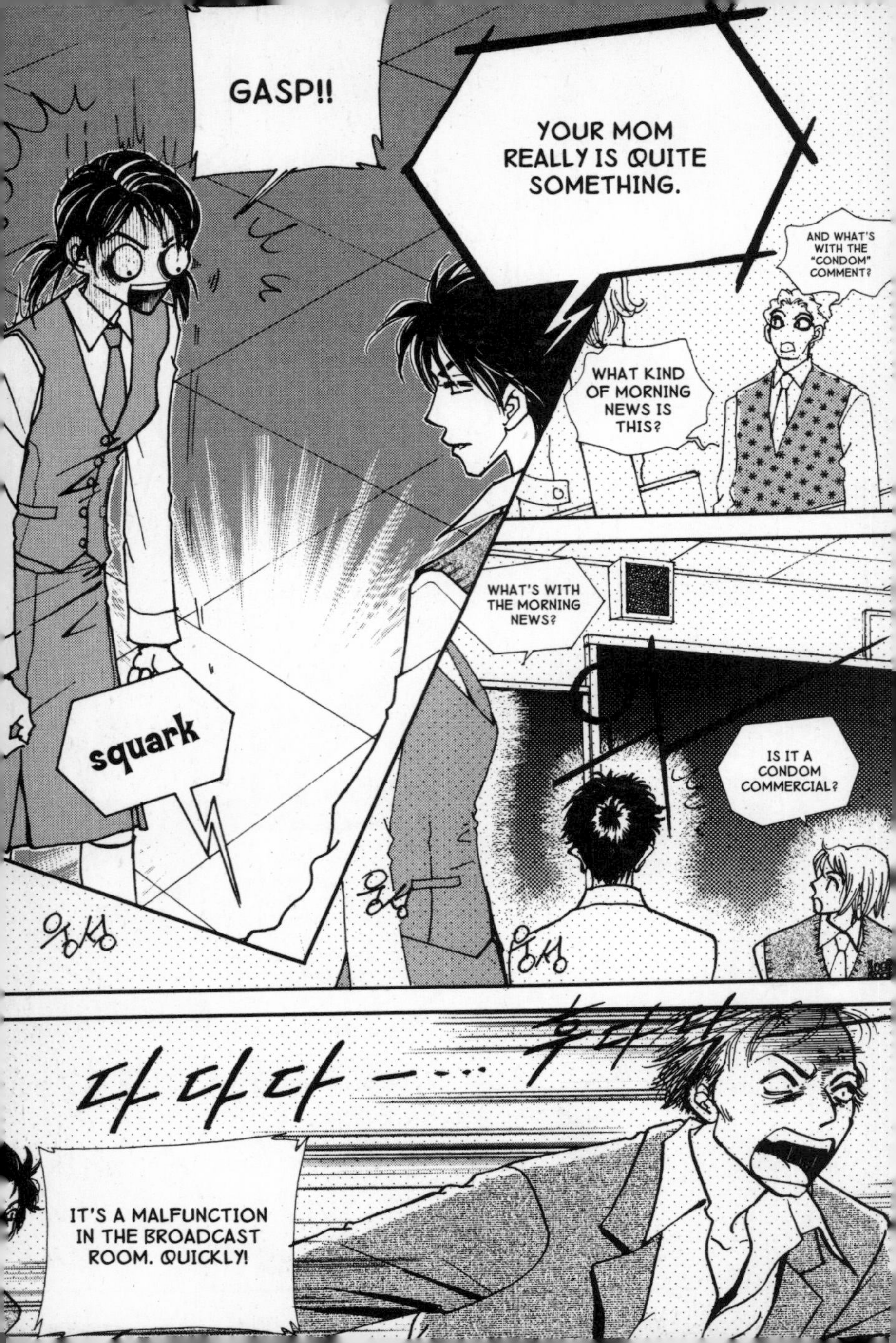
GASP!!
squark
웅성
YOUR MOM REALLY IS QUITE SOMETHING.
웅성
WHAT KIND OF MORNING NEWS IS THIS?
AND WHAT'S WITH THE "CONDOM" COMMENT?
WHAT'S WITH THE MORNING NEWS?
IS IT A CONDOM COMMERCIAL?
웅성
다다다—
후다닥
IT'S A MALFUNCTION IN THE BROADCAST ROOM. QUICKLY!

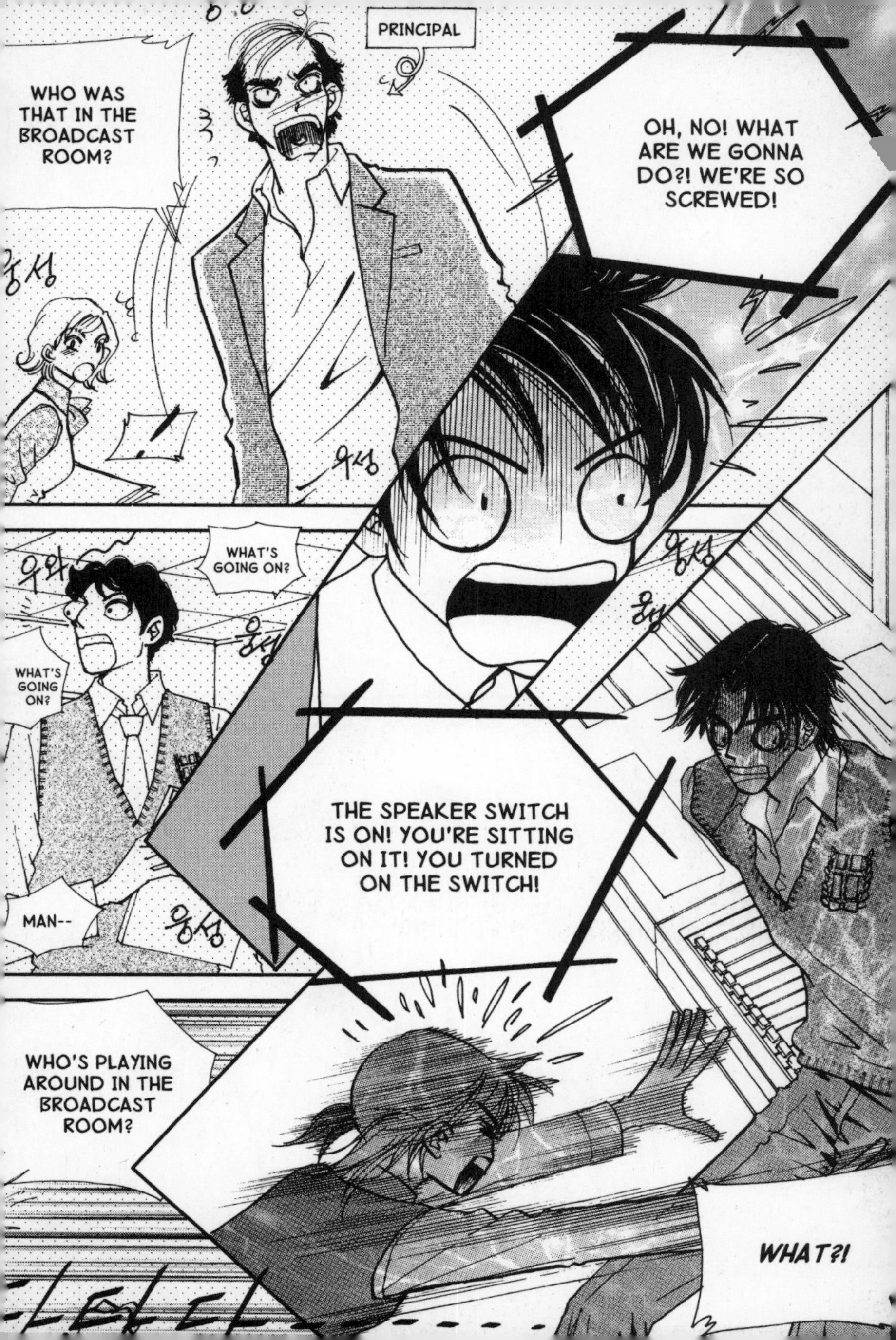
PRINCIPAL
WHO WAS THAT IN THE BROADCAST ROOM?
OH, NO! WHAT ARE WE GONNA DO?! WE'RE SO SCREWED!
WHAT'S GOING ON?
WHAT'S GOING ON?
MAN--
THE SPEAKER SWITCH IS ON! YOU'RE SITTING ON IT! YOU TURNED ON THE SWITCH!
WHO'S PLAYING AROUND IN THE BROADCAST ROOM?
WHAT?!

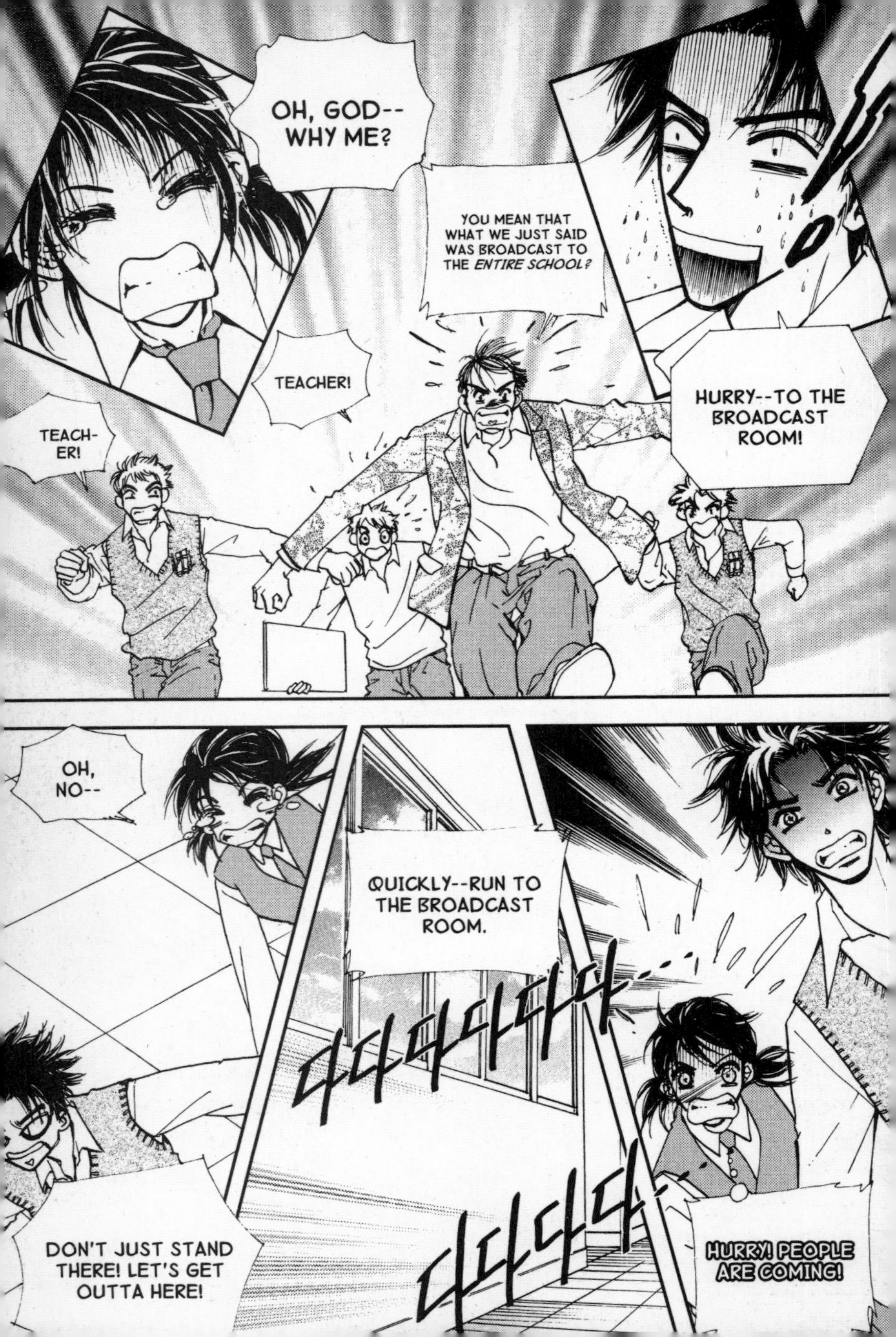
OH, GOD--
WHY ME?
YOU MEAN THAT WHAT WE JUST SAID WAS BROADCAST TO THE *ENTIRE SCHOOL?*
TEACH-
ER!
TEACHER!
HURRY--TO THE BROADCAST ROOM!
OH,
NO--
DON'T JUST STAND THERE! LET'S GET OUTTA HERE!
QUICKLY--RUN TO THE BROADCAST ROOM.
HURRY! PEOPLE ARE COMING!

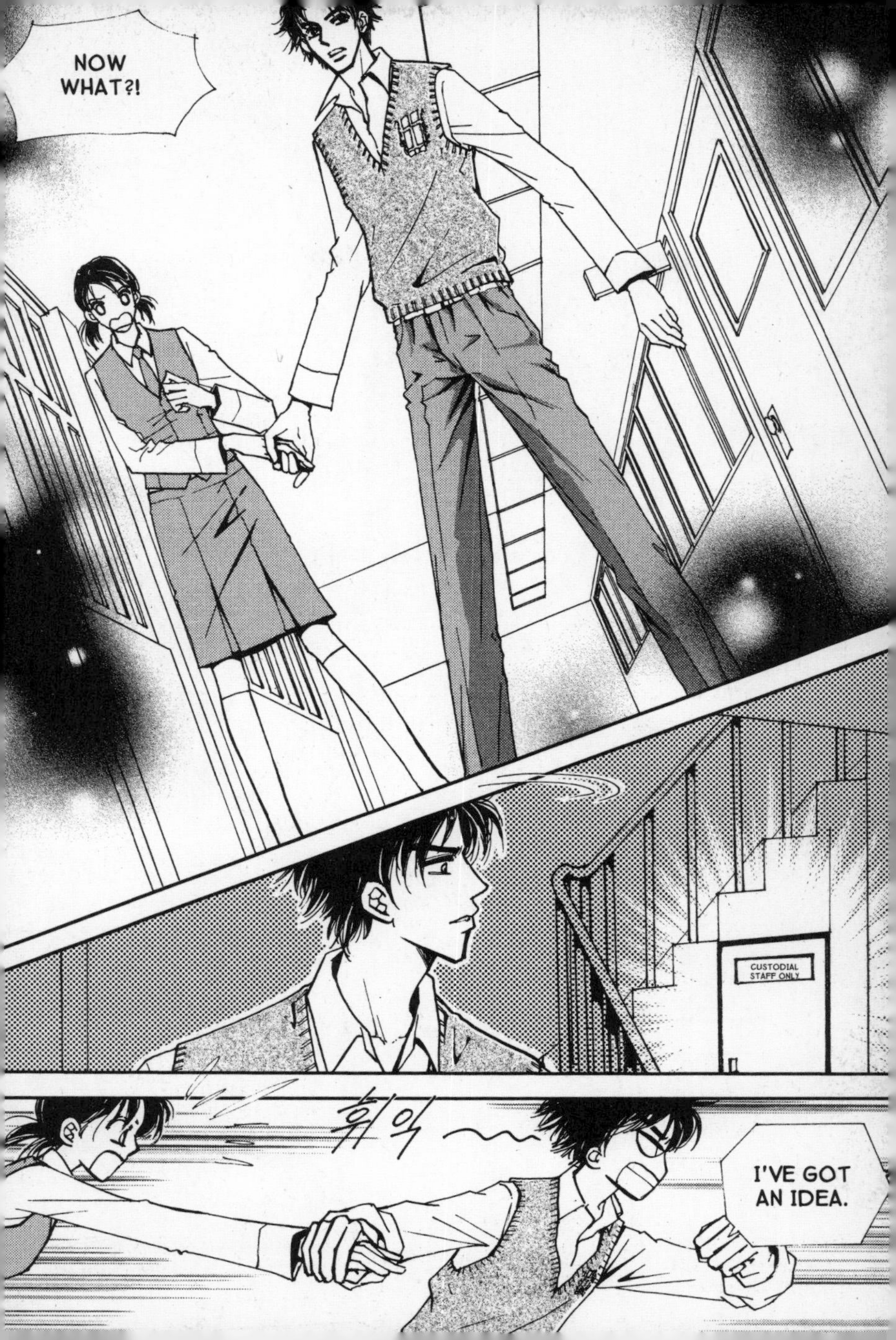
NOW WHAT?!
CUSTODIAL STAFF ONLY
휘익
I'VE GOT AN IDEA.

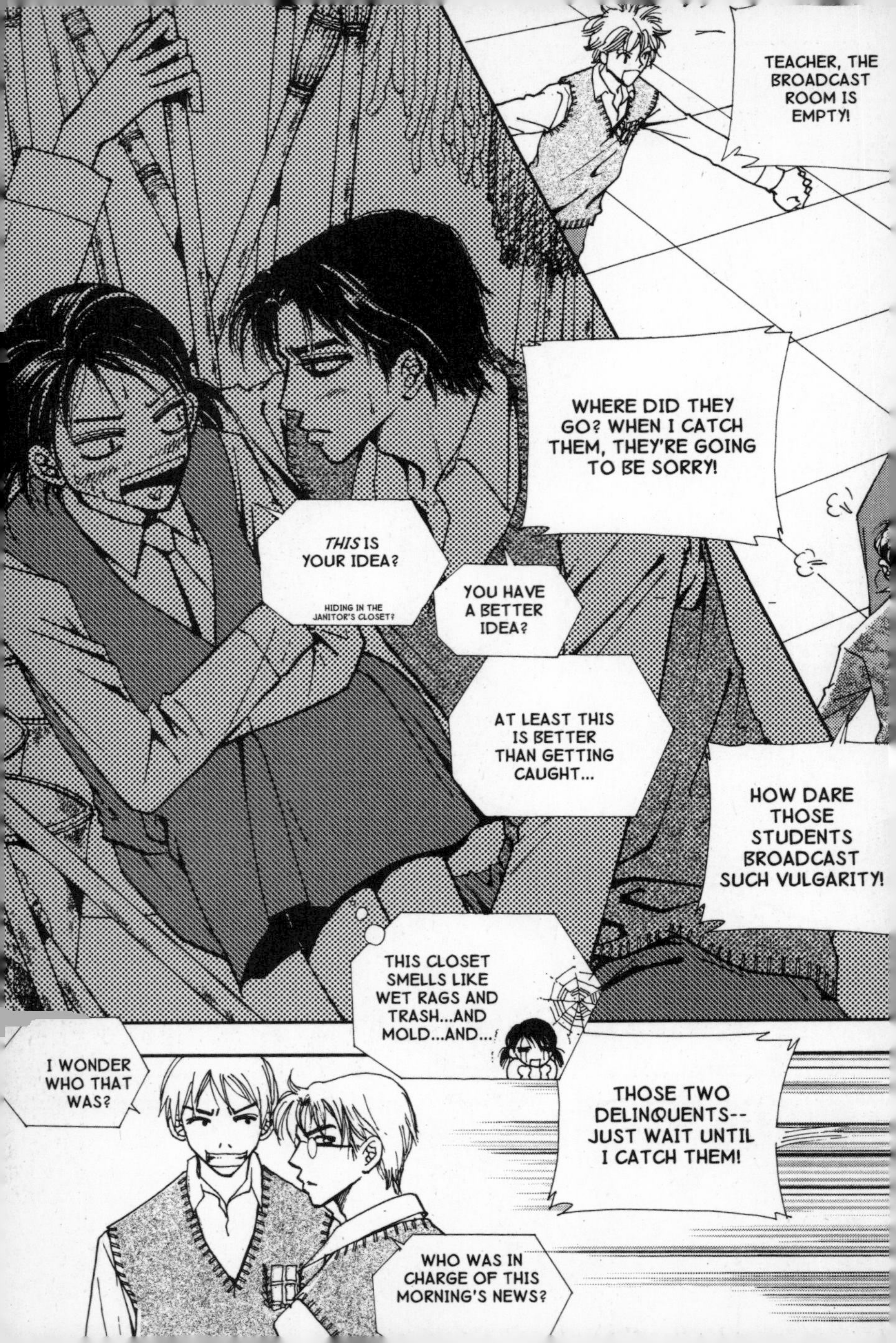
TEACHER, THE BROADCAST ROOM IS EMPTY!
WHERE DID THEY GO? WHEN I CATCH THEM, THEY'RE GOING TO BE SORRY!
HOW DARE THOSE STUDENTS BROADCAST SUCH VULGARITY!
THIS IS YOUR IDEA?
HIDING IN THE JANITOR'S CLOSET?
YOU HAVE A BETTER IDEA?
AT LEAST THIS IS BETTER THAN GETTING CAUGHT...
THIS CLOSET SMELLS LIKE WET RAGS AND TRASH...AND MOLD...AND...
THOSE TWO DELINQUENTS--JUST WAIT UNTIL I CATCH THEM!
I WONDER WHO THAT WAS?
WHO WAS IN CHARGE OF THIS MORNING'S NEWS?

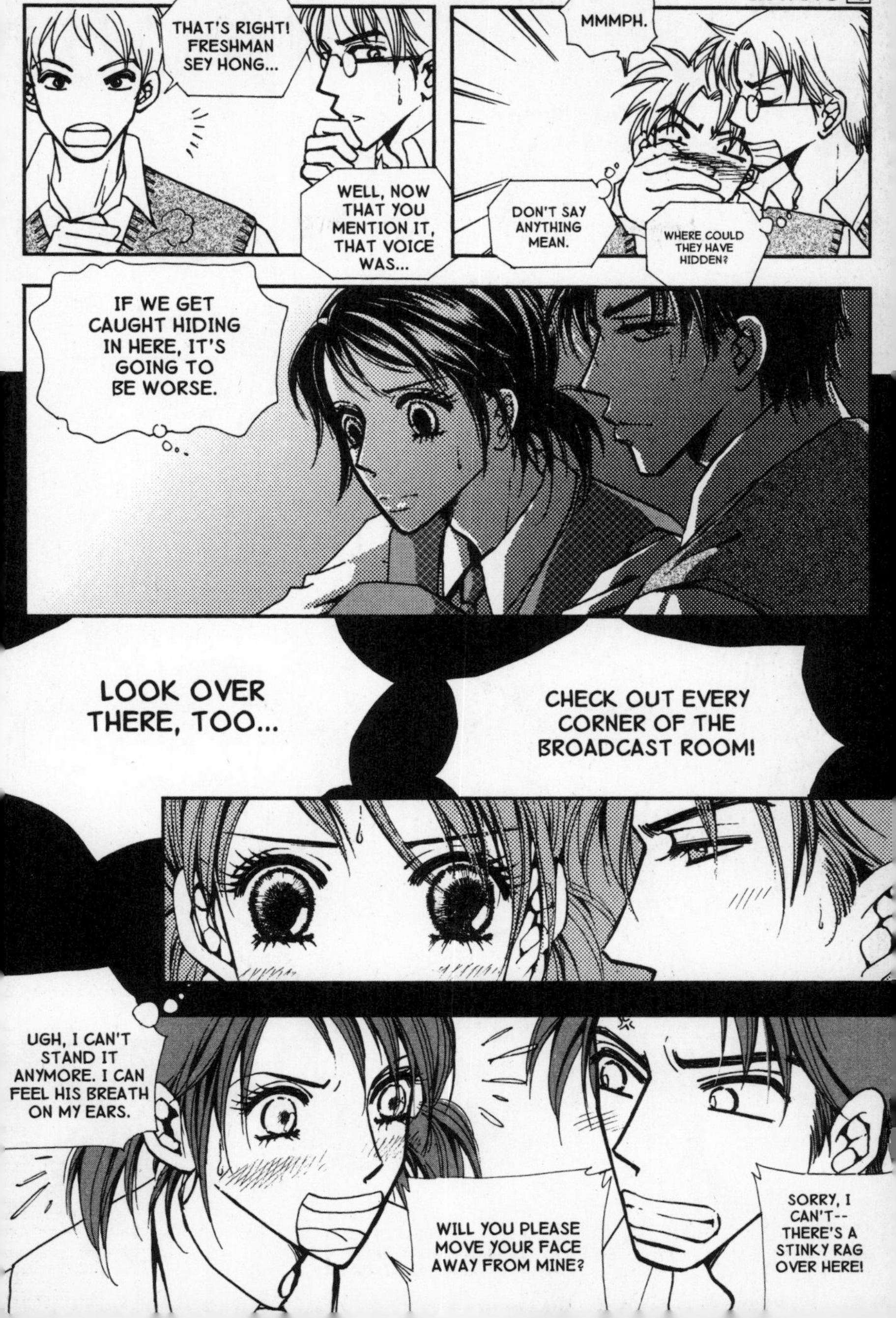
THAT'S RIGHT! FRESHMAN SEY HONG...
WELL, NOW THAT YOU MENTION IT, THAT VOICE WAS...
MMMPH.
DON'T SAY ANYTHING MEAN.
WHERE COULD THEY HAVE HIDDEN?
IF WE GET CAUGHT HIDING IN HERE, IT'S GOING TO BE WORSE.
LOOK OVER THERE, TOO...
CHECK OUT EVERY CORNER OF THE BROADCAST ROOM!
UGH, I CAN'T STAND IT ANYMORE. I CAN FEEL HIS BREATH ON MY EARS.
WILL YOU PLEASE MOVE YOUR FACE AWAY FROM MINE?
SORRY, I CAN'T-- THERE'S A STINKY RAG OVER HERE!

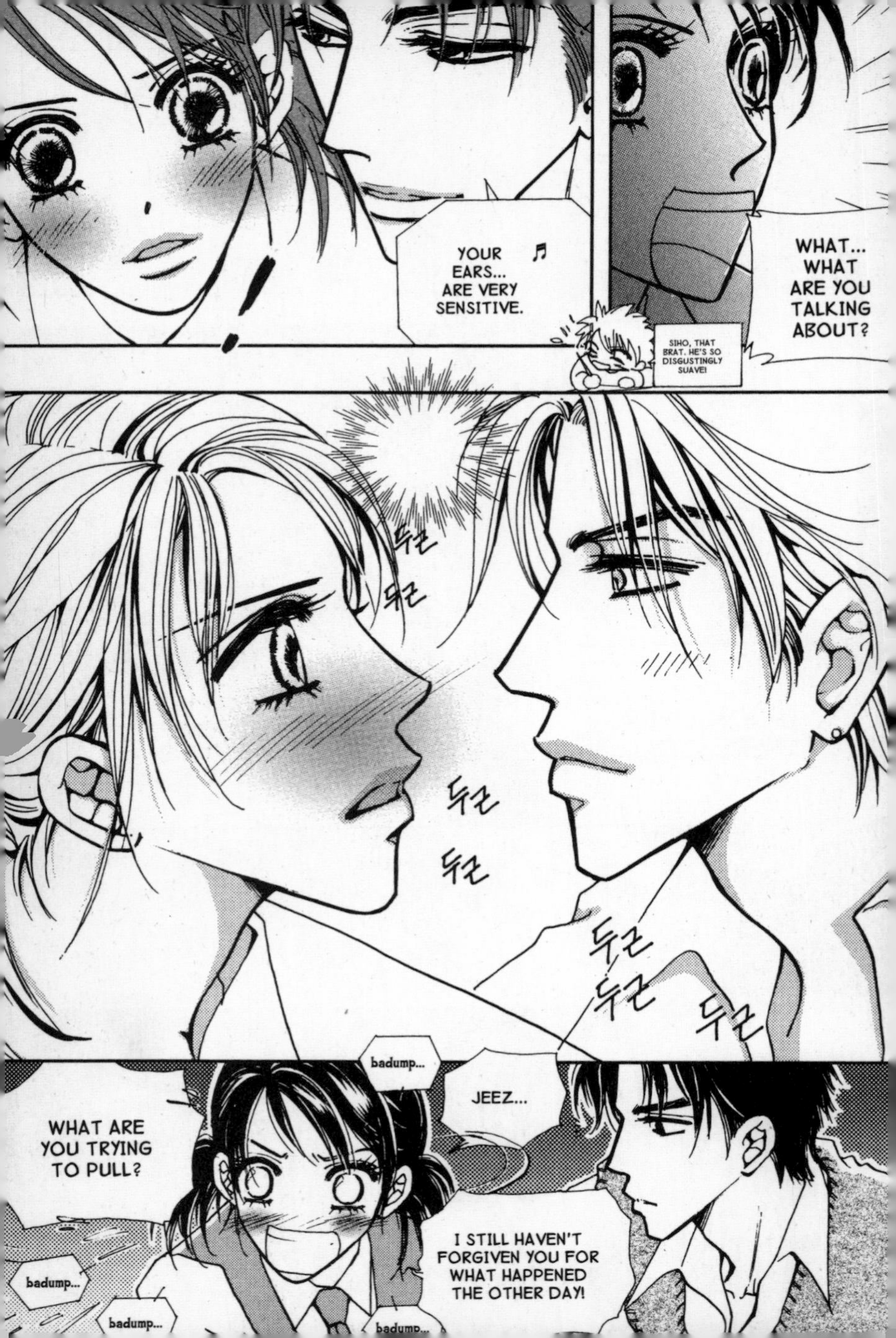
YOUR EARS... ARE VERY SENSITIVE. ♬
WHAT... WHAT ARE YOU TALKING ABOUT?
SIHO, THAT BRAT. HE'S SO DISGUSTINGLY SUAVE!
두근
두근
두근
두근
두근
두근
두근
badump...
JEEZ...
WHAT ARE YOU TRYING TO PULL?
I STILL HAVEN'T FORGIVEN YOU FOR WHAT HAPPENED THE OTHER DAY!
badump...
badump...
badump...

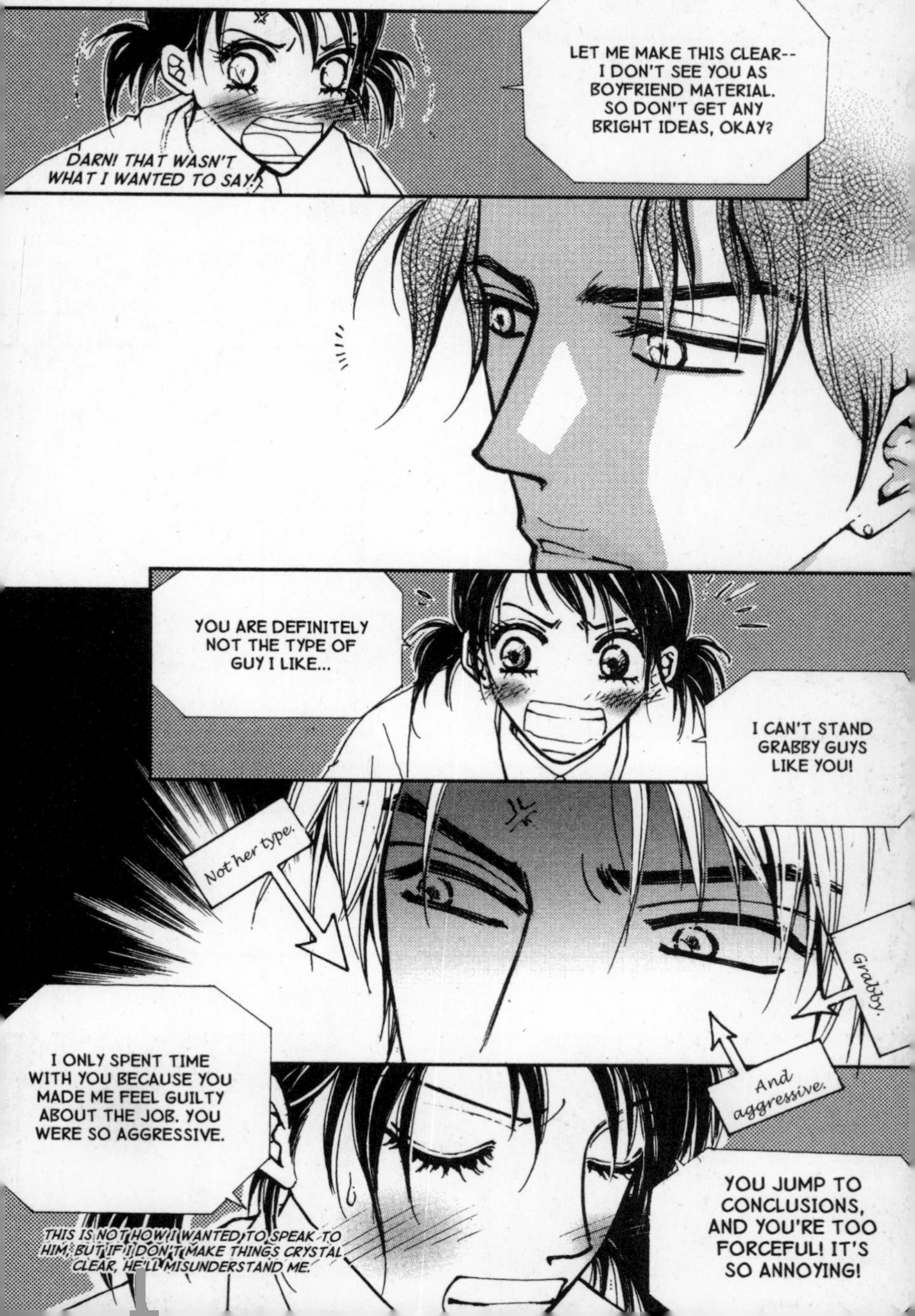
LET ME MAKE THIS CLEAR-- I DON'T SEE YOU AS BOYFRIEND MATERIAL. SO DON'T GET ANY BRIGHT IDEAS, OKAY?
DARN! THAT WASN'T WHAT I WANTED TO SAY!
I CAN'T STAND GRABBY GUYS LIKE YOU!
YOU ARE DEFINITELY NOT THE TYPE OF GUY I LIKE...
Not her type.
Grabby.
And aggressive.
YOU JUMP TO CONCLUSIONS, AND YOU'RE TOO FORCEFUL! IT'S SO ANNOYING!
I ONLY SPENT TIME WITH YOU BECAUSE YOU MADE ME FEEL GUILTY ABOUT THE JOB. YOU WERE SO AGGRESSIVE.
THIS IS NOT HOW I WANTED TO SPEAK TO HIM, BUT IF I DON'T MAKE THINGS CRYSTAL CLEAR, HE'LL MISUNDERSTAND ME.

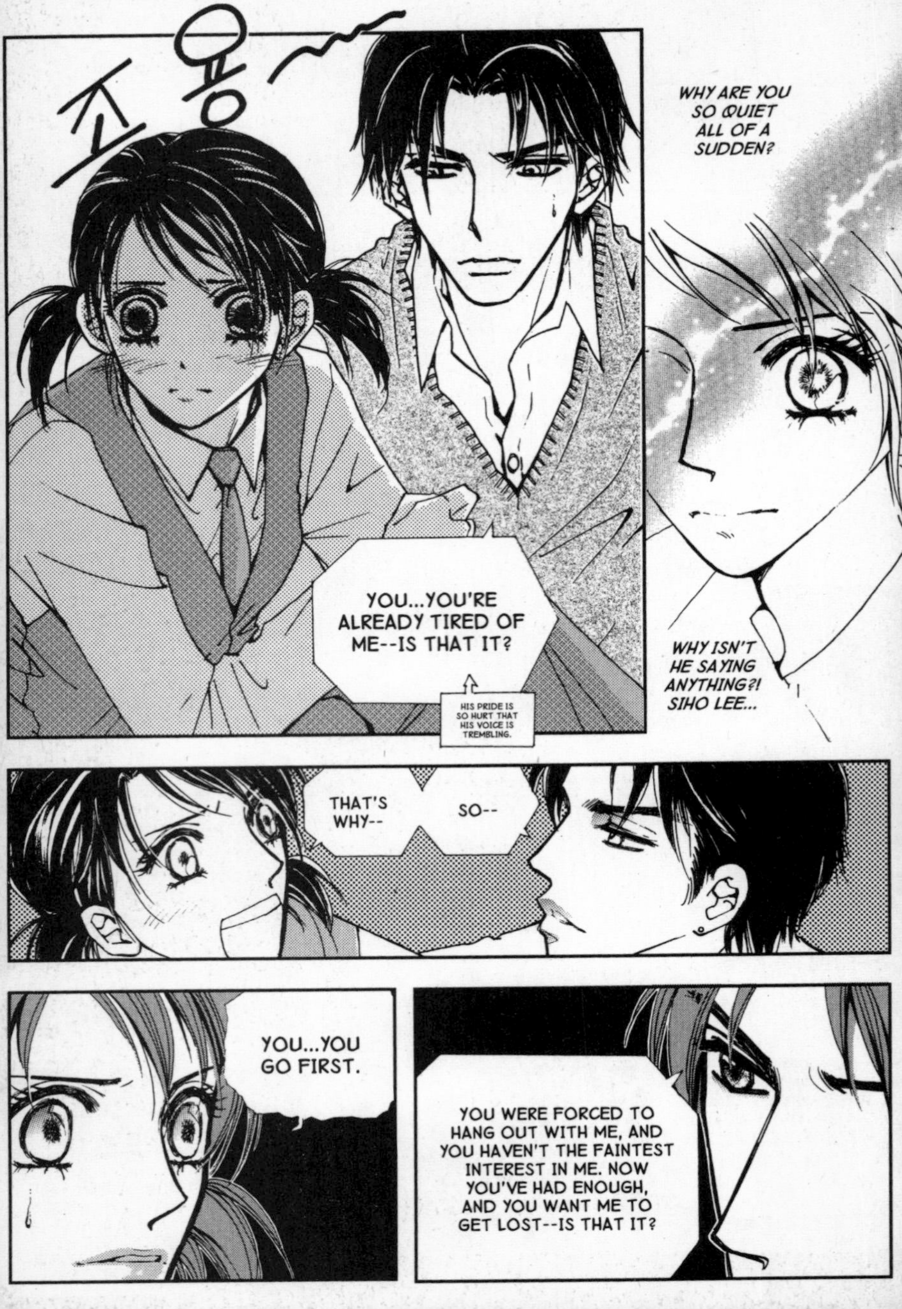

조용~~
YOU...YOU'RE ALREADY TIRED OF ME--IS THAT IT?
HIS PRIDE IS SO HURT THAT HIS VOICE IS TREMBLING.
WHY ARE YOU SO QUIET ALL OF A SUDDEN?
WHY ISN'T HE SAYING ANYTHING?! SIHO LEE...
THAT'S WHY--
SO--
YOU...YOU GO FIRST.
YOU WERE FORCED TO HANG OUT WITH ME, AND YOU HAVEN'T THE FAINTEST INTEREST IN ME. NOW YOU'VE HAD ENOUGH, AND YOU WANT ME TO GET LOST--IS THAT IT?

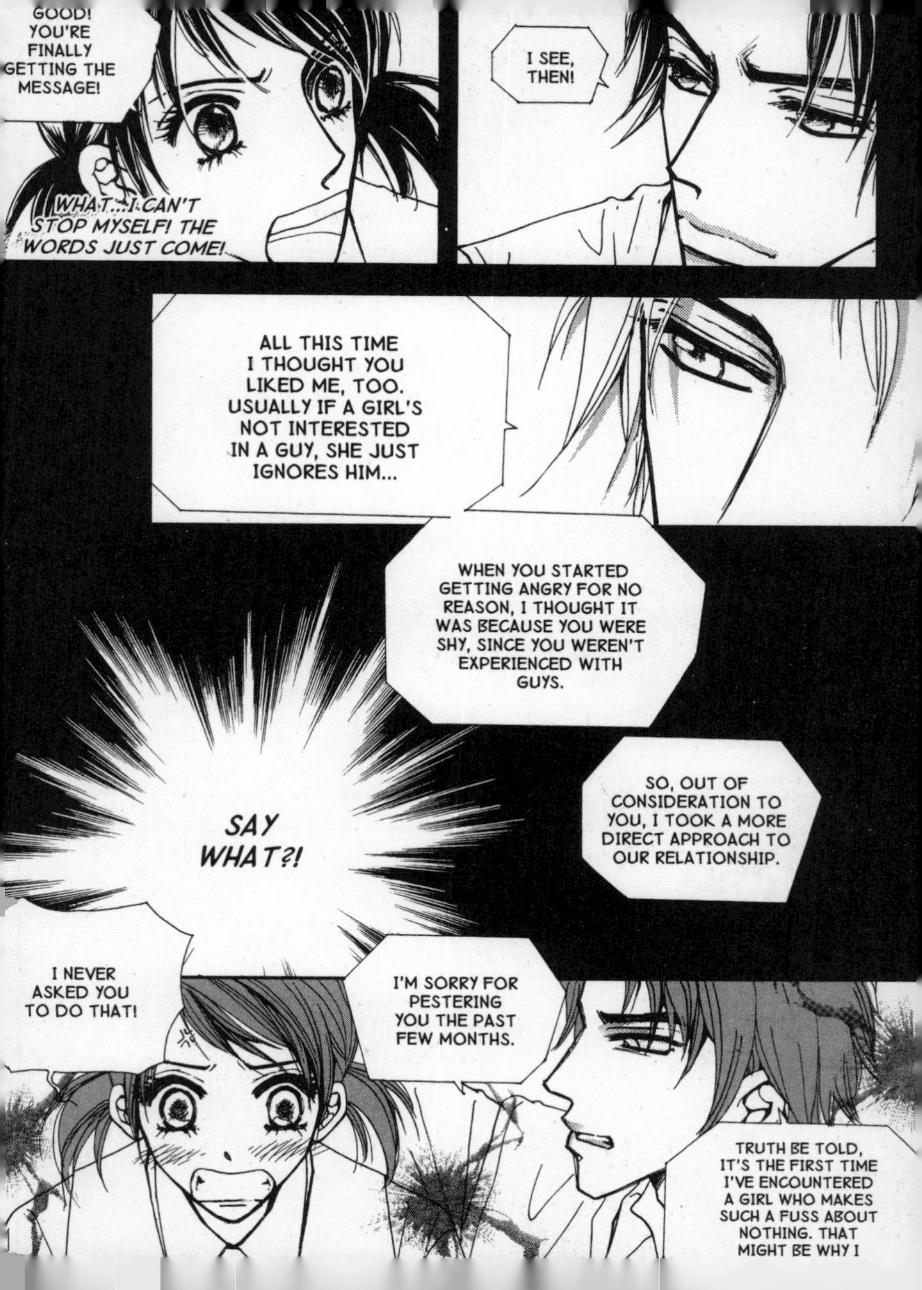
I SEE, THEN!
GOOD! YOU'RE FINALLY GETTING THE MESSAGE!
WHAT...I CAN'T STOP MYSELF! THE WORDS JUST COME!
ALL THIS TIME I THOUGHT YOU LIKED ME, TOO. USUALLY IF A GIRL'S NOT INTERESTED IN A GUY, SHE JUST IGNORES HIM...
WHEN YOU STARTED GETTING ANGRY FOR NO REASON, I THOUGHT IT WAS BECAUSE YOU WERE SHY, SINCE YOU WEREN'T EXPERIENCED WITH GUYS.
SO, OUT OF CONSIDERATION TO YOU, I TOOK A MORE DIRECT APPROACH TO OUR RELATIONSHIP.
SAY WHAT?!
I'M SORRY FOR PESTERING YOU THE PAST FEW MONTHS.
TRUTH BE TOLD, IT'S THE FIRST TIME I'VE ENCOUNTERED A GIRL WHO MAKES SUCH A FUSS ABOUT NOTHING. THAT MIGHT BE WHY I
I NEVER ASKED YOU TO DO THAT!

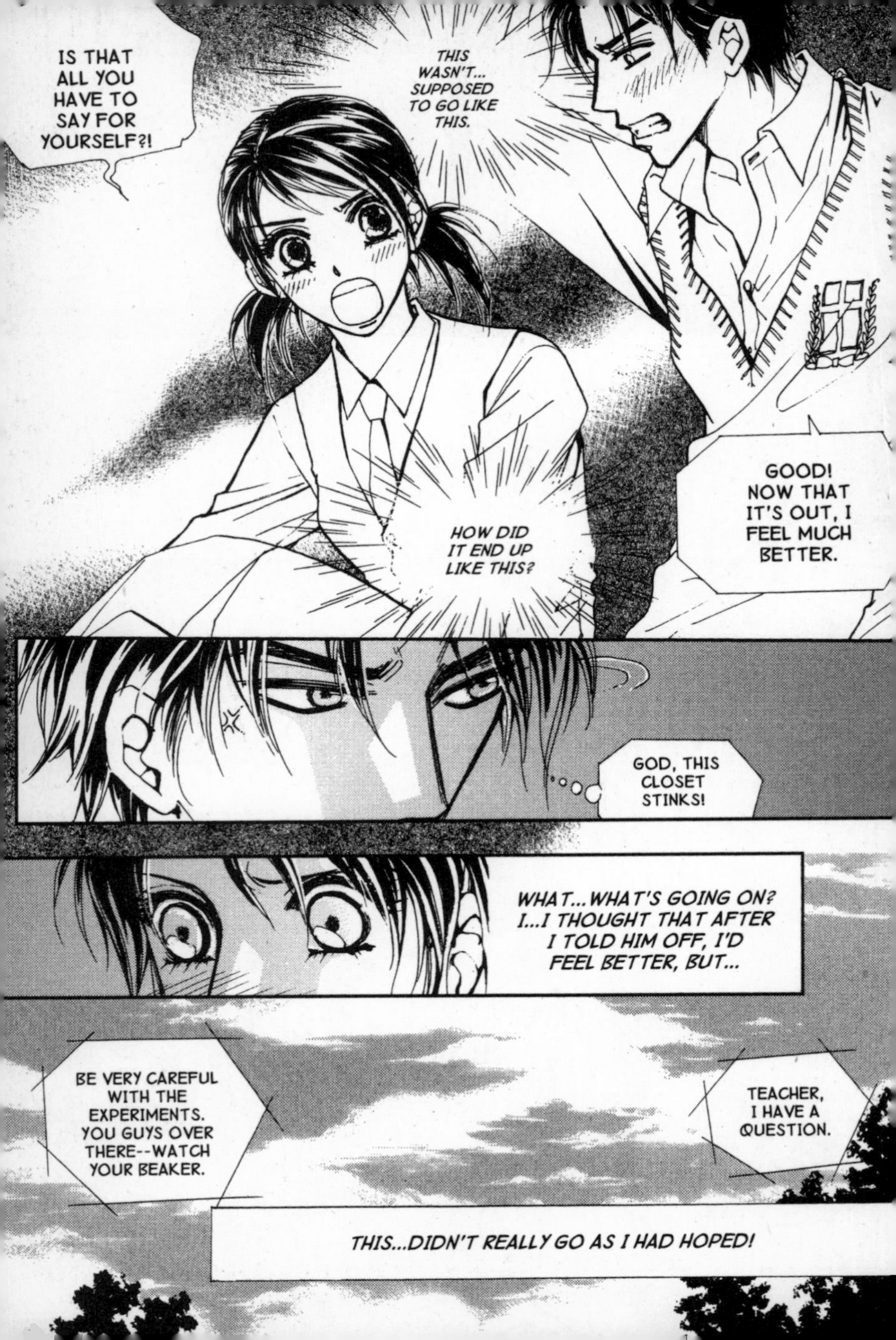
THIS WASN'T... SUPPOSED TO GO LIKE THIS.
IS THAT ALL YOU HAVE TO SAY FOR YOURSELF?!
GOOD! NOW THAT IT'S OUT, I FEEL MUCH BETTER.
HOW DID IT END UP LIKE THIS?
GOD, THIS CLOSET STINKS!
WHAT...WHAT'S GOING ON? I...I THOUGHT THAT AFTER I TOLD HIM OFF, I'D FEEL BETTER, BUT...
TEACHER, I HAVE A QUESTION.
BE VERY CAREFUL WITH THE EXPERIMENTS. YOU GUYS OVER THERE--WATCH YOUR BEAKER.
THIS...DIDN'T REALLY GO AS I HAD HOPED!

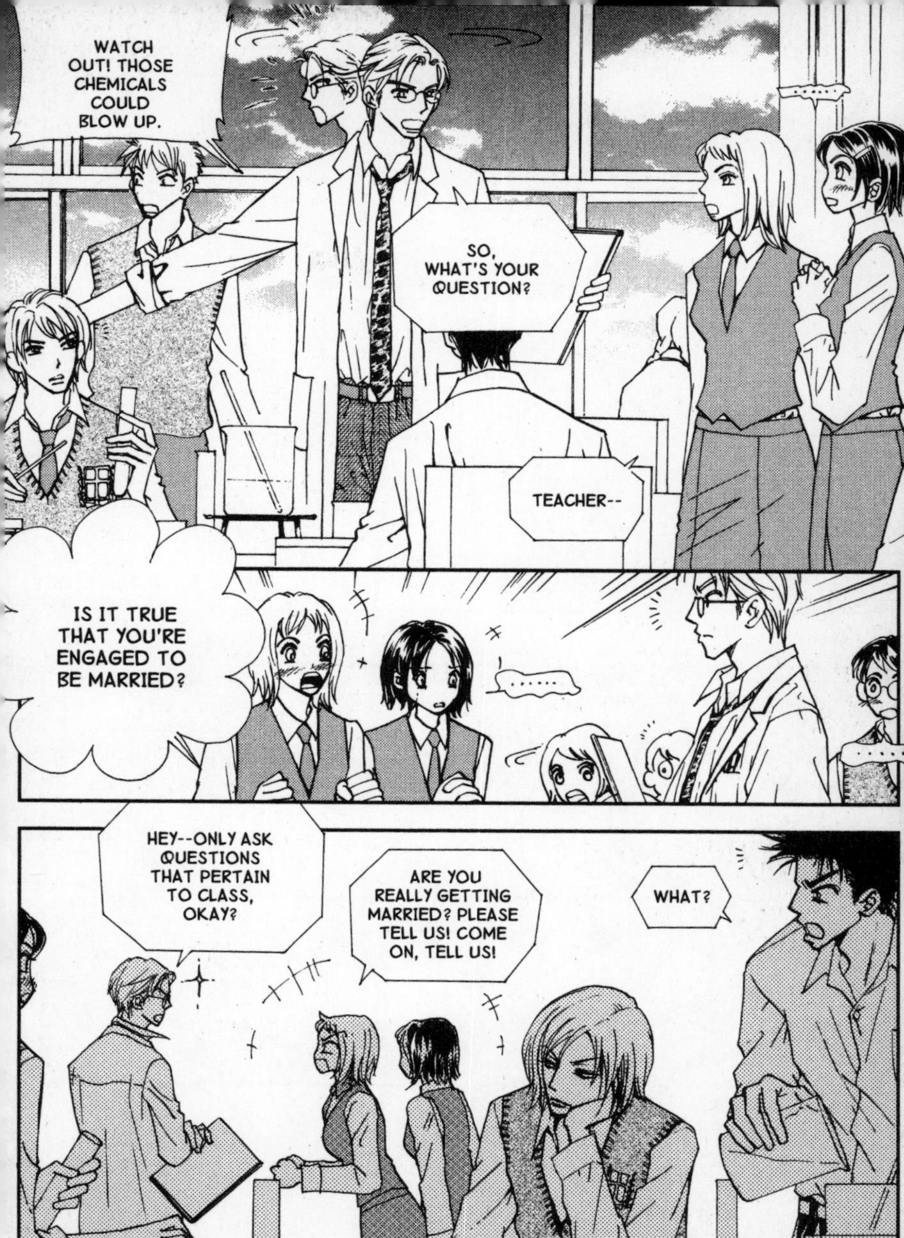
WATCH OUT! THOSE CHEMICALS COULD BLOW UP.
SO, WHAT'S YOUR QUESTION?
TEACHER--
IS IT TRUE THAT YOU'RE ENGAGED TO BE MARRIED?
......
WHAT?
ARE YOU REALLY GETTING MARRIED? PLEASE TELL US! COME ON, TELL US!
HEY--ONLY ASK QUESTIONS THAT PERTAIN TO CLASS, OKAY?

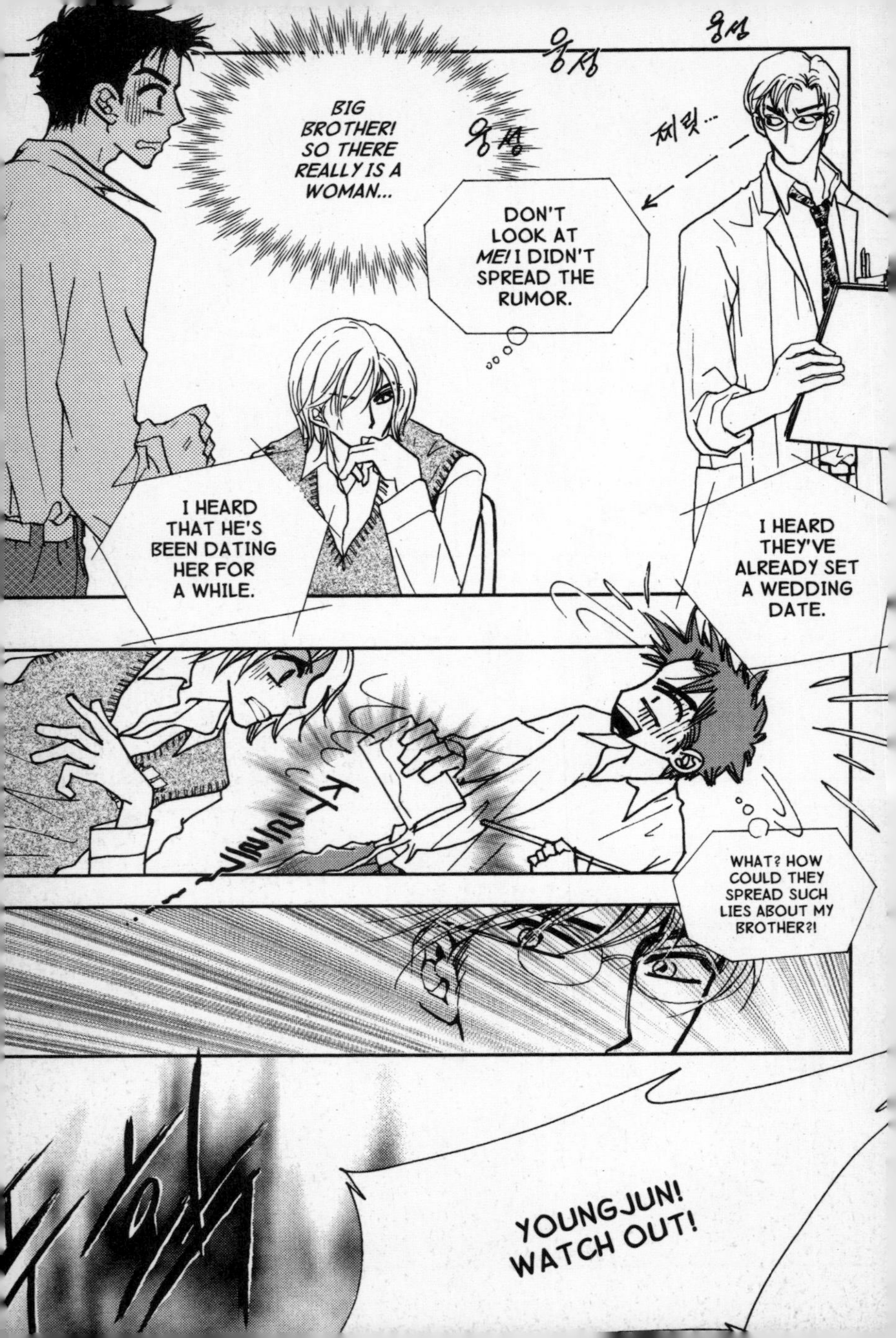
웅성
웅성
BIG BROTHER! SO THERE REALLY IS A WOMAN...
웅성
찌릿...
DON'T LOOK AT ME! I DIDN'T SPREAD THE RUMOR.
I HEARD THAT HE'S BEEN DATING HER FOR A WHILE.
I HEARD THEY'VE ALREADY SET A WEDDING DATE.
WHAT? HOW COULD THEY SPREAD SUCH LIES ABOUT MY BROTHER?!
YOUNGJUN! WATCH OUT!

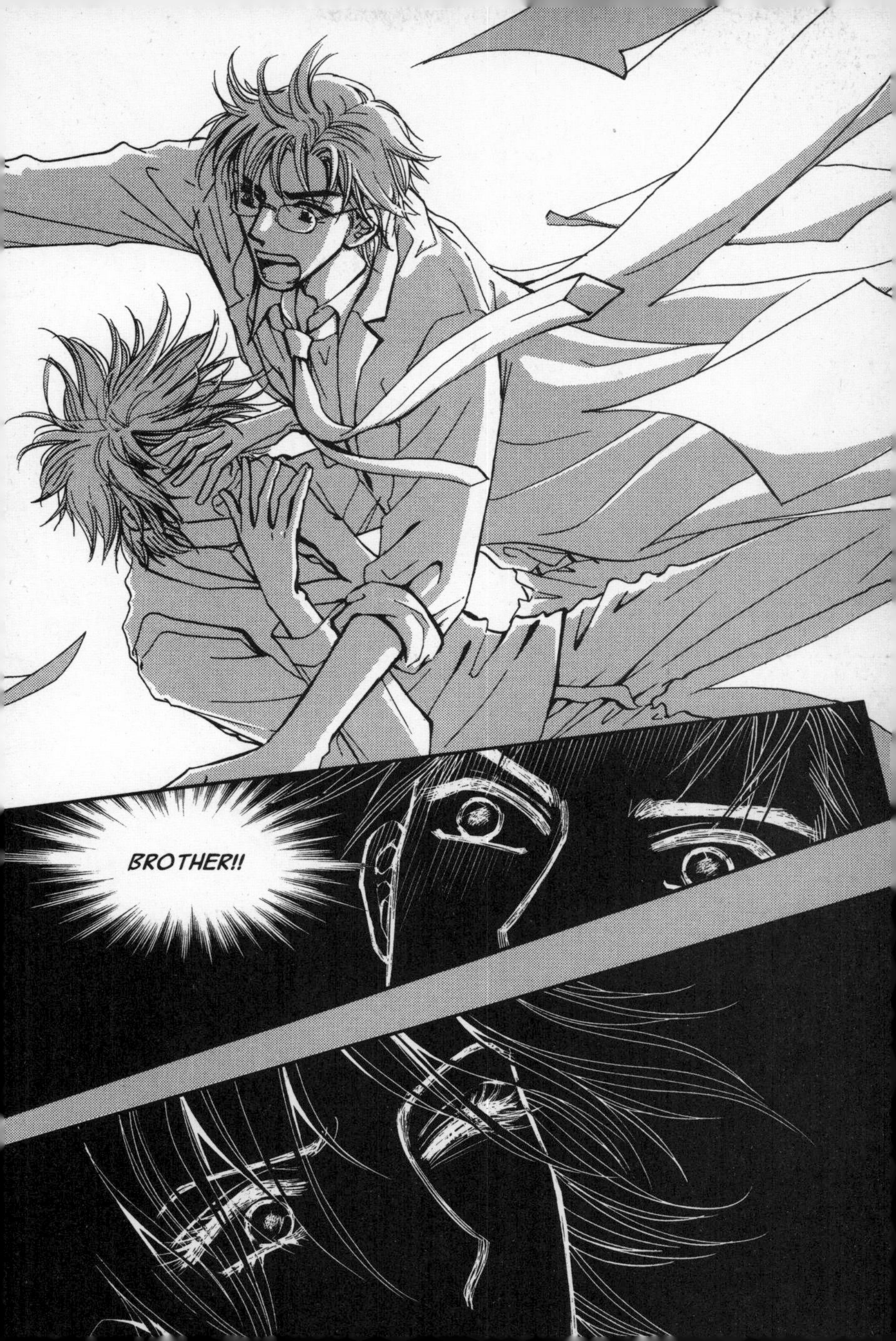
BROTHER!!

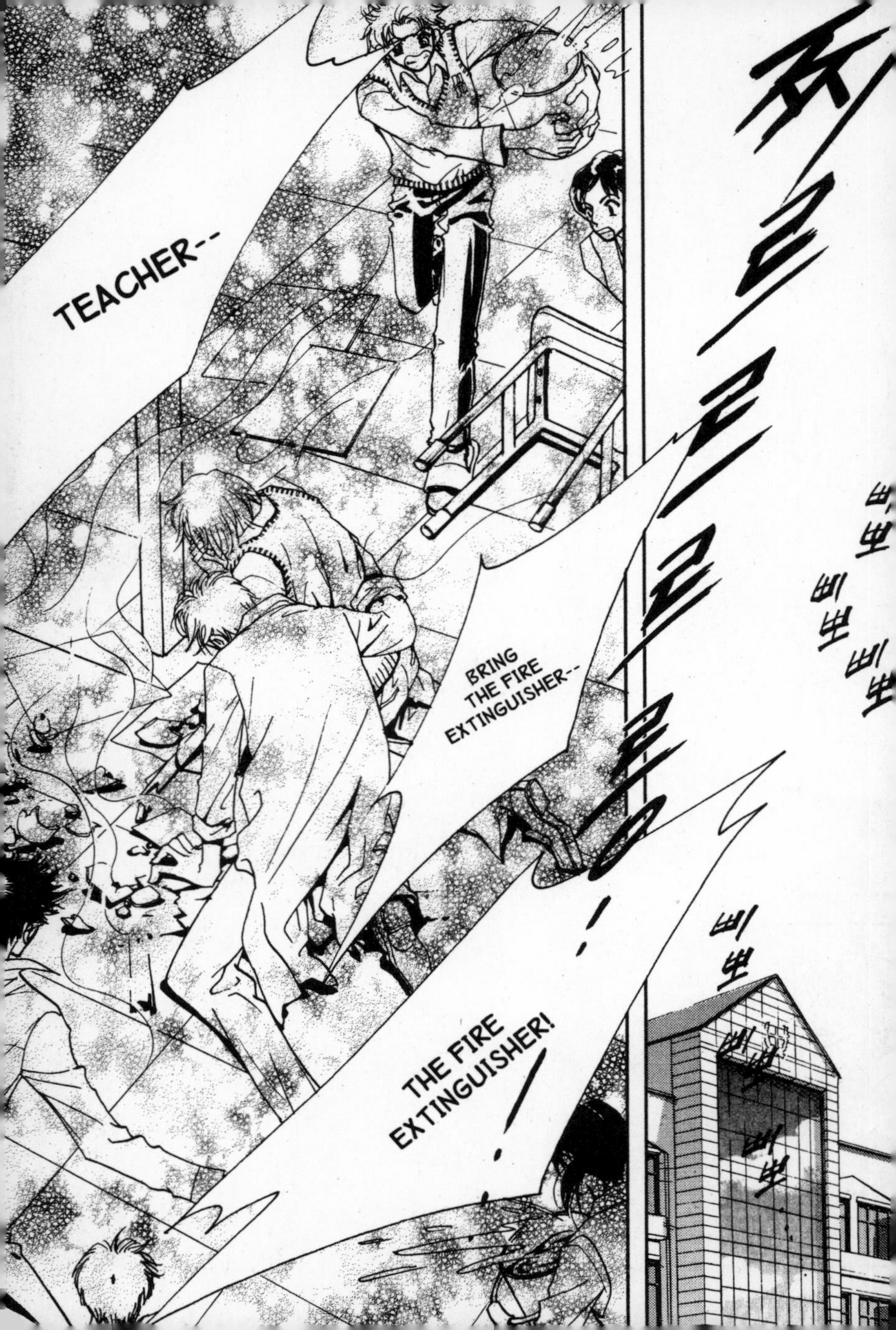
삐뽀 삐뽀 삐뽀
TEACHER--
BRING THE FIRE EXTINGUISHER--
THE FIRE EXTINGUISHER!
삐뽀 삐뽀 삐뽀

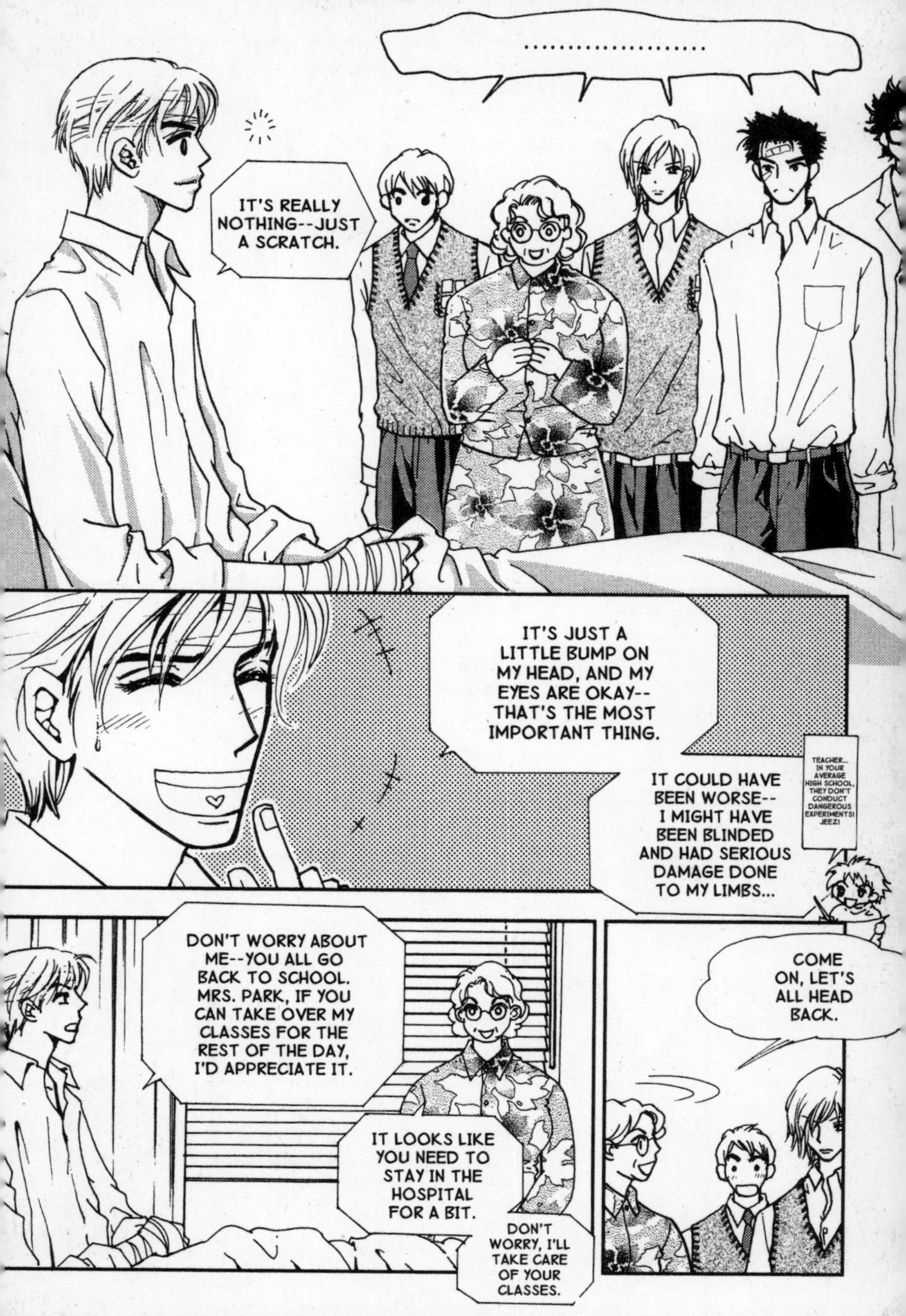
....
IT'S REALLY NOTHING--JUST A SCRATCH.
IT'S JUST A LITTLE BUMP ON MY HEAD, AND MY EYES ARE OKAY-- THAT'S THE MOST IMPORTANT THING.
IT COULD HAVE BEEN WORSE-- I MIGHT HAVE BEEN BLINDED AND HAD SERIOUS DAMAGE DONE TO MY LIMBS...
TEACHER... IN YOUR AVERAGE HIGH SCHOOL, THEY DON'T CONDUCT DANGEROUS EXPERIMENTS! JEEZ!
DON'T WORRY ABOUT ME--YOU ALL GO BACK TO SCHOOL. MRS. PARK, IF YOU CAN TAKE OVER MY CLASSES FOR THE REST OF THE DAY, I'D APPRECIATE IT.
IT LOOKS LIKE YOU NEED TO STAY IN THE HOSPITAL FOR A BIT.
DON'T WORRY, I'LL TAKE CARE OF YOUR CLASSES.
COME ON, LET'S ALL HEAD BACK.

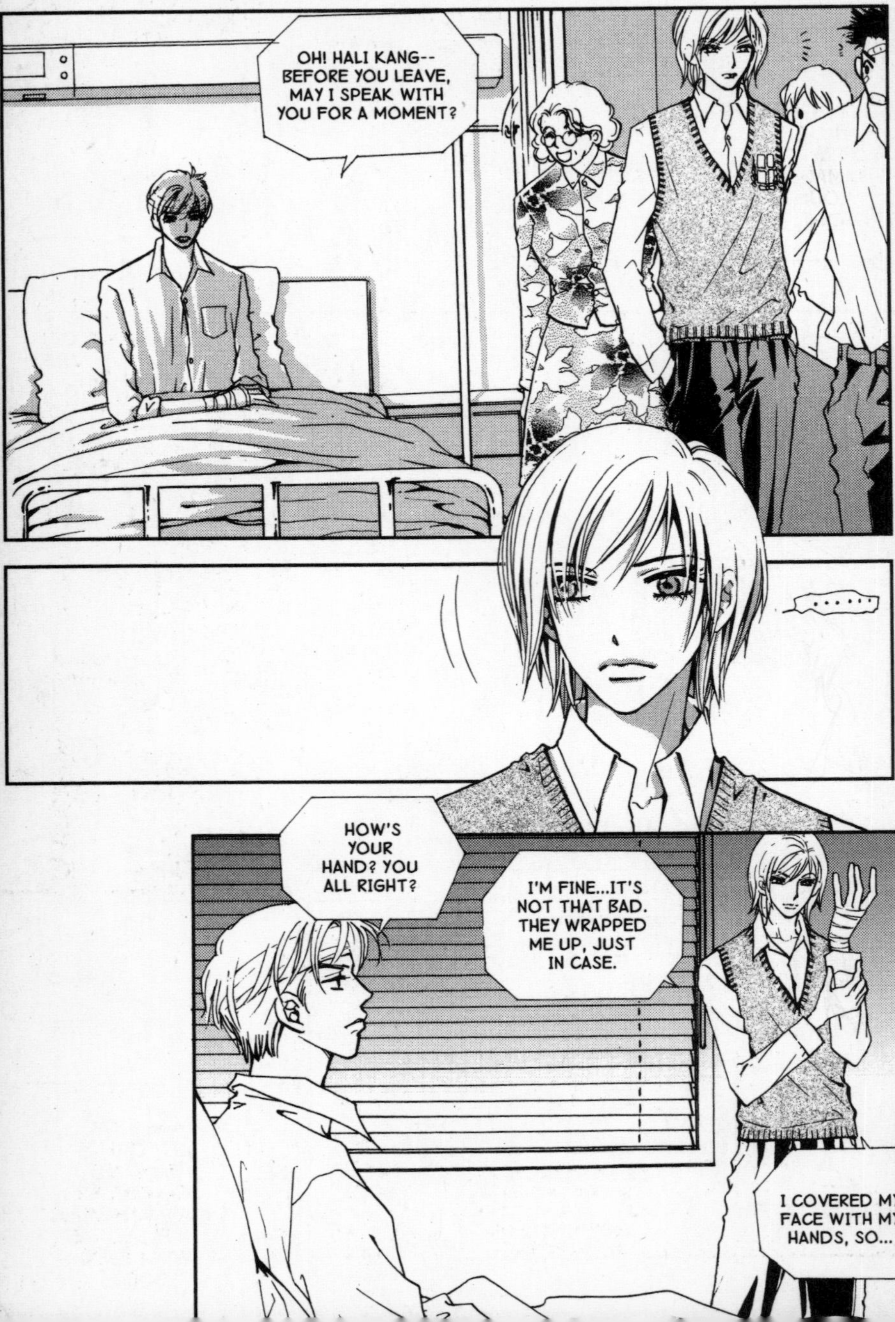
OH! HALI KANG-- BEFORE YOU LEAVE, MAY I SPEAK WITH YOU FOR A MOMENT?
......
HOW'S YOUR HAND? YOU ALL RIGHT?
I'M FINE...IT'S NOT THAT BAD. THEY WRAPPED ME UP, JUST IN CASE.
I COVERED MY FACE WITH MY HANDS, SO...

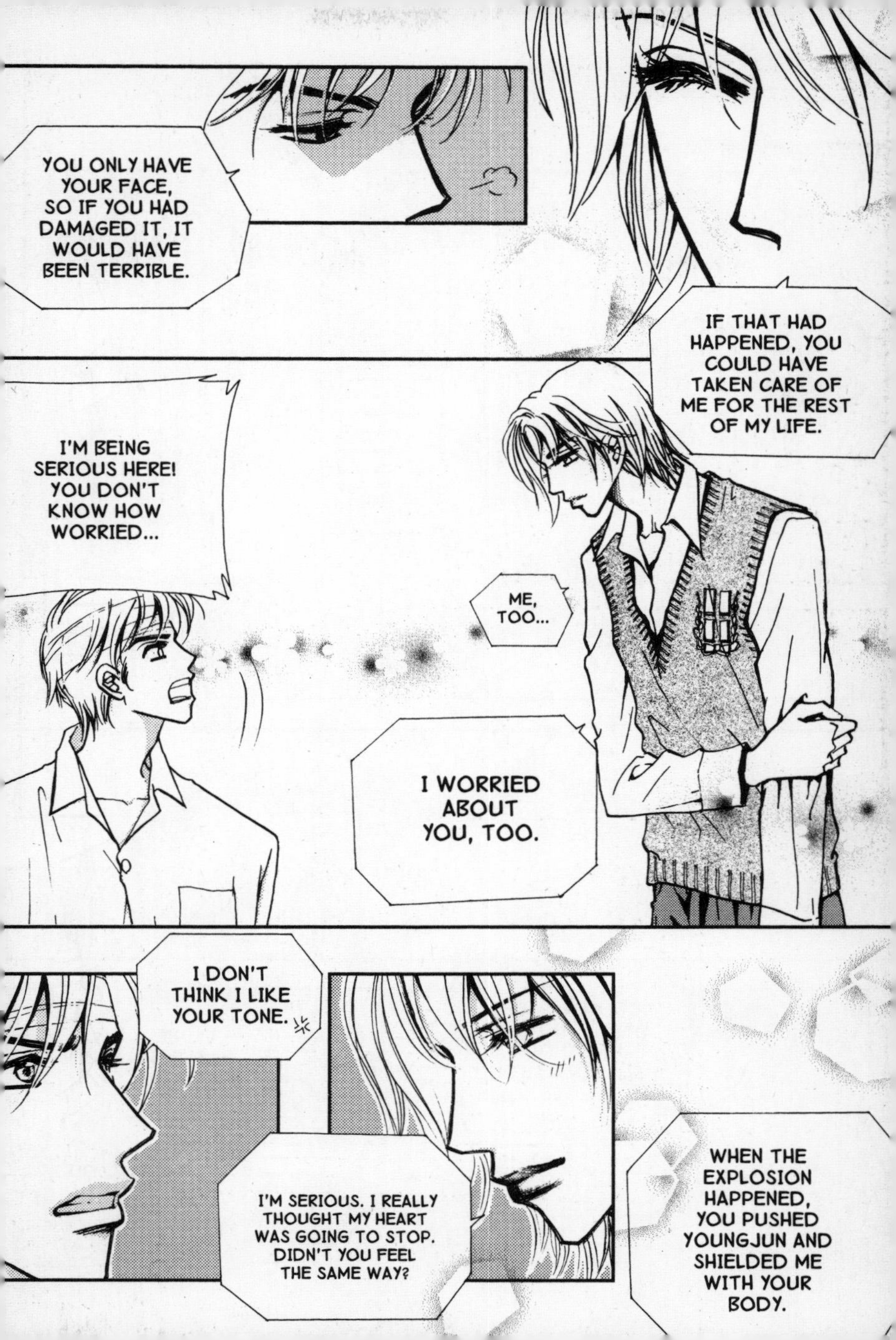
YOU ONLY HAVE YOUR FACE, SO IF YOU HAD DAMAGED IT, IT WOULD HAVE BEEN TERRIBLE.
IF THAT HAD HAPPENED, YOU COULD HAVE TAKEN CARE OF ME FOR THE REST OF MY LIFE.
I'M BEING SERIOUS HERE! YOU DON'T KNOW HOW WORRIED...
ME, TOO...
I WORRIED ABOUT YOU, TOO.
I DON'T THINK I LIKE YOUR TONE.
I'M SERIOUS. I REALLY THOUGHT MY HEART WAS GOING TO STOP. DIDN'T YOU FEEL THE SAME WAY?
WHEN THE EXPLOSION HAPPENED, YOU PUSHED YOUNGJUN AND SHIELDED ME WITH YOUR BODY.

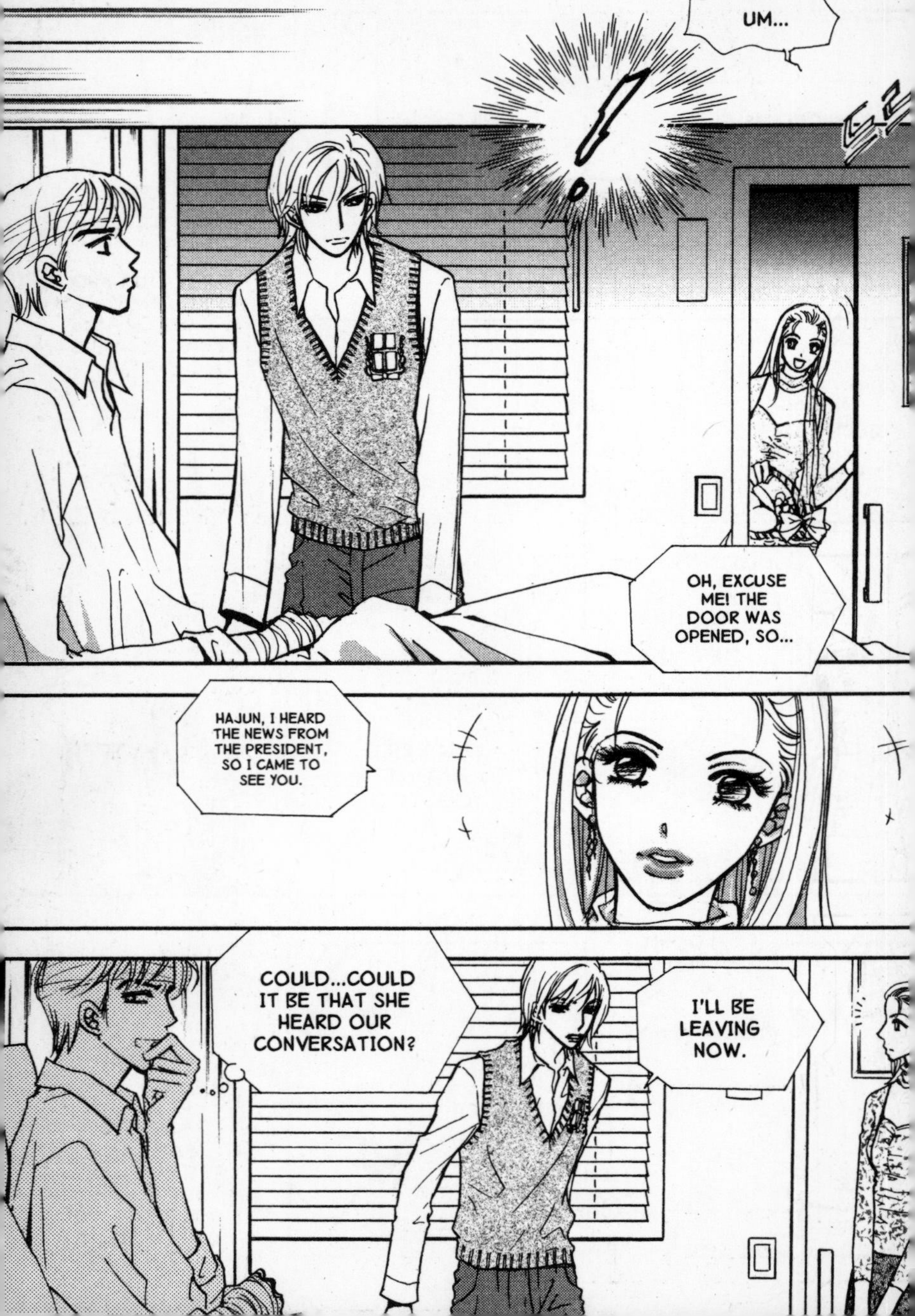
UM...
OH, EXCUSE ME! THE DOOR WAS OPENED, SO...
HAJUN, I HEARD THE NEWS FROM THE PRESIDENT, SO I CAME TO SEE YOU.
COULD...COULD IT BE THAT SHE HEARD OUR CONVERSATION?
I'LL BE LEAVING NOW.

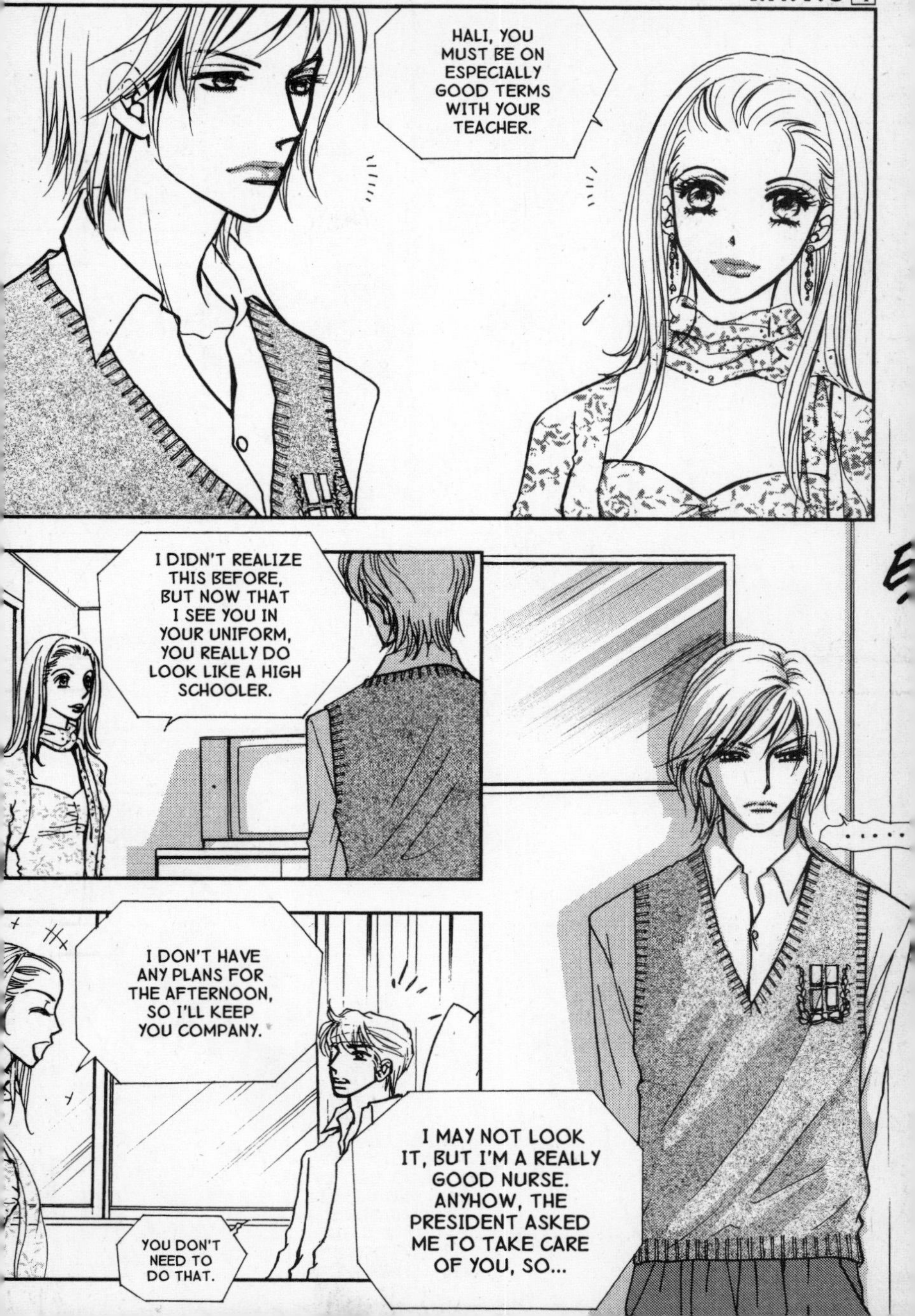
HALI, YOU MUST BE ON ESPECIALLY GOOD TERMS WITH YOUR TEACHER.
I DIDN'T REALIZE THIS BEFORE, BUT NOW THAT I SEE YOU IN YOUR UNIFORM, YOU REALLY DO LOOK LIKE A HIGH SCHOOLER.
....
I DON'T HAVE ANY PLANS FOR THE AFTERNOON, SO I'LL KEEP YOU COMPANY.
YOU DON'T NEED TO DO THAT.
I MAY NOT LOOK IT, BUT I'M A REALLY GOOD NURSE. ANYHOW, THE PRESIDENT ASKED ME TO TAKE CARE OF YOU, SO...

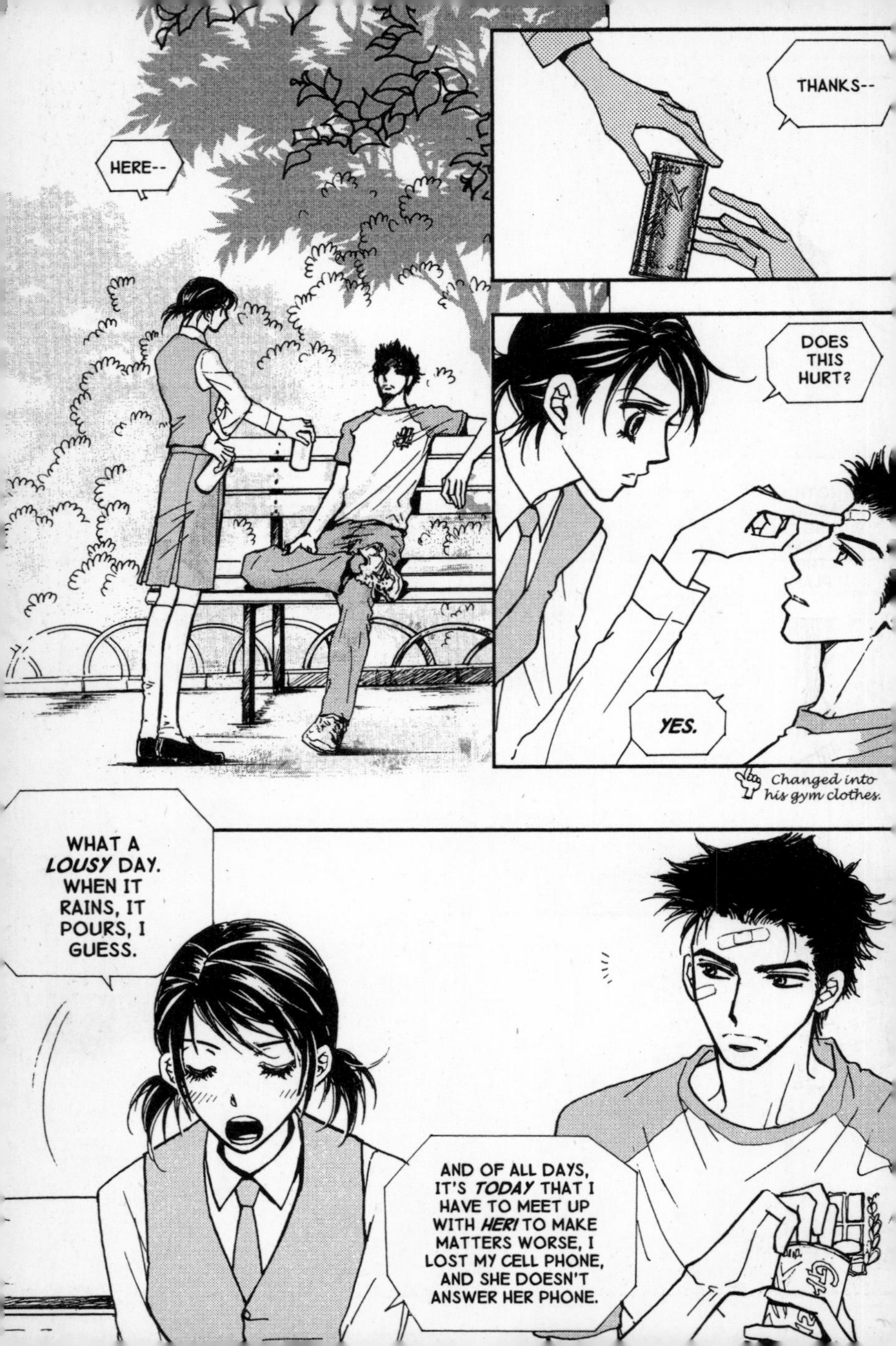
HERE--
THANKS--
DOES THIS HURT?
YES.
Changed into his gym clothes.
WHAT A LOUSY DAY. WHEN IT RAINS, IT POURS, I GUESS.
AND OF ALL DAYS, IT'S TODAY THAT I HAVE TO MEET UP WITH HERI TO MAKE MATTERS WORSE, I LOST MY CELL PHONE, AND SHE DOESN'T ANSWER HER PHONE.

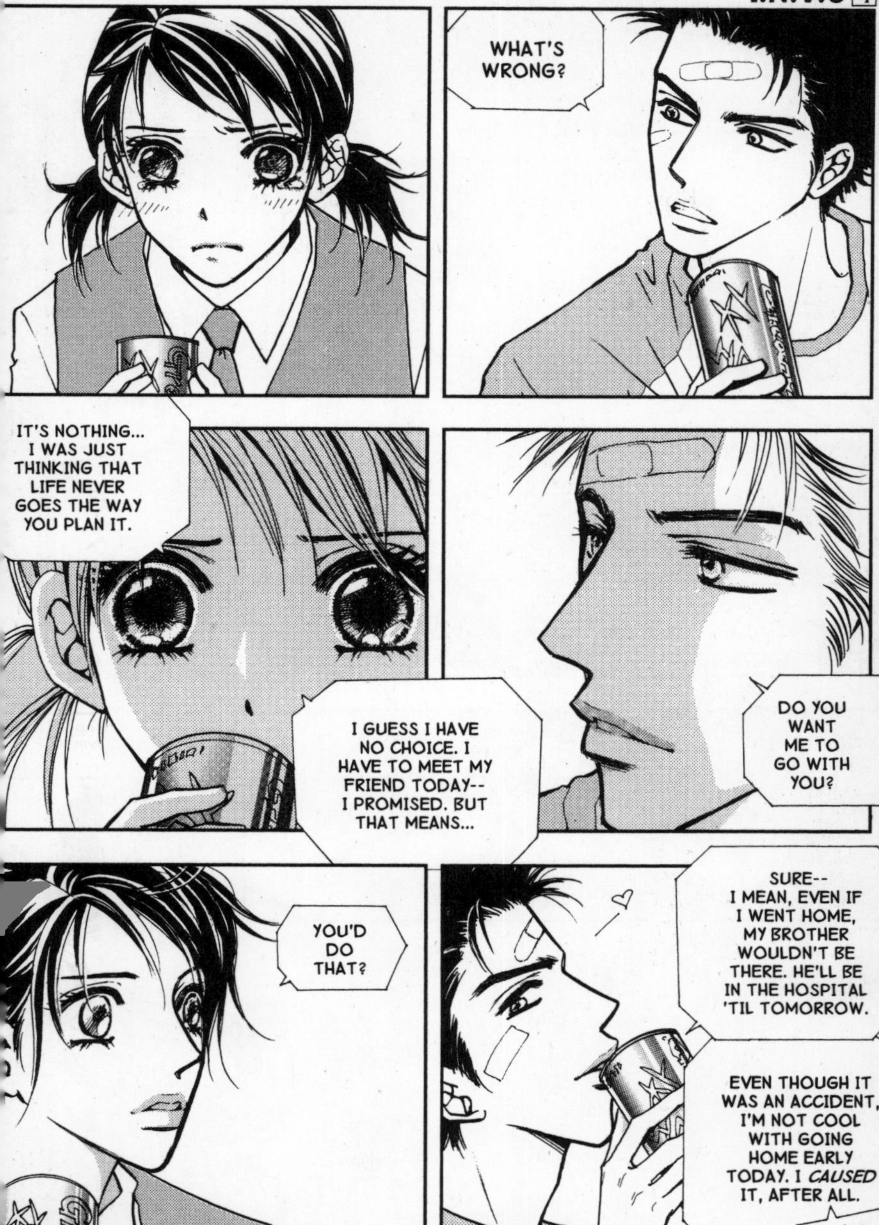
WHAT'S WRONG?
IT'S NOTHING... I WAS JUST THINKING THAT LIFE NEVER GOES THE WAY YOU PLAN IT.
I GUESS I HAVE NO CHOICE. I HAVE TO MEET MY FRIEND TODAY-- I PROMISED. BUT THAT MEANS...
DO YOU WANT ME TO GO WITH YOU?
YOU'D DO THAT?
SURE-- I MEAN, EVEN IF I WENT HOME, MY BROTHER WOULDN'T BE THERE. HE'LL BE IN THE HOSPITAL 'TIL TOMORROW.
EVEN THOUGH IT WAS AN ACCIDENT, I'M NOT COOL WITH GOING HOME EARLY TODAY. I *CAUSED* IT, AFTER ALL.
I feel so guilty...

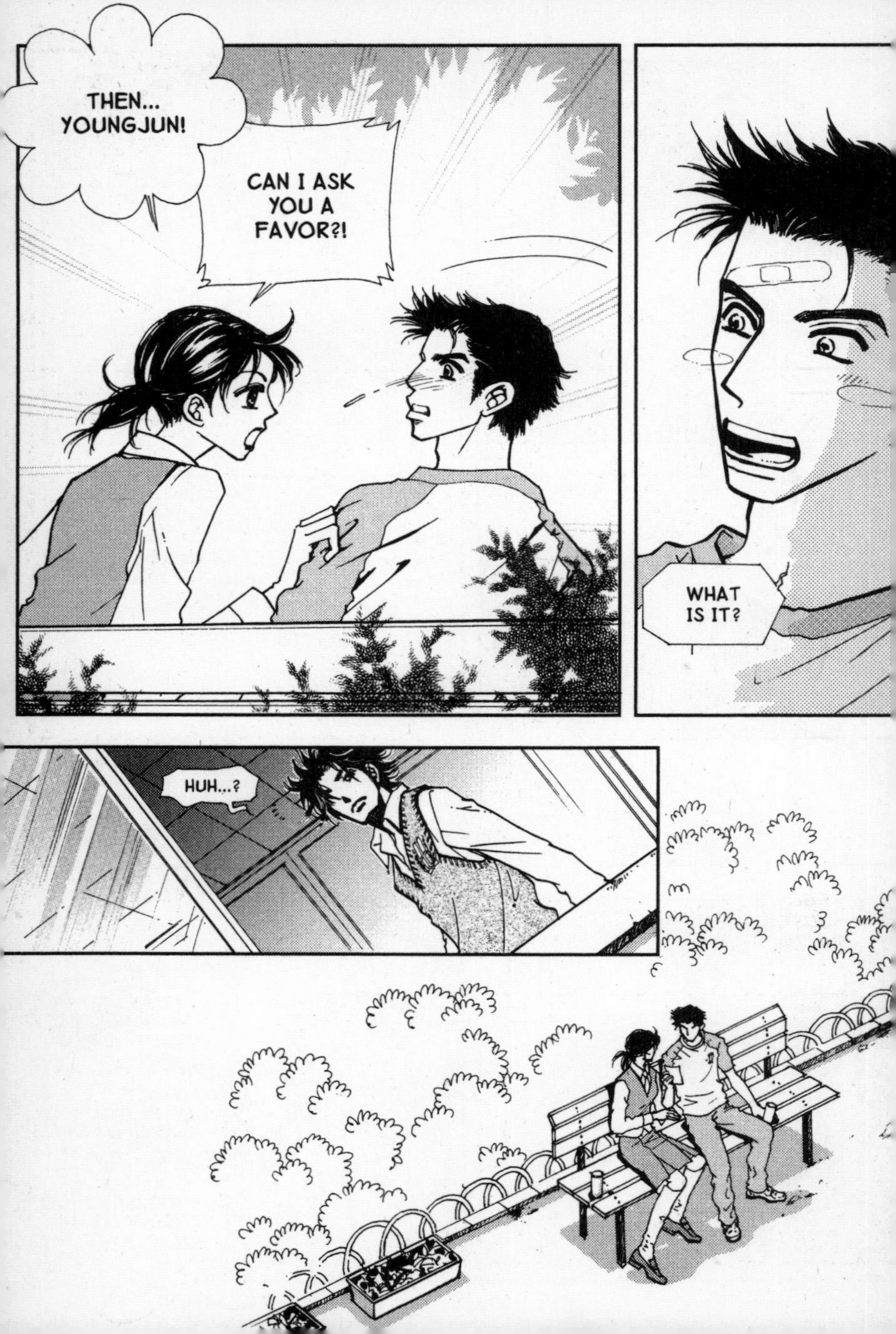
THEN... YOUNGJUN!
CAN I ASK YOU A FAVOR?!
WHAT IS IT?
HUH...?

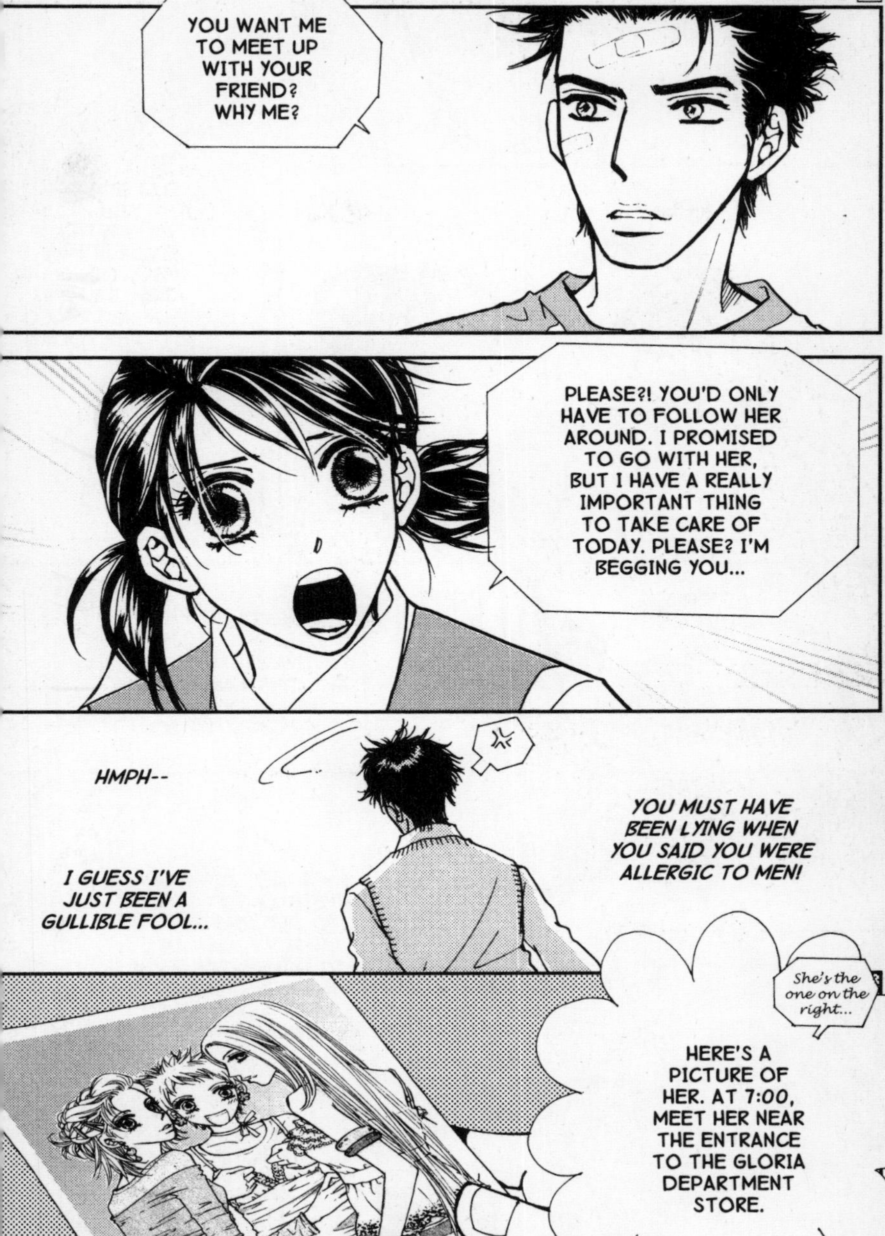
YOU WANT ME TO MEET UP WITH YOUR FRIEND? WHY ME?
PLEASE?! YOU'D ONLY HAVE TO FOLLOW HER AROUND. I PROMISED TO GO WITH HER, BUT I HAVE A REALLY IMPORTANT THING TO TAKE CARE OF TODAY. PLEASE? I'M BEGGING YOU...
HMPH--
YOU MUST HAVE BEEN LYING WHEN YOU SAID YOU WERE ALLERGIC TO MEN!
I GUESS I'VE JUST BEEN A GULLIBLE FOOL...
HERE'S A PICTURE OF HER. AT 7:00, MEET HER NEAR THE ENTRANCE TO THE GLORIA DEPARTMENT STORE.
She's the one on the right...

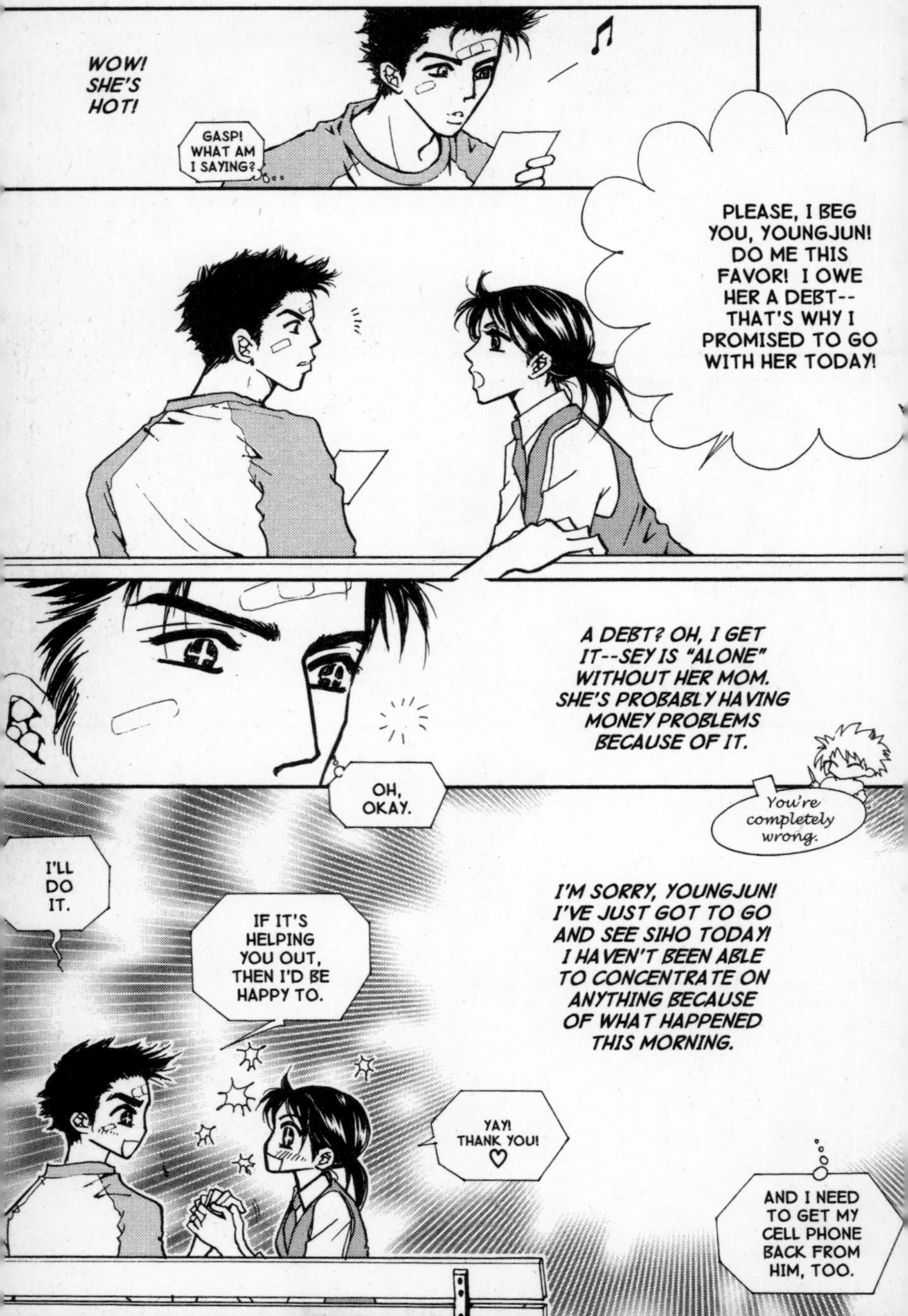
WOW! SHE'S HOT!
GASP! WHAT AM I SAYING?
PLEASE, I BEG YOU, YOUNGJUN! DO ME THIS FAVOR! I OWE HER A DEBT-- THAT'S WHY I PROMISED TO GO WITH HER TODAY!
A DEBT? OH, I GET IT--SEY IS "ALONE" WITHOUT HER MOM. SHE'S PROBABLY HAVING MONEY PROBLEMS BECAUSE OF IT.
OH, OKAY.
You're completely wrong.
I'LL DO IT.
IF IT'S HELPING YOU OUT, THEN I'D BE HAPPY TO.
YAY! THANK YOU! ♡
I'M SORRY, YOUNGJUN! I'VE JUST GOT TO GO AND SEE SIHO TODAY! I HAVEN'T BEEN ABLE TO CONCENTRATE ON ANYTHING BECAUSE OF WHAT HAPPENED THIS MORNING.
AND I NEED TO GET MY CELL PHONE BACK FROM HIM, TOO.

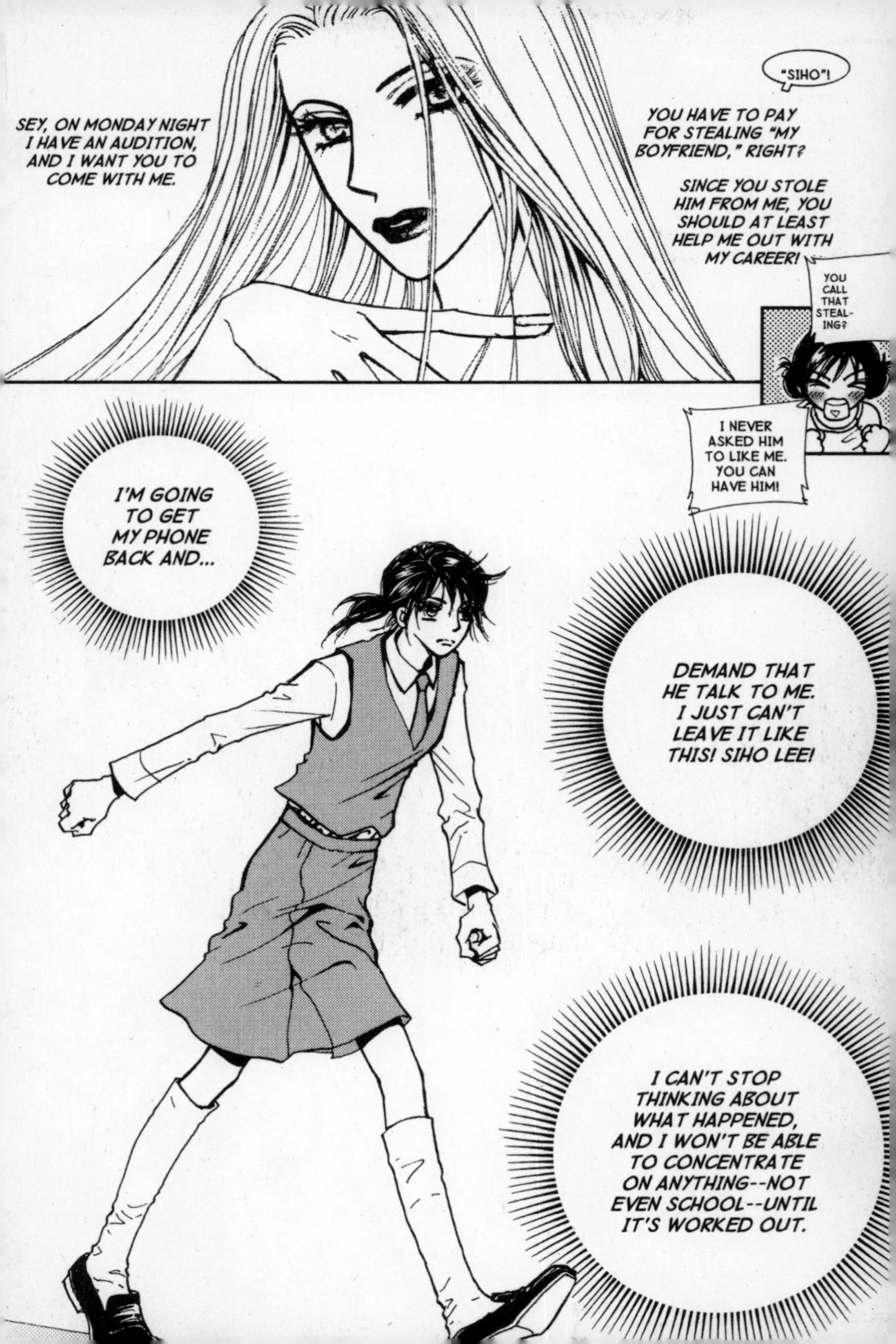
SEY, ON MONDAY NIGHT I HAVE AN AUDITION, AND I WANT YOU TO COME WITH ME.
"SIHO"!
YOU HAVE TO PAY FOR STEALING "MY BOYFRIEND," RIGHT?
SINCE YOU STOLE HIM FROM ME, YOU SHOULD AT LEAST HELP ME OUT WITH MY CAREER!
YOU CALL THAT STEAL-ING?
I NEVER ASKED HIM TO LIKE ME. YOU CAN HAVE HIM!
I'M GOING TO GET MY PHONE BACK AND...
DEMAND THAT HE TALK TO ME. I JUST CAN'T LEAVE IT LIKE THIS! SIHO LEE!
I CAN'T STOP THINKING ABOUT WHAT HAPPENED, AND I WON'T BE ABLE TO CONCENTRATE ON ANYTHING--NOT EVEN SCHOOL--UNTIL IT'S WORKED OUT.

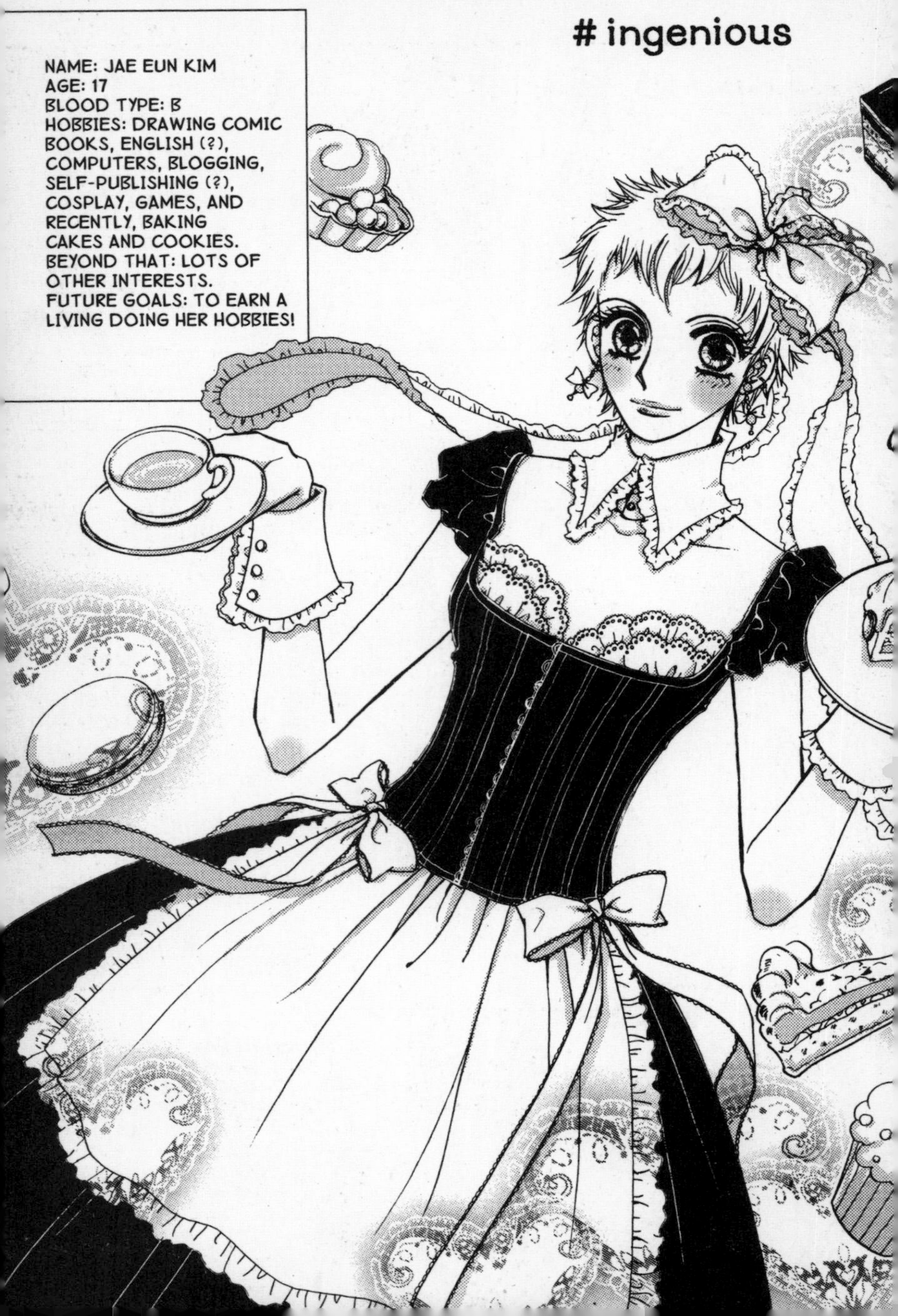
ingenious
NAME: JAE EUN KIM
AGE: 17
BLOOD TYPE: B
HOBBIES: DRAWING COMIC BOOKS, ENGLISH (?), COMPUTERS, BLOGGING, SELF-PUBLISHING (?), COSPLAY, GAMES, AND RECENTLY, BAKING CAKES AND COOKIES.
BEYOND THAT: LOTS OF OTHER INTERESTS.
FUTURE GOALS: TO EARN A LIVING DOING HER HOBBIES!

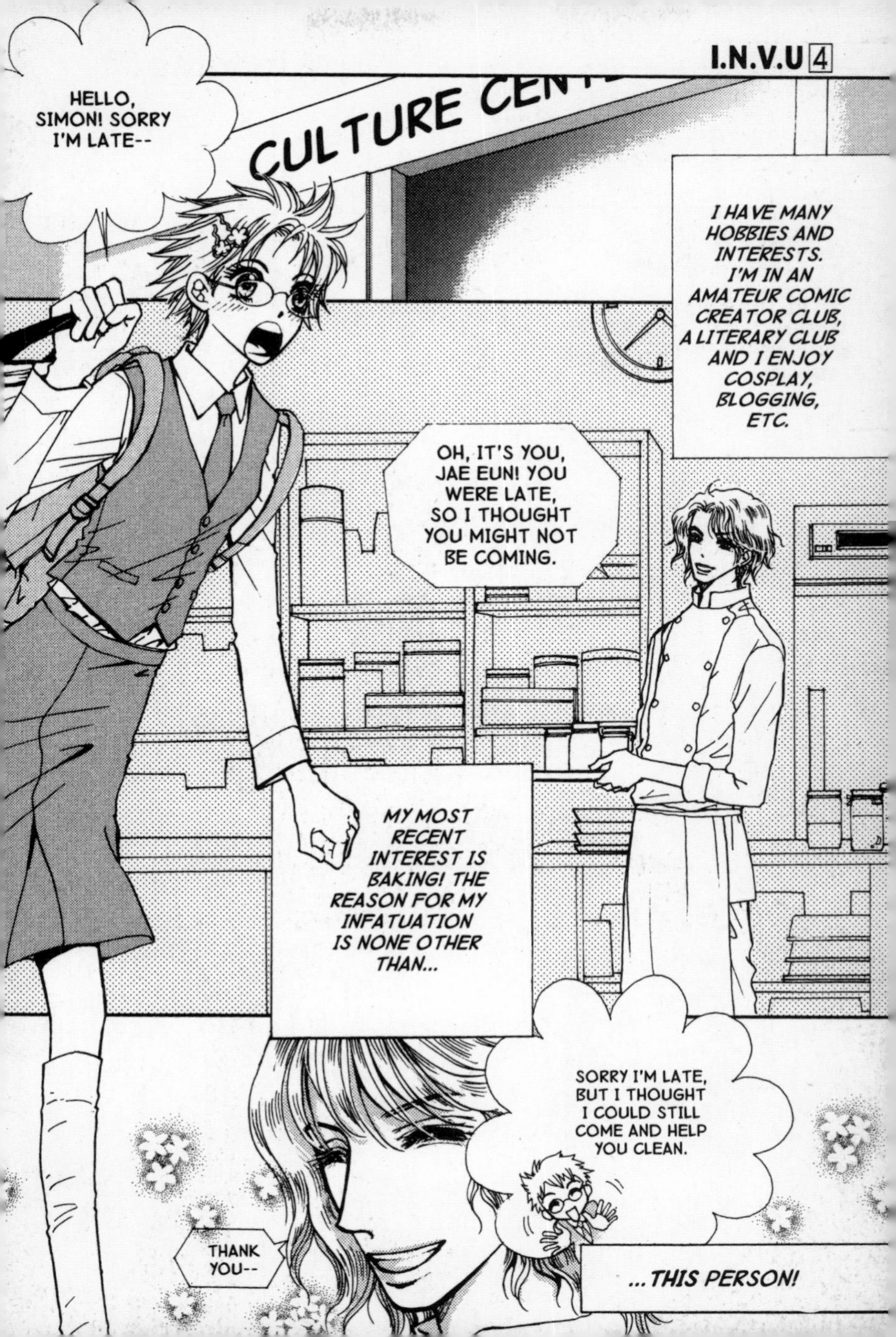
HELLO, SIMON! SORRY I'M LATE--
CULTURE CENT
I HAVE MANY HOBBIES AND INTERESTS. I'M IN AN AMATEUR COMIC CREATOR CLUB, A LITERARY CLUB AND I ENJOY COSPLAY, BLOGGING, ETC.
OH, IT'S YOU, JAE EUN! YOU WERE LATE, SO I THOUGHT YOU MIGHT NOT BE COMING.
MY MOST RECENT INTEREST IS BAKING! THE REASON FOR MY INFATUATION IS NONE OTHER THAN...
SORRY I'M LATE, BUT I THOUGHT I COULD STILL COME AND HELP YOU CLEAN.
THANK YOU--
...THIS PERSON!

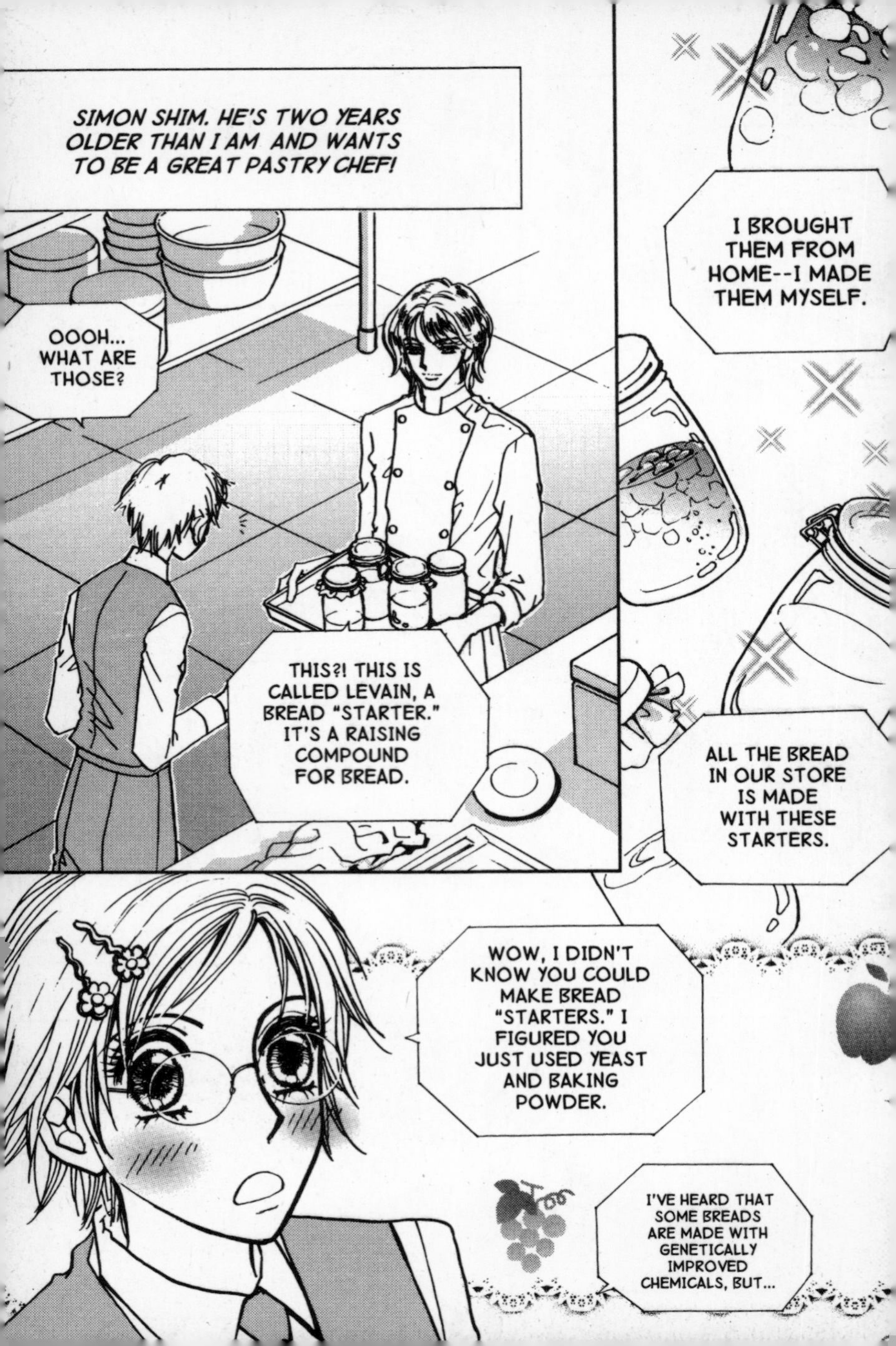
SIMON SHIM. HE'S TWO YEARS OLDER THAN I AM AND WANTS TO BE A GREAT PASTRY CHEF!
OOOH... WHAT ARE THOSE?
THIS?! THIS IS CALLED LEVAIN, A BREAD "STARTER." IT'S A RAISING COMPOUND FOR BREAD.
I BROUGHT THEM FROM HOME--I MADE THEM MYSELF.
ALL THE BREAD IN OUR STORE IS MADE WITH THESE STARTERS.
WOW, I DIDN'T KNOW YOU COULD MAKE BREAD "STARTERS." I FIGURED YOU JUST USED YEAST AND BAKING POWDER.
I'VE HEARD THAT SOME BREADS ARE MADE WITH GENETICALLY IMPROVED CHEMICALS, BUT...

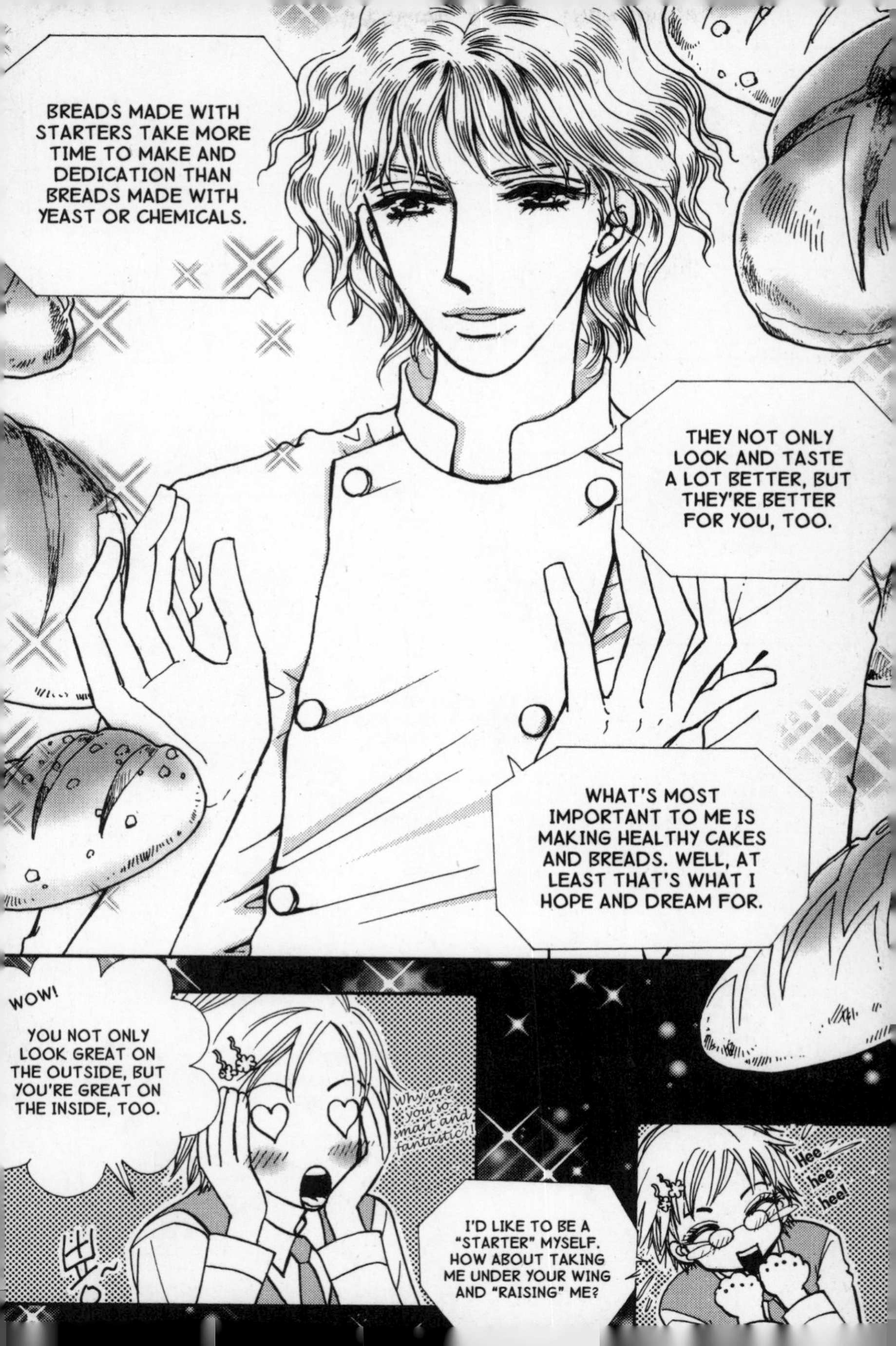
BREADS MADE WITH STARTERS TAKE MORE TIME TO MAKE AND DEDICATION THAN BREADS MADE WITH YEAST OR CHEMICALS.
THEY NOT ONLY LOOK AND TASTE A LOT BETTER, BUT THEY'RE BETTER FOR YOU, TOO.
WHAT'S MOST IMPORTANT TO ME IS MAKING HEALTHY CAKES AND BREADS. WELL, AT LEAST THAT'S WHAT I HOPE AND DREAM FOR.
WOW!
YOU NOT ONLY LOOK GREAT ON THE OUTSIDE, BUT YOU'RE GREAT ON THE INSIDE, TOO.
Why are you so smart and fantastic?!
I'D LIKE TO BE A "STARTER" MYSELF. HOW ABOUT TAKING ME UNDER YOUR WING AND "RAISING" ME?
Hee hee hee!

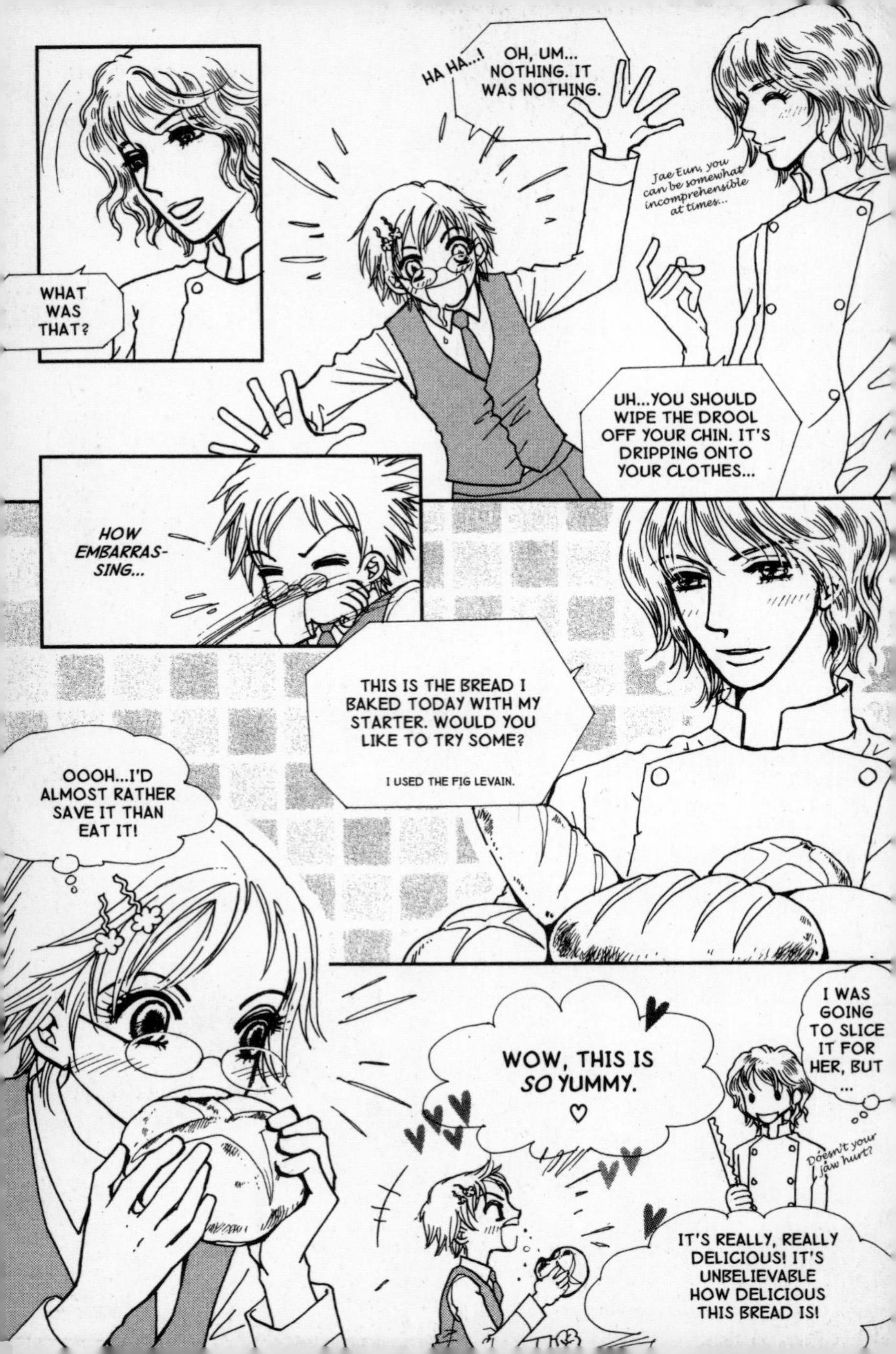
WHAT WAS THAT?
HA HA...!
OH, UM... NOTHING. IT WAS NOTHING.
Jae Eun, you can be somewhat incomprehensible at times...
UH...YOU SHOULD WIPE THE DROOL OFF YOUR CHIN. IT'S DRIPPING ONTO YOUR CLOTHES...
HOW EMBARRAS-SING...
THIS IS THE BREAD I BAKED TODAY WITH MY STARTER. WOULD YOU LIKE TO TRY SOME?
I USED THE FIG LEVAIN.
OOOH...I'D ALMOST RATHER SAVE IT THAN EAT IT!
WOW, THIS IS *SO* YUMMY. ♡
I WAS GOING TO SLICE IT FOR HER, BUT ...
Doesn't your jaw hurt?
IT'S REALLY, REALLY DELICIOUS! IT'S UNBELIEVABLE HOW DELICIOUS THIS BREAD IS!

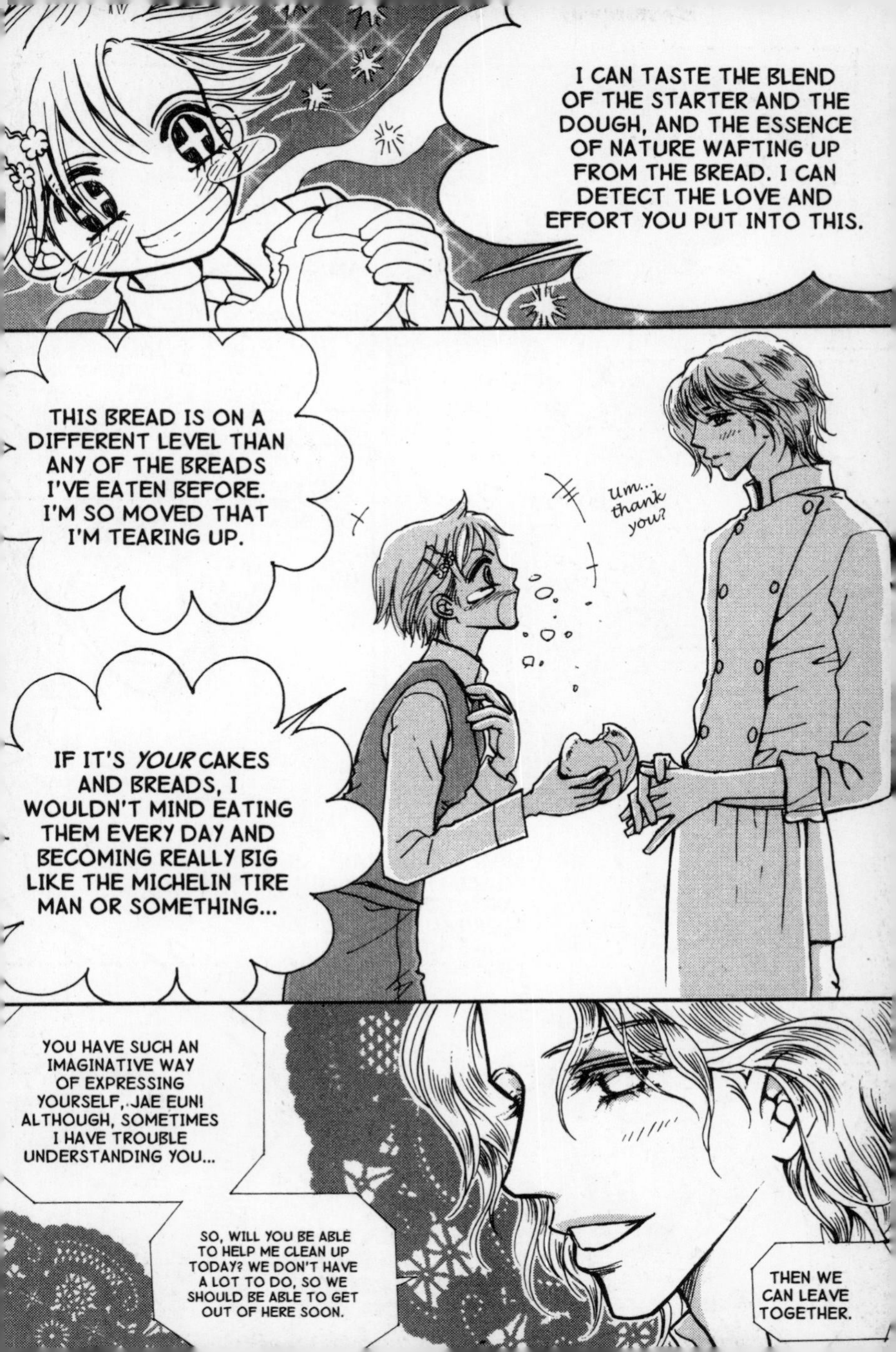
I CAN TASTE THE BLEND OF THE STARTER AND THE DOUGH, AND THE ESSENCE OF NATURE WAFTING UP FROM THE BREAD. I CAN DETECT THE LOVE AND EFFORT YOU PUT INTO THIS.
THIS BREAD IS ON A DIFFERENT LEVEL THAN ANY OF THE BREADS I'VE EATEN BEFORE. I'M SO MOVED THAT I'M TEARING UP.
IF IT'S *YOUR* CAKES AND BREADS, I WOULDN'T MIND EATING THEM EVERY DAY AND BECOMING REALLY BIG LIKE THE MICHELIN TIRE MAN OR SOMETHING...
um... thank you?
YOU HAVE SUCH AN IMAGINATIVE WAY OF EXPRESSING YOURSELF, JAE EUN! ALTHOUGH, SOMETIMES I HAVE TROUBLE UNDERSTANDING YOU...
SO, WILL YOU BE ABLE TO HELP ME CLEAN UP TODAY? WE DON'T HAVE A LOT TO DO, SO WE SHOULD BE ABLE TO GET OUT OF HERE SOON.
THEN WE CAN LEAVE TOGETHER.

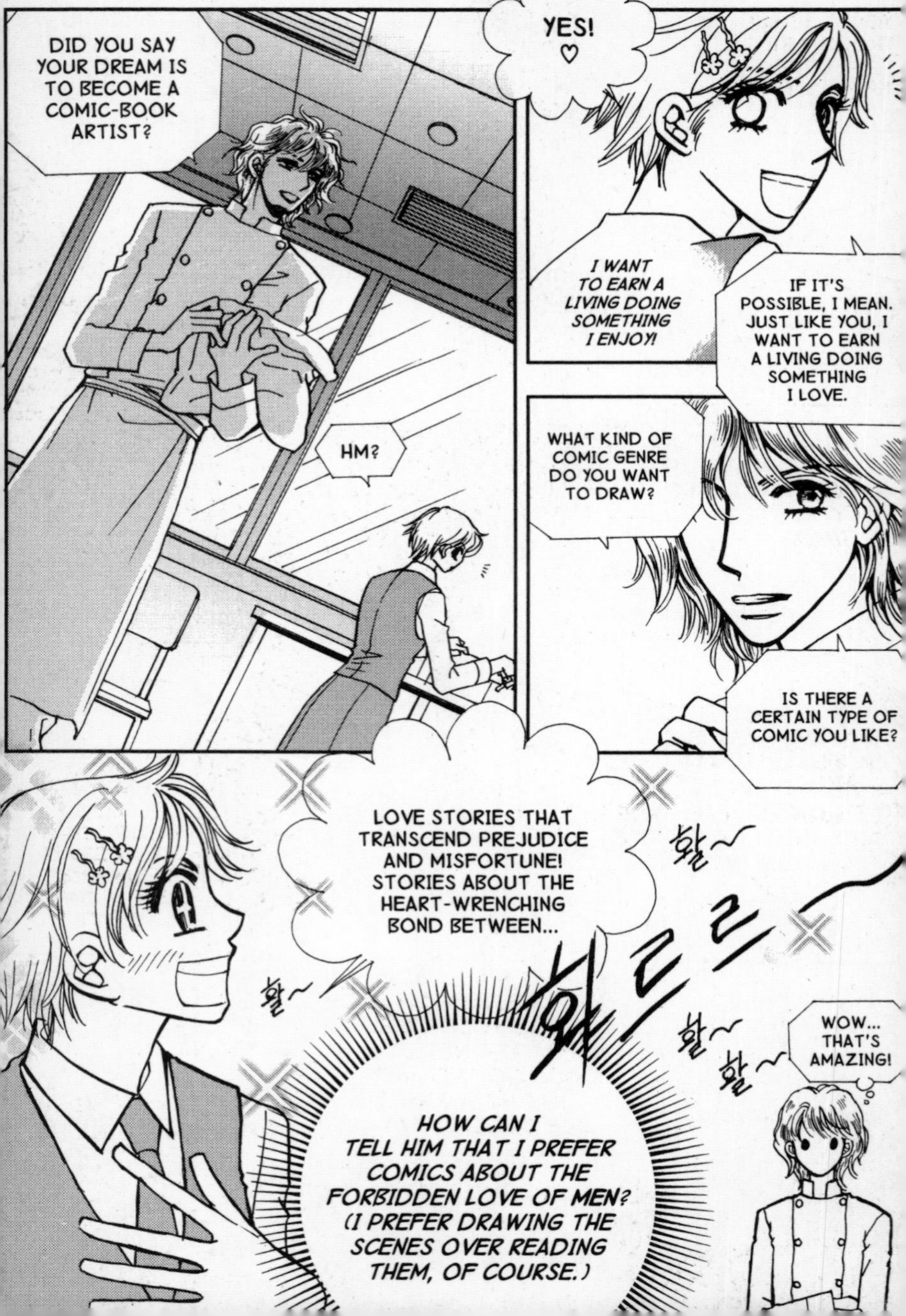
DID YOU SAY YOUR DREAM IS TO BECOME A COMIC-BOOK ARTIST?
HM?
YES! ♡
I WANT TO EARN A LIVING DOING SOMETHING I ENJOY!
IF IT'S POSSIBLE, I MEAN. JUST LIKE YOU, I WANT TO EARN A LIVING DOING SOMETHING I LOVE.
WHAT KIND OF COMIC GENRE DO YOU WANT TO DRAW?
IS THERE A CERTAIN TYPE OF COMIC YOU LIKE?
LOVE STORIES THAT TRANSCEND PREJUDICE AND MISFORTUNE! STORIES ABOUT THE HEART-WRENCHING BOND BETWEEN...
활~
활~
활~
활~
HOW CAN I TELL HIM THAT I PREFER COMICS ABOUT THE FORBIDDEN LOVE OF MEN? (I PREFER DRAWING THE SCENES OVER READING THEM, OF COURSE.)
WOW... THAT'S AMAZING!

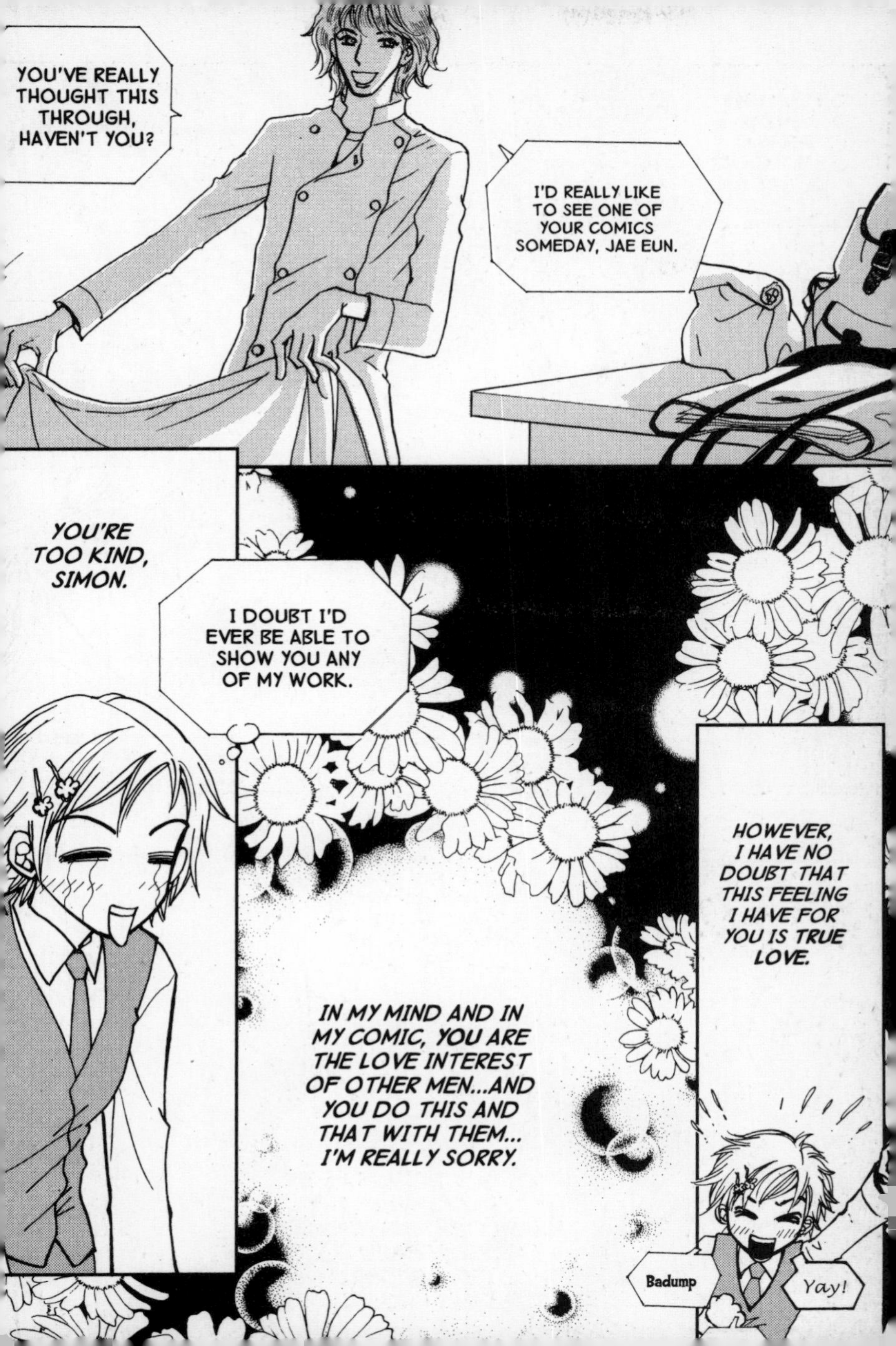
YOU'VE REALLY THOUGHT THIS THROUGH, HAVEN'T YOU?
I'D REALLY LIKE TO SEE ONE OF YOUR COMICS SOMEDAY, JAE EUN.
YOU'RE TOO KIND, SIMON.
I DOUBT I'D EVER BE ABLE TO SHOW YOU ANY OF MY WORK.
IN MY MIND AND IN MY COMIC, YOU ARE THE LOVE INTEREST OF OTHER MEN...AND YOU DO THIS AND THAT WITH THEM... I'M REALLY SORRY.
HOWEVER, I HAVE NO DOUBT THAT THIS FEELING I HAVE FOR YOU IS TRUE LOVE.
Badump
Yay!

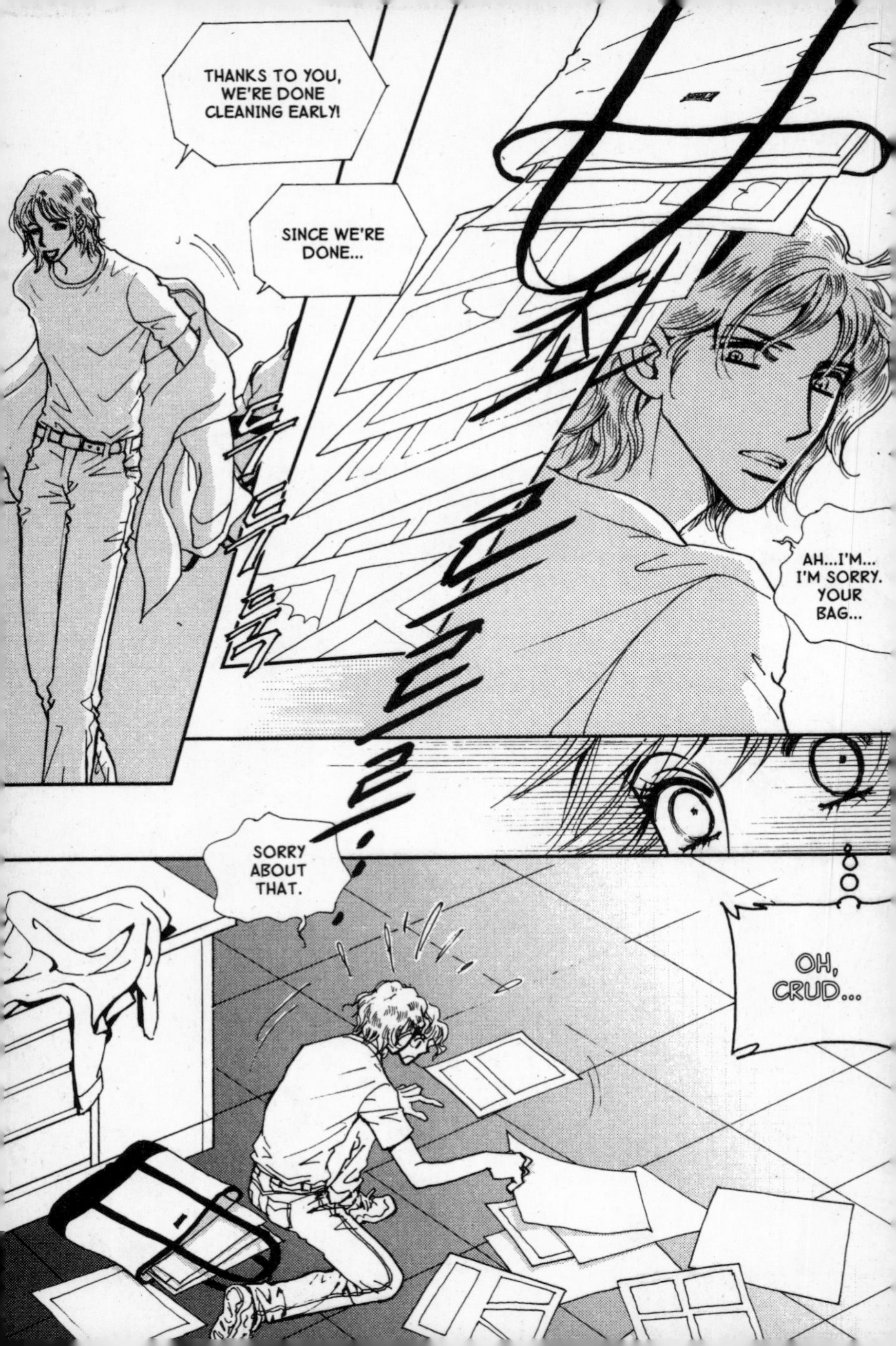
THANKS TO YOU, WE'RE DONE CLEANING EARLY!
SINCE WE'RE DONE...
AH...I'M... I'M SORRY. YOUR BAG...
SORRY ABOUT THAT.
OH, CRUD...

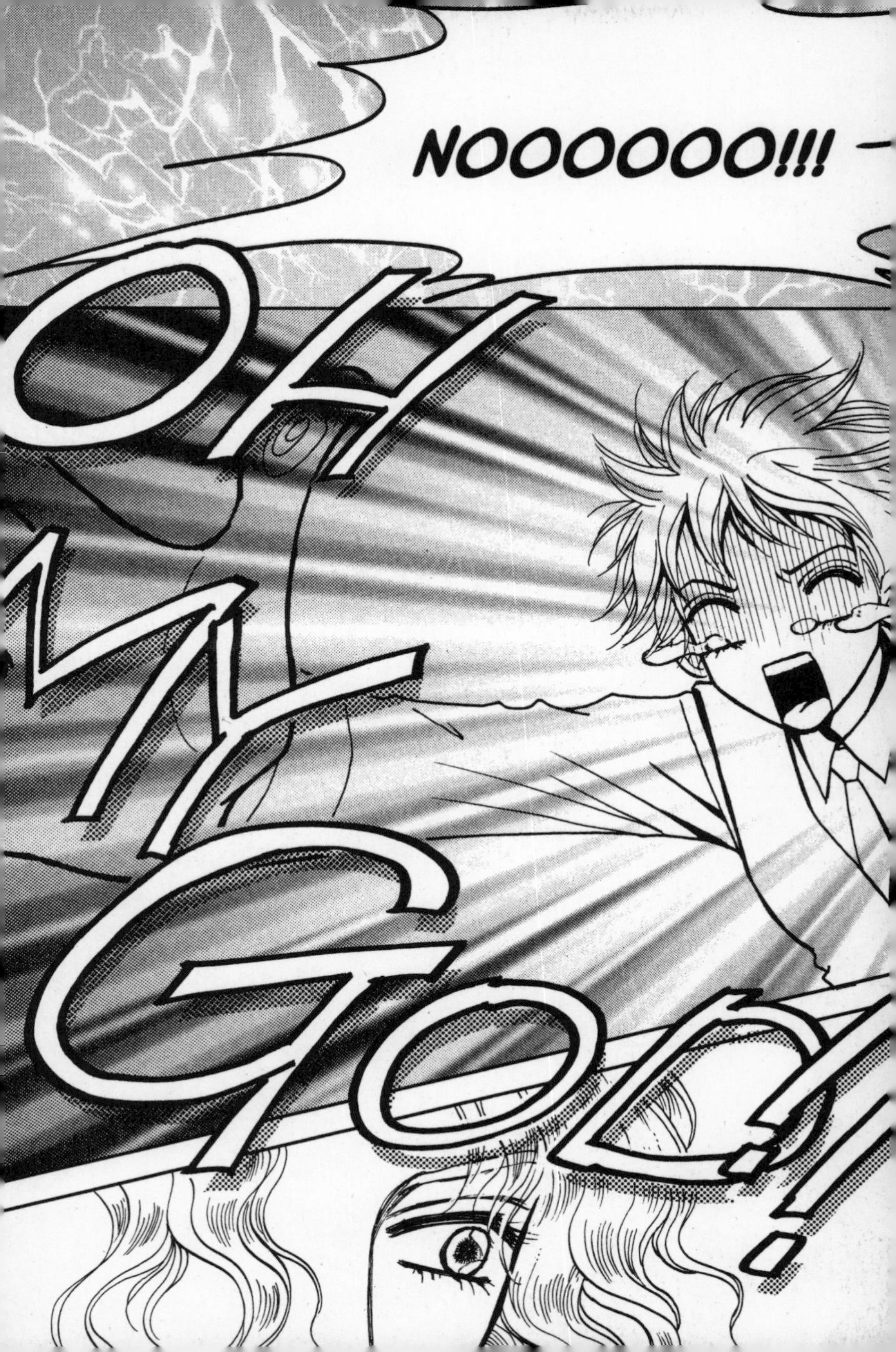
NOOOOOO!!!
OH MY GOD!!

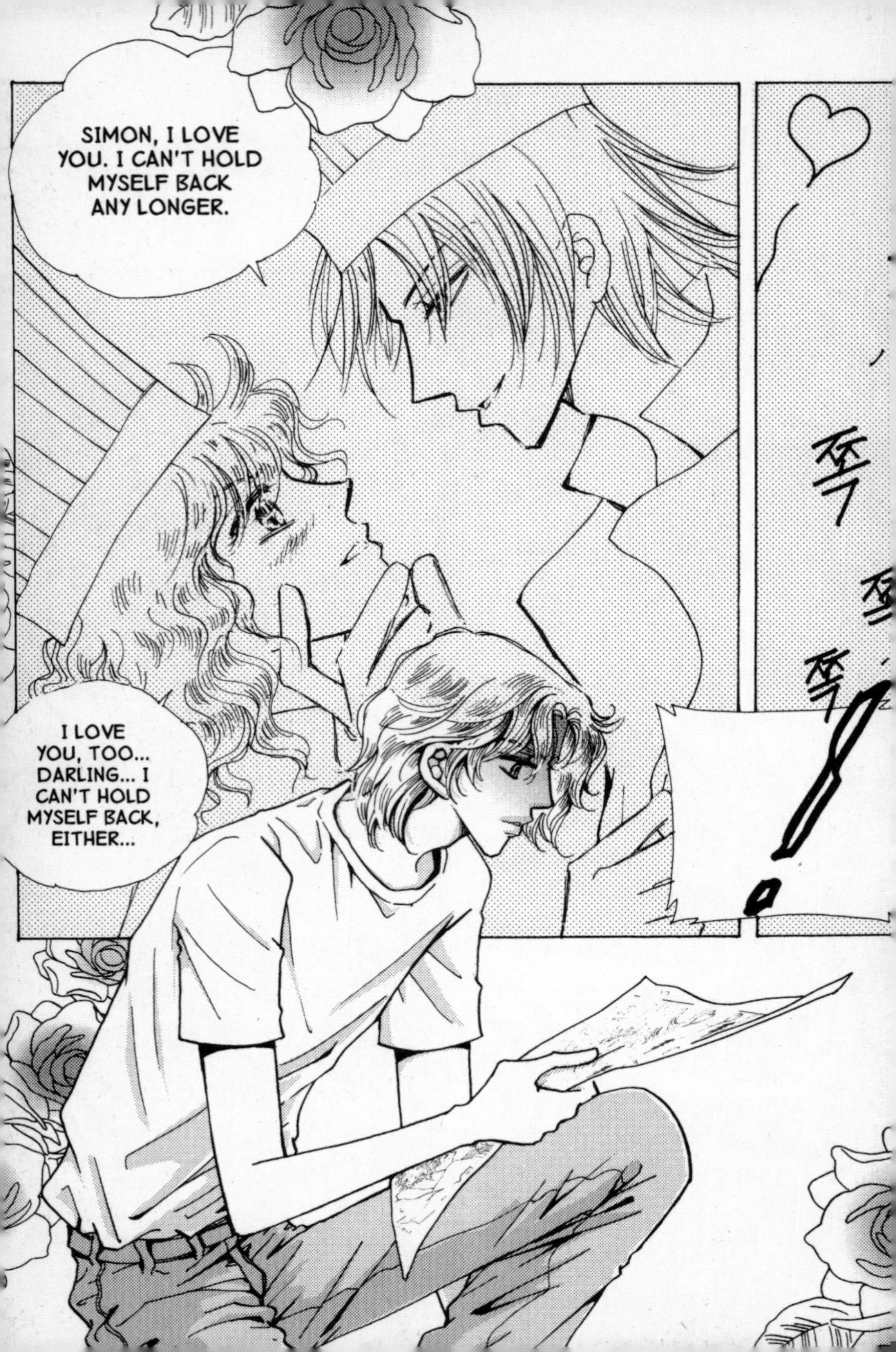
SIMON, I LOVE YOU. I CAN'T HOLD MYSELF BACK ANY LONGER.
I LOVE YOU, TOO... DARLING... I CAN'T HOLD MYSELF BACK, EITHER...

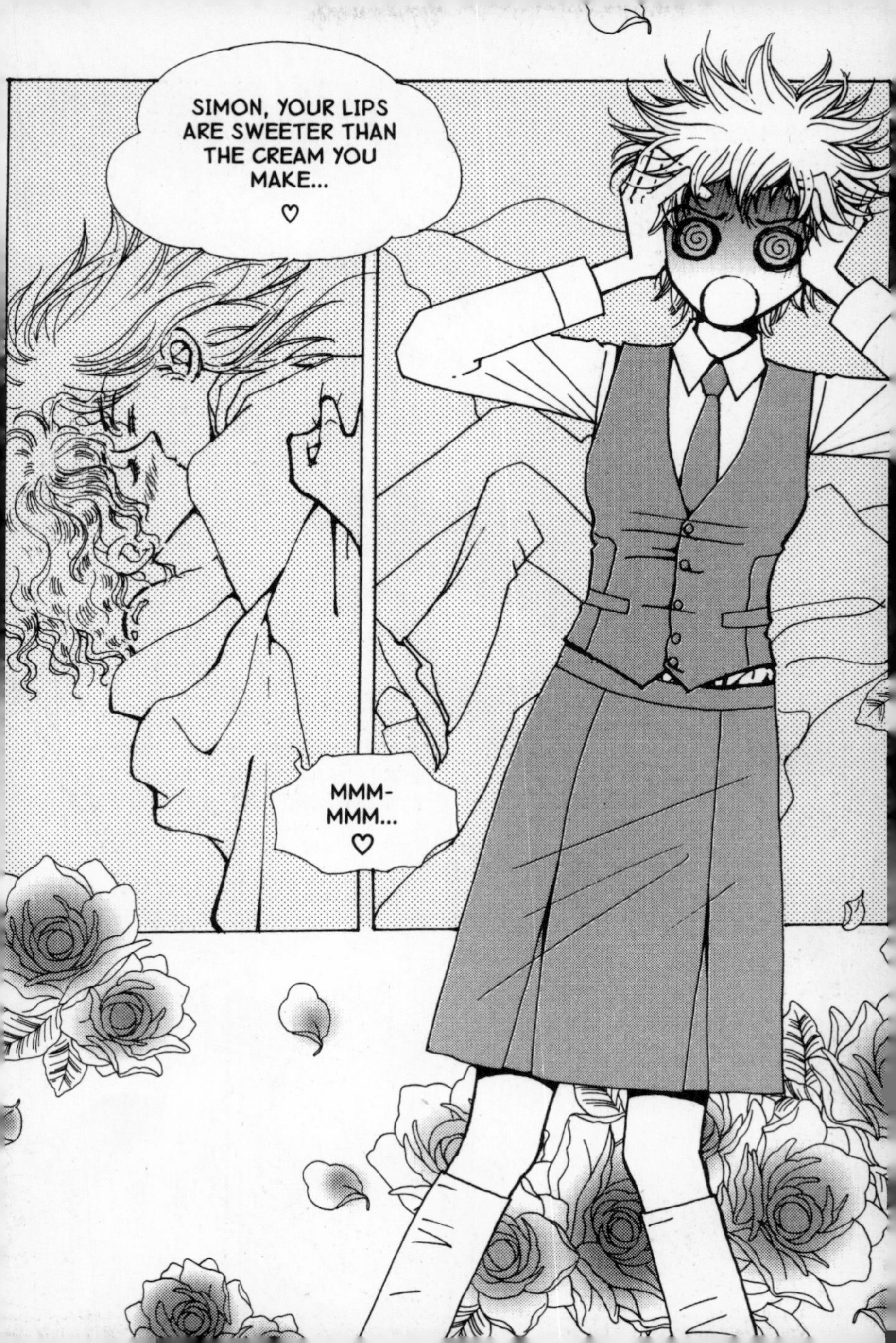
SIMON, YOUR LIPS ARE SWEETER THAN THE CREAM YOU MAKE... ♡
MMM-MMM... ♡

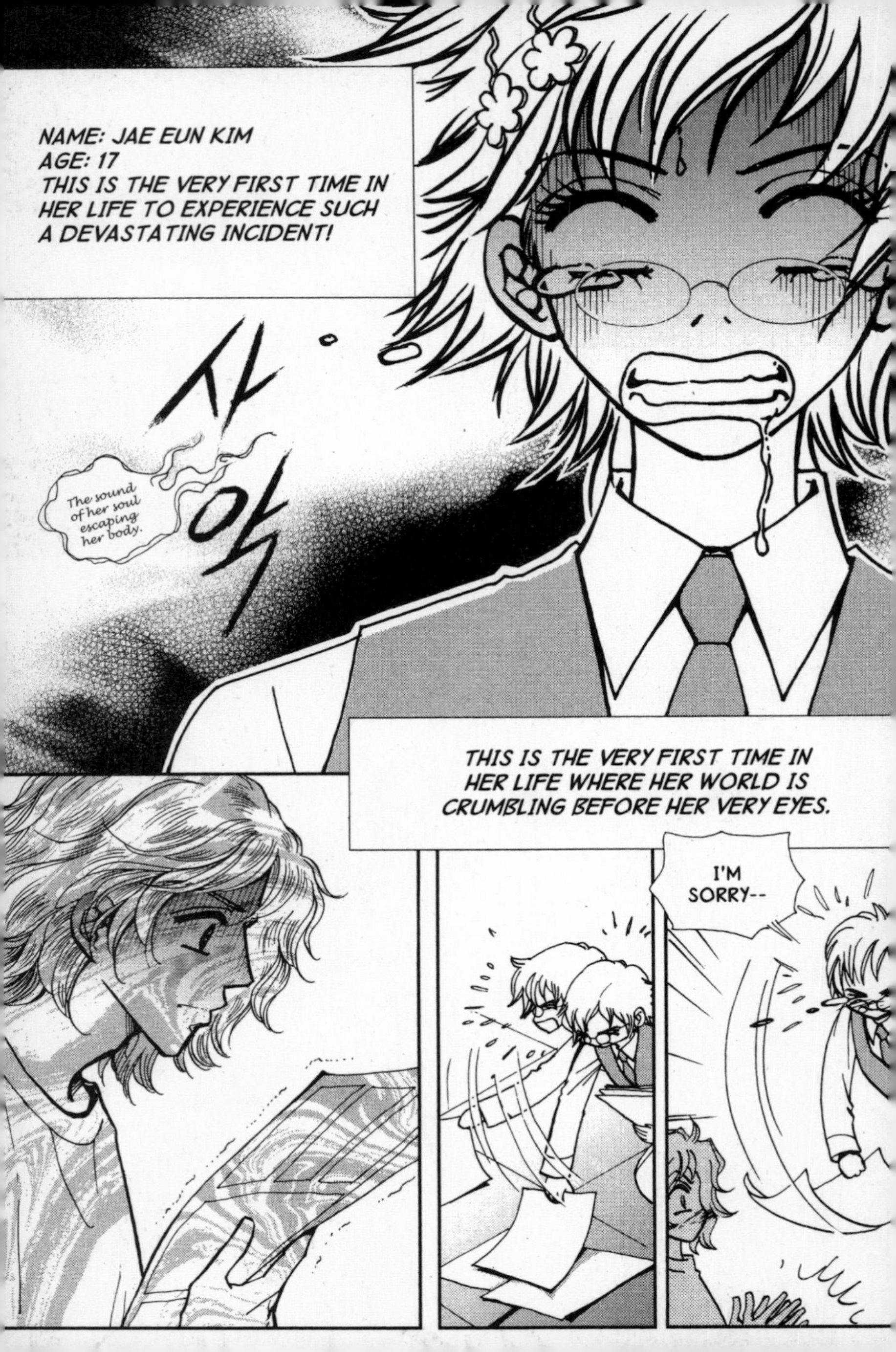
NAME: JAE EUN KIM
AGE: 17
THIS IS THE VERY FIRST TIME IN HER LIFE TO EXPERIENCE SUCH A DEVASTATING INCIDENT!
The sound of her soul escaping her body.
THIS IS THE VERY FIRST TIME IN HER LIFE WHERE HER WORLD IS CRUMBLING BEFORE HER VERY EYES.
I'M SORRY--

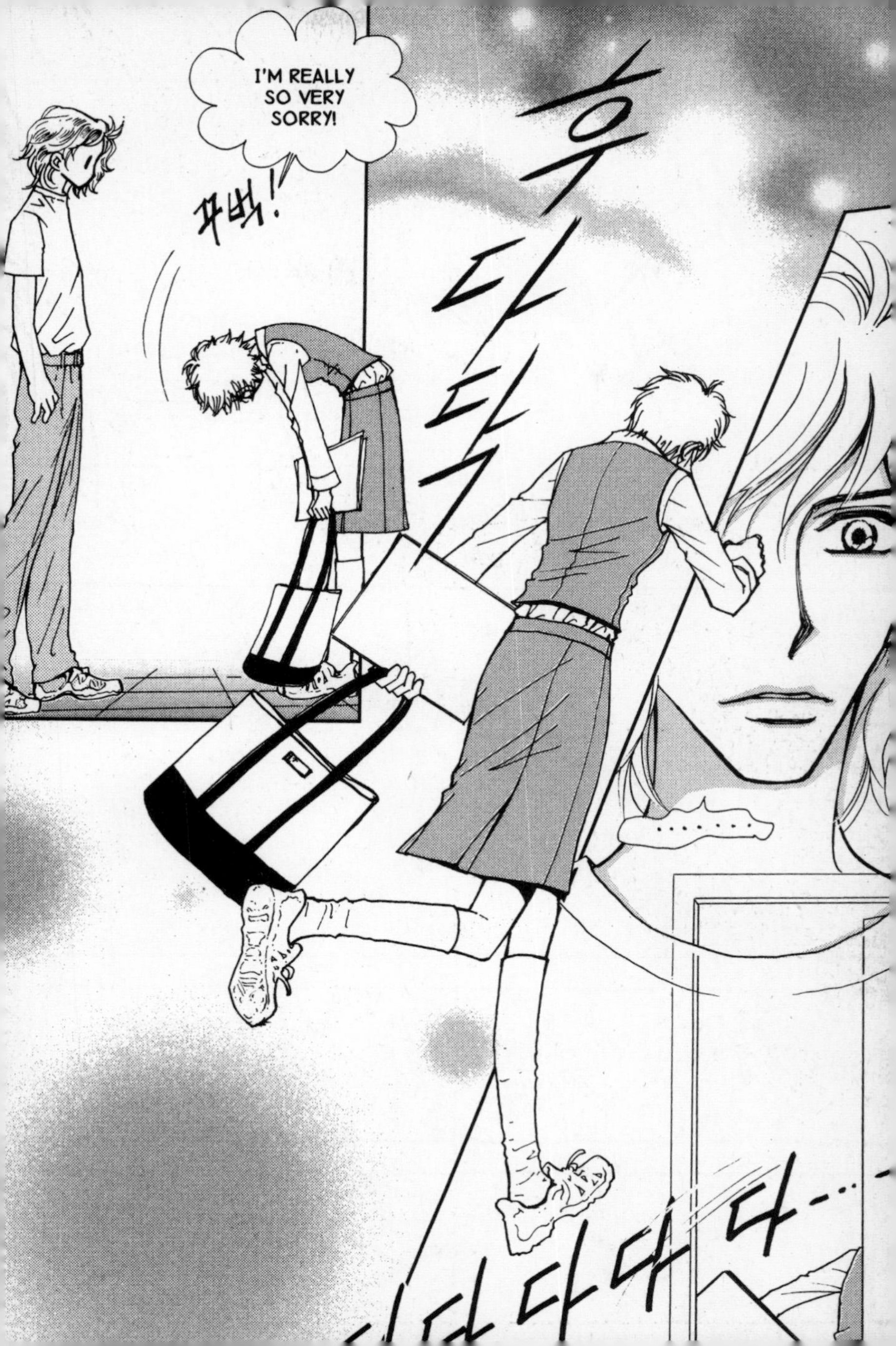
I'M REALLY SO VERY SORRY!
꾸벅!
후다닥

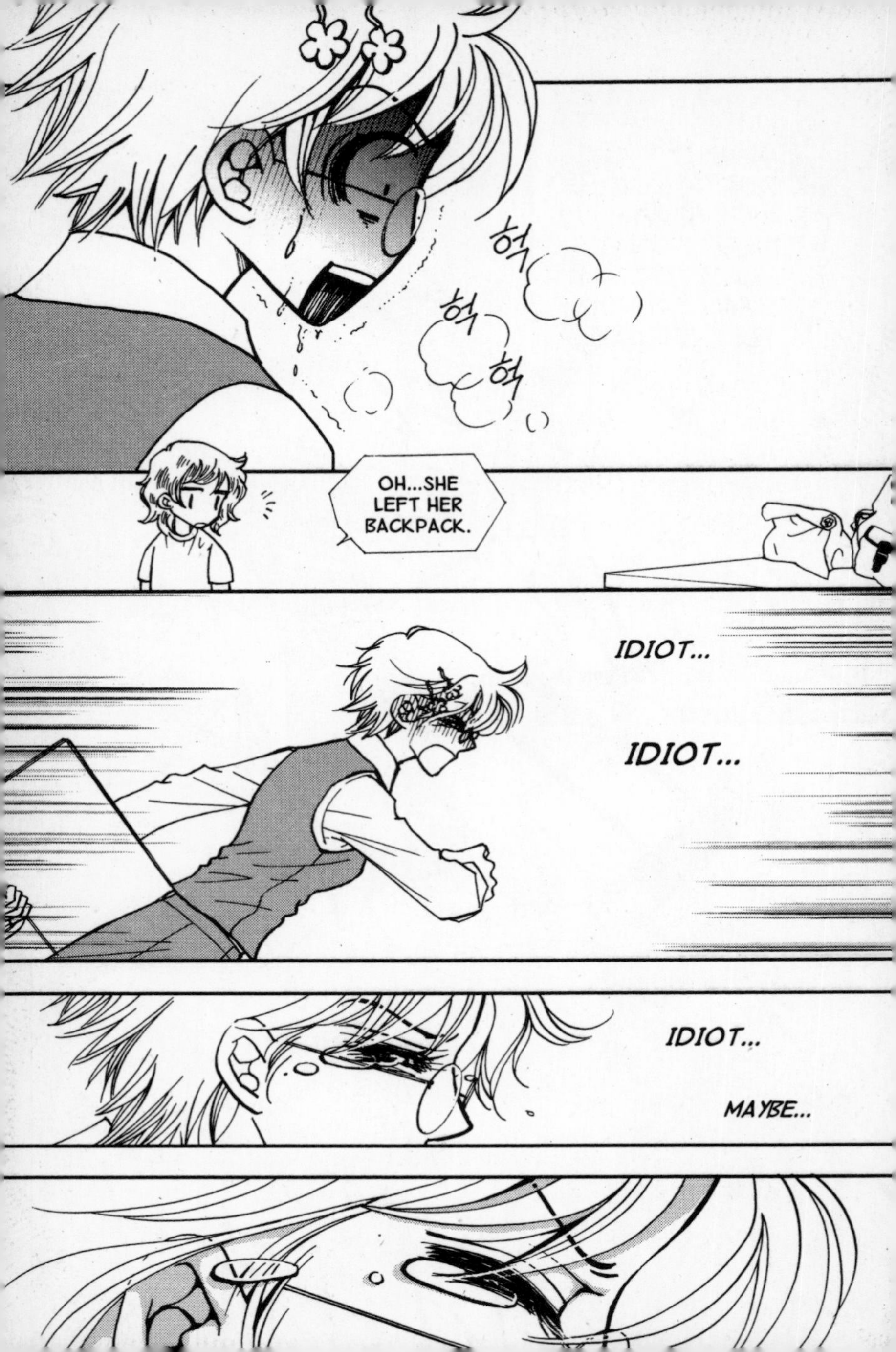
헉
헉
헉
OH...SHE LEFT HER BACKPACK.
IDIOT...
IDIOT...
IDIOT...
MAYBE...

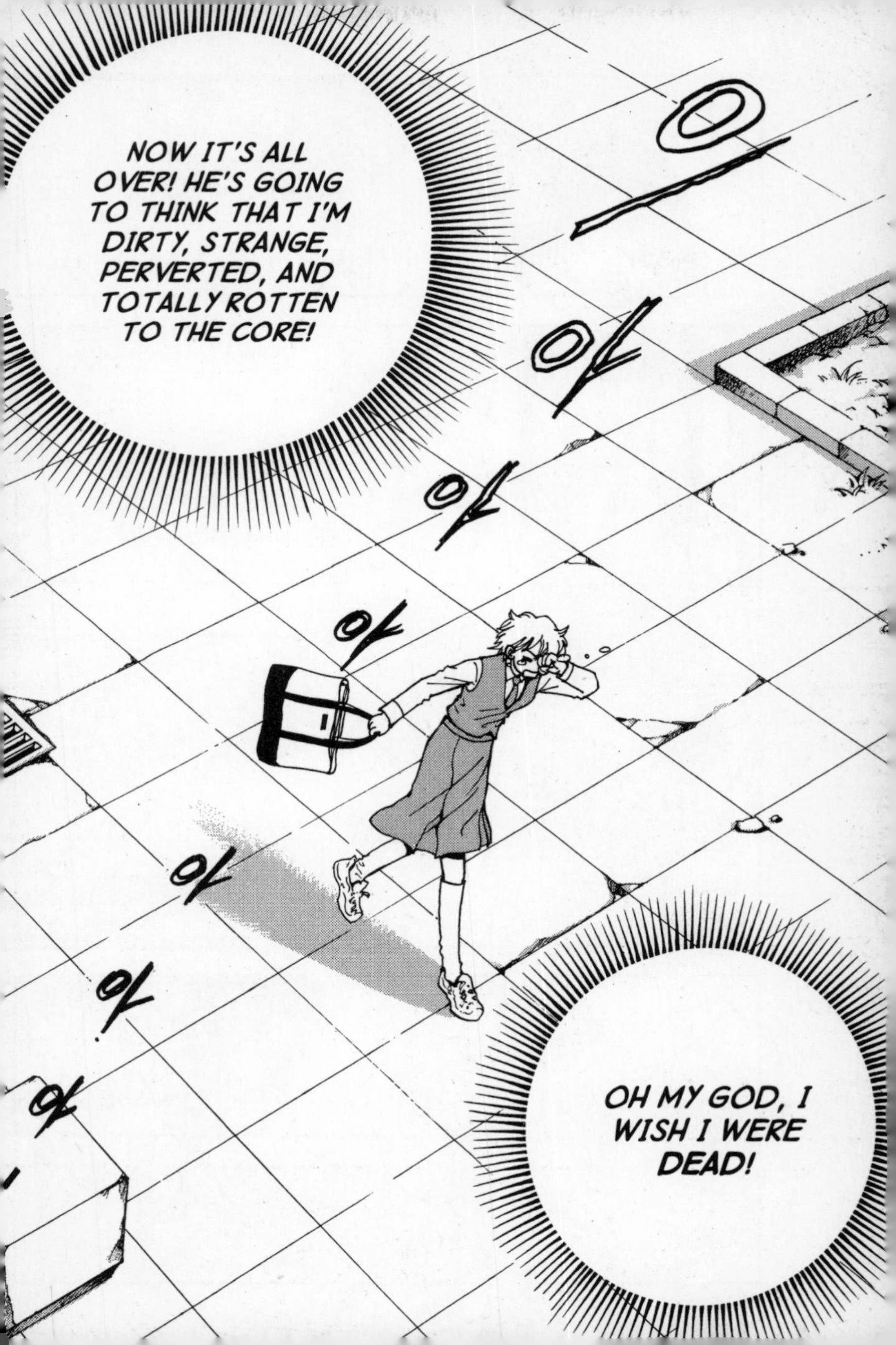
NOW IT'S ALL OVER! HE'S GOING TO THINK THAT I'M DIRTY, STRANGE, PERVERTED, AND TOTALLY ROTTEN TO THE CORE!
OH MY GOD, I WISH I WERE DEAD!

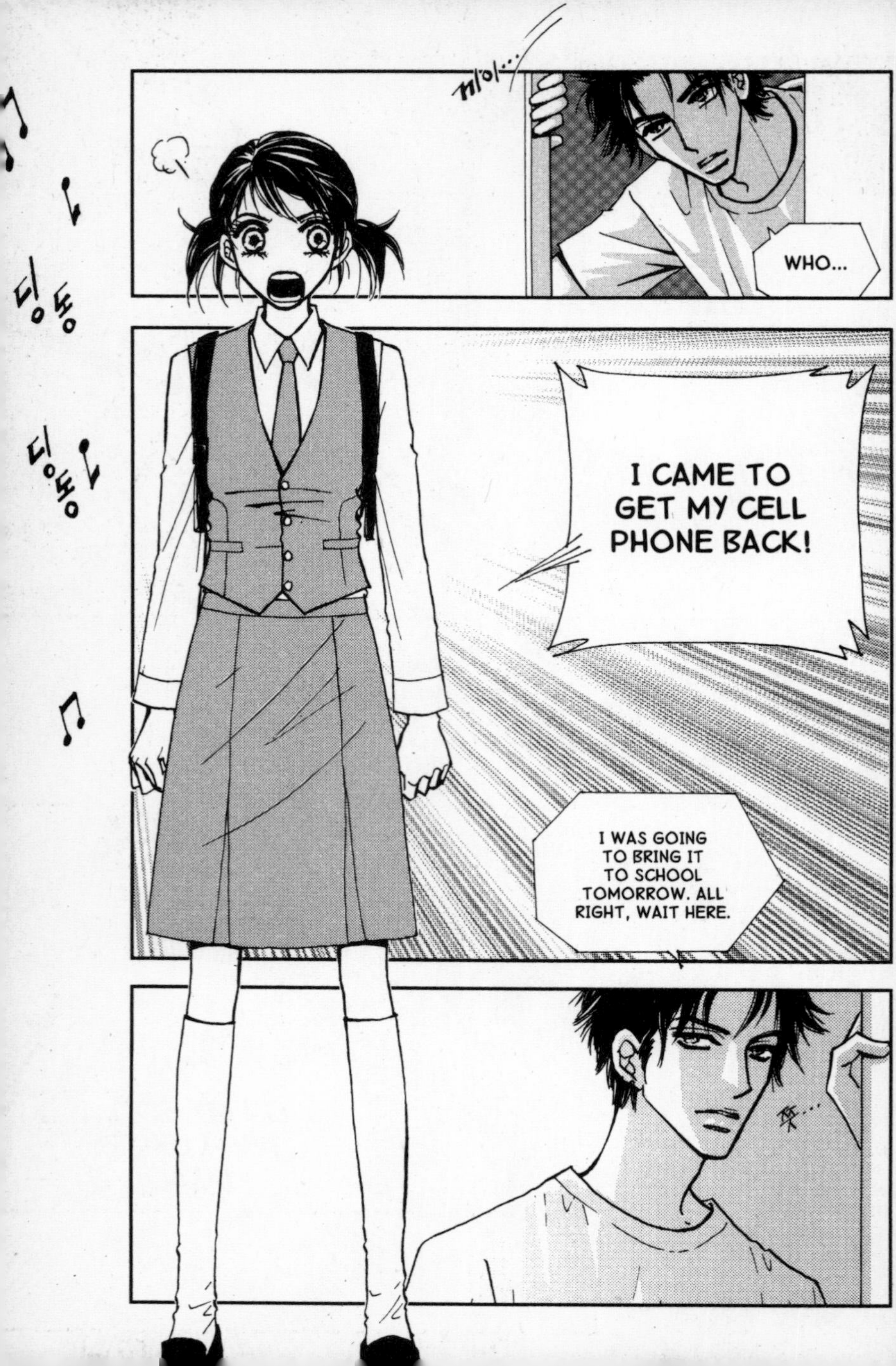
딩동
딩동
WHO...
I CAME TO GET MY CELL PHONE BACK!
I WAS GOING TO BRING IT TO SCHOOL TOMORROW. ALL RIGHT, WAIT HERE.

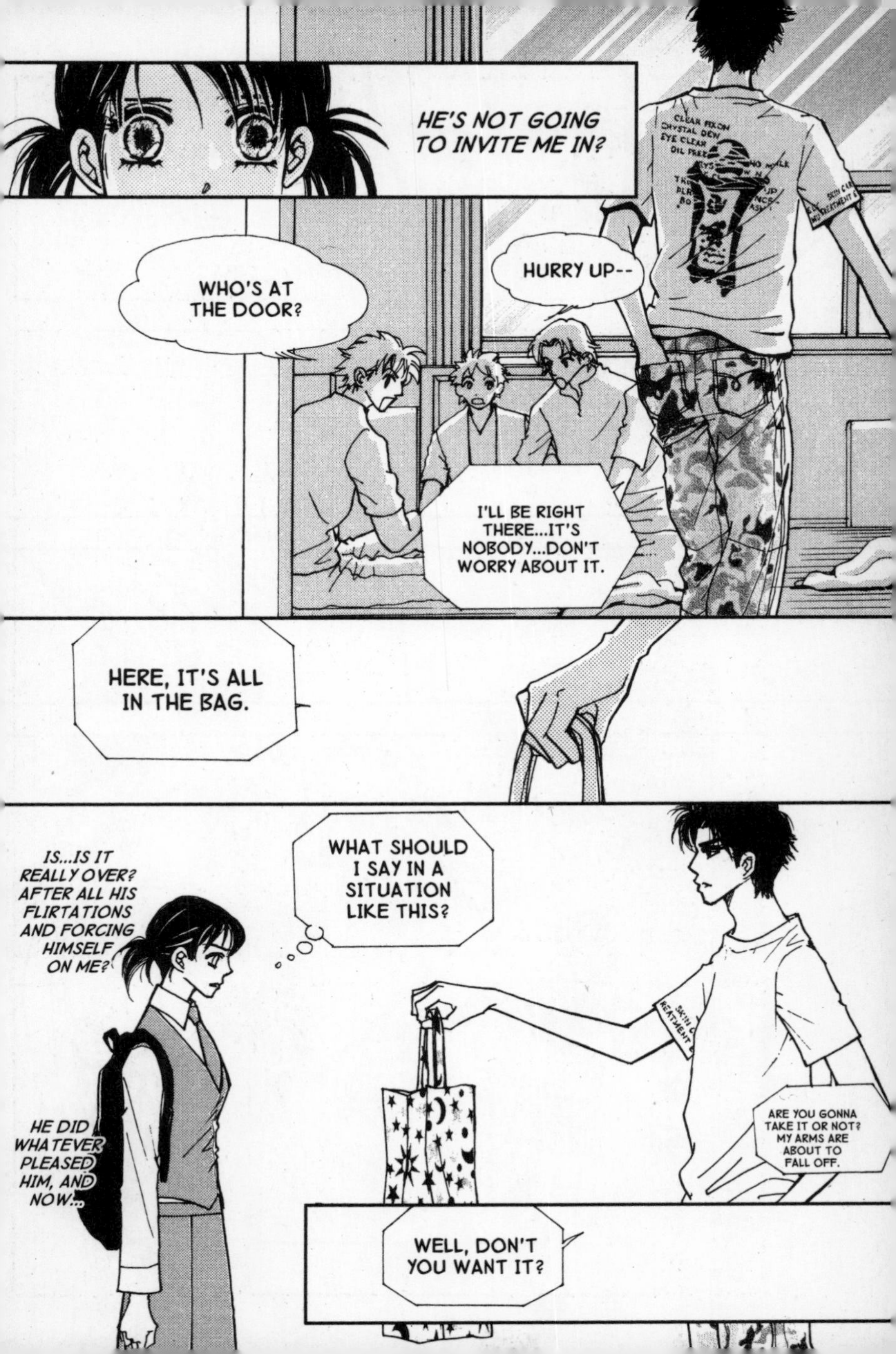
HE'S NOT GOING TO INVITE ME IN?
HURRY UP--
WHO'S AT THE DOOR?
I'LL BE RIGHT THERE...IT'S NOBODY...DON'T WORRY ABOUT IT.
HERE, IT'S ALL IN THE BAG.
WHAT SHOULD I SAY IN A SITUATION LIKE THIS?
IS...IS IT REALLY OVER? AFTER ALL HIS FLIRTATIONS AND FORCING HIMSELF ON ME?
ARE YOU GONNA TAKE IT OR NOT? MY ARMS ARE ABOUT TO FALL OFF.
HE DID WHATEVER PLEASED HIM, AND NOW...
WELL, DON'T YOU WANT IT?

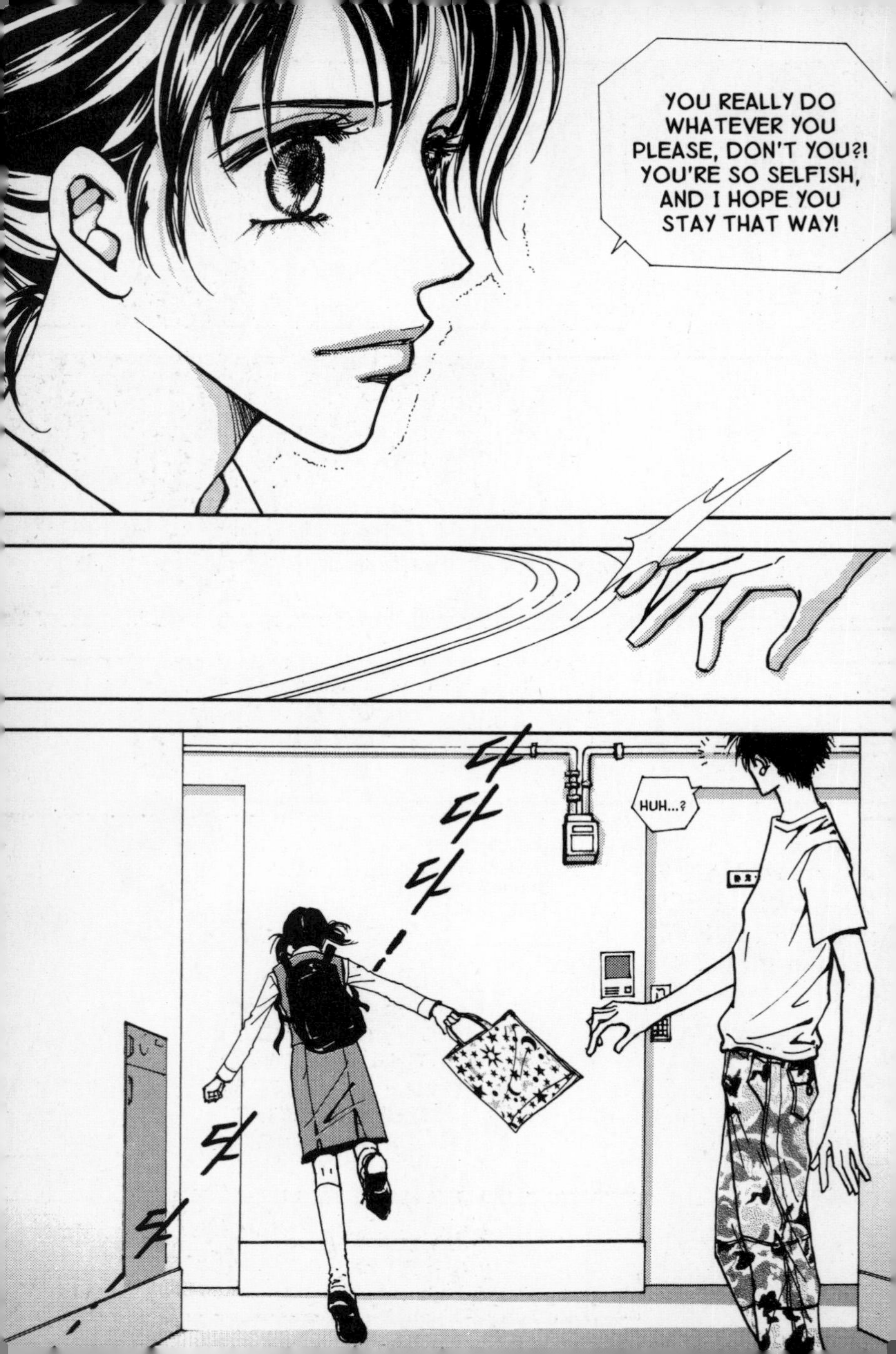
YOU REALLY DO WHATEVER YOU PLEASE, DON'T YOU?! YOU'RE SO SELFISH, AND I HOPE YOU STAY THAT WAY!
다다다
HUH...?
다 다

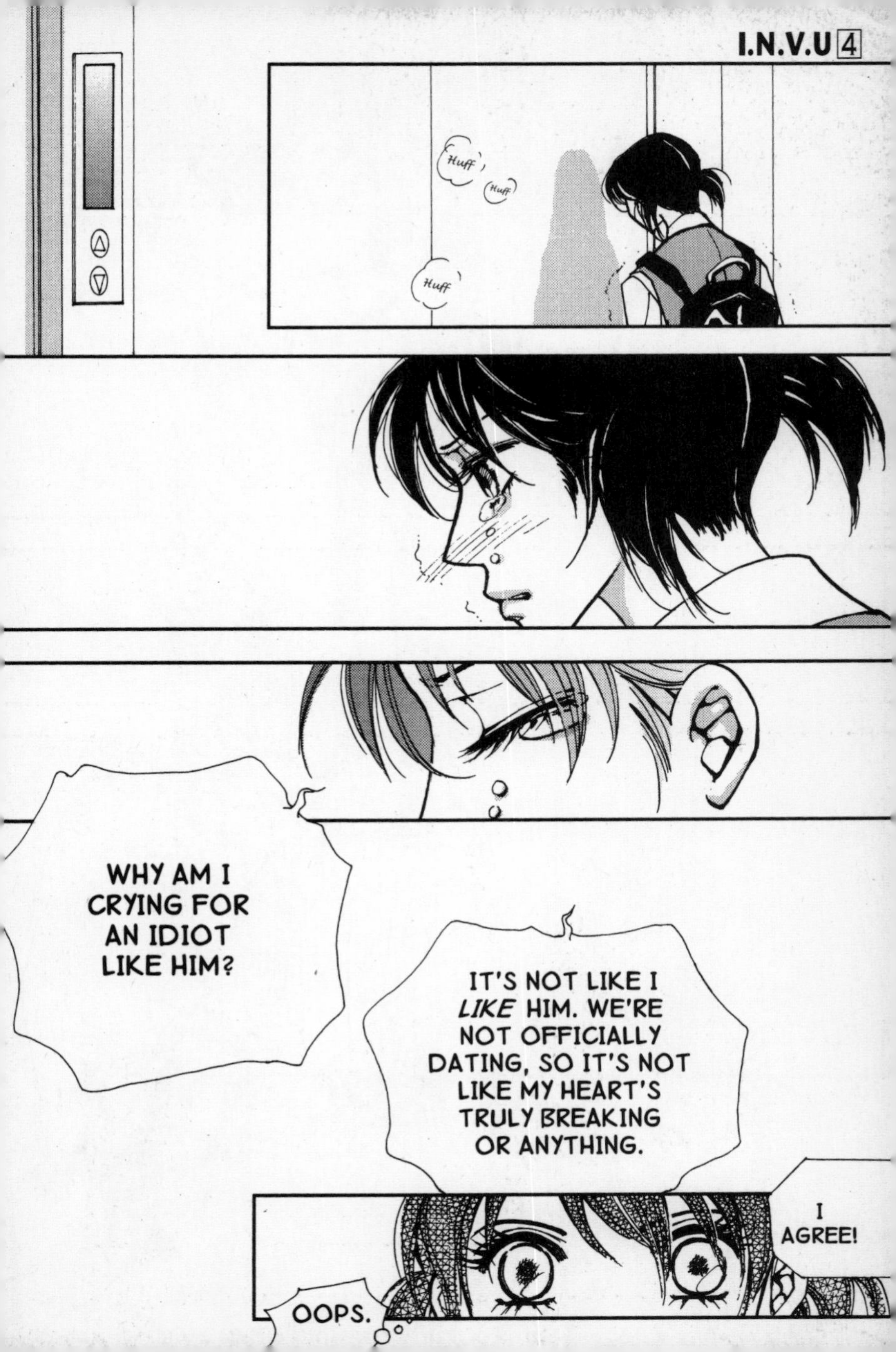
Huff
Huff
Huff
WHY AM I CRYING FOR AN IDIOT LIKE HIM?
IT'S NOT LIKE I *LIKE* HIM. WE'RE NOT OFFICIALLY DATING, SO IT'S NOT LIKE MY HEART'S TRULY BREAKING OR ANYTHING.
I AGREE!
OOPS.

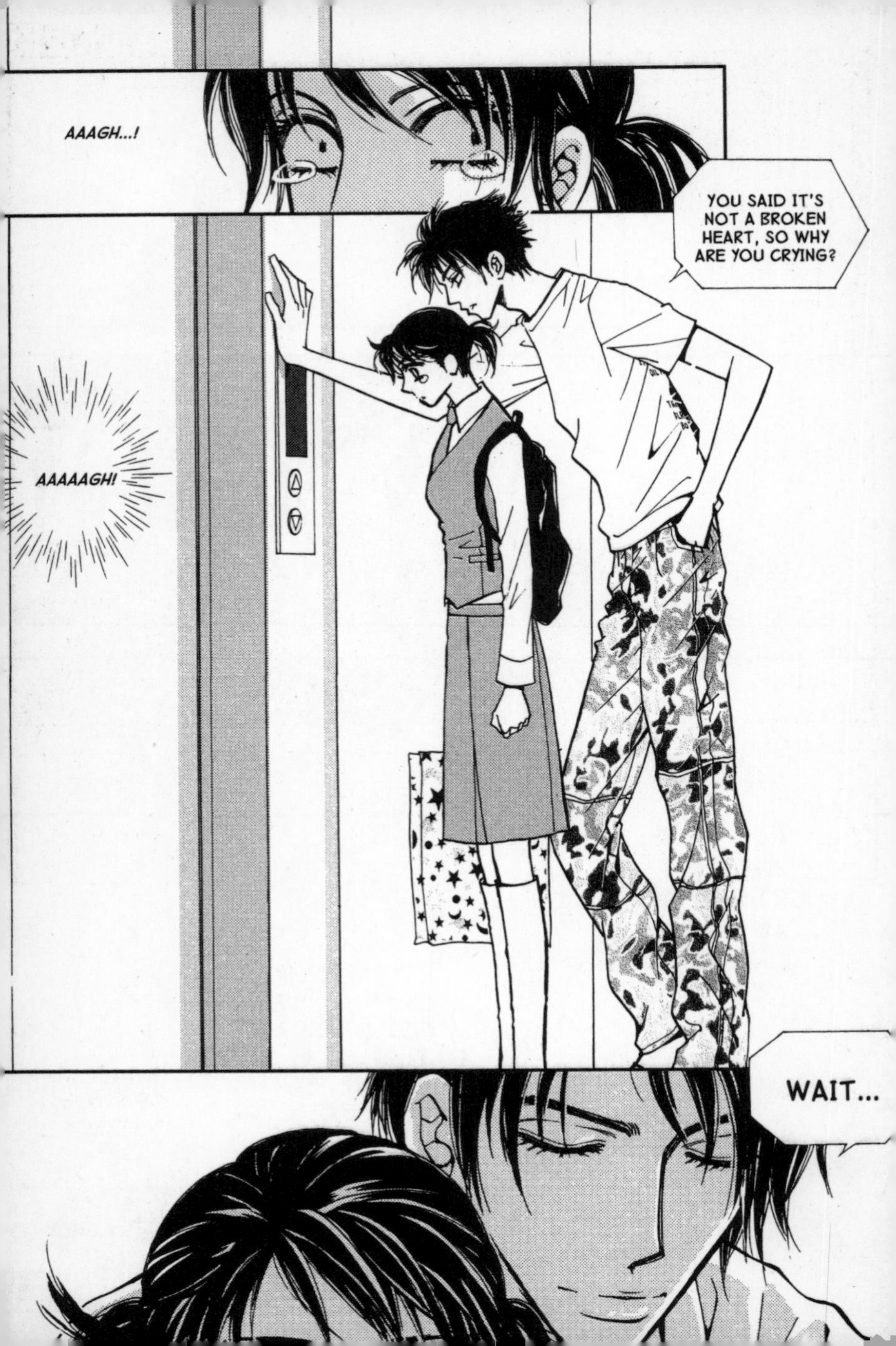
AAAGH...!
YOU SAID IT'S NOT A BROKEN HEART, SO WHY ARE YOU CRYING?
AAAAAGH!
WAIT...

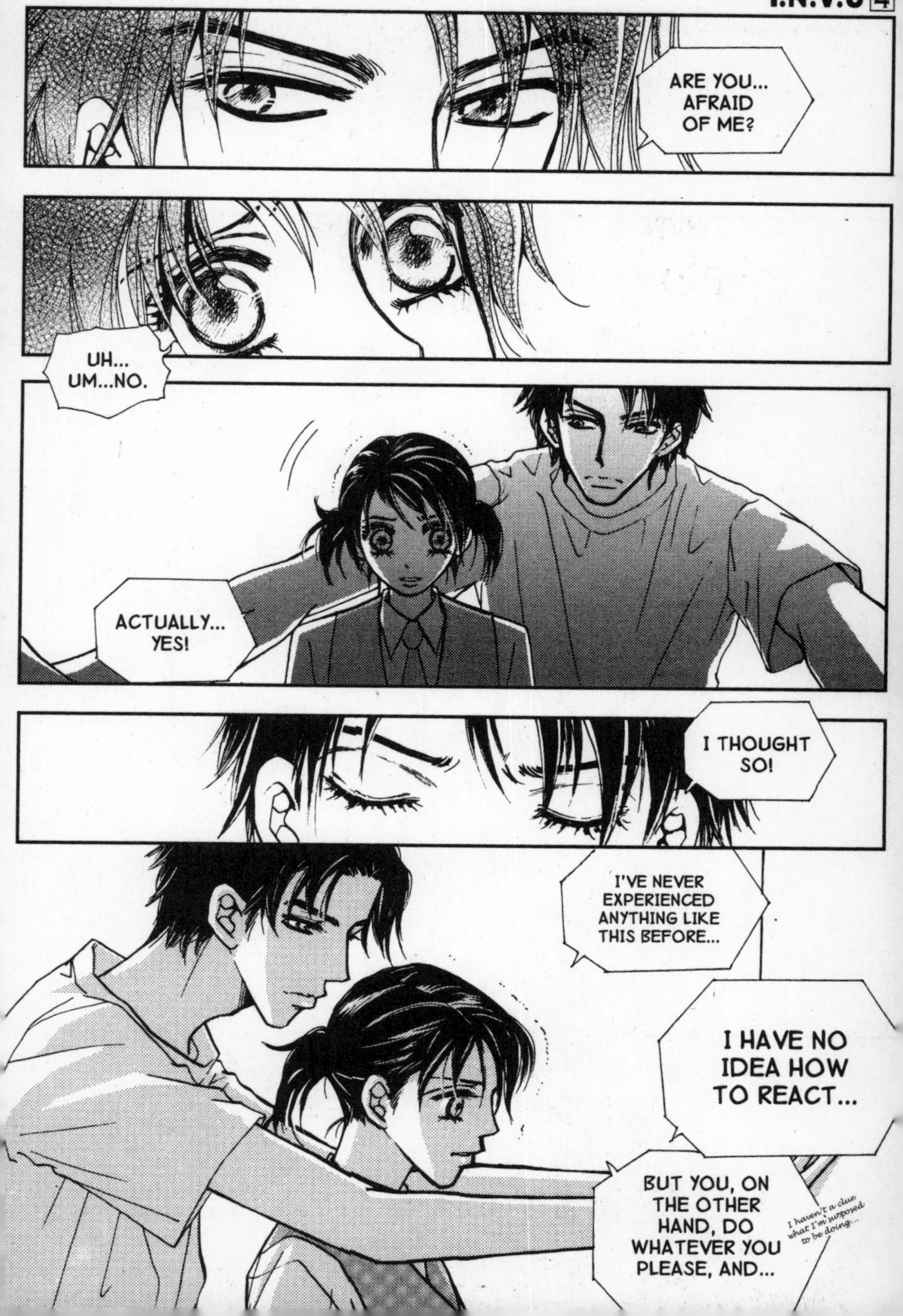
ARE YOU... AFRAID OF ME?
UH... UM...NO.
ACTUALLY... YES!
I THOUGHT SO!
I'VE NEVER EXPERIENCED ANYTHING LIKE THIS BEFORE...
I HAVE NO IDEA HOW TO REACT...
BUT YOU, ON THE OTHER HAND, DO WHATEVER YOU PLEASE, AND...
I haven't a clue what I'm supposed to be doing...

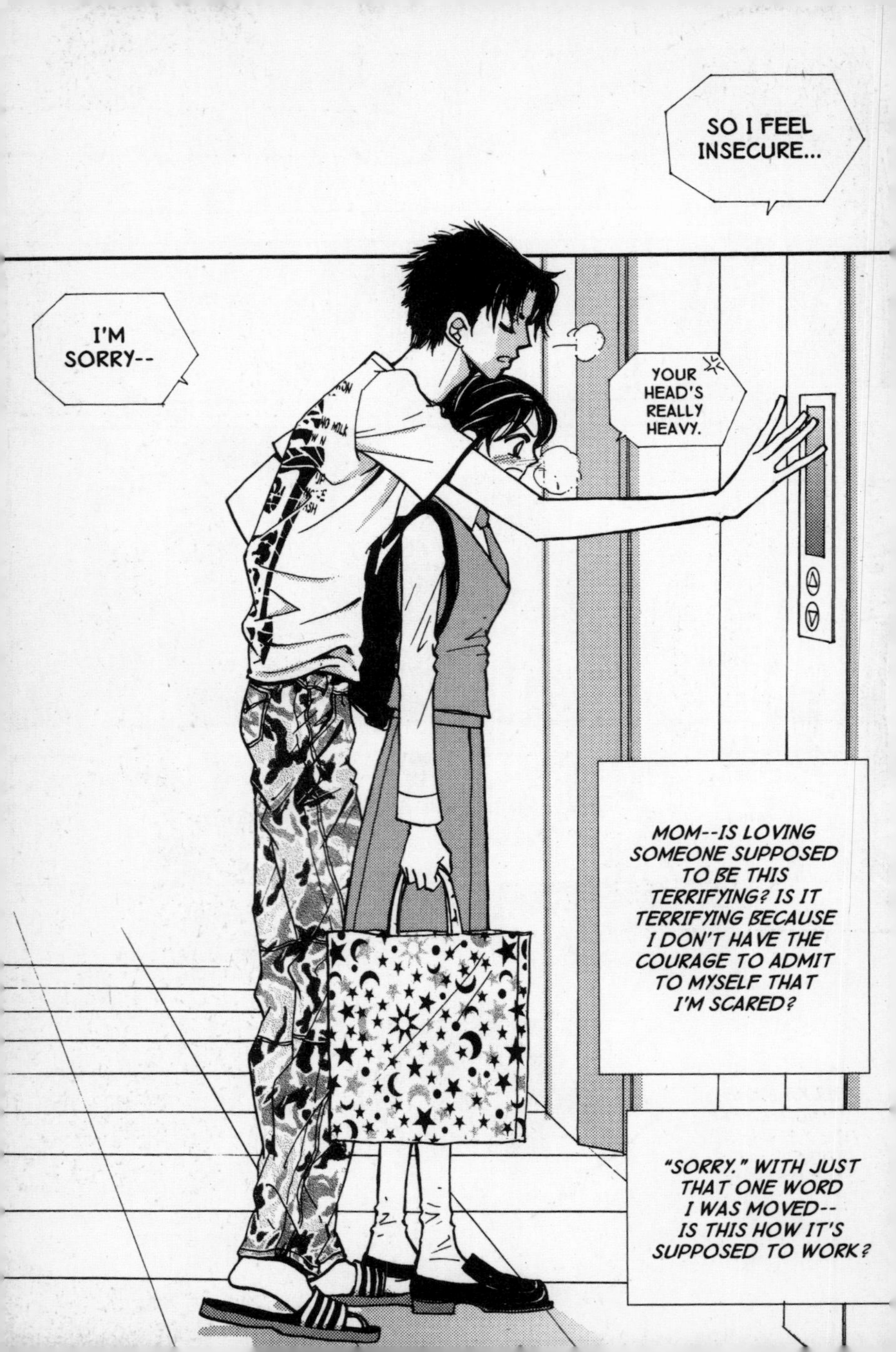
SO I FEEL INSECURE...
I'M SORRY--
YOUR HEAD'S REALLY HEAVY.
MOM--IS LOVING SOMEONE SUPPOSED TO BE THIS TERRIFYING? IS IT TERRIFYING BECAUSE I DON'T HAVE THE COURAGE TO ADMIT TO MYSELF THAT I'M SCARED?
"SORRY." WITH JUST THAT ONE WORD I WAS MOVED-- IS THIS HOW IT'S SUPPOSED TO WORK?

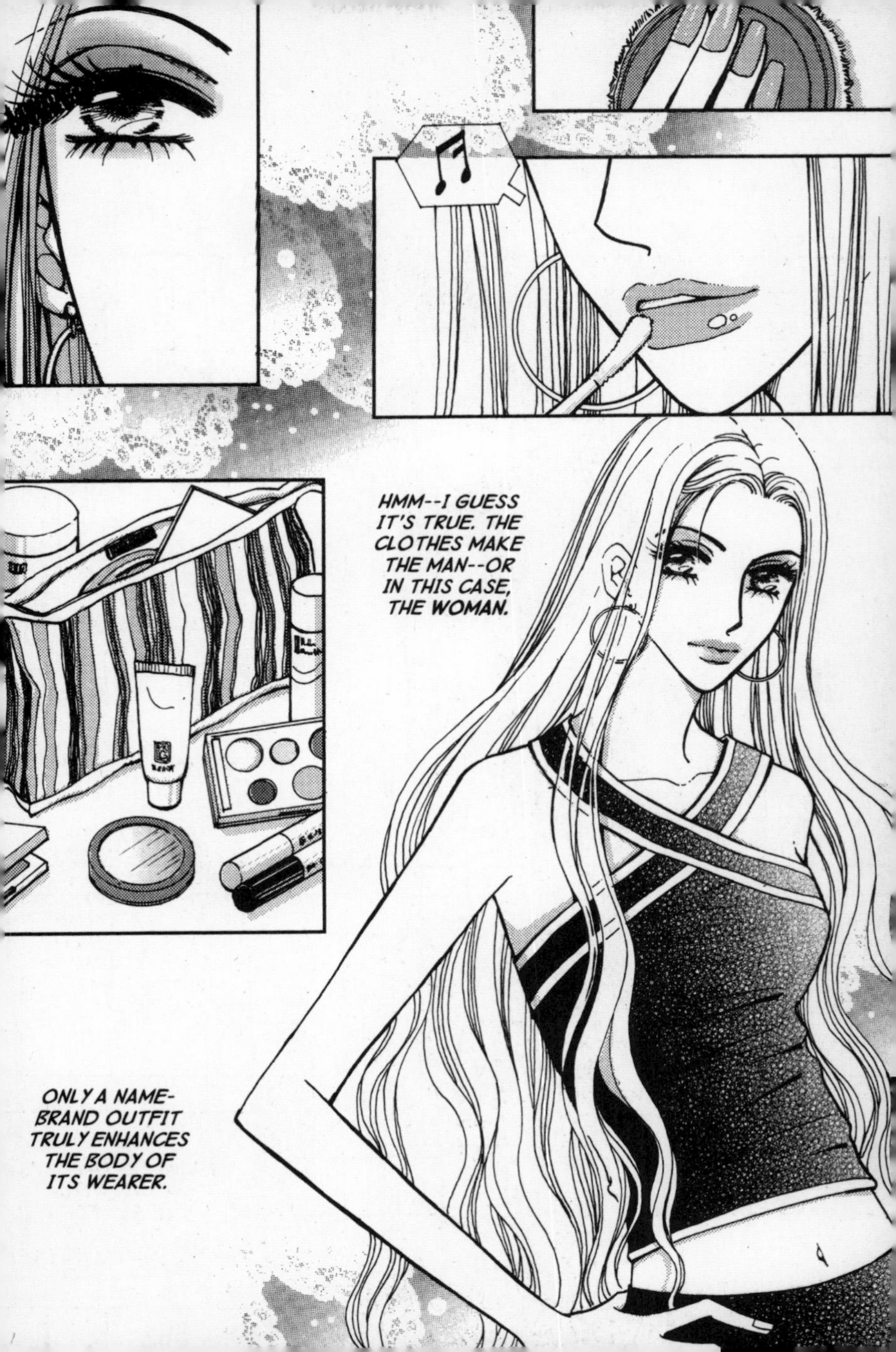
HMM--I GUESS IT'S TRUE. THE CLOTHES MAKE THE MAN--OR IN THIS CASE, THE WOMAN.
ONLY A NAME-BRAND OUTFIT TRULY ENHANCES THE BODY OF ITS WEARER.

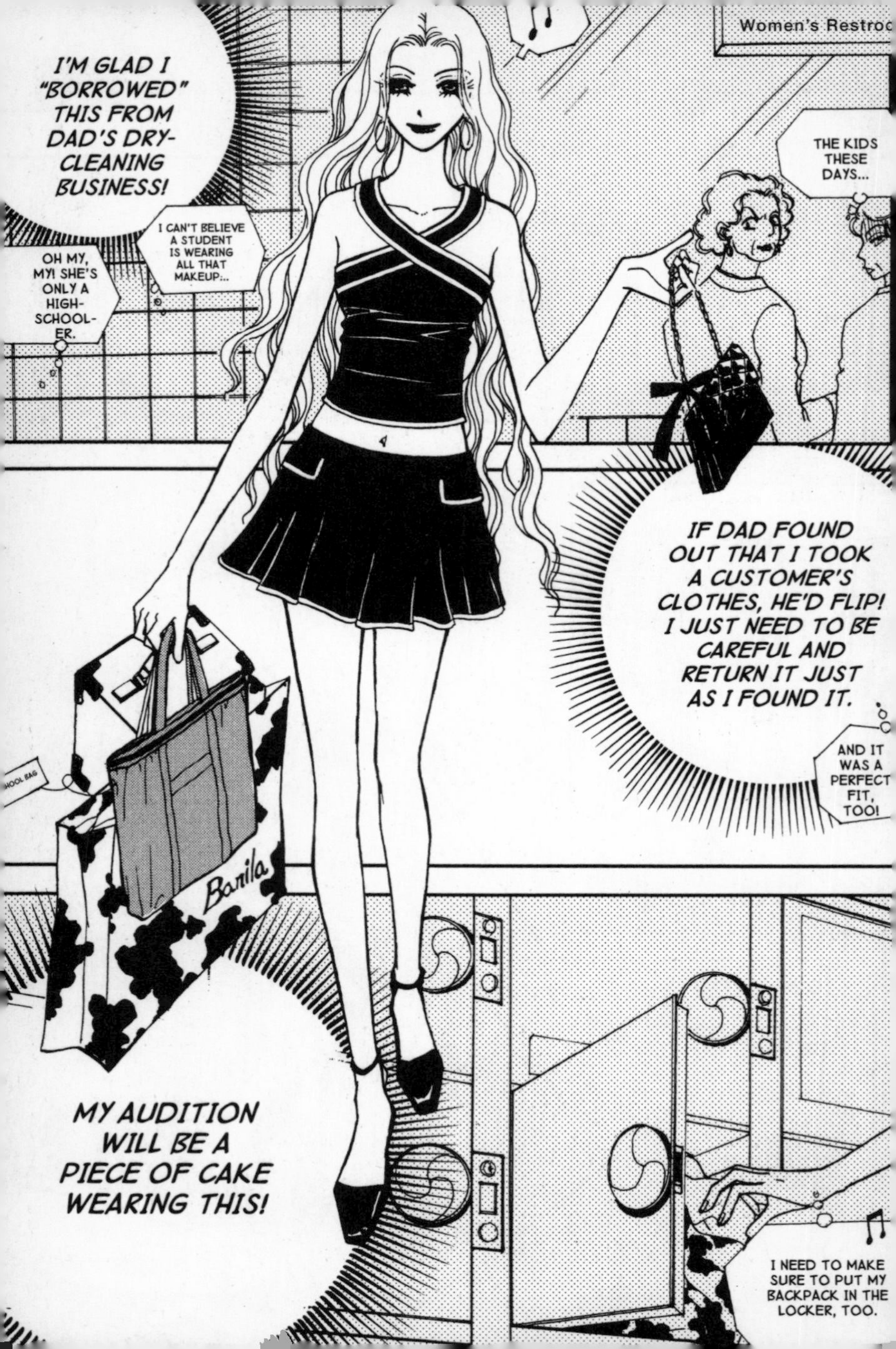
Women's Restroc
THE KIDS THESE DAYS...
I CAN'T BELIEVE A STUDENT IS WEARING ALL THAT MAKEUP...
OH MY, MY! SHE'S ONLY A HIGH-SCHOOL-ER.
I'M GLAD I "BORROWED" THIS FROM DAD'S DRY-CLEANING BUSINESS!
IF DAD FOUND OUT THAT I TOOK A CUSTOMER'S CLOTHES, HE'D FLIP! I JUST NEED TO BE CAREFUL AND RETURN IT JUST AS I FOUND IT.
AND IT WAS A PERFECT FIT, TOO!
Barila
I NEED TO MAKE SURE TO PUT MY BACKPACK IN THE LOCKER, TOO.
MY AUDITION WILL BE A PIECE OF CAKE WEARING THIS!

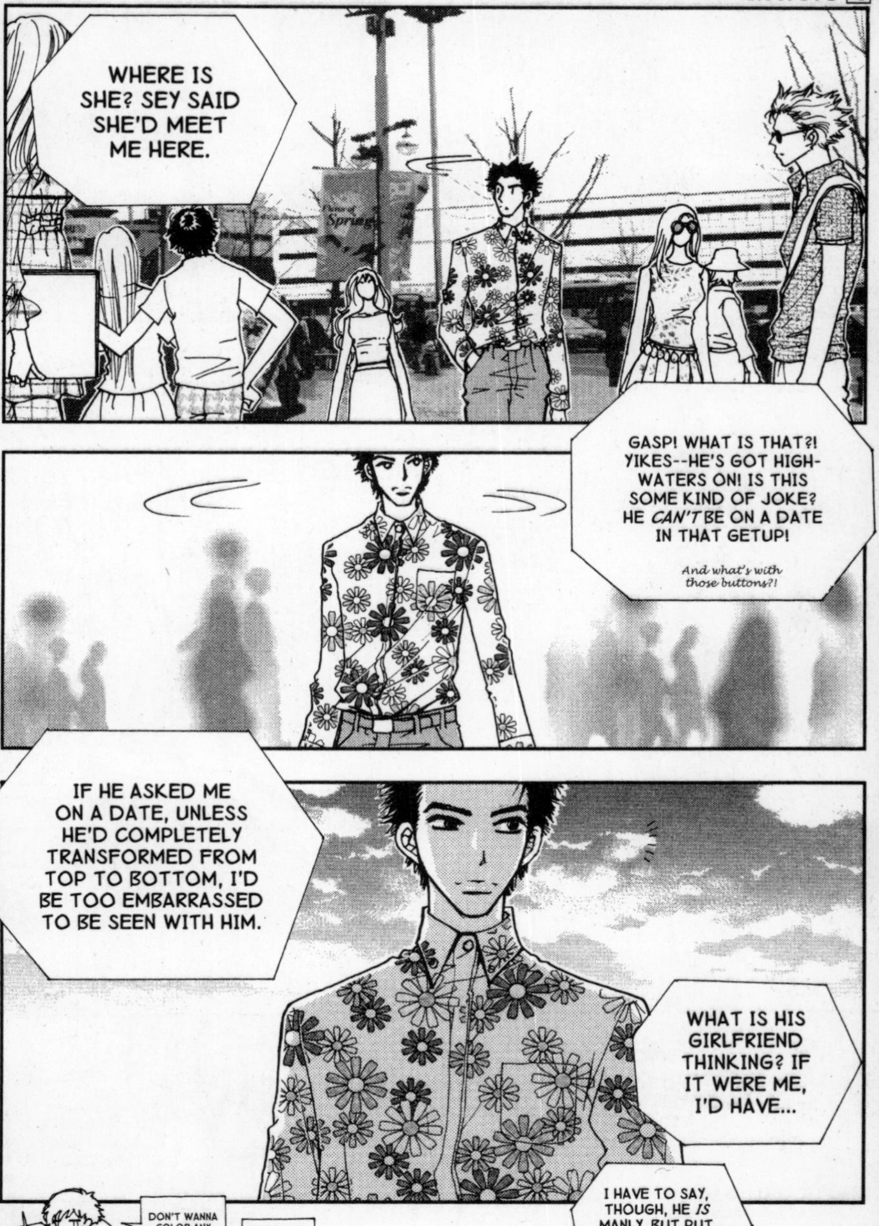
WHERE IS SHE? SEY SAID SHE'D MEET ME HERE.
GASP! WHAT IS THAT?! YIKES--HE'S GOT HIGH-WATERS ON! IS THIS SOME KIND OF JOKE? HE *CAN'T* BE ON A DATE IN THAT GETUP!
And what's with those buttons?!
IF HE ASKED ME ON A DATE, UNLESS HE'D COMPLETELY TRANSFORMED FROM TOP TO BOTTOM, I'D BE TOO EMBARRASSED TO BE SEEN WITH HIM.
WHAT IS HIS GIRLFRIEND THINKING? IF IT WERE ME, I'D HAVE...
DON'T WANNA COLOR ANY MORE...
DUE TO THE HUMIDITY, IT'S HARD TO USE THE TONES.
I HAVE TO SAY, THOUGH, HE *IS* MANLY. BUT PUT SOME EFFORT INTO HOW YOU LOOK!

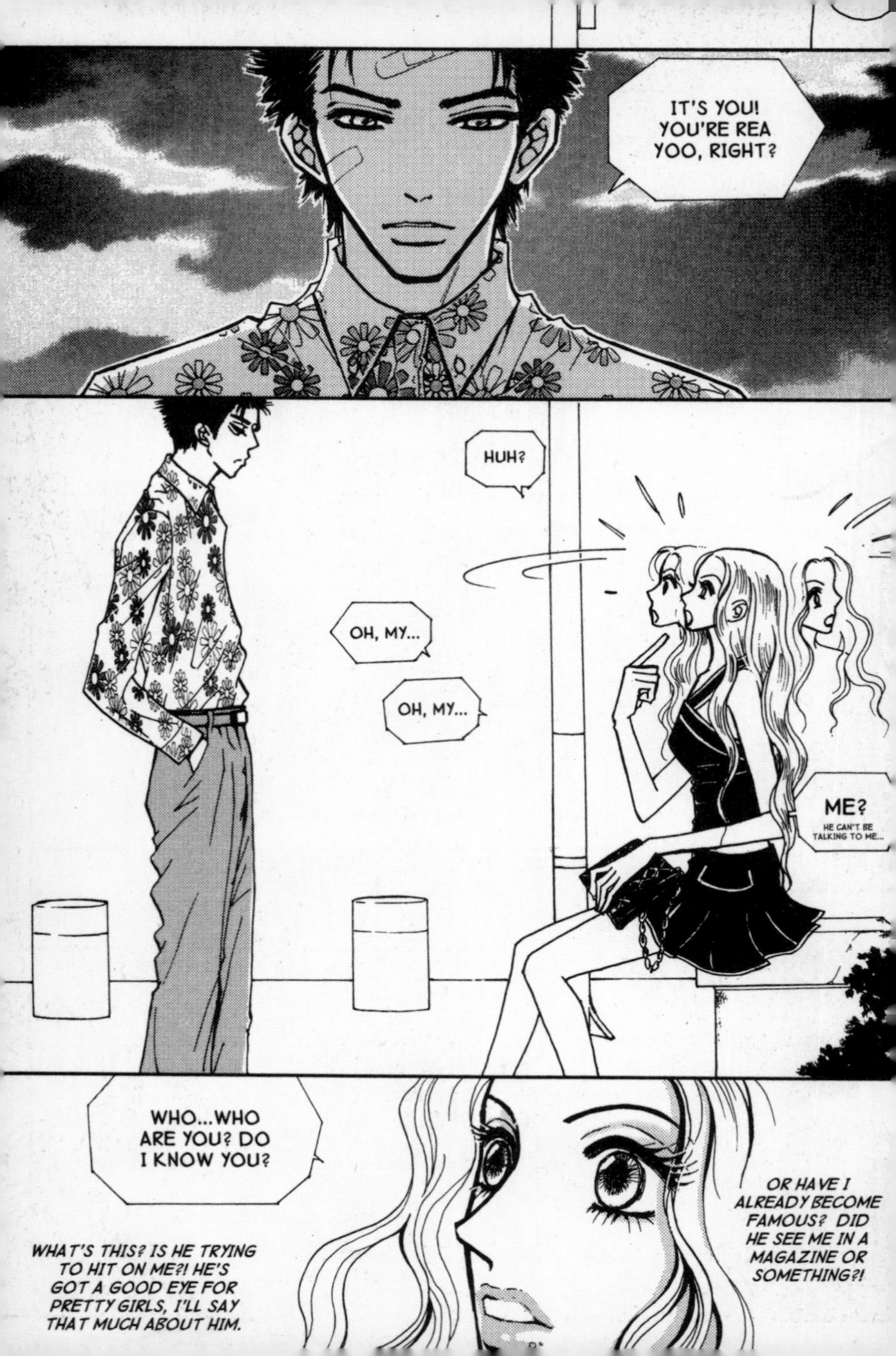
IT'S YOU! YOU'RE REA YOO, RIGHT?
HUH?
OH, MY...
OH, MY...
ME?
HE CAN'T BE TALKING TO ME...
WHO...WHO ARE YOU? DO I KNOW YOU?
WHAT'S THIS? IS HE TRYING TO HIT ON ME?! HE'S GOT A GOOD EYE FOR PRETTY GIRLS, I'LL SAY THAT MUCH ABOUT HIM.
OR HAVE I ALREADY BECOME FAMOUS? DID HE SEE ME IN A MAGAZINE OR SOMETHING?!

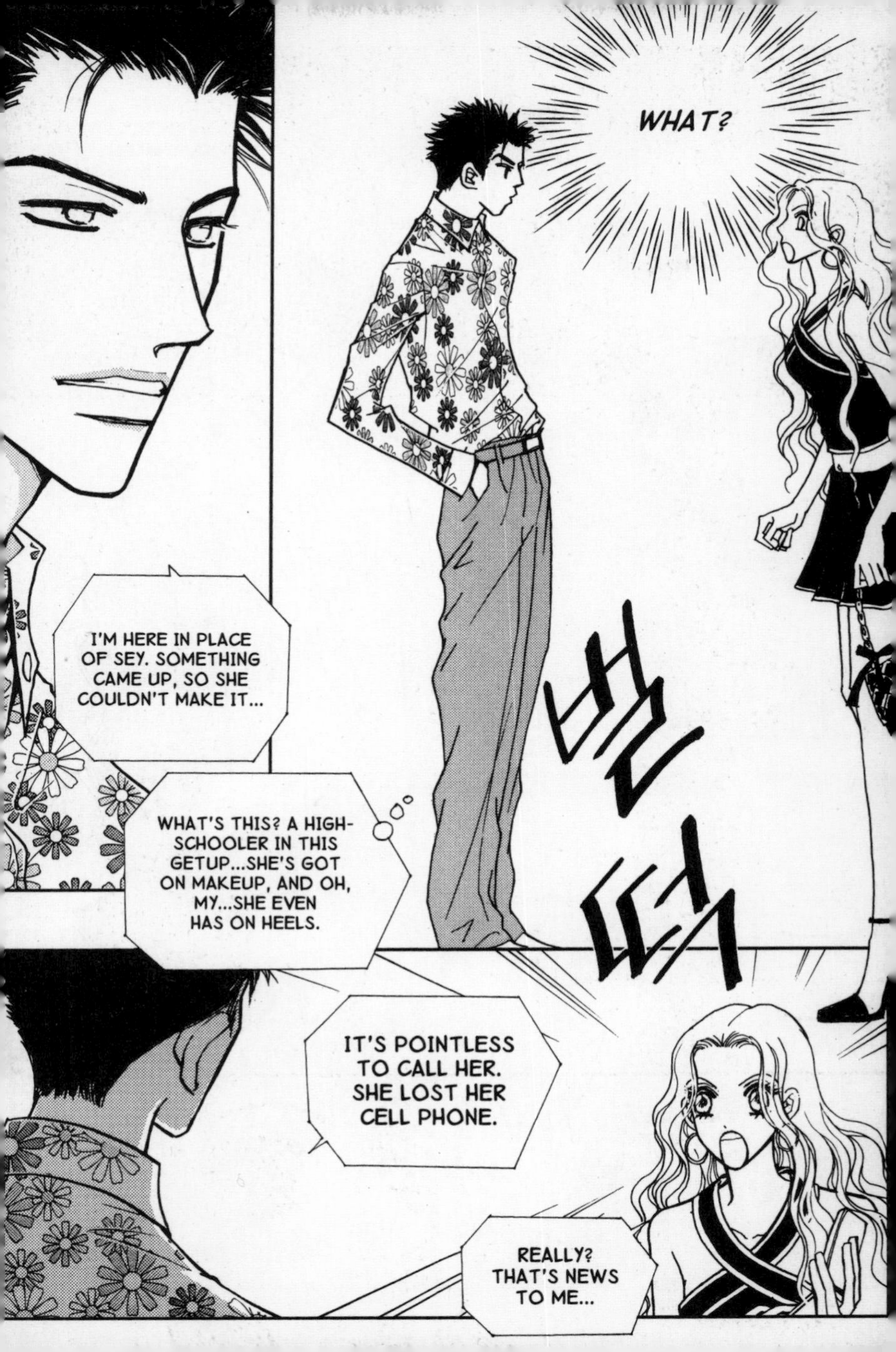
I'M HERE IN PLACE OF SEY. SOMETHING CAME UP, SO SHE COULDN'T MAKE IT...
WHAT?
WHAT'S THIS? A HIGH-SCHOOLER IN THIS GETUP...SHE'S GOT ON MAKEUP, AND OH, MY...SHE EVEN HAS ON HEELS.
IT'S POINTLESS TO CALL HER. SHE LOST HER CELL PHONE.
REALLY? THAT'S NEWS TO ME...

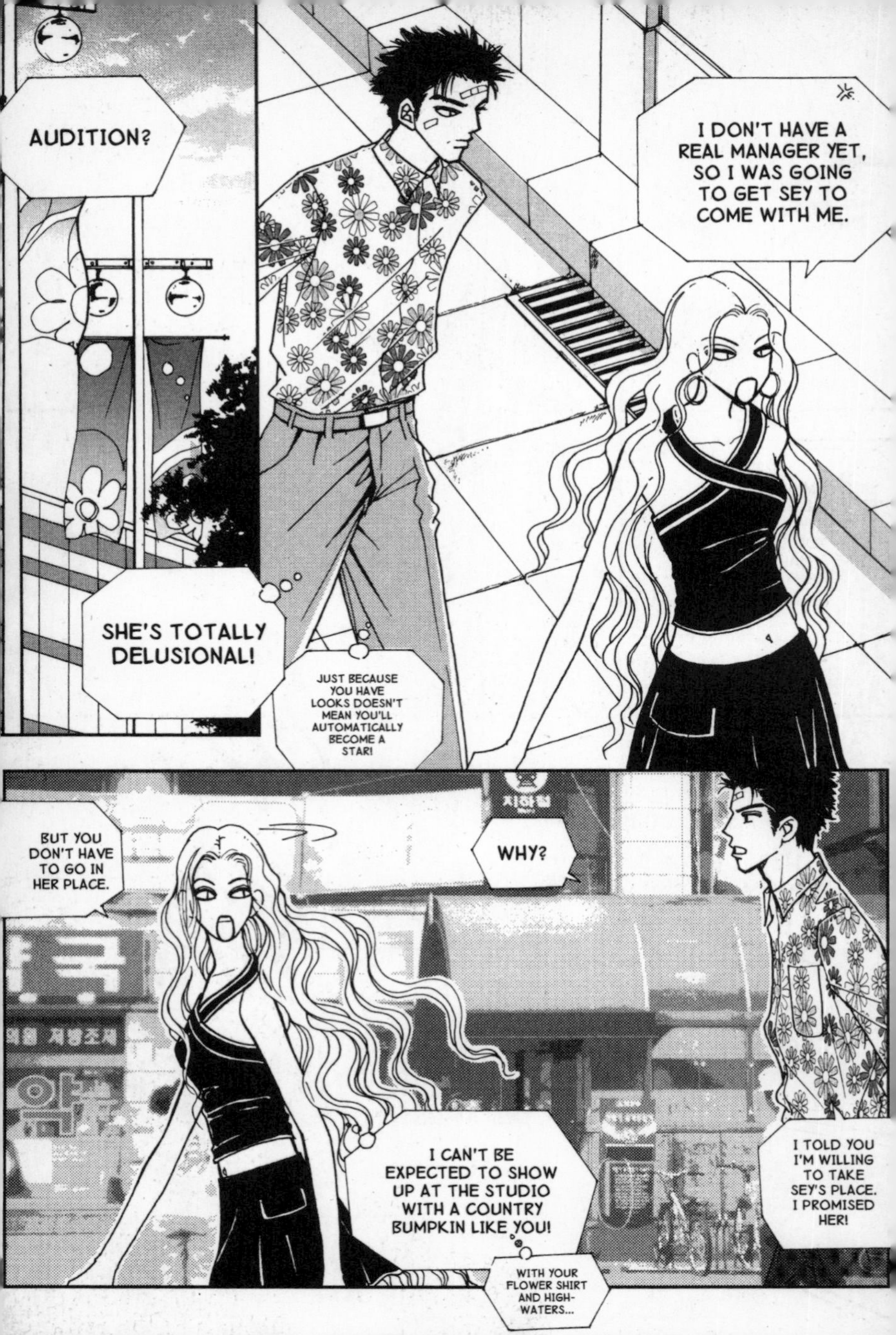
AUDITION?
I DON'T HAVE A REAL MANAGER YET, SO I WAS GOING TO GET SEY TO COME WITH ME.
SHE'S TOTALLY DELUSIONAL!
JUST BECAUSE YOU HAVE LOOKS DOESN'T MEAN YOU'LL AUTOMATICALLY BECOME A STAR!
BUT YOU DON'T HAVE TO GO IN HER PLACE.
WHY?
I CAN'T BE EXPECTED TO SHOW UP AT THE STUDIO WITH A COUNTRY BUMPKIN LIKE YOU!
WITH YOUR FLOWER SHIRT AND HIGH-WATERS...
I TOLD YOU I'M WILLING TO TAKE SEY'S PLACE. I PROMISED HER!

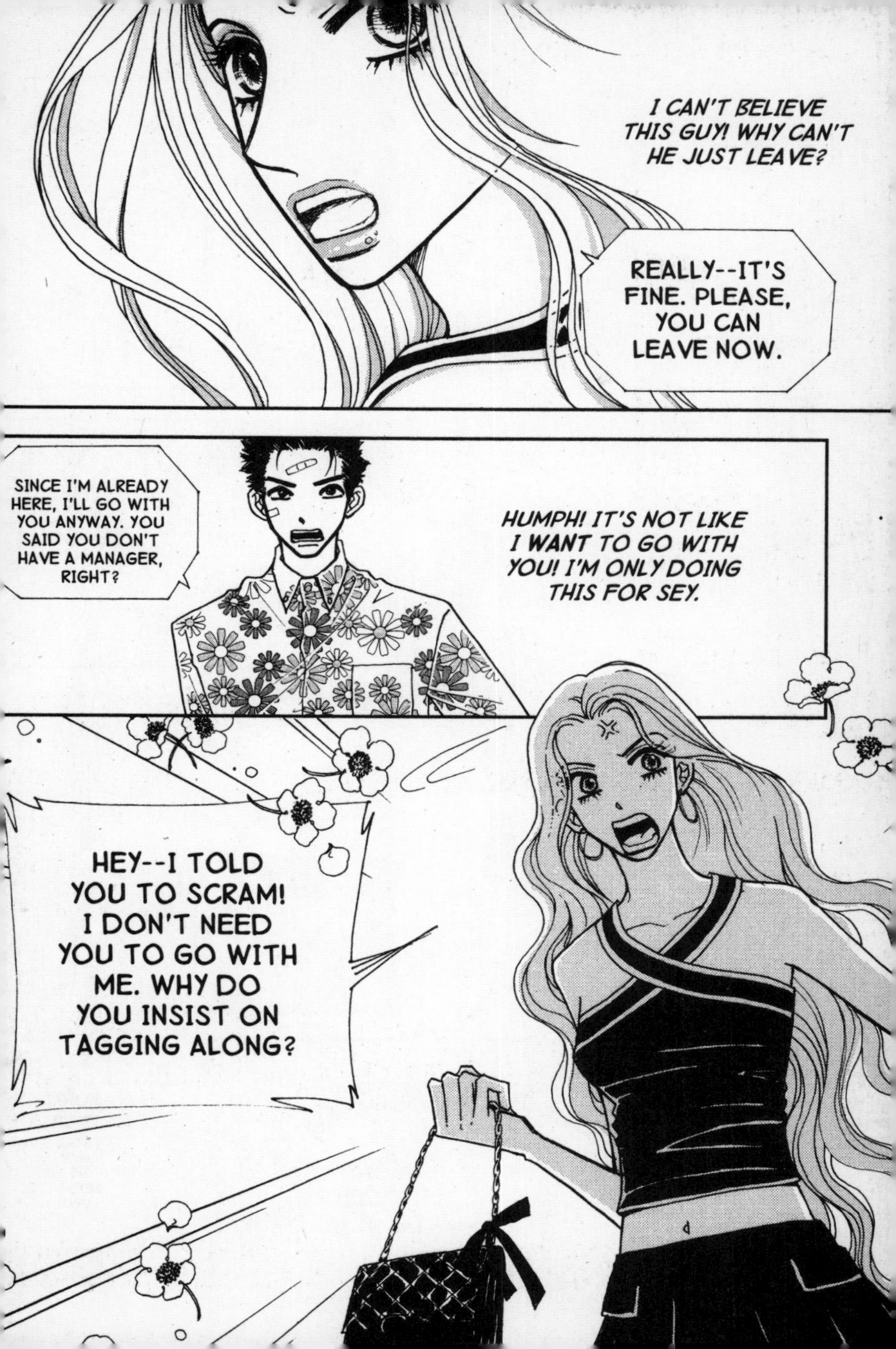
I CAN'T BELIEVE THIS GUY! WHY CAN'T HE JUST LEAVE?
REALLY--IT'S FINE. PLEASE, YOU CAN LEAVE NOW.
SINCE I'M ALREADY HERE, I'LL GO WITH YOU ANYWAY. YOU SAID YOU DON'T HAVE A MANAGER, RIGHT?
HUMPH! IT'S NOT LIKE I WANT TO GO WITH YOU! I'M ONLY DOING THIS FOR SEY.
HEY--I TOLD YOU TO SCRAM! I DON'T NEED YOU TO GO WITH ME. WHY DO YOU INSIST ON TAGGING ALONG?

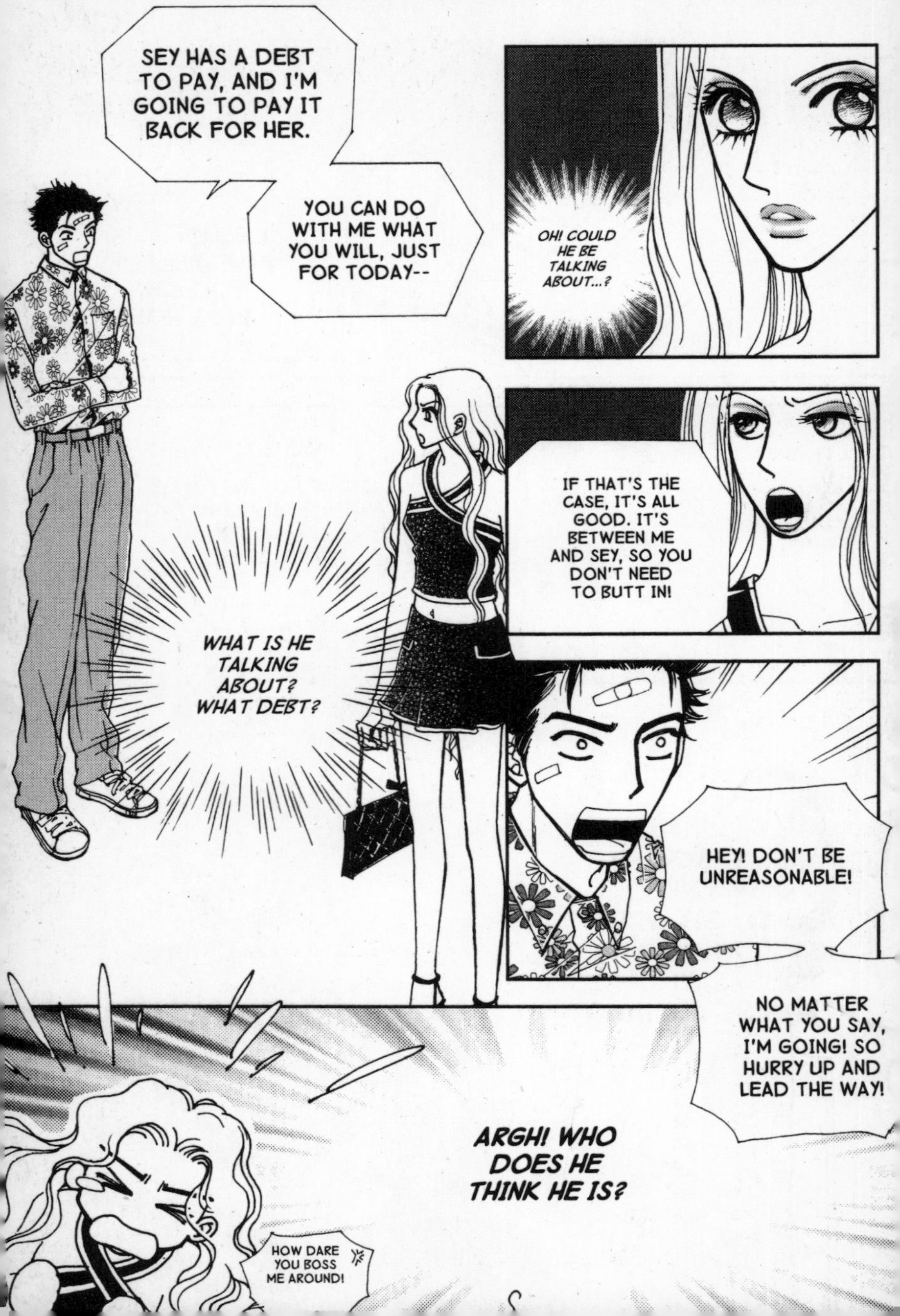
SEY HAS A DEBT TO PAY, AND I'M GOING TO PAY IT BACK FOR HER.
YOU CAN DO WITH ME WHAT YOU WILL, JUST FOR TODAY--
WHAT IS HE TALKING ABOUT? WHAT DEBT?
OH! COULD HE BE TALKING ABOUT...?
IF THAT'S THE CASE, IT'S ALL GOOD. IT'S BETWEEN ME AND SEY, SO YOU DON'T NEED TO BUTT IN!
HEY! DON'T BE UNREASONABLE!
NO MATTER WHAT YOU SAY, I'M GOING! SO HURRY UP AND LEAD THE WAY!
ARGH! WHO DOES HE THINK HE IS?
HOW DARE YOU BOSS ME AROUND!

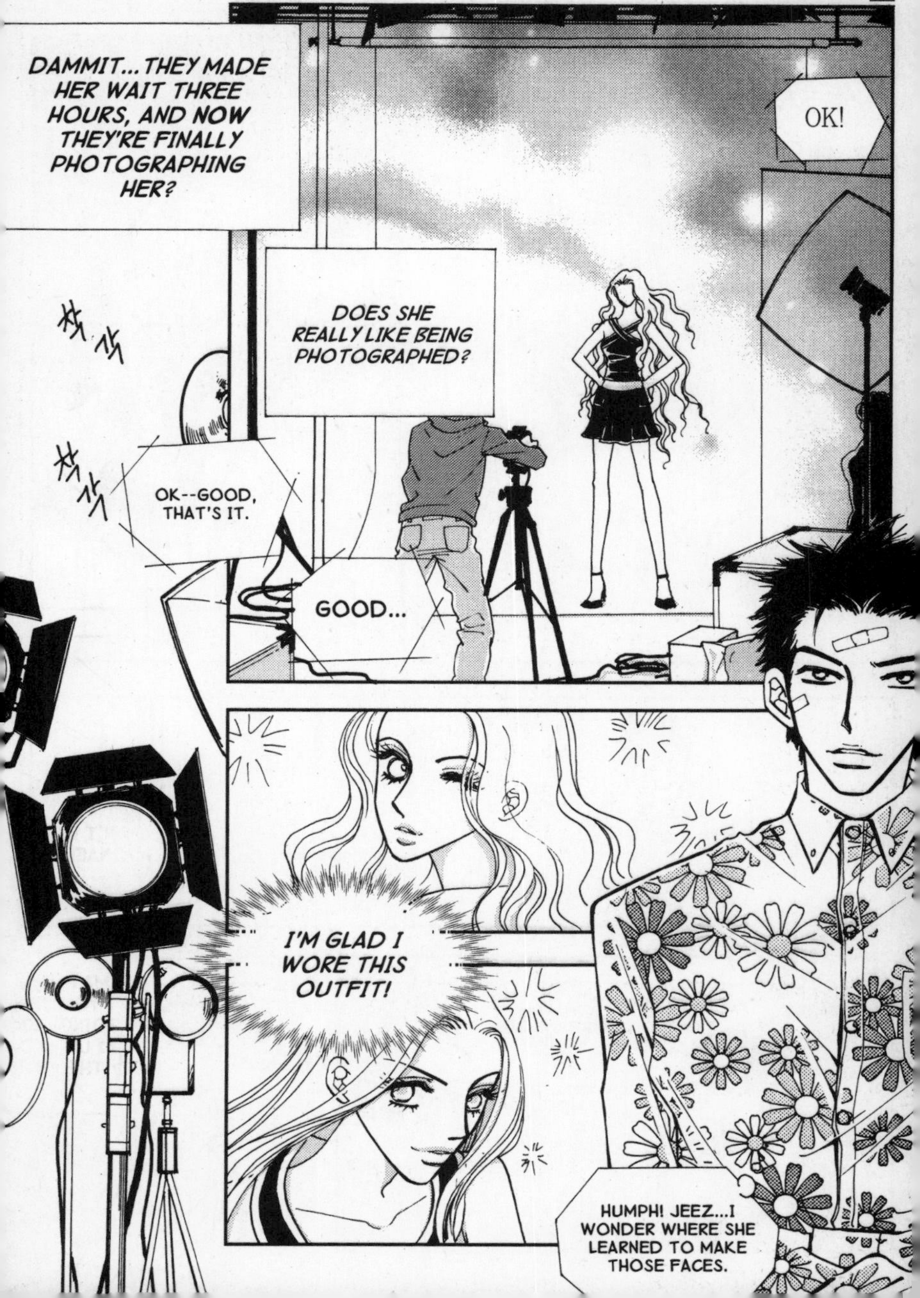
DAMMIT...THEY MADE HER WAIT THREE HOURS, AND NOW THEY'RE FINALLY PHOTOGRAPHING HER?
OK!
DOES SHE REALLY LIKE BEING PHOTOGRAPHED?
OK--GOOD, THAT'S IT.
GOOD...
I'M GLAD I WORE THIS OUTFIT!
HUMPH! JEEZ...I WONDER WHERE SHE LEARNED TO MAKE THOSE FACES.

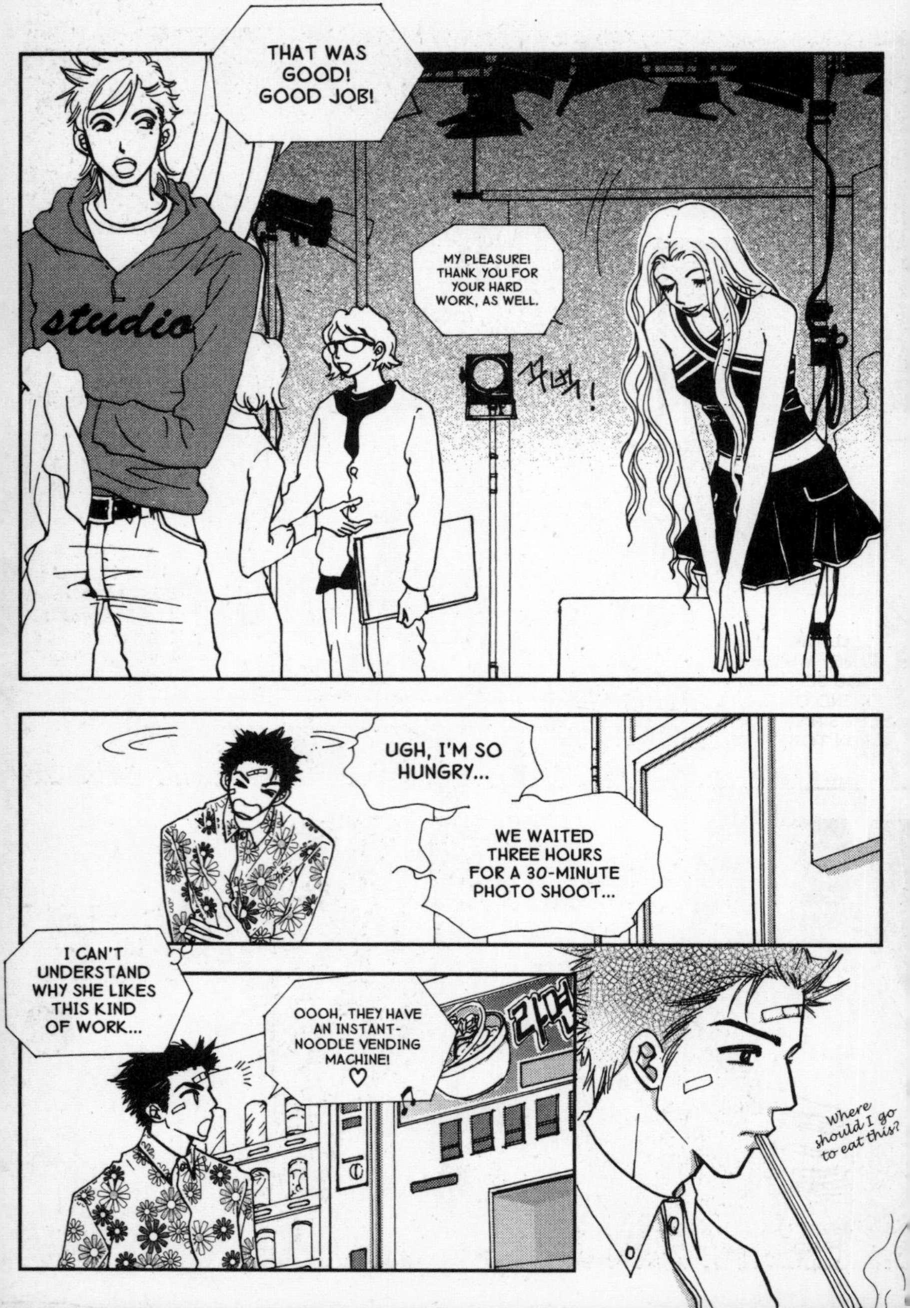
THAT WAS GOOD! GOOD JOB!
MY PLEASURE! THANK YOU FOR YOUR HARD WORK, AS WELL.
UGH, I'M SO HUNGRY...
WE WAITED THREE HOURS FOR A 30-MINUTE PHOTO SHOOT...
I CAN'T UNDERSTAND WHY SHE LIKES THIS KIND OF WORK...
OOOH, THEY HAVE AN INSTANT-NOODLE VENDING MACHINE! ♡
Where should I go to eat this?

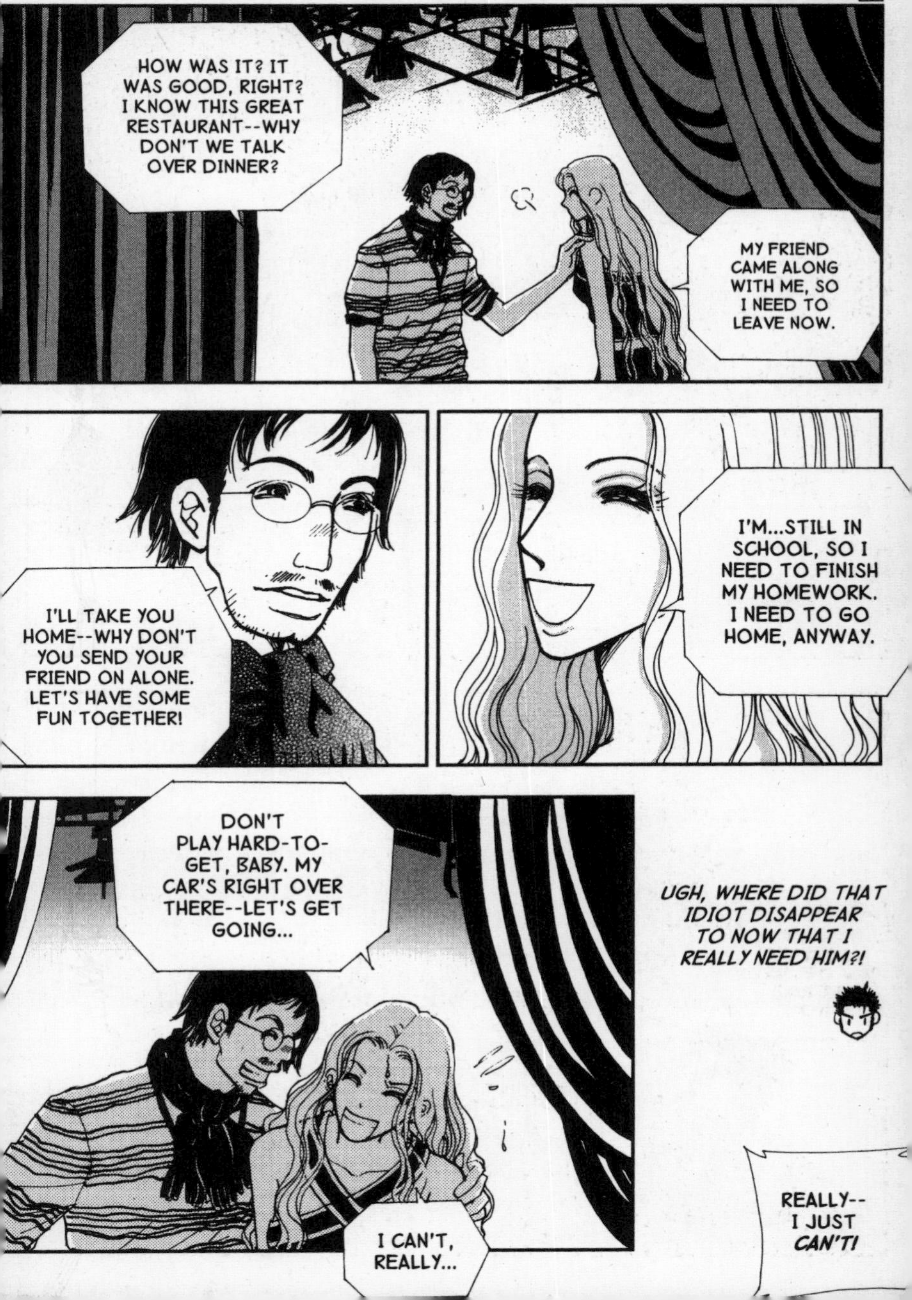
HOW WAS IT? IT WAS GOOD, RIGHT? I KNOW THIS GREAT RESTAURANT--WHY DON'T WE TALK OVER DINNER?
MY FRIEND CAME ALONG WITH ME, SO I NEED TO LEAVE NOW.
I'LL TAKE YOU HOME--WHY DON'T YOU SEND YOUR FRIEND ON ALONE. LET'S HAVE SOME FUN TOGETHER!
I'M...STILL IN SCHOOL, SO I NEED TO FINISH MY HOMEWORK. I NEED TO GO HOME, ANYWAY.
DON'T PLAY HARD-TO-GET, BABY. MY CAR'S RIGHT OVER THERE--LET'S GET GOING...
UGH, WHERE DID THAT IDIOT DISAPPEAR TO NOW THAT I REALLY NEED HIM?!
I CAN'T, REALLY...
REALLY--I JUST CAN'T!

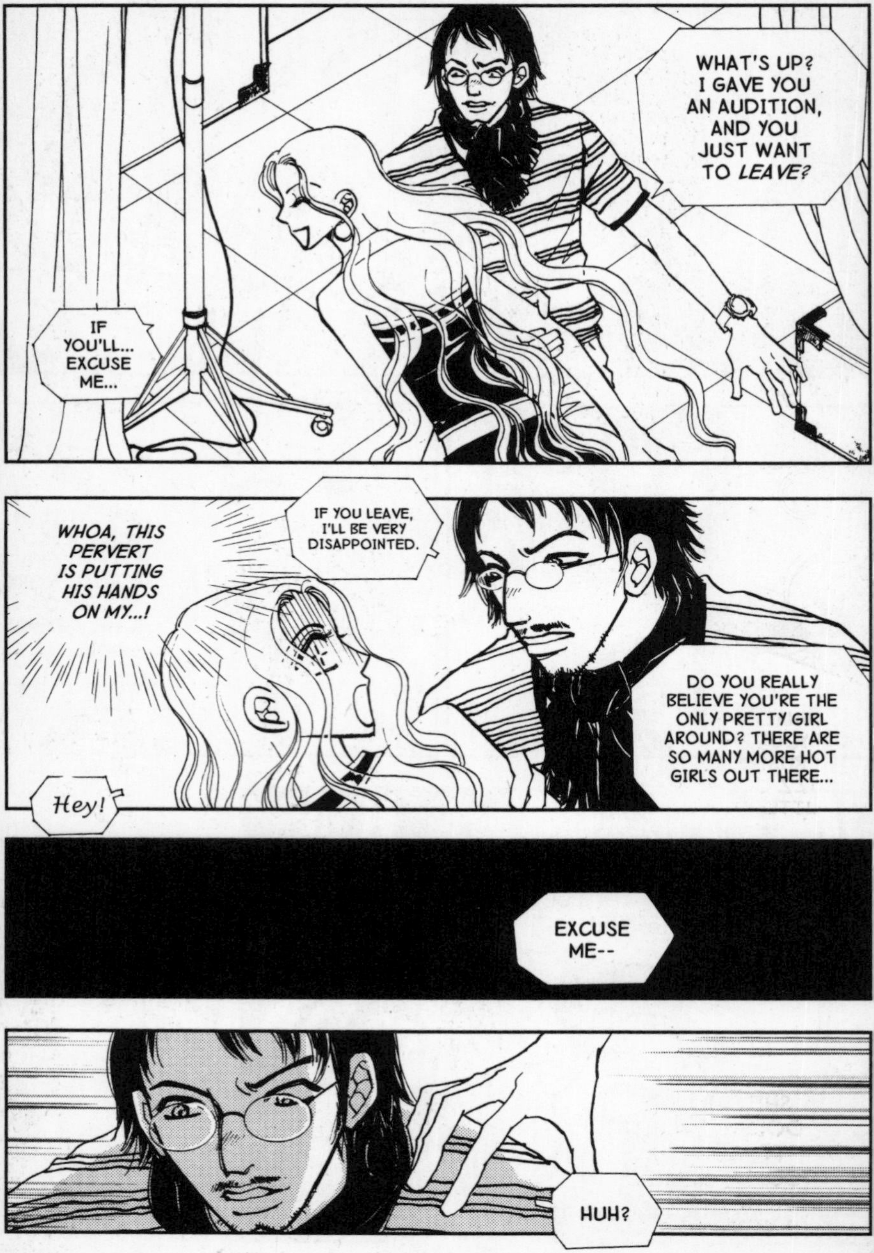
IF YOU'LL... EXCUSE ME...
WHAT'S UP? I GAVE YOU AN AUDITION, AND YOU JUST WANT TO *LEAVE?*
IF YOU LEAVE, I'LL BE VERY DISAPPOINTED.
WHOA, THIS PERVERT IS PUTTING HIS HANDS ON MY...!
Hey!
DO YOU REALLY BELIEVE YOU'RE THE ONLY PRETTY GIRL AROUND? THERE ARE SO MANY MORE HOT GIRLS OUT THERE...
EXCUSE ME--
HUH?

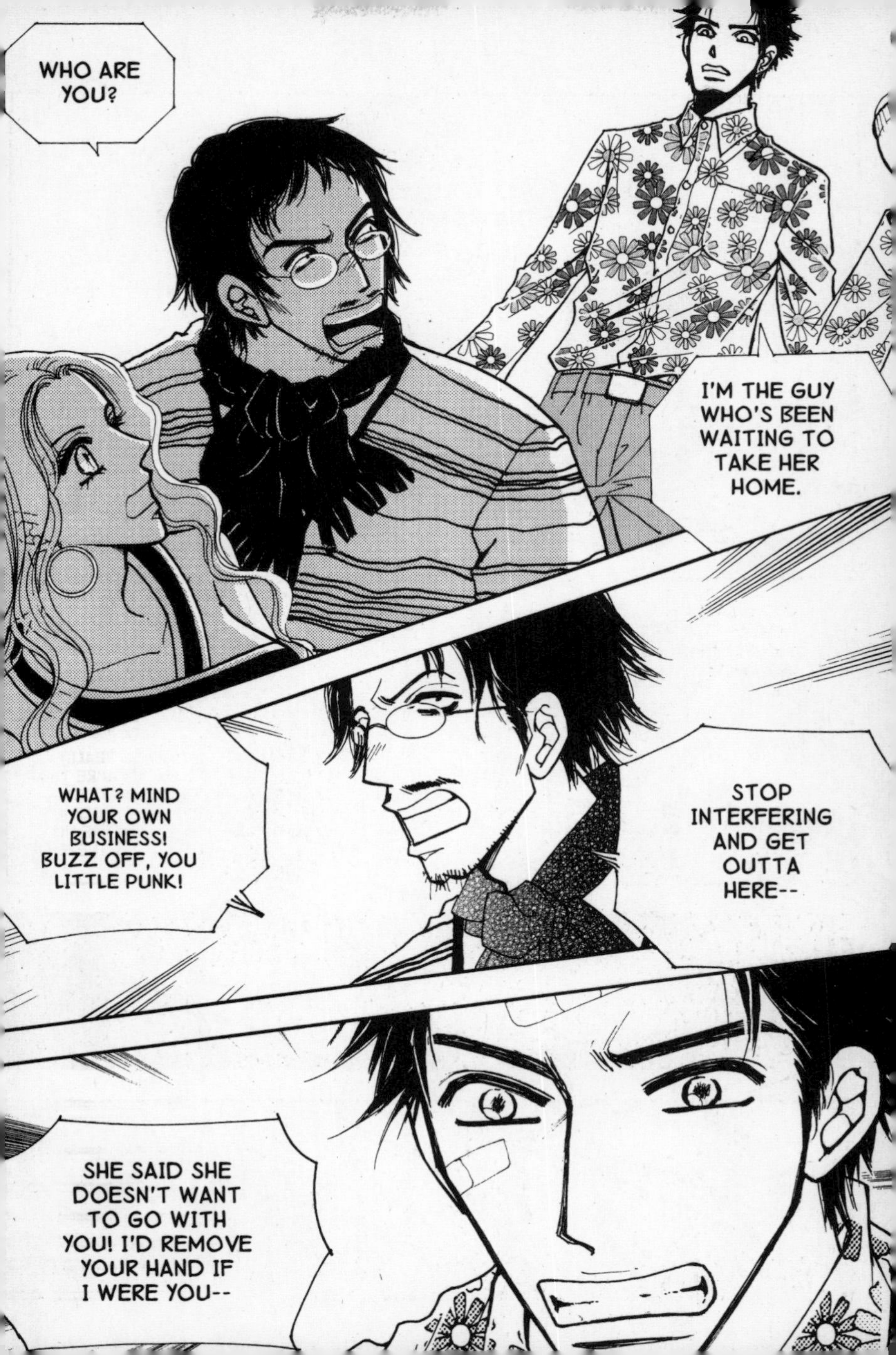
WHO ARE YOU?
I'M THE GUY WHO'S BEEN WAITING TO TAKE HER HOME.
WHAT? MIND YOUR OWN BUSINESS! BUZZ OFF, YOU LITTLE PUNK!
STOP INTERFERING AND GET OUTTA HERE--
SHE SAID SHE DOESN'T WANT TO GO WITH YOU! I'D REMOVE YOUR HAND IF I WERE YOU--

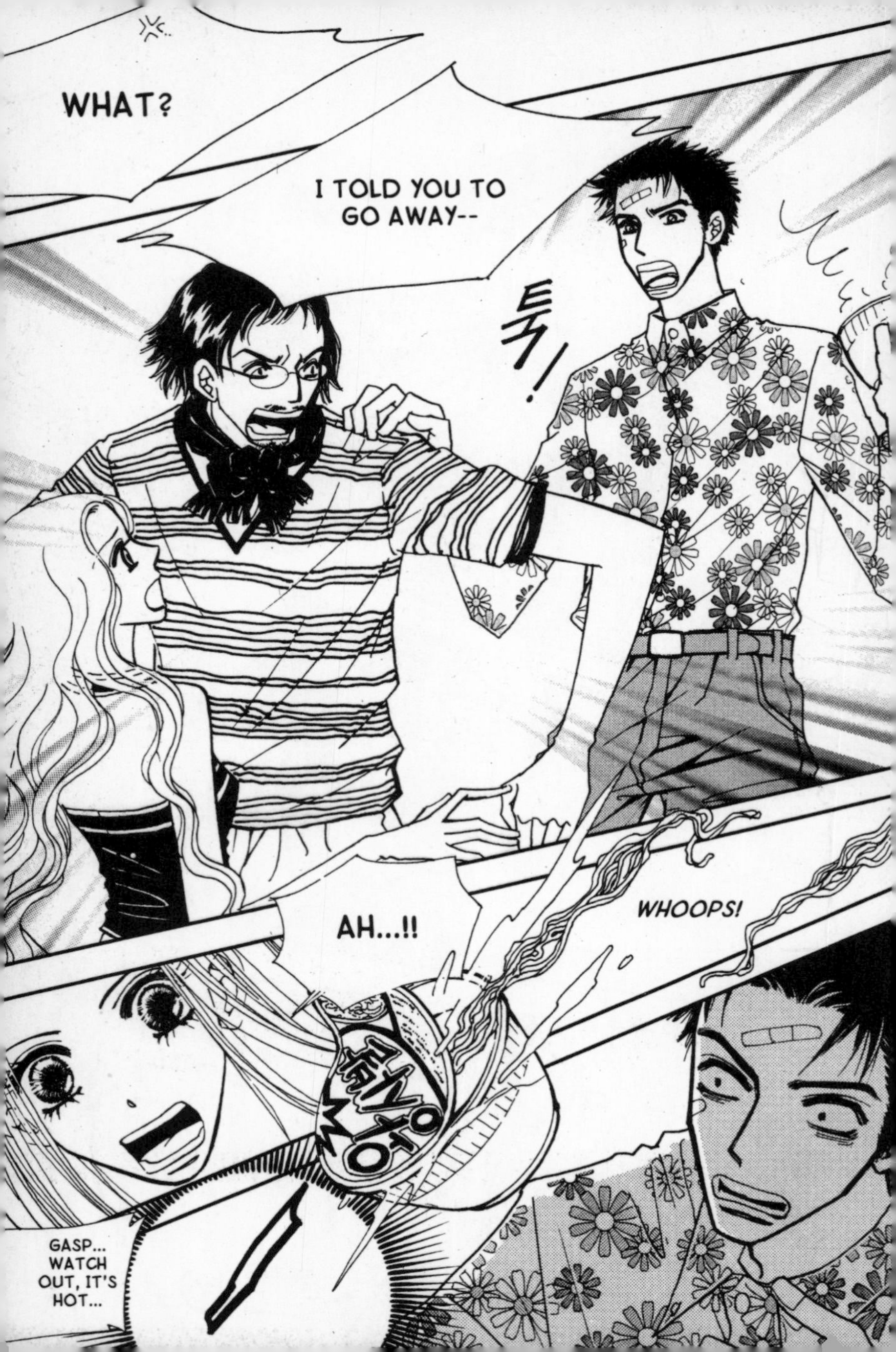
WHAT?
I TOLD YOU TO GO AWAY--
WHOOPS!
AH...!!
GASP... WATCH OUT, IT'S HOT...

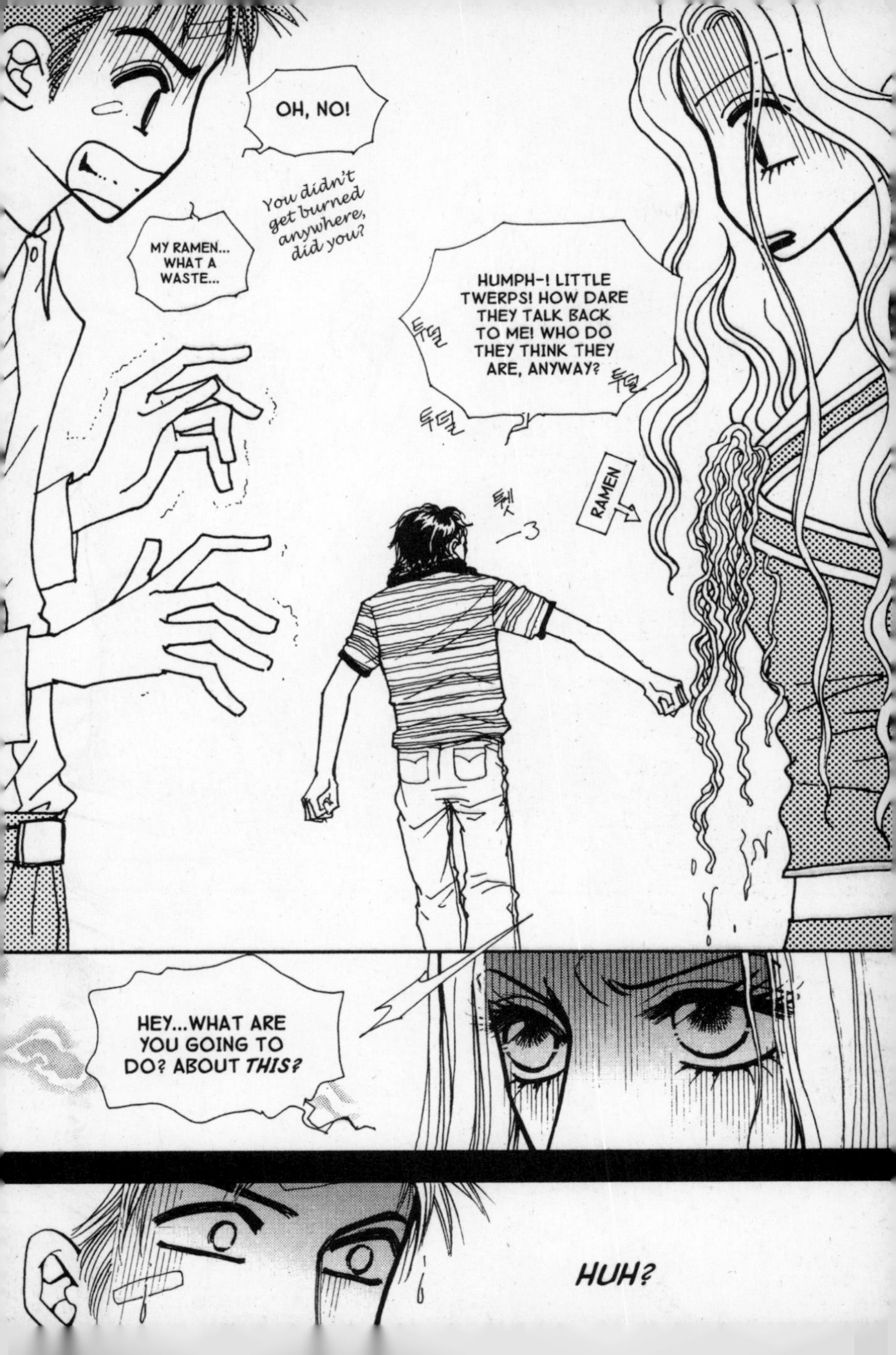
OH, NO!
MY RAMEN... WHAT A WASTE...
You didn't get burned anywhere, did you?
HUMPH-! LITTLE TWERPS! HOW DARE THEY TALK BACK TO ME! WHO DO THEY THINK THEY ARE, ANYWAY?
투덜
투덜
투덜
RAMEN
HEY...WHAT ARE YOU GOING TO DO? ABOUT THIS?
HUH?

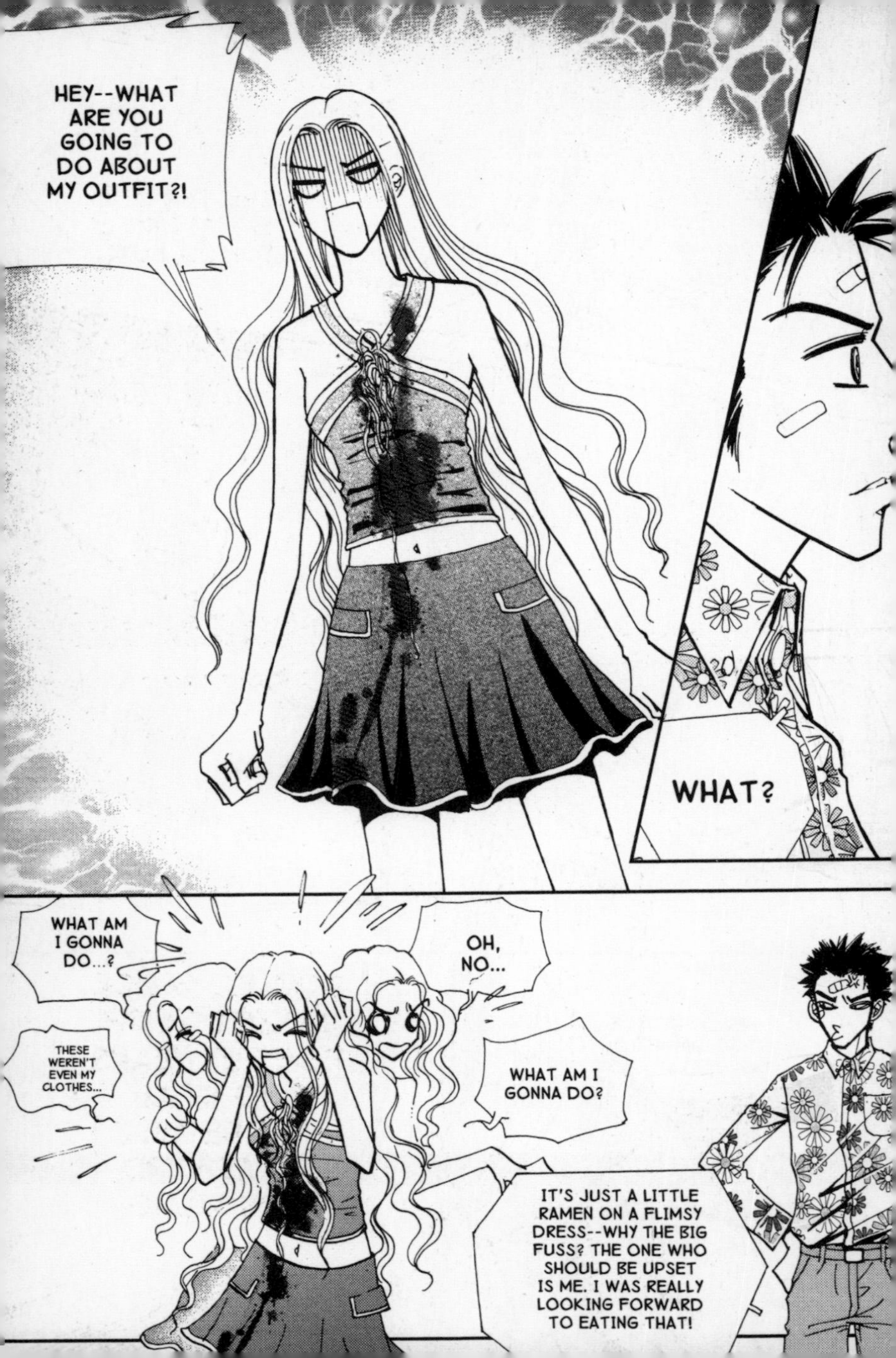
HEY--WHAT ARE YOU GOING TO DO ABOUT MY OUTFIT?!
WHAT?
OH, NO...
WHAT AM I GONNA DO...?
WHAT AM I GONNA DO?
THESE WEREN'T EVEN MY CLOTHES...
IT'S JUST A LITTLE RAMEN ON A FLIMSY DRESS--WHY THE BIG FUSS? THE ONE WHO SHOULD BE UPSET IS ME. I WAS REALLY LOOKING FORWARD TO EATING THAT!

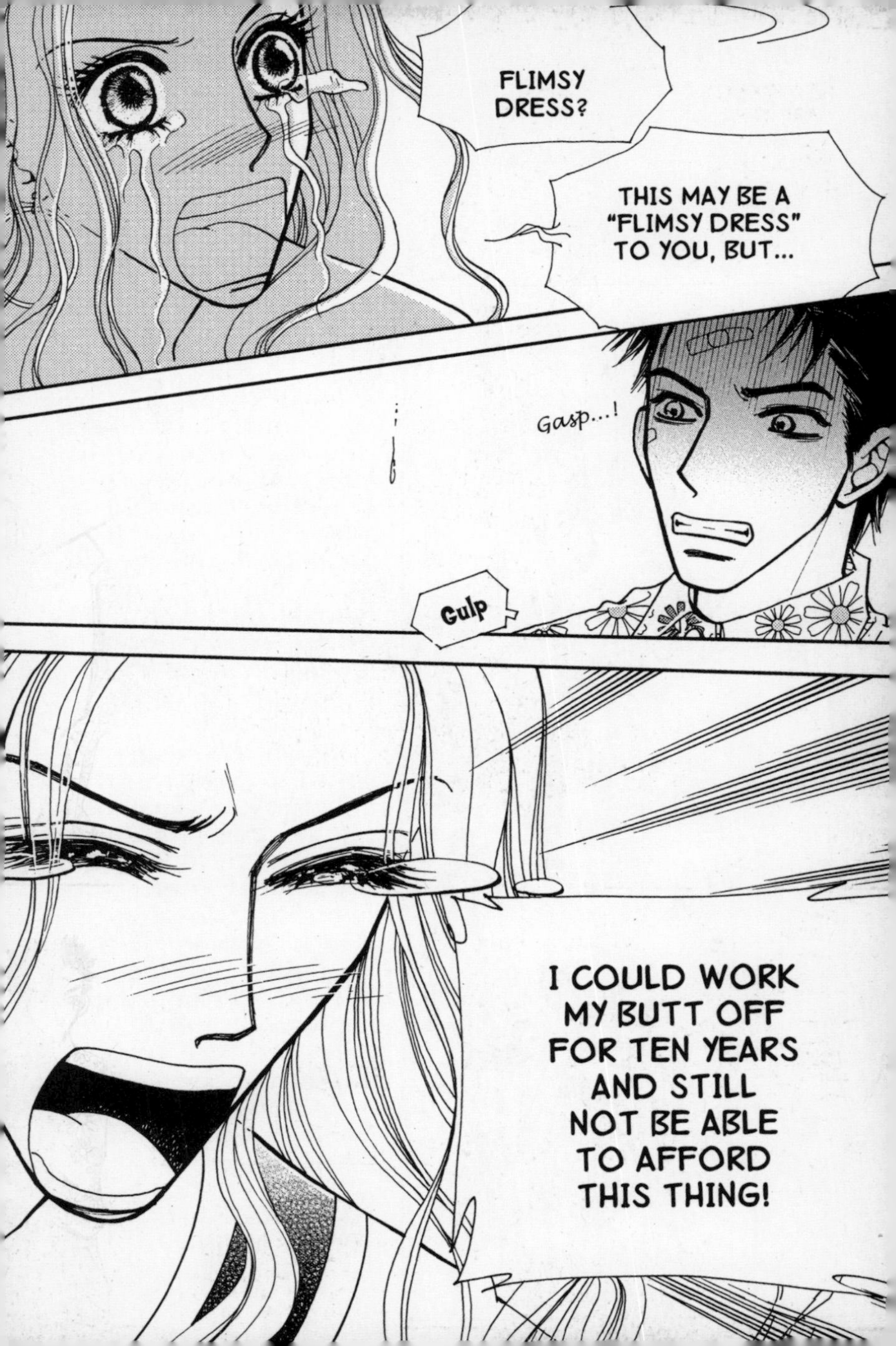
FLIMSY DRESS?
THIS MAY BE A "FLIMSY DRESS" TO YOU, BUT...
Gasp...!
Gulp
I COULD WORK MY BUTT OFF FOR TEN YEARS AND STILL NOT BE ABLE TO AFFORD THIS THING!

IN THE NEXT VOLUME OF
I.N.V.U.

It looks like Sey and Siho may finally take a stab at a real romance, but has Jae Eun already killed her chances with Simon? Will he really be as shocked and appalled at her hobbies (and her feelings) as Jae Eun imagines, or perhaps our sweet baker has a soft spot for fangirls...?

Meanwhile, things continue to heat up between Hajun and Hali, but what will Hajun's fiancée, not to mention his wealthy family, think about the situation? And speaking of hot, Youngjun is certainly in hot water after dumping his afternoon snack on Rea's designer dress. His fashion sense may be lacking, but the boy does know trouble when he sees it!

Stay tuned for the next volume of I.N.V.U.!

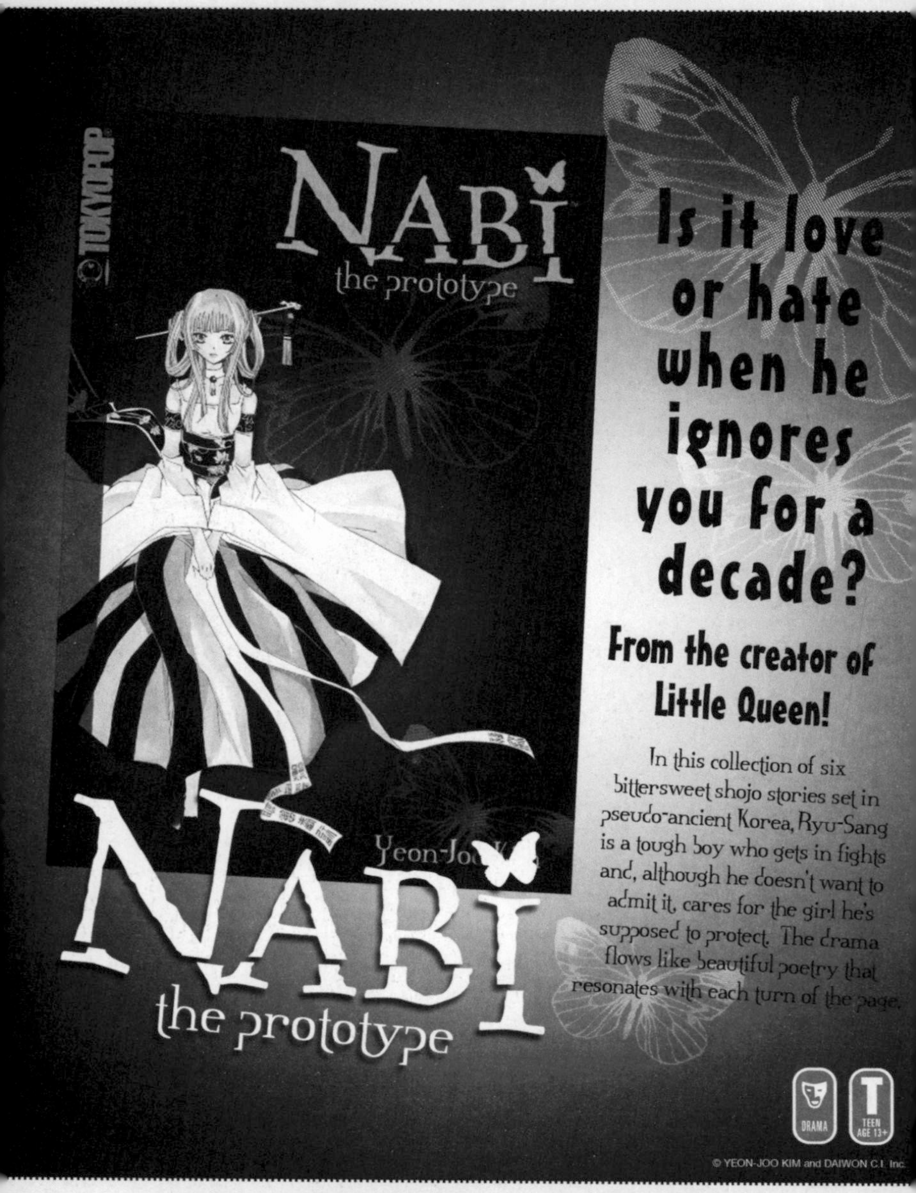
TOKYOPOP
NABI the prototype
Yeon-Joo Kim
NABI the prototype
Is it love or hate when he ignores you for a decade?
From the creator of Little Queen!
In this collection of six bittersweet shojo stories set in pseudo-ancient Korea, Ryu-Sang is a tough boy who gets in fights and, although he doesn't want to admit it, cares for the girl he's supposed to protect. The drama flows like beautiful poetry that resonates with each turn of the page.
DRAMA
T
TEEN AGE 13+
© YEON-JOO KIM and DAIWON C.I. Inc.

TOKYOPOP
WARCRAFT
THE SUNWELL TRILOGY
ULTIMATE EDITION
RICHARD A. KNAAK · JAE-HWAN KIM

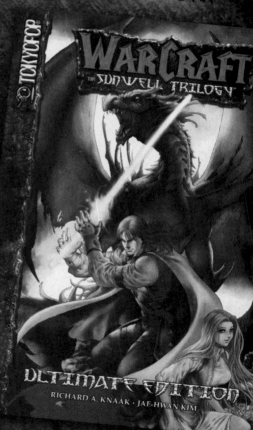

Beautiful Color Images from
CLAMP's Most Popular Series!

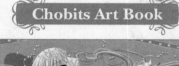

Chobits Art Book

ART NOT FINAL

Your Eyes Only

CLAMP

Luscious, full-color art from the world's most popular
manga studio, CLAMP, fills this stunningly gorgeous book.
This book is a feast for the eyes of any Chobits fan!

FOR MORE INFORMATION VISIT: WWW.TOKYOPOP.COM